LYING AND DECE

Thomas Carson offers the most comprehensive a   ....
moral and conceptual questions about lying and deception. Part I addresses
conceptual questions and offers definitions of lying, deception, and related
concepts such as withholding information, 'keeping someone in the dark', and
'half-truths'. Part II deals with questions in ethical theory. Carson argues that
standard debates about lying and deception between act-utilitarians and their
critics are inconclusive because they rest on appeals to disputed moral intuitions.
He defends a version of the golden rule and a theory of moral reasoning. His
theory implies that there is a moral presumption against lying and deception
that causes harm—a presumption at least as strong as that endorsed by act-
utilitarianism. He uses this theory to justify his claims about the issues he
addresses in Part III: deception and withholding information in sales, deception
in advertising, bluffing in negotiations, the duties of professionals to inform
clients, lying and deception by leaders as a pretext for fighting wars, and lying
and deception about history (with special attention to the Holocaust), and cases
of distorting the historical record by telling half-truths. The book concludes with
a qualified defence of the view that honesty is a virtue.

Thomas L. Carson is Professor of Philosophy at Loyola University Chicago.

Lying and Deception

Theory and Practice

THOMAS L. CARSON

OXFORD

UNIVERSITY PRESS

OXFORD
UNIVERSITY PRESS

Great Clarendon Street, Oxford OX2 6DP,
United Kingdom

Oxford University Press is a department of the University of Oxford.
It furthers the University's objective of excellence in research, scholarship,
and education by publishing worldwide. Oxford is a registered trade mark of
Oxford University Press in the UK and in certain other countries

First published 2010
First published in paperback 2012

British Library Cataloguing in Publication Data

Data available

Library of Congress Cataloging in Publication Data
Library of Congress Control Number 2010920521

ISBN 978-0-19-957741-5 (Hbk)
ISBN 978-0-19-965480-2 (Pbk)

Printed in the United Kingdom by
Lightning Source UK Ltd., Milton Keynes

In Memory of My Mother and For My Father

Contents

Contents

Detailed Contents

PART II: MORAL THEORY

IIA NORMATIVE ETHICAL THEORY

IIC THE IMPLICATIONS OF IIA AND IIB FOR QUESTIONS ABOUT LYING AND DECEPTION

PART III APPLICATIONS

Acknowledgments

I have received a great deal of help from many people. It is a pleasure to acknowledge these debts here.

My greatest debt is to Joe Mendola. He and I have met regularly to drink coffee and discuss philosophy since 2001. He has patiently read numerous drafts of the book and has given me many helpful ideas and criticisms. His influence and suggestions are everywhere in the book and have enabled me to improve the book in many ways.

I have benefited greatly from the comments and suggestions of my two Oxford referees, Tom Beauchamp and James Mahon. (Tom may not recall that he commented on a very distant ancestor of Chapter 10 at a conference long ago in 1979.)

My Oxford Editors, Catherine Berry and Abigail Coulson, and my Oxford proofreader, Andrew Hawkey, have shepherded the book to completion and given me a great deal of help and advice.

Roy Sorensen read and commented on the penultimate draft of the book and offered many helpful criticisms and suggestions. Brad Hooker read the entire manuscript; his penetrating criticisms of Chapters 5 and 6 were particularly helpful. Alan Strudler also read the entire manuscript and offered numerous helpful comments and criticisms. The late Betsy Postow gave me long and penetrating criticisms of Chapters 5 and 6 and saved me from several embarrassing mistakes in Chapter 5.

For comments on my version of the golden rule in Chapter 6, I thank Harry Gensler, Jason Kawall, Russ Shaffer Landau, J. D. Trout, David Schweickart, David Ozar, Chris Meyers, Grant Sterling, and Alvin Goldman. I owe special thanks to Harry Gensler. His own work on the golden rule inspired me to defend my own version of the golden rule and apply it to issues in applied ethics. My work on Chapters 1 and 2 benefited greatly from the help of Bruce Russell, Bill Tolhurst, Al Mele, Mike Gorr, Kent Machina, Don Fallis, Bill Mann, Bill Lycan, Uriah Kriegel, Clancy Martin, J. D. Trout, Catherine Womack, and Laura Lenhart. For help with my interpretation of Kant, I thank Marcia Baron, Victoria Wike, David Yandell, and Paul Abella. Henry West offered very helpful criticisms of Chapter 4 and answered a number of scholarly questions about Mill.

My first work on these topics began long ago at Virginia Tech where I collaborated with Rich Wokutch on several papers on bluffing in negotiations and deceptive advertising (Kent Murmann and Richard Cox were co-authors on two of these papers). I thank Rich for all that I have learned from him. Later on, Alexei Marcoux, Ian Maitland, Ivan Preston, and Norm Bowie gave me a great deal of help with Chapters 8–10. Dave Ozar and Alexei Marcoux gave me very helpful comments and suggestions about Chapter 11. Chapters 8–11 include a considerable amount of material taken from my paper "Deception in Business and Professional Ethics," in the *Oxford Handbook of Business Ethics* edited by Tom Beauchamp and George Brenkert. Tom and George read several versions of this paper and made many helpful suggestions.

Chapters 12 and 13 present the results of my foray into historical research. I greatly enjoyed this work, though it proved to be quite difficult. I am indebted to David Dennis, Tom Knapp, Mark Allee, Elliot Levcowitz, and Ted Karmanski of the Loyola University History Department. I also wish to thank Professors Ian Kershaw, Bruce Cumings, Bill Astoree, James McPherson, Drew Bergerson, and Michael Neiberg for their very generous and helpful responses to my email inquires. The work of McPherson, Kershaw, Cummings, and Astore figures importantly in these chapters. Fred Stoutland and David Schweickart gave me helpful comments on Chapter 12.

I have gained a great appreciation for historians and their work. However, the examples I discuss in Chapter 13 show how badly things can go when the historical record is falsified and not approached honestly. History is often abused for evil purposes.

Thanks also to Jeff Tullis and Bernard Gert for helpful advice and correspondence on matters relating to the book.

I have benefited from the help of my graduate assistants at Loyola University Chicago. I particularly want to thank Chris Meyers, Jason Beyer, Jean Tan, Micah Lehner, Mark Chakoian, Christina Drogalis, and Marcella Russo. Chris was particularly helpful with my work on the golden rule; he has also taken up the cause of Hare/prescriptivism in some of his published work. Micah, Mark, and Christina were my TAs during the last four years I worked on this book. They patiently suffered though innumerable drafts of the manuscript and gave me many helpful criticisms on matters of style and substance. Their questions and corrections have done much to improve the style, coherence, and substance of the manuscript.

Work on this book was supported by a paid leave of absence, three summer research grants, and two smaller research grants from Loyola University Chicago.

Finally, I thank my daughter Nora for her careful reading of the manuscript.

No doubt there are others who helped me but who I have overlooked and not mentioned here. I beg their forgivingness for not calling them to mind.

I thank my family (Judy, Nora, and Dan) for their patience and support.

This book is dedicated to the memory of my mother, Jane M. Carson and to my father James E. Carson. It has been my great good fortune to be their son. I also want to acknowledge my indebtedness to my extended family (both living and dead)—to my sister, grandparents, uncles and aunts, my mother in law, nieces and nephews, cousins, and in-laws. Throughout my life, I have been surrounded and sustained by their love.

Material from the following publications is used with the permission of the publishers:

Conflicts of interest and self-dealing in the professions: a review essay. *Business Ethics Quarterly* **14** (2004): 161–182.

Deception and withholding information in sales. *Business Ethics Quarterly* **11** (2001): 275–306.

Deception in business and professional ethics. *Oxford Handbook of Business Ethics*, Tom Beauchamp and George Brenkert, eds. (Oxford University Press, 2010), pp. 335–365.

Ethical issues in selling and advertising. *Companion to Business Ethics*, Norman Bowie, ed. (Boston: Blackwell's, 2002), pp. 186–205.

Liar liar. *International Journal of Applied Philosophy* **22** (2008): 189–210.

Lying, deception, and related concepts. In *The Philosophy of Deception*, Clancy Martin, ed. (Oxford University Press, 2009), pp. 153–187.

Ross and utilitarianism on promise keeping and lying: self-evidence and the data of ethics. *Philosophical Issues* (Annual Supplement to the journal *Nous*), Volume 15, 2005, pp. 140–157.

Second thoughts on bluffing. *Business Ethics Quarterly* **3** (1993): 317–341.

The definition of lying. *Nous* **40** (2006): 284–306.

I also wish to thank the editors of these journals and books from which these papers are taken and to all who helped with these papers. Finally, I want to thank the *Chicago Tribune* for permission to quote at length from the article by Ron Grossman.

Introduction and Précis

Few, if any, moral questions have greater bearing on the conduct of our everyday lives than questions about lying and deception. These questions arise in a wide range of settings from personal relationships to actions undertaken in professional roles and the public sphere; they are also important for ethical theory. An important test of any theory of right and wrong or moral obligation is whether it gives an adequate account of the morality of lying and deception. This book addresses questions in ethical theory and practical questions about lying, deception, and information disclosure in public affairs, business and professional ethics, and personal relationships.

Part I (Chapters 1 and 2) is a conceptual map for the rest of the book. It proposes an analysis of the concepts of lying and deception and explains the relationship between the notions of lying, deception, "keeping someone in the dark," concealing information, withholding information, bullshit, spin, and "half-truths."

Part IIA (Chapters 3–5) addresses questions in moral theory and examines the implications of Kant's theory, act-utilitarianism, Ross's theory, and rule-consequentialism for questions about the morality of lying and deception. The historical figures in question have much more to say about lying than deception, though I am equally concerned with deception in this book. Kant is a notorious absolutist about lying, but I argue that Kant's basic moral theory does not commit him to the view that there is an absolute moral prohibition against lying. Many critics contend that utilitarianism often permits lying when lying is wrong. Mill attempts to answer this objection in *Utilitarianism* where he claims that lying always has indirect bad consequences (lying makes one less honest and undermines trust between people). Mill claims that, therefore, utilitarianism implies that there is a strong moral presumption against lying. Even so, Ross and rule-consequentialists argue that act-utilitarianism is too permissive about lying and present cases in which they claim that the theory conflicts with our moral intuitions or "considered moral judgments" about the wrongness of lying. I argue that the standard debate between act-utilitarians, Rossians, and rule-consequentialists about this issue is inconclusive because it involves an appeal to disputed moral intuitions or disputed "considered moral judgments." Each of the parties appeals to his/her own moral intuitions or considered moral judgments, without doing enough to justify them.

In order to avoid the dialectical impasse of appealing to moral intuitions (or considered moral judgments) that are rejected by ostensibly rational and competent people, I defend a theory of moral reasoning that does not rest on an appeal to moral intuitions. My theory, which I present in Part IIB (Chapter 6), is a version of the golden rule and a broadly Kantian theory. It enables me to justify and defend moral judgments about a wide range of cases without appealing to disputed moral intuitions. In particular, it allows us to see that the negative judgments about lying and deception, on which the traditional theories agree, are correct.

In Part IIC (Chapter 7), I explain the implications of my theory of moral reasoning for the issues of lying and deception. My theory implies that there is a strong moral presumption against lying and deception when they cause harm, a presumption that is at least as strong as that endorsed by act-utilitarianism. At a minimum, lying and deception are wrong in those cases in which act-utilitarianism implies that they are wrong. Lying and deception may be wrong in other cases as well, but they are clearly wrong in these cases. I also argue that lying and deception are sometimes permissible, and thus (though I appeal to a Kantian theory of moral reasoning) Kant's absolutism is not a reasonable view about the morality of lying/deception. My theory does not settle all of the debates in normative ethical theory discussed in IIA. It is compatible with the truth of act-utilitarianism, Ross's theory, and rule-consequentialism; each of these theories passes the rationality tests of my theory of moral reasoning. To that extent, my theory leaves open the possibility that moral relativism is true. However, the kind of relativism that may be consistent with my theory is not an "anything goes" relativism, because there is considerable overlap or convergence between what these reasonable views say about the morality of lying and deception. Roughly, they agree that lying and deception are wrong in those cases in which act-utilitarianism implies that they are wrong. In these and other cases in which reasonable views all agree/converge, there are objective moral truths. My theory leaves some questions open, but it enables me to justify moral judgments about lying and deception in a wide range of cases and provides a basis for answering the practical moral questions addressed in Part III.

Part III (Chapters 8–14) applies the conclusions reached in Parts I and II to a broad range of practical moral issues: deception and withholding information in sales, deception in advertising, bluffing and deception in negotiations, the duty of professionals to inform their clients, lying and deception by leaders as a pretext for fighting wars (or avoiding wars), distorting the historical record by lying and deception, and distorting the historical record by spinning the facts or telling half truths. I distinguish between "honesty in a negative sense" (having a strong principled disinclination to tell lies or deceive others) and "honesty in a positive sense," which (in addition to involving being disinclined to tell lies or deceive others) involves being candid, open, and willing to reveal information. I argue that honesty in the negative sense (or something that closely resembles it) is a cardinal virtue in ordinary circumstances but that often honesty in the positive sense is not a virtue.

PART I

Chapter 1: Lying

I define lying roughly as follows: a lie is a deliberate false statement that the speaker warrants to be true. Two features of my definition are noteworthy. First, contrary to most standard definitions, I argue that lying does not require that the liar intends to deceive others. (I appeal to cases in which one is compelled or enticed to make false statements, cases of lying in which one can benefit by making false statements even if they do not deceive others, and cases of bald-faced lies in which the liar knows that others know she is lying and therefore has no hope or intention of deceiving them.) Second, I hold that in order to tell a lie, one must make a statement that one warrants to be true. According to my definition, any lie violates an implicit promise or guarantee that what one says is true. My definition makes sense of the common view that lying involves a breach of trust. To lie, on my view, is to invite others to trust and rely on what one says by warranting its truth, and at the same time to betray that trust by making a false statement that one does not believe to be true.

I discuss several published criticisms of my definition. I isolate several criticisms that, while it is not certain, may require a refinement of my basic definition, and I formulate a revised version of my definition that clearly answers them. According to the revised definition, lying requires that one *intends to warrant* the truth of what one says but does not require that one actually warrants its truth, as in my original definition. Nothing that I say in the book depends on the subtle difference between these two definitions.

Chapter 2: Deception and Related Concepts

Deception can be defined roughly as intentionally causing someone to have false beliefs, but this definition needs to be qualified to deal with certain cases, including the following. I intentionally cause you to believe statement X and X is false, but I neither believe that X is true nor believe that X is false. I also discuss several other cases that may require modifications of this definition and formulate several revised versions of the definition; I count cases in which people intentionally cause others to persist in false beliefs as cases of deception.

There are two main differences between lying and deception. First, unlike "lying," "deception" implies success. An act must actually cause someone to have false beliefs in order to count as a case of deception. Intentional false statements need not succeed in deceiving others in order to count as lies. Second, although a lie must be a false statement, deception need not involve making a false statement; true statements can be deceptive, and many forms of deception do not involve making statements of any sort. Thus, many instances of deception do not constitute lying.

I also explain the relationship between deception and the notions of withholding information, concealing information, "keeping someone in the dark," "spin," and "half-truths," and I analyze the relationship between lying, deception, and bullshit. Harry Frankfurt to the contrary, bullshit does not require the intent to deceive and bullshit can constitute lying. I also argue that Frankfurt's famous claim that bullshitters, *qua* bullshitters, are unlike liars in that they are unconcerned with the truth (unconcerned with knowing "how things are") is mistaken. Since Frankfurt claims that unconcern with the truth is the essence of bullshit, this shows that his analysis of bullshit is mistaken.

PART IIA

Chapter 3: Kant and the Absolute Prohibition against Lying

In several works, Kant claims that lying is always wrong, no matter what. He is probably the most well-known defender of an absolute prohibition against lying in the history of Western philosophy. I survey what Kant says about lying in his writings. It is noteworthy that he never directly appeals to the categorical imperative in any of his arguments to show that lying is always wrong. I argue that the universal law version of the categorical imperative does not imply that lying is always wrong—one can consistently will that everyone follows maxims or principles that sometimes permit lying. Korsgaard to the contrary, the second version of the categorical imperative, which says that we should never treat another person as a mere means, does not imply that lying is never permissible. I contend that Korsgaard's arguments rest on contentious interpretations of several ambiguous passages in Kant. None of the versions of the categorical imperative commits Kant to an absolute prohibition against lying.

Not only does Kant fail to give a compelling argument for an absolute prohibition against lying, there are positive reasons to reject his absolutism. The duty not to lie can conflict with other moral duties. If lying is always wrong no matter what, then the duty not to lie must always be more important than any conflicting duty. However, it is most implausible to hold that the duty not to lie is always more important than any conflicting duty. Kant's own example of lying to thwart the plans of a would-be murderer is one of the best illustrations of this.

Chapter 4: Act-Utilitarianism

Act-utilitarianism implies that lying is morally permissible when, and only when, there is no alternative course of action open to one that has better consequences than lying. Many critics contend that utilitarianism is too permissive about the morality of lying. Mill attempts to answer this objection in *Utilitarianism* where he claims that lying always has indirect bad consequences (lying makes one less honest and undermines trust between people). Mill claims that, therefore, utilitarianism implies that there is a strong moral presumption against lying. I defend Mill's argument and note two ways in which it can be extended and strengthened. First, there is another indirect bad consequence of lying that Mill does not mention—the difficulties that liars incur in trying to "keep their stories straight." Second, in addition to the indirect bad consequences of lying (and deception), there are also direct bad consequences. We are (generally) harmed when we are deceived because we cannot effectively pursue our ends and interests if we act on the basis of false beliefs.

Chapter 5: Ross and Rule-Consequentialism

Even if we grant the success of Mill's arguments and the additional arguments I give in Chapter 4, the act-utilitarian view about the morality of lying is still open to a serious objection. If lying and not lying will have exactly the same consequences, then, according to act-utilitarianism, it does not matter whether or not one lies. Ross claims that lying is *prima facie* wrong, or wrong other things being equal; it is wrong to lie unless one has a conflicting obligation that is more important than (or as important as) the duty not to lie. Ross claims that it is "self-evident" that it is wrong to lie, other things being equal. He also thinks that it is obvious that it is wrong to lie when lying produces only slightly better consequences than not lying. Ross likens our knowledge of basic moral principles to our knowledge of axioms and postulates of mathematics (and our knowledge of the validity of certain forms of argument). This analogy is mistaken because there is far more disagreement (among competent people and those we might call "experts") about morality than math or logic. In contrast with Ross, Moore claims that it is self-evident that we should always do whatever has the best consequences. Moore's claim is flatly inconsistent with what Ross says about cases in which lying produces slightly better consequences than not lying. Neither Ross nor Moore gives convincing reasons for thinking that his own moral intuitions are correct and that the other's are mistaken. The debate between Ross and Moore about the morality of lying is inconclusive because both parties appeal to disputed intuitions. Appeals to moral intuitions are not adequate to justify judgments about controversial moral questions.

Rule-consequentialism or rule-utilitarianism represents a substantial modification of traditional act-utilitarianism. Roughly, rule-consequentialism holds that an act is morally right provided that it is consistent with the moral code the general acceptance of which would produce the best consequences. I examine Brad Hooker's well-known version of rule-consequentialism. Hooker claims that the ideal moral code that determines the rightness and wrongness of our actions includes the Rossian *prima facie* duty not to lie. Hooker appeals to the method of reflective equilibrium. He claims that his theory matches better with "our considered moral judgments" than act-utilitarianism. Hooker's arguments against act-utilitarianism depend entirely on the reliability of the considered moral judgments to which he appeals. (He has no other argument against act-utilitarianism other than its inconsistency with these judgments.) However, many ostensibly reasonable people disagree with the considered moral judgments to which he appeals in his arguments against act-utilitarianism, and he does not do enough to show that his considered moral judgments are correct/reliable and that the judgments of those who disagree with him are incorrect/unreliable. In the absence of some convincing defense of the reliability of these judgments, Hooker's arguments are unsuccessful.

PART IIB

Chapter 6: The Golden Rule and a Theory of Moral Reasoning

In order to avoid the sort of dialectical impasse noted in Chapter 5, we need to address metaethical questions about the justification of moral judgments. Chapter 6 develops a theory of moral reasoning in the form of rationality conditions for moral judgments. I argue that moral judges must be: (1) consistent; (2) adequately informed by knowledge of relevant facts (this requires vividly understanding relevant considerations, including the feelings of others—to lack empathy is to be deficient in knowledge and understanding required for being an informed moral judge); and (3) able to reason properly and have properly functioning cognitive abilities. These three rationality requirements are at least necessary conditions for rational moral judgments. The focus of this chapter is the first requirement (consistency).

I defend the following two consistency principles: (1) We must judge acts done to ourselves in the same way that we judge acts done to others, unless there are morally relevant differences between the acts, and (2) our attitudes must be consistent with our moral judgments (among other things, this implies that if I think that it is morally permissible for someone to do something to me (or someone I love), then I cannot object to her doing it to me (or someone I love)). Together, these two consistency principles entail the following version of the golden rule:

GR. Consistency requires that if I think it would be morally permissible for someone to do a certain act to another person, then I must not object to someone doing the same act to me (or someone I love) in relevantly similar circumstances. [I am inconsistent if I think that it would be morally permissible for someone to do something to another person, but object to someone doing the same act to me or someone I love in relevantly similar circumstances.]

I also give arguments for several other closely related consistency principles.

GR implies that if I claim that it is permissible for someone to do something to another person, then, on pain of inconsistency, I cannot object if someone else does the same thing to me in relevantly similar circumstances. The force of this version of the golden rule derives from the fact that, since there are certain things that we do object to other people doing to us, we cannot say that it would be morally permissible for us to do these same things to others in relevantly similar circumstances. Similarly, because there are actions we object to if they are done to our friends and loved ones, we cannot hold that it is permissible for us to do those things to others in relevantly similar circumstances.

I answer several well-known objections to the golden rule, including the objection that it permits people with unusual preferences, e.g., masochists, to perform wrong actions, and the objection that it makes it wrong to do anything to another person that she does not like, e.g., punish her. I also answer the objection that my version of the golden rule is useless for justifying moral judgments because claims to the effect that certain differences are or are not morally relevant presuppose answers to controversial questions.

I illustrate how the golden rule applies to cases and argue that (when supplemented by the other rationality conditions) it can justify certain moral judgments. My examples are moral judgments about the Holocaust and acts of fraud and deception by members of professions that increase their earnings but cause great harm to their clients. My theory also provides a basis for disproving ethical egoism. No one can be a consistent egoist, because ethical egoism requires that individuals sometimes harm others in ways that everyone objects to being harmed. The success of these arguments disproves extreme versions of moral relativism and moral skepticism. Since we can justify certain moral judgments, we know that at least some moral judgments are true/correct.

My proposal about moral reasoning is broadly Kantian in form, and also similar to Hare's universal prescriptivism. My consistency arguments are similar to Hare's in that they have the following limitation—they apply only to people who make moral judgments. My version of the golden rule does not provide any basis for arguing against moral nihilists who refrain from making any moral judgments. I offer pragmatic reasons to not be a moral nihilist. I also venture an answer to the questions "Why should I be consistent?" and "Why should I care about whether or not I am consistent?"

It is generally conceded that Hare's moral theory is a powerful and sophisticated theory of moral reasoning and moral argument. However, Hare makes unwise and implausible claims about what his theory can and cannot show. He famously grants the possibility of a consistent Nazi. He shows why it is very difficult to be a consistent Nazi, but grants that people who are willing to have Nazi principles applied against themselves and those they love could be consistent Nazis. Hare ignores the easy and obvious move of saying that consistent Nazis are not (and cannot be) adequately informed. Among other things, consistent Nazis have many false beliefs about their victims and lack an adequate understanding of the feelings of their victims. Although a Nazi could be consistent, a Nazi could not be both adequately informed and consistent. In *Moral Thinking*, Hare makes much more ambitious claims for his theory and offers a "proof" of utilitarianism. The proof depends on Hare's very implausible denial of the possibility of moral weakness and other dubious assumptions that I detail. I avoid some of Hare's most serious mistakes and offer a more reasonable view about what consistency arguments can and cannot show.

PART IIC

Chapter 7: The Partial Overlap/Convergence of Reasonable Views

The rationality and consistency tests defended in Chapter 6 can be used to discredit and rule out certain moral principles and moral judgments. We must reject principles and judgments that we cannot accept if we are consistent, rational, and informed. Thus, these tests can indirectly establish the truth of certain moral judgments and moral principles.

I argue that there is a large overlap or convergence in the moral judgments about lying and deception of people whose judgments satisfy rationality/consistency requirements. Thus, there is a large and important class of moral judgments about lying and deception that is true or justified. With some qualifications, we can claim the following:

The moral principles and moral judgments about lying and deception that survive consistency and rationality tests support a moral presumption against harmful lying and deception that is at least as strong as that endorsed by (welfare maximizing versions of) act-utilitarianism. Moral principles and moral judgments that claim or imply that lying or deception is permissible in cases in which it harms others and the harm it causes outweighs the benefits it produces fail rationality/consistency tests. In addition, the view that lying and/or deception are always wrong no matter what does not survive consistency and rationality tests.

I also propose an improved version of Rawls's and Hooker's reflective equilibrium; on my view, acceptable initial moral judgments must pass rationality/consistency tests. This improved version of reflective equilibrium yields roughly the same results for the issues of lying and deception as the direct application of consistency tests. It does not permit us to say that there is a single correct view about the morality of lying and deception, but there is a large convergence in the reasonable views that can be held in reflective equilibrium. All such views imply that there is a presumption against harmful lying and deception that is at least as strong as that endorsed by act-utilitarianism. Ross's theory, several modified versions of Ross's theory, and rule-consequentialism are also consistent with this result and, thus, they are also reasonable views about the morality of lying and deception. My improved version of reflective equilibrium also implies that the view that lying/deception are wrong no matter what is not a reasonable view.

These results enable me to justify moral judgments about lying and deception in a broad range of cases and provide a basis for answering most of the practical moral questions I address in Chapters 8–13. However, my theory also leaves some questions open—rational consistent moral judges can (and sometimes do) disagree about questions of lying and deception. They can disagree about the questions that divide the proponents of act-utilitarianism, rule-consequentialism, and Ross's theory.

PART III

Chapter 8: Deception and Withholding Information in Sales

I argue that salespeople have *prima facie* duties to: (1) warn customers of potential hazards; (2) refrain from lying and deception; (3) fully and honestly answer questions about what they are selling (insofar as their knowledge and time constraints permit); and (4) refrain from steering customers toward purchases they have reason to think will be harmful to customers. I defend this theory by appeal to the version of golden rule and the strong presumption against harmful lying and deception established in Chapters 6 and 7. I also analyze cases of deception and withholding information in sales. This chapter gives my most detailed application of the golden rule to particular cases.

Chapter 9: Deception in Advertising

Deceptive advertising harms people in much the same ways as deception in sales and tends to be wrong for the same reasons. Deceptive ads harm consumers by causing them to have false beliefs about the nature of the products being advertised and thereby causing them to make different purchasing decisions than they would have made otherwise (and purchase things unsuitable for their needs). I present examples of deceptive ads that harm consumers and argue that running such ads is morally wrong. My arguments appeal to the presumption against harmful deception established in Chapters 6–8. I then examine US laws regarding deceptive advertising. The law prohibits deceptive advertising, but it defines "deceptive advertising" too narrowly. US law frequently permits what is, in fact, deceptive advertising; therefore, following US laws is not an adequate ethical standard for advertisers. I also address the objection that deceptive advertising is permissible if one's competitors are putting one at a disadvantage by means of their own deceptive practices.

Chapter 10: Bluffing and Deception in Negotiations

This chapter discusses deception and bluffing in negotiations and focuses on the following kind of case: I am selling a house and tell a prospective buyer that $350 000 is absolutely the lowest price that I will accept, when I know that I would be willing to accept as little as $320 000 for the house. In this case, I make a deliberate false statement about my intentions and bargaining position. Despite the strong presumption against harmful lying and deception in commercial transactions, lying and deception in negotiations can sometimes be justified for reasons of "self-defense" if others are engaging in lying/deception and thereby gaining an advantage over one.

Chapter 11: Honesty, Professionals, and the Vulnerability of the Public

Often, professionals are in a position to advance their own financial interests by means of lying and deception, e.g., lying to a client to manipulate her into purchasing unneeded services. This creates very serious ethical problems because clients often have no way to assess the truth of what professionals tell them. We are at the mercy of professionals and need to rely on their honesty. I present examples that illustrate this important and widespread phenomenon and argue that the financial benefits professionals often derive from deception create systemic conflicts of interest. Professionals should adhere to a strong presumption against lying and deception in their dealings with their clients. In addition, all, or almost all, professionals have a duty to warn others of potential health and safety hazards and refrain from steering clients/customers toward decisions they have reason to think will be harmful to them. Professionals who work on the understanding that they are acting as fiduciaries (or quasi-fiduciaries) for the benefit of their clients/employers are obligated to do much more than this. They must be candid and provide salient information that clients/employers need. Those who have fiduciary duties to others have extensive positive duties to provide information to others—they must do more than refrain from lying and deception.

Perhaps the most fully developed account of the obligation of individuals to provide information is found in the principle of informed consent in medicine. I explain this principle and ask how far it can or should be extended to other professions. I argue that informed consent is a good model for professionals who are hired and paid by their clients and have fiduciary duties to act for the benefit of their clients, but not for professionals who do not have fiduciary duties to their clients/customers.

Chapter 12: Lying and Deception about Questions of War and Peace: Case Studies

This chapter examines cases in which political leaders and public figures told lies or engaged in deception as a pretext for fighting wars. My examples include William Randolph Hearst, Franklin Roosevelt, Lyndon Johnson, George W. Bush, and Dick Cheney. I devote particular attention to the case of Bush and Cheney and argue that they lied and attempted to deceive the public. Although this claim will strike many readers as obvious, it has not been adequately defended by those who make it. The journalists, public officials, and commentators who have accused Bush and Cheney of lying and deception do not offer careful definitions of lying and deception, much less a careful application of those definitions to the cases at issue. Certain features of my definition of lying are salient in these cases and help to show that Bush and Cheney lied and attempted to deceive the public—they strongly warranted the truth of claims that they knew were open to serious doubts. In most of these cases, lying and deception led to disastrous consequences and were morally wrong. However, I argue that Franklin Roosevelt was morally justified in his lying and deception in order to aid Britain during the early stages of WWII. I also discuss cases in which Dean Acheson, John Foster Dulles, and Dwight Eisenhower may have engaged in lying and deception in order to avoid wars. These also seem be to cases of justifiable lying/deception.

Chapter 13: Honesty, Conflicts, and the Telling of History: More Case Studies

The main thesis of this chapter is that deception and dishonesty about the historical record can create or aggravate conflicts and sometimes lead to disastrous consequences and, that, therefore, this sort of deception and dishonesty is morally wrong. I provide a detailed account the myth of the "stab in the back" (*Dolchstosslegende*) and Germany's defeat in WWI. The widespread acceptance of this myth by the German people was one of the central causes of the rise of Nazism and the Holocaust. I discuss other cases of deception and lying that distorted the historical record and led to very bad consequences; my examples are the dishonest version of history defended by neo-Confederates in the aftermath of the US Civil War and lies denying the crimes of Joseph Stalin by the New York correspondent Walter Duranty. Then I explicate the important concept of "half-truths." Half-truths mislead people and distort the truth but fall short of lying (often, they fall short of deception). Even when it falls short of lying and deception, endorsing half-truths is often a form of intellectual dishonesty. I discuss several cases in which half-truths have distorted the historical record and thereby aggravated social/political conflicts. The concept of half-truths has widespread application in personal relationships. I conclude by offering a brief account of the virtue of intellectual honesty (with particular attention to intellectual honesty about political questions).

Chapter 14: Honesty as a Virtue

Honesty is generally regarded as a cardinal virtue. In order to assess this conventional wisdom I examine the arguments of several dissenters who reject it. Some argue that since lying and deception are frequently justified in certain spheres of life/activity, honesty is not a virtue (in those spheres). We need to distinguish between what, for lack of better terms, I will call "honesty in a negative sense" (having a strong principled disinclination to tell lies or deceive others) and "honesty in a positive sense," which (in addition to involving being disinclined to tell lies or deceive others) involves being candid, open, and willing to reveal information. I argue that honesty in the negative sense (or something that closely resembles it) is a cardinal virtue in ordinary circumstances, but often honesty in the positive sense is not a virtue. I also identify spheres of activity in which candor and openness are virtues.

A NOTE ON READING THIS BOOK

Those readers who want to read a comprehensive treatment of moral and conceptual questions about lying and deception should read the entire book. Readers who are interested only in questions related to ethical theory and major traditions in the history of ethics should read Chapters 1–7 and 14. Readers who are interested in questions of business and professional ethics should read Chapters 1, 2, 6–11, and 14. Those interested in conceptual questions should read Chapters 1, 2, 9, and 11–14. Readers interested in questions about lying and deception in politics and lying and deception about the historical record should read Chapters 1, 2, 12, and 13.

I

CONCEPTS

Conceptual questions about the nature of lying and deception are prior to questions about the moral status of lying and deception because whether or not lying/deception is wrong depends on what lying/deception is. Chapters 1 and 2 are a conceptual roadmap for the rest of the book. I offer definitions of lying and deception and explain the relationships between the notions of lying, deception, "keeping someone in the dark," concealing information, withholding information, bullshit, spin, and "half-truths."

1

Lying

INTRODUCTION

This chapter proposes a definition of lying. Roughly, a lie is a deliberate false statement that the speaker warrants to be true. Two features of my definition are noteworthy. First, contrary to almost all standard definitions, I argue that lying does not require that the liar intends to deceive others. (I appeal to cases in which one is compelled or enticed to make false statements, cases of lying in which one can benefit by making false statements, even if they do not deceive others, and cases of bald-faced lies in which the liar knows that others know she is lying and, therefore, has no hope or intention of deceiving them.) Second, I hold that in order to tell a lie, one must make a statement that one warrants to be true. According to my definition (L5, see p. 30), any lie violates an implicit promise or guarantee that what one says is true. My definition makes sense of the common view that lying involves a *breach of trust*. To lie, on my view, is to invite others to trust and rely on what one says by warranting its truth and, at the same time, to betray that trust by making a false statement that one does not believe to be true. In the second part of this chapter, I answer published criticisms of my definition by Roy Sorensen and Don Fallis. Several of these objections may be serious, and I formulate a revised version of my definition that avoids them. According to my revised definition (L7, see p. 37), lying requires that one *intends to warrant* the truth of what one says, but does not require that one actually warrants its truth. Nothing that I say in the book depends on the difference between these two definitions (see p. 39–40).

1.I. MY DEFINITION OF LYING

1.I.1. Lies and Falsehoods

In order to tell a lie, one must make a false statement. Showing that a statement is true is always sufficient to counter the accusation that one has told a lie. Often people choose their words with great care in order to mislead others without saying anything that is literally false. For example, suppose that I know that a used car I am selling frequently overheats. A prospective buyer asks me whether the car overheats. If I say "no," I am lying. If I answer by making the true statement," I drove this car across the Mojave Desert on a very hot day and had no problems," I am not lying. This true statement is still very misleading—I drove the car across the desert four years ago and have had lots of trouble with it overheating since then. Often, people engage in this kind of verbal trickery because they take themselves to be avoiding lying and they regard lying as morally worse than deception. It is difficult to account for this widespread phenomenon unless we concede that ordinary language does not count such statements as lies. The recent controversy about whether or not President Clinton lied to the Starr Grand Jury when he denied having a "sexual relationship" with Monica Lewinsky illustrates this point. Clinton claims that his statement that he "did not have sexual relations with Monica Lewinsky" was not a lie because it was true, given the definition of "sexual relationship" specified in the questions he was asked by the grand jury. Clinton went through verbal contortions attempting to avoid acknowledging his relationship with Lewinsky without saying anything false. Clinton admits that what he said was misleading or deceptive, but he claims that he did not say anything false and, thus, did not lie or perjure himself. Those who hold that Clinton's statement was a lie are claiming (among other things) that what he said was false. (Perjury is defined as lying under oath in court. The law counts someone's testimony as perjurious only if what she says is false. Therefore, the law presupposes that a lie must be a false statement.)

A more difficult case for my view that a lie must be a false statement is the following:

I go fishing on a boat with a friend, John. He and I both catch a fish at the same time. Although we don't realize it, our lines are crossed. I have caught a very big fish and John has caught a little one, but we mistakenly believe that I caught the small fish and John caught the big one. We throw the two fish back into the water. I go home thinking that I caught a small fish. When I return, my father, an avid fisherman, asks me how I did. I say that I caught a very large fish and threw it back into the water, thereby intending to deceive him about size of the fish that I caught.[1]

My linguistic intuitions tell me that a lie must be a false statement, and that, therefore, what I say in this case is not a lie. I intend to lie in this case but I do not. Others report conflicting intuitions about this case and the question of whether a lie must be a false statement. (Fried, Isenberg, Williams, Bok, Kant, and Chisholm and Feehan all defend definitions of lying according to which a lie need not be a false statement.) To the extent that it rests on disputed intuitions, my claim that a lie must be a false statement is open to question. William Lycan reports empirical evidence that people's linguistic intuitions are divided on this point. He has on numerous occasions presented his students with a case from Sartre, who thinks that saying something false is necessary for lying. Sartre gives a case in which someone wants another person to believe that p is true. The person believes that p is false and asserts p to the other person, but p is true. According to Sartre, the person's statement cannot be a lie because p is true. Lycan (2006) reports that 40% of his students disagree with Sartre's claim and the view that saying something false is necessary for lying. I will not pursue this issue further here, but in note 22 I explain how my definition can be modified to accommodate the view that a lie need not be a false statement.

1.I.2. Falsehoods and Lies

All lies are false statements, but not all false statements are lies. I do not lie if faulty memory causes me to state something false when I am trying my best to be accurate and truthful. If I say something that is clearly false as a joke that is not intended to be taken seriously, I am not lying.

What is the difference between a lie and (the broader notion of) a false statement? Standard dictionary definitions of lying say that a lie is a false statement made with the intent to deceive others. The first definition of the word "lie" in the *Oxford English Dictionary* (1989) is the following: "a false statement made with the intent to deceive." *Webster's International Dictionary of the English Language* (1929) gives the following definition: "to utter a falsehood with the intent to deceive." However, these two definitions overlook an essential feature of lying. If a statement is a lie, then the person who makes it cannot believe that it is true.[2] Suppose that I tell you that Joe is away from his home because I hope to deceive you into thinking that you can easily break into his house and steal his paintings. In fact, I know that he has a sophisticated burglar alarm with a video camera that is likely to catch you in the act. I believe that Joe is away from home, but contrary to what I believe, he is at home. My statement is false and it is intended to deceive you, but it is not a lie, because I *believe* that it is true.

The definition of lying needs a condition to rule out the possibility that one believes that what one says is true. However, it is unclear exactly how this condition should be formulated. We might say that in order to lie one must make a false statement that one believes is false (or believes is probably false). Alternatively, we might say that in order to tell a lie one must make a false statement that one does not believe to be true. These two different ways of formulating the condition yield different results in the following sort of case: I make a false statement when I do not have the slightest idea whether or not it is true. Such statements are characteristic of bullshit. According to the strong condition (above), this statement cannot possibly be a lie (no matter what other conditions it satisfies), because I do not believe that the statement is false or probably false. The weaker condition allows for the possibility that statements of this sort are lies. (In such cases, the person who makes the statement does not believe that it is true.) I do not know of any decisive reason to prefer the stronger condition to the weaker condition or vice versa. Rather than attempt to show that the correct definition of lying must incorporate the stronger condition (or the weaker condition), I think that we should simply say that there are broader and narrower concepts of lying.

1.I.3. A Reformulation of the Dictionary Definitions

The foregoing objection to the dictionary definitions of lying and the uncertainty about how to formulate the condition that the liar must believe that what he says is false (or not believe that it is true), suggest the following definition of lying:

L1. A person S tells a lie iff: 1. S makes a false statement X, 2. S believes that X is false or probably false (or, alternatively, S doesn't believe that X is true), and 3. S intends to deceive another person by means of stating X (by stating X, S intends to cause another person to have false beliefs).[3]

The first condition of this definition needs explanation and clarification. What does it mean to say that a person, S, makes a false statement? This means roughly that: (1) S produces (utters, writes, signs, etc.) a linguistic token, t, that expresses a proposition, X; (2) X is false; and (3) S does this with the intention of communicating X to someone or some group of people. The last clause is clearly necessary. I might idly or absentmindedly produce linguistic tokens that express propositions with no intention of communicating those propositions to anyone. For example, while being bored by a committee meeting, I might write a sentence expressing a proposition on a piece of paper. Alternatively, in an empty room, I might read aloud statements from a book I am looking at. Doing this does not constitute stating anything unless I somehow intend to communicate to others. (I say more about this and the question whether successfully communicating with others is necessary for lying in 1.I.13.)

Consider this revised version of L1:

L1'. A person S lies or tells a lie iff: 1. S makes a false statement X, 2. S believes that X is false or probably false (or, alternatively, S does not believe that X is true), and 3. by stating X, S intends to cause others to believe X.

L1 and L1' differ only in their formulation of condition 3—they differ in cases in which a person intends to deceive others by means of stating something false (X) but does not intend to cause them to believe X.

1.I.4. Lying and the Right to Know the Truth

Those who are attracted to the absolutist view that lying is always wrong sometimes try to deal with objections by appealing to very narrow definitions of lying according to which the examples posed as cases of permissible lying are not genuine cases of lying (cf. Bok, 1979, pp. 14–15). The most well-known version of this kind of definition is the view that a necessary condition of one's lying is that the person to whom one's statement is directed has a right to know the truth.

According to this view, speaking falsely to someone who has no right to know the truth cannot be a lie. According to this definition, my making a deliberate false statement to a thief who asks me where I hid my money would not be a lie because the thief does not have a right to know the truth about the matter in question.[4] This kind of constraint can be incorporated into the definition of lying as follows:

L2. A person S tells a lie iff: 1. S makes a false statement X, 2. S believes that X is false or probably false (or, alternatively, S doesn't believe that X is true), 3. S intends to deceive another person by means of stating X (S intends his statement to cause another person to have false beliefs), and 4. the person to whom he makes the statement has the right to know the truth about the matter in question.

L2 is the result of adding condition 4 to L1. Given such definitions, some of the strongest examples commonly adduced against the claim that lying is always wrong are not genuine instances of lying. Consider the following variation on Kant's infamous example from "On a Supposed Right to Lie from Philanthropic Concerns." Suppose that someone comes to your door and asks you the whereabouts of a personal enemy. He evidently wants to murder the other person. You deliberately say that she (the man's enemy) is at a certain location when you know that she is not. You do this in the hope of misleading the man and saving her life. I would call this a case of permissible lying. According to L2, this is not a case of lying. I have no substantive moral disagreement with defenders of L2 about this case. We both agree that it is morally permissible to speak falsely to the man and mislead him. Our only disagreement is about whether we should count this example as a case of lying.

The sort of definition under consideration is sharply at variance with ordinary language. Ordinary language counts the example in question as a case of lying. There is a strong presumption against any definition of lying so much at odds with ordinary language. Using the term "lying" in accordance with this definition is likely to engender confusion. Pragmatic considerations also weigh against this definition of lying. L2 makes it impossible for us to determine whether or not certain acts are lies until we have first resolved difficult and controversial moral questions about whether someone has a right to know the truth (cf. Bok, 1979, pp. 14–15).[5] If we accept L2 (or any similar definition), then we cannot call a statement a lie unless we have reason to think that the audience has a right to know the truth. There are good pragmatic reasons for us to use the concept of lying to help point out and distinguish between salient features of actions and thereby assist us in making moral judgments. In order to serve this purpose, the concept of lying must be defined independently of *controversial* moral assumptions.

Some people endorse definitions such as L2 in order to defend the absolutist view that lying is always wrong. However, L2 does not rule out as lies clear cases of morally permissible lying. Suppose that a man has just had open heart surgery and is temporarily in a precarious state of health. His surgeon says that he must be shielded from any emotional distress for the next few days. Unbeknown to the patient, his only child, Bob, has been killed in an automobile accident. When the patient awakens after the surgery, he is surprised that Bob is not there and asks, "Where is Bob?" You fear that in his condition, the shock of learning about Bob's death might cause the man to die. So you lie and say that his son has been delayed. Given appropriate qualifications, it is morally permissible to lie to the patient. L2 does not exclude this as a case of lying—surely, the father has a right to know the truth about his son's death. This seems to be a case of morally permissible lying that violates someone's right to know the truth. Not every case of making a false statement to save the life of an innocent person is a case of making a false statement to someone who has no right to know the truth. L2 cannot rule out the possibility that there are cases in which it is necessary to lie in order to save the life of an innocent person and, therefore, it does not allow defenders of the absolute prohibition against lying to make their position palatable to common sense.

1.1.5. That the Intent to Deceive is not Necessary for Lying

L1 seems to me to be fairly close to the mark. However, some clear cases of lying in which one is compelled or enticed to make false statements (and some cases of lying in which one can benefit by making false statements) do not involve any intention to deceive others. These cases are counterexamples to L1 and most standard definitions of lying (such as the dictionary definitions noted earlier) according to which the intent to deceive others is necessary for lying. Suppose that I witness a crime and clearly see that a particular individual committed the crime. Later, the same person is accused of the crime and, as a witness in court, I am asked whether or not I saw the defendant commit the crime. I make the false statement that I did not see the defendant commit the crime, for fear of being harmed or killed by him. However, I do not intend that my false statements deceive anyone. (I hope that no one believes my testimony and that he is convicted in spite of it.) Deceiving the jury is not a means to preserving my life. Giving false testimony is necessary to save my life, but deceiving others is not; the deception is merely an unintended "side effect." I do not intend to deceive the jury in this case, but it seems clear that my false testimony would constitute a lie.

Here, it might be objected that, although I do not intend to deceive the members of the jury about the defendant's guilt, I still intend to deceive them into falsely believing *something else*, namely, that I *believe* that what I am saying is true. However, this reply does not work for every version of this example. Suppose that I know that the crime and my presence at the scene of the crime were recorded on a video camera so that there is almost no chance that the jury will believe that I believe what I am saying. Further, suppose that (1) I am confident that I will not be charged with perjury, even if everyone believes that I am lying, and (2) I am indifferent to other people's opinion about my character. Given all of this, I do not intend to deceive anyone into thinking that I believe what I am saying.

In the example in which I am the witness, I lie by making a false statement, even though I have no intention of deceiving anyone about anything. This case demonstrates that, at least sometimes, there is a performative act involved in making a statement. Sometimes we want to "go on record" and claim the truth of a particular statement. When we go on record to claim something, we warrant the truth of what we say. It is possible for me to go on record to claim the truth of something that I know is false without intending to deceive anyone. In my witness example, I go on record to claim that I did not see the defendant commit the crime in order to avoid being killed or harmed. (If I am being bribed, I might lie by testifying and saying something false "on the record" without having any intention to deceive others; I might simply want to receive my reward for giving the testimony and hope that it does not deceive anyone.)

A person can lie without intending to deceive anyone if she "goes on record" and warrants the truth of something she knows to be false in order to avoid institutional punishment of one sort or another. Suppose that a college Dean is cowed whenever he fears that someone *might* threaten a law suit and has a firm, but unofficial, policy of never upholding a professor's charge that a student cheated on an exam unless the student confesses in writing to having cheated. The Dean is very cynical about this and believes that students are guilty *whenever* they are charged. A student is caught in the act of cheating on an exam by copying from a crib sheet. The professor fails the student for the course and the student appeals the professor's decision to the Dean who has the ultimate authority to assign the grade. The student is privy to information about the Dean's *de facto* policy and, when called before the Dean, he (the student) affirms that he did not cheat on the exam. He claims that he was not copying from the crib sheet. He claims that he inadvertently forgot to put his "review sheet" away when the exam began and that he never looked at it during the exam. The student says this on the record in an official proceeding and thereby warrants the truth of statements he knows to be false. He intends to avoid punishment by doing this. He may have no intention of deceiving the Dean that he did not cheat. (If he is really hard-boiled, he may take pleasure in thinking that the Dean knows that he is guilty.) An objector might continue and say that surely the student intends to deceive *someone*—his parents or future employers. However, this is not necessarily the case. The student may not care whether or not others know that he cheated, but simply want to have his grade changed. (If it helps, suppose that the will of a deceased relative calls for the student to inherit a great deal of money if he graduates from the college in question with a certain grade-point average.) Since the student will get the money whether or not he deceives anyone, and since he knows that what he says will not cause anyone to have false beliefs, he lies although he clearly does not intend to deceive anyone.

Here is a third example of lying without the intent to deceive. Suppose that while working in his office, I happen upon evidence that my uncle perpetrated large-scale fraud in his capacity as a financial advisor. I ask him about this, and he admits to having committed fraud. He calls in my brother and sister who also work in the office and know about the fraud. My uncle then tells us the whole story but asks us to solemnly swear on our mother's grave that we will never tell anyone else or speak to anyone else (anyone other than the four of us) about this. We all swear to never mention or reveal any of this to anyone else.

After my uncle's death, there is a lawsuit against his estate by the victims of his fraud. There is conclusive evidence of his fraud. The evidence includes the testimony of numerous people (including my brother and sister), secret records of the funds he stole, and records of secret bank accounts my uncle created to hide the money. There is also conclusive evidence that I knew about the fraud—a handwritten letter from me to my uncle, the testimony of my brother and sister, and wire-tapped phone conversations between my siblings and me.

Under oath in court, I am asked if I knew anything about his fraud and whether I ever came across evidence that he committed fraud. Since I believe that I am morally bound by my oath to my uncle (but not by my oath to the court), I deny any knowledge of his fraud and claim that, to the best of my knowledge, no fraud ever occurred. My statement is a lie. What I say is false, I know that it is false, and, because I make the statement under oath, I strongly warrant its truth.

My false testimony is not intended to deceive anyone about matters relating to the lawsuit. I know that my testimony will not cause anyone to believe that my uncle is innocent. Nor do I intend or hope to deceive anyone about what I believe or about *anything* else. My only intention in this case is to remain faithful to my oath to my uncle. The motives for my actions have been revealed by the testimony of my brother and sister, and I expect everyone to believe their testimony about the time when my uncle told us of his fraud and made us swear not to tell others about it. I am quite happy if everyone knows the whole truth (I think that others will respect my true motives, and I have no fear of being charged with perjury for my testimony). Given all of this, I do not expect or intend my testimony to deceive anyone about anything.[6]

These cases of lying without intending to deceive others are crucial for my argument in this chapter. Later in the chapter (Section 1.I.10), I will return to these cases and explain why my definition counts them both as cases of lying.

Let me digress briefly to clarify the notion of an intentional act. Roughly, the intended consequences of an act are those that one either (1) aims at for their own sake, or (2) foresees and regards as part of a causal chain leading to consequences that one desires or aims at for their own sake (cf. Goldman, 1970, chapter 3, and Walzer, 1977, pp. 153–156).[7] Consider the following example. The leader of nation X plans an air attack on armaments factories in nation Y. The ultimate aim of the attack is to end the death and suffering caused by the war. The leader of X regards the destruction of these factories as a necessary means to ending the war and the attendant suffering. The leader foresees that the attack will kill civilians living in areas adjacent to the factories.[8] The death of these people is not a means that (causally) contributes to the goal of ending the war, rather, it is an unavoidable "side effect" of the bombing. This consequence is not "intended" but merely foreseen. "Terror bombing," on the other hand, involves the intention to kill innocent civilians. Suppose that the leader of a nation at war orders the bombing of an enemy city. S/he aims to end the war by demoralizing the civilian population of the enemy country.[9] Demoralizing the civilian population is to be accomplished by killing large numbers of civilians. Here, the killing of the civilians is not just a side effect but an essential part of the causal chain leading to the ultimate goal of the bombing. Leaders who order the bombing of cities for these reasons *intend* to kill civilians. (This holds even if the leaders in question do not desire the killing of the civilians as an end in itself and even if they deeply regret the killing of the civilians.[10])

1.1.6. Chisholm and Feehan's Definition

My examples in the preceding section are counterexamples to the definition proposed by Chisholm and Feehan (1977) in their well-known paper, "The Intent to Deceive." They define lying as follows: "[Person] *L* lies to [person] D = df There is a proposition p such that (i) either L believes that p is not true or L believes that p is false and (ii) L asserts p to D" (p. 152).[11] This definition makes use of the concept of asserting a proposition. Chisholm and Feehan (1977) define this notion as follows: "*L* asserts p to D = df L states p to D and does so under conditions which, he believes, justify D in believing that he, L, not only accepts p, but also intends to contribute causally to D's believing that he, L, accepts p" (p. 152). They comment on this definition as follows:

A statement that is made merely in play, or in irony, is thus not an assertion, for the speaker is not justified in taking it seriously. When one speaks ironically, one plays oneself down, but one gives a "signal of irony"—perhaps by means of tone and choice of words—and this signal indicates that one is not to be taken seriously and hence one is not making an assertion.   (p. 152)

The example in which I am the witness is also a counterexample to Chisholm and Feehan's (1977) definition. The witness clearly lies in this example, but their definition does not count this statement as a lie. Because the defendant's crime was videotaped, the witness knows that the jury will not be justified in believing that he believes (accepts) what he says. This objection can be strengthened if we further stipulate that the witness is known to be an extremely dishonest person. Given all of this, the witness knows that the jury will not be justified in believing that he believes (accepts) what he says. Chisholm and Feehan's definition has the very odd and unacceptable result that a notoriously dishonest person cannot lie to people who he knows distrust him. Their definition implies that it is self-contradictory to say that I lie when I know that others know that I am lying (and thus are not justified in believing that I believe (accept) what I say).[12]

1.I.7. My Definition of Lying (A Preliminary Version)

Standard definitions of lying claim that the intention to deceive others is necessary for lying. As we have seen, this is a mistake, and we need to find some alternative condition(s) to replace this in our definition of lying. W. D. Ross (1930) hints at this needed condition. He holds that all lies are *prima facie* wrong because they are instances of promise-breaking; it is *prima facie* wrong to lie because to lie is to break an implicit promise to tell the truth that one makes whenever one uses language to make statements.[13] Ross himself does not define lying. However, his view implies that all lies involve breaking a promise to speak (or communicate) truthfully. I agree with Ross that lying involves breaking a promise (or something very similar to a promise) to communicate truthfully.[14] The expression "it's true that" is redundant in the context of ordinary statements. Consider the following:

1. The sky is blue.
2. It is true that the sky is blue.

(1) and (2) have exactly the same meaning. In ordinary contexts, the expression "it is true that" adds nothing to the meaning of a statement. This is so because, ordinarily, when one makes a statement, one is understood to be warranting its truth.

Taken together with our earlier criticisms of L1 and L2, the view that making a statement (ordinarily) involves warranting that what one says is true suggests the following definition of "lying":

L3. A person S tells a lie iff: 1. S makes a false statement X, 2. S believes that X is false or probably false (or, alternatively, S does not believe that X is true), and 3. S states X in a context in which S thereby warrants the truth of X.

This definition avoids the earlier counterexamples. It counts the witness's testimony in court as a lie. When the witness testifies in court, he warrants the truth of what he says by explicitly promising to tell the truth under oath. L3 allows us to say that it is possible for me to lie to you when I know that you know that I am lying so that I have no hope of deceiving you either about the truth of what I say or about what I believe. (For more on the implications of my definition for the cases from Section 1.I.5, see Section 1.I.10.)

1.I.8. "A Defense of the Transparency Thesis"

My definition of lying is motivated by the "transparency thesis"—the view that the expression "it is true that" adds nothing to the meaning of a statement. The classic statements of the transparency thesis are found in Frege (p. 151) and Frank Ramsey. Ramsey (1931) writes: ' "It is true that Caesar was murdered" means no more than that Caesar was murdered, and "It is false that Caesar was murdered" means no more than that Caesar was not murdered' (p. 142). Strawson (1949) offers a noteworthy criticism of the transparency thesis in his essay "Truth." He argues that "X" and "it's true that X" cannot always be used interchangeably. For example, suppose that I say that Ingrid is having an extramarital affair and you deny it. My responding with "But it's *true* that she is having an affair," can constitute a stronger, more emphatic response than simply repeating "she is having an affair." In many borderline cases, it is unclear whether or not making a statement involves warranting its truth. In such cases, saying that X is true warrants the truth of X, but merely saying that X (without saying that X is true) does not. For example, suppose that I know of a humorous and improbable fact about Judy. I wish to state this fact and warrant its truth in the context of a humorous "bull-session." Simply stating the fact in this situation probably does not constitute warranting its truth. In order to accomplish this it may be necessary for me to say something like "It's *true* that _____ I'm not kidding." Strawson's criticisms of the very strong version of the transparency thesis according to which "X" and "it's true that X" can *always* be used interchangeably are consistent with my view that, *in ordinary contexts*, the expression "it's true that" adds nothing to the meaning of a statement. The fact that saying "it's true that X" sometimes constitutes a *stronger warranty of the truth of X* than just saying "X" is consistent with my view that, ordinarily, a person who states something warrants its truth (indeed, this fact presupposes the truth of my view).

1.I.9. The Concept of Warranting

A warranty of truth is a kind of guarantee or promise that what one says is true. Following Austin and Searle, contemporary philosophers generally take promising to be a performative act. To make a promise is to place oneself under an obligation to do something. This explains the difference between promising to do X and stating an intention to do X (see Searle, 1968).[15] There seems to be no satisfactory alternative explanation. However, special problems arise if we attempt to extend this account of promising as an analysis of warranting the truth of a statement. If one promises to do X, one is placing oneself under an obligation to perform a specific act (one is placing oneself under an obligation to do X). However, often when one warrants the truth of a statement, one is not placing oneself under an obligation to perform any *particular action* or kind of action. To warrant the truth of a statement X is not necessarily to place oneself under an obligation to make it true that X, for one is usually not in a position to affect the truth of the statements one makes. If I warrant the truth of my statement that the moon is 250 000 miles from the earth, I am not placing myself under an obligation to make it the case that the moon is 250 000 miles from the earth. Nor does warranting the truth of X place one under an obligation to perform acts of compensation in case X turns out not to be true and others are harmed as a result of relying on one's statements. There is no general understanding about what (if anything) we owe others when they suffer harm as a result of accepting false claims that we make.

In our linguistic community, and almost all others of which I am aware, there is a *presumption* that the warranty of truth is in force in any situation.[16] *Convention* dictates that one warrants the truth of one's statements in the absence of special contexts, special signals, or cues to the contrary. In the context of a work of fiction or when saying something in jest, one is not guaranteeing the truth of what one says. So, for example, one is not implicitly guaranteeing that what one says is true if one says something manifestly false as a joke to a friend in an ironic tone of voice.

In many cases, it is unclear whether those who speak are warranting the truth of what they say. For example, suppose that I deliberately make a false statement to a person whom I know to be very gullible, but give a very subtle indication that I might be joking (I might, for example, raise an eyebrow very slightly). In such a case, it is unclear whether I am warranting the truth of what I say and, therefore, unclear whether or not this should be considered a lie. Such cases should be considered borderline cases for the concept of lying. It is a virtue of my analysis that they count as such.[17] Many instances of bluffing are borderline cases of warranting/lying (see Chapter 10 and Carson, 1993b).

1.I.10. Conditions for Warranting the Truth of a Statement

If one warrants the truth of a statement, then one promises or guarantees, either explicitly or implicitly, that what one says is true. The idea of explicitly promising to tell the truth is straightforward and needs no explanation here. A witness who swears an oath explicitly promises that what she says is true. One can also explicitly promise that what one says is true by means of such locutions as "I swear on my honor . . . " In ordinary circumstances, statements are warranted to be true. Because of this default warranty of truth, statements ordinarily invite trust and reliance.

Sometimes people lie when they know that others know that they are lying. In such cases of bald-faced lying, a person can lie in stating that X, even if she does not intend to deceive anyone about the truth of X or about what she believes. In such cases, one invites reliance on what one says by warranting its truth. It is possible for me to issue you an invitation, even if I know that you know that I know that you will not accept the invitation (and even if I know that you know that I hope you will not accept the invitation). I can invite my estranged uncle to attend my wedding while knowing and hoping that he won't come. This invitation is not voided by our mutual understanding of the fact that I know and hope that he will not accept the invitation. (To help see this, imagine that there is a guard at the door of the wedding who admits only invited guests.) Similarly, lies can and do invite reliance on what is stated, even if the liar hopes and knows that her audience will not believe or rely on her statements.

The cases presented in Section 1.I.5 illustrate the kinds of reasons one can have for lying in such cases. It might be the case that one will benefit simply by making the false statement in question, e.g., by receiving a bribery payment or avoiding a harm that was threatened. So, one might lie by making a false statement in order to receive the benefit or avoid the harm. In addition, one might lie in order to "go on record" as saying something, as in the case of the man who lies in order to keep his promise to his uncle.

Convention dictates that there are circumstances, for example, when people tell stories or attempt to be humorous, which remove the default warranty of truth from our statements. The linguistic conventions of our society imply that, in the case of statements that are clearly not intended be humorous or tell a story, the default warranty of truth is usually very strong. The student's statement to the Dean is such a case. If the student's response to the Dean's questions includes obvious winks and nods and unguarded nervous laughter, then the warranty of truth may be removed (or at least it is cast into doubt).[18] However, if the student "plays it straight" and looks grave and serious, then his statements are warranted to be true and count as lies according to my definition. It is not paradoxical or contradictory for me to promise you that a statement is true, when I know that you know that I know it is not true. I can promise you something, even if you and I both know that I will not keep the promise; I can also make a promise to you in bad faith even if I know that you know that I am making the promise in bad faith. In such a case, my promise invites your reliance, but you would not be justified in relying on what I say. Thus, my warranting the truth of something I say to you justifies you in complaining to me if it is not true, although it does not always justify you in relying on it.

Whether a person warrants the truth of what s/he says on a given occasion depends largely on the context and the relevant local conventions embedded in that context. Far too many possible contextual factors are relevant for it to be possible to state necessary and sufficient conditions for warranting the truth of a statement. However, the following observations help explicate the notion of warranting the truth of a statement.

1. Whether or not a speaker (communicator) warrants the truth of what she says is at least partly independent of her intentions. One can warrant the truth of a statement without intending to, and one can even warrant the truth of a statement contrary to one's intentions. The following example illustrates this. Suppose that I am asked to speak at two different banquets. At the first banquet I am asked to give a serious talk about the current political situation and the job performance of the new President of the United States. At the second banquet I am expected to give a humorous or satirical talk about current politics and political figures. I become confused about which talk is supposed to be serious and which is supposed to be humorous. I deliver my humorous satirical talk to the group that has asked me to give a

serious talk. I tell them a story about the President having "broken wind" during a meeting with foreign dignitaries. I warrant the truth of this story to my audience, although I do not intend to. I give my serious talk to an audience expecting a humorous talk. During my talk, I relate certain curious news about the President's health. The audience takes it to be a lame joke. Even though I take myself to be warranting the truth of what I say, I am not. Extending the last example further, suppose that I concoct a false, but humorous, story to discredit a political figure before an election. I intend to tell this story and warrant its truth to an audience interested in current events, but, unbeknownst to me, I am speaking to an audience expecting to hear political satire and humor. My statements about the politician are false, I know that they are false, and I intend to warrant their truth. However, my definition implies that I have not lied, because, contrary to my intentions, I did not warrant the truth of my statement. In this case, I intended to lie but failed due to my failure to warrant the truth of what I said.

2. Whether or not the truth of a statement is warranted to an audience is partly independent of whether the members of the audience believe that the speaker (writer) warrants its truth to them. I can be mistaken in believing that the truth of a statement is or is not warranted to me. Sometimes people are obtuse and fail to perceive that the things they are told are said in jest. In such cases, they can be mistaken in believing that the speaker (writer) warrants the truth of what s/he says (writes). Similarly, a member of an audience can be mistaken in believing that a speaker (writer) is *not* warranting the truth of what s/he says (writes). Suppose that a historical society and an association of comedians are both holding meetings in a particular hotel. I enter a conference room of the hotel expecting to hear a comedian perform. However, unbeknownst to me, the speaker in the room is a member of the historical society. As I walk in, the speaker is relating a humorous event in the life a well-known historical figure. Although I do not believe that the speaker is warranting the truth of what he says, he is.

In many contexts it is unclear whether the speaker/writer warrants the truth of what s/he says. Suppose that an English-speaking acquaintance from a non-Western country tells me a very bizarre story on April Fool's Day. I do not know whether he knows anything about American practices and understandings about April Fool's Day. In the absence of other contextual clues, it is unclear whether he warrants the truth of what he says. Suppose that a professor is well known for her animated, humorous, and Socratic style of teaching. She often makes false statements to her classes to see if they are paying attention. When she does this, she berates her students if they fail to catch her. She begins her lecture with an improbable sounding historical anecdote. In this context, it is unclear whether the professor warrants the truth of what she says. In the course of Socratic classroom debates in which professors play devil's advocate, it is often unclear whether they warrant the truth of what they say—philosophy classrooms are rife with this kind of ambiguity.

This sort of ambiguity is increased if the speaker (writer) and the audience are members of different societies that have different conventions and expectations about truth-telling and warranting the truth of statements. There are often contexts in which one party expects that what is said is warranted to be true and the other party does not.[19]

1.I.11. Yet Another Revision

The foregoing example of a person who warrants the truth of a statement when he intends not to raises problems for my definition of lying. According to my definition, the speaker in the earlier example who mistakenly believes that his audience is expecting a humorous talk tells a lie (albeit unintentionally) when he tells the story about the President's flatulence. His statement is false, he knows that it is false, and he warrants its truth to his audience. It seems counterintuitive to call this a lie, even if we stress that it is an unintentional lie. Our definition of lying seems to need another condition, namely, that it is not the case that the speaker takes himself to be not warranting the truth of what he says. The speaker in the present example does not satisfy this condition because he takes himself to be not warranting the truth of what he says. With this additional condition, the definition reads as follows:

L4. A person S tells a lie iff: 1. S makes a false statement X, 2. S believes that X is false or probably false (or, alternatively, S does not believe that X is true), 3. S states X in a context in which S thereby warrants the truth of X, and 4. S does not take herself to be not warranting the truth of what she says.[20]

1.I.12. A Complication and My Final Definition

Problems are created by cases in which statements are made to groups of individuals who have differing levels of knowledge and sophistication, so that the truth of a given statement on a given occasion is warranted to some, but not all, of the people to whom it is made. Consider, for example, a greatly exaggerated account of a past event told to a mixed group containing both sophisticated adults and young children: "The dog who was chasing me was huge; he was at least ten feet tall." (Note, I am supposing that the context of this is not just "a story" but an account of something that was alleged to have actually happened.) In such a case, one warrants the truth of what one says to the children but not to the adults. The very content of the narrative makes it clear to the adults that its truth is not being warranted to them. However, there is nothing one does and nothing about the context or content of what one says that removes the default warranty of truth to the children. We need to relativize our concept of lying and allow for the possibility that, in making a given statement or utterance on a particular occasion, one might be lying to some members of one's audience, but not to others.[21] I propose the following:

L5. A person S tells a lie to another person S1 iff: 1. S makes a false statement X to S1, 2. S believes that X is false or probably false (or, alternatively, S does not believe that X is true), 3. S states X in a context in which S thereby warrants the truth of X to S1, and 4. S does not take herself to be not warranting the truth of what she says to S1.[22]

1.I.13. Some Comments on this Definition

Condition 1 says that a statement must be false in order to be a lie. Whether we count a statement as true or false sometimes depends on the standards of precision and accuracy we employ. For example, suppose that someone asks me what time it is. My watch is very accurate and displays the following time "10:01:15" (one minute fifteen seconds after 10). I tell the person "it's ten o'clock." Is my statement true? It depends on the context. If someone asks this question in a context in which it is understood by all that the answer needs to be extremely accurate and precise (e.g., an engineer at a radio station who needs to know when to begin broadcasting a program or an astronaut who needs to know when to begin a maneuver) then my statement is false. On the other hand, if I am asked this question by my wife while taking a leisurely walk on our vacation when neither of us needs to know exactly what time it is, my answer should count as a true statement. My concept of warranting proves useful for dealing with this issue. In some contexts one warrants what one says as true to a high degree of accuracy and precision. In other contexts, statements are not warranted to be true to a high degree of accuracy.

Some hold that a necessary condition for telling a lie is that communication actually occurs, i.e., that what is said is actually conveyed or communicated to another person (for example, Siegler, 1966; Fried, 1978, p. 57). (This could also be construed as a necessary condition for making a statement.) According to this view, I can attempt to lie but fail if I do not communicate successfully. Suppose that I speak to someone and intentionally say something that is false in circumstances that I know constitute warranting the truth of what I say. On the view in question, my utterance cannot be a lie unless I succeed in communicating with the other person. If the person to whom I am speaking is deaf or does not speak the language I am using, then I have not succeeded in making a statement to her and I cannot be said to have lied to her (although I attempted to). Alternatively, to take another example, suppose that I am talking to you in a different room of a house so that we cannot see each other. The conversation stops for half an hour. After this interval, I intentionally say something I know to be false intending to warrant the truth of what I say. However, unbeknownst to me, you have left the house (you are many miles away) and do not hear what I say. I am inclined to think that in this case I did not lie to you, although I intended to. Others report very different intuitions about this case. I do not have any decisive arguments that settle this question. In any case, we can leave the definition of lying as it is. To endorse my definition we do not need to settle the question of whether making a (false) statement requires that one succeeds in communicating with another. This question concerns the proper interpretation of the first condition of the definition. The question is whether successfully communicating with another person is necessary for making a statement.

Some related issues and puzzles should be briefly noted here. What should we say about statements that are successfully conveyed to others, but only long after they are made? Suppose that an historical figure writes many false things in his diary in the hope of misleading future readers and historians. The diary is not read by anyone until 100 years later. When he writes this, can we say that he is lying? Can we say that he *is* lying, but that his lying (now) depends on what will happen in the future? Suppose that a politician writes a false account in his diary hoping to mislead future historians. The diary is later destroyed and no one else ever reads it. Should we say that he intended to lie but failed to because his statements were never successfully conveyed to anyone else? Roy Sorensen gave me the following cases in correspondence:

Consider time delay cases. I write a lie in a letter. I mail the letter. It is read three days later. When did I lie? If I only lie when it is read, then I can lie while asleep or dead. The time delay can be long so that I can lie to a person who does not yet exist. Consider a sperm donor who writes a letter to his future child. The letter could have a lie in it.

1.I.14. An Objection: The Concept of Assertion

A number of alternative definitions of lying discussed in this chapter employ the notion of making an assertion. One might argue that lying should be defined in terms of making an assertion rather than warranting the truth of a statement.[23] Taking this suggestion, one might claim that the following is preferable to (and simpler than) my definition of lying:

L6. A person S tells a lie to another person S1 iff: 1. S asserts a false proposition X to S1, 2. S believes that X is false or probably false (or, alternatively, S does not believe that X is true), and 3. S does not take herself to be not asserting X to S1.

Whether or not L6 is a plausible definition depends on what sort of explanation of "asserting a proposition" is provided. Without a detailed account of what is meant by "asserting a proposition," L6 is vague and ambiguous. As some understand the concept of an assertion, asserting a proposition is roughly the same as warranting its truth. Given this, L6 is equivalent or nearly equivalent to my L5 and the details of my account of warranting the truth of a statement are still needed to give content to the concept of assertion used in L6. L6 has a superficial appearance of greater simplicity created by the fact that it includes three conditions instead of four.

If L6 is combined with a concept of assertion substantially different from my notion of warranting an assertion, it does not yield an acceptable definition of lying. I will attempt to show that this is the case for the other alternative accounts of asserting a proposition presented earlier in this chapter. Fried (1978), B. Williams (2002), and Chisholm and Feehan (1977) each define lying in terms of the concept of an assertion. I have offered criticisms of their definitions of lying. Still, we might ask whether any of their analyses of the concept of assertion yields a plausible definition of lying when combined with L6.

Fried

Fried writes: "As a first approximation: to assert X is to utter X in a context such that the utterance is intended to cause belief." If we combine L6 with Fried's (1978) account of assertion, we are committed to the view that in order for my stating X to be a lie I must intend that others believe X (p. 56). However, this is not the case, for reasons that we saw in earlier in 1.I.5 and 1.I.10. I can lie even if I do not intend to cause you to believe what I say. L6 is not a plausible definition of lying when combined with Fried's concept of assertion.

Williams

B. Williams (2002) defines what it is to assert a proposition in the following passage: "A utters sentence 'S,' where 'S' means that P, in doing which either he expresses his belief that P, or he intends the person addressed to take it that he believes that P" (p. 74).When combined with L6, Williams's concept of making an assertion implies that a necessary condition of one's telling a lie in saying X is that either one expresses one's belief that X or one intends to cause the person(s) one addresses to believe that one believes that X. This is also false for reasons we saw in 1.I.5 and 1.I.10.

Chisholm and Feehan

Chisholm and Feehan (1977) define asserting a proposition in the following passage: "*L* asserts p to D = df L states p to D and does so under conditions which, he believes, justify D in believing that he, L, not only accepts p, but also intends to contribute causally to D's believing that he, L, accepts p" (p. 152).When combined with L6, this definition of assertion implies that, in order to lie to you in stating proposition X, I must state X to you in conditions that I believe justify you in believing that I accept X and intend to contribute to your believing that I accept X. As we have seen, however, a notoriously dishonest person can lie to you in stating X, even if he knows that you are not justified in believing that he accepts X and even if he knows that you are not justified in believing that he aims or intends to cause you to believe that he believes that X.

1.I.15. Reasons to Accept My Definition

Lying is a concept used in everyday language, and moral questions about lying arise in people's everyday experience. There are no compelling reasons to revise or reject the ordinary language concept of lying—at least the burden of proof rests with those who would revise or reject it. Therefore, consistency with ordinary language and people's linguistic intuitions about what does and does not count as a lie is a desideratum of any definition of lying. My definition provides a better account of our shared linguistic intuitions about what does and does not count as a lie than any of the alternative definitions considered in this chapter. My definition also explains why many cases are unclear or borderline cases for the concept of lying. (In many cases it is unclear whether or not one warrants the truth of what one says.) My definition is near the mark in terms of ordinary language, but no definition can be completely consistent with everyone's linguistic intuitions about what does and does not constitute lying. People have conflicting intuitions about certain cases and certain issues, e.g., whether a lie must be a false statement.

In every language and culture there are contextual understandings about whether a given utterance or use of language should be taken to be a statement that is warranted to be true.[24] These understandings often determine whether or not an utterance or linguistic act constitutes a lie. One and the same utterance can be a lie in some contexts but not others. For example, a false utterance that would ordinarily count as a lie may not be a lie if it is uttered on April Fool's Day (see J. A. Barnes, 1993, p. 113). A sentence that would be a lie if it appeared in a police report or history book would not be a lie if it appeared in a novel (cf. J. A. Barnes, 1993, p. 166). J. A. Barnes holds that the best explanation of why such cases do or do not constitute lying is that lying requires the intention to deceive others (pp. 15, 113–114). According to Barnes, an utterance that is not intended to be a statement that purports to be true is not a lie, because it is not made with the intention to deceive others. Barnes's explanation is implausible for reasons given earlier in 1.I.5 and 1.I.10. My definition provides a better explanation of this than Barnes's or alternative definitions. My definition also provides a good explanation of why there is often disagreement about whether a given utterance made by a member of one society to a member of another society constitutes lying. The explanation is that when members of two different societies interact, they often do not share the same implicit understandings about how statements are to be taken in given contexts. A context that a member of one society takes to involve warranting the truth of what one says is not taken to involve a warranty of truth by a member of the other society.[25]

Strawson's (1949) criticisms of the "transparency thesis" show that there are weaker and stronger ways of warranting the truth of a statement. To count as a lie, a statement must be warranted to a certain minimum degree, but some lies are warranted to a much greater degree. One's expressions of confidence or lack of confidence in the certitude of one's statements also strengthen or weaken the degree to which one warrants them as true. The strength with which a lie is warranted to be true is arguably relevant to its moral assessment. Perhaps the wrongness or culpability of a lie is determined, in part, by the strength with which it is warranted to be true.[26] (This is relevant in 12.III where I discuss the repeated claims by members of the Bush administration to the effect that it was "certain" that Iraq possessed "weapons of mass destruction.") My definition of lying has the virtue of making perspicuous what is arguably a morally relevant consideration; it also helps us to identify and diagnose an important type of deception (see Chapter 2.I).

My definition does not beg any controversial moral questions about lying, e.g., "is lying *prima facie* wrong?" or "Is lying always wrong?" My definition helps illuminate moral questions by identifying morally salient features of actions.

A final virtue of my analysis is that it makes sense of the common view that lying involves a breach of trust. To lie, on my view, is to invite others to trust and rely on what one says by warranting its truth, but, at the same time, to betray that trust by making false statements that one does not believe.[27]

1.II. REPLIES TO CRITICISMS OF MY DEFINITION

My definition, which I defend in Carson (2006), has been criticized in recent papers by Roy Sorensen (2007) and Don Fallis (2009).

1.II.1. Sorensen

Sorensen (2007) endorses my criticisms of the view that lying requires the intent to deceive and makes use of some of my arguments in support of his own views. However, he thinks that my definition of lying is too narrow and cannot account for cases of bald-faced lying:

Carson's counterexamples show that standard definitions of lying are too narrow. However, Carson's definition does not relieve the narrowness. The concept of warrant is not broad enough to explain how we can lie in the face of common knowledge. One can warrant p only if p might be the case. When the falsehood of p is common knowledge, no party to the common knowledge can warrant p because p is epistemically impossible. (p. 254)

Sorensen claims that my definition of lying is too narrow because, in the case of bald-faced lies, the falsity of what one says is obvious and common knowledge, and thus it is impossible for one to warrant the truth of what one says. Consider one of Sorensen's examples of a bald-faced lie. The Norwegian journalist Asne Seierstad went to a civilian hospital in Iraq during the 2003 war. Sorensen (2007) writes:

She is surprised to see a ward with wounded soldiers. This suggests that Iraqi military hospitals are already overcrowded. [Seierstad writes:]

– How many soldiers have you admitted today? I ask a Doctor.
– There are no soldiers here, the doctor says.
– But they are wearing uniforms?
– I see no uniforms he says, and pushes me out.—You must go now, do you hear?
  (p. 253)

In this case, Sorensen would say that the doctor cannot warrant the truth of his claim that there are no soldiers there and that he sees no uniforms, because he and Seierstead both know that it is false (and each knows that the other knows this). However, Sorensen, to the contrary, the doctor still warrants the truth of what he says because he invites Seierstad to trust and rely on the truth of what he says and guarantees the truth of what he says. The fact that the bald-faced liar has no hope of getting others to trust him does not make it impossible for him to invite them to trust him. Similarly, as we saw earlier (1.1.10), I can invite someone to come to an event, even though I know that he will not accept the invitation—our mutual knowledge that he will not accept the invitation does not cancel the performative force of issuing it.

To the extent that there is any doubt about the adequacy of this answer to Sorensen, my alternative definition, L7 (see p. 37), allows me to count Sorensen's example as a clear case of lying. L7 drops the requirement that the liar must warrant the truth of what she says and replaces it with the requirement that the liar *intends to warrant the truth of what she says*. The doctor in Sorensen's example intends to warrant the truth of what he says, and L7 clearly counts the doctor's statement as a case of lying.

Sorensen (2007) also claims that my definition is too broad in certain respects:

Carson says that the warranter guarantees the truth of p. But this conception of warrant is too broad. Consider a witness who says "Rocco shot the Mafia boss but I give my word that Rocco did not shoot him." This is not even a lie. Nor can the witness make it a lie by meeting obligations incurred by saying "Rocco did not shoot him."   (p. 254)

However, Sorensen to the contrary, I do not have to count "Rocco shot the Mafia boss but I give my word that Rocco did not shoot him" as a lie. This utterance is not a lie because it does not warrant the truth of any statement to the effect that Rocco did or did not shoot the Mafia boss. In ordinary contexts, utterances such as this are self-undermining and do not warrant or guarantee the truth of *anything*. "Rocco shot the Mafia boss but I give my word that Rocco did not shoot him" does not warrant or guarantee the truth of the statement that Rocco shot the Mafia boss because the second part of the utterance undermines the first part. Similarly, this utterance does not warrant or guarantee the truth of the statement that Rocco did not shoot the Mafia boss.

Sorensen also says things that constitute an objection to my account of the notion of warranting the truth of a statement. Roughly, I define warranting the truth of a statement as promising or guaranteeing that it is true. I also claim that when one warrants a statement as true one invites others to trust it or rely on it. However, Sorensen (2007) says things that raise problems for this later claim. He writes: "Assertion does not entail an invitation to agree with the speaker. A captured American spy could tell Saddam Hussein, 'President, there is a large force of American soldiers hidden along the Turkish border but I am not inviting you to agree with me; I hope that you disagree and are blind-sided by those soldiers' " (p. 255). Although he does not present this example as a case of lying or as a counterexample to my definition, this case is clearly an objection to my view because it implies that one can lie without inviting belief. (According to Sorensen, such an assertion could be a lie if the speaker believes that it is false.[28])

This objection can be rebutted. Warranting the truth of a statement presupposes that the statement is being used to invite or influence belief. It does not make sense for one to guarantee the truth of something that one is not inviting or influencing others to believe. Saying "I am not inviting you to agree with" cancels something ordinarily implied by asserting something. Thus, in this example, it is unclear that one is warranting or standing behind the statement that there is a large force of American soldiers along the Turkish border, and, therefore, in my view, it is doubtful that this is a lie. However, suppose that we grant Sorensen that this is a case of warranting an assertion and thus a case of lying without inviting others to rely on the truth of what one says. Given *that*, I can not claim that one invites belief whenever one warrants the truth of a statement. However, I can still say that when one warrants the truth of a statement or assertion *the default* is that one invites others to believe it (in other words, when one warrants the truth of a statement, one thereby invites others to believe it short of doing or saying something to nullify or call into question the implicit invitation conveyed by warranting the statement). Because warranting the truth of a statement is necessary for lying, when one lies one thereby invites others to believe it, short of doing or saying something to nullify or call into question the implicit invitation conveyed by warranting the statement. Therefore, even if I grant everything that Sorensen says about this case, I only need to make a minor adjustment in my view that warranting the truth of a statement involves inviting others to believe it.

Sorensen (2007) defines lying as follows: "Lying is just asserting what one does not believe." The plausibility of this definition depends on his account of asserting a proposition.[29] Sorensen does not offer a definition of asserting a proposition (with necessary and sufficient conditions), but he says that asserting a proposition requires narrow plausibility (the proposition must be such that "someone who only had access to the assertion might believe it") but not wide probability (the proposition need not have "credibility relative to one's total evidence") (p. 255). To the extent that he does not fully analyze the concept of assertion, Sorensen's definition of lying is unclear. In order for his definition of lying to be defensible, his notion of asserting a proposition must involve something like my idea of warranting the truth of a statement.

1.II.2. Fallis

Fallis's paper (2009) "What is Lying?" discusses my definition at considerable length. Fallis endorses my criticisms of the view that lying requires the intent to deceive and makes use of some of my arguments in support of his own views. However, he also presents two cases that he contends are clear cases of lying that my definition cannot account for. Here, I defend my definition against Fallis's second case, though I concede that his first case may require me to modify my definition. My modified definition clearly answers his first objection.

According to Fallis (2009), my own example of the politician who mistakenly delivers a speech to the wrong audience (1.I.10) constitutes a clear counterexample to my definition of lying.

Given that he believes that his audience expects a serious speech, my strong intuition is that the politician *is* lying in this case if he makes statements that he believes to be false. However, since this is a context where his audience actually expects a humorous speech, the politician does not (according to Carson's definition) warrant the truth of his statements. Thus, according to Carson's definition of lying, the politician is not lying. (p. 48)

I myself think that the politician's statement in this case is *not* a clear case of lying; at best, it is a borderline case. This is a puzzling case in which both the speaker and the audience misunderstand what is going on. Therefore, it is not the kind of case that can be used to test the adequacy of definitions of lying. Suppose, however, that I am mistaken and that most people would regard this case as a clear unambiguous case of lying. If future work in experimental philosophy[30] should vindicate Fallis' claim that this is a clear case of lying, I would have to concede that my definition is inadequate. However, even in that case, a slightly modified version of my definition suffices to handle Fallis' objection. Consider the following:

L7. A person S tells a lie to another person S1 iff: 1. S makes a false statement X to S1, 2. S believes that X is false or probably false (or, alternatively, S does not believe that X is true), and 3. S intends to warrant the truth of X to S1.[31]

This modified definition easily handles Fallis' first objection. In his example, the politician *intends* to warrant the truth of what he says so my modified definition allows me to agree with Fallis that this is (clearly) a case of lying. L7 deals better than L5 with my case of the politician who unwittingly warrants the truth of what he says to an audience because he mistakenly believes that the audience is expecting a humorous satirical speech. Like my L5, L7 allows me to say that this is not a lie, and it does so without resorting to the ad hoc condition 4 ("S does not take herself to be not warranting the truth of what she says to S1") of L5. As we saw earlier, L7 may also be preferable to L5 in that it more clearly avoids Sorensen's first objection.

Fallis (2009) presents his second objection to my definition in the following passage:

suppose that the witness follows up his statement that "Tony was with me at the time of the murder" by saying, "Of course, you know I am really bad with dates and times." This proviso makes it clear that the witness is not *guaranteeing* that Tony was with him at the time of the murder. Thus he is clearly not (according to Carson's definition) warranting the truth of what he says . . . However, if he believes that Tony was not with him at the time of the murder, it still seems pretty clear that he has lied to the jury . . . .   (p. 49)

Contrary to what Fallis claims, it's not clear from his description of the case that the person does not warrant the truth of what he says. At most, this is a borderline case for the concept of warranting.

There are two possibilities. First, it is possible that saying "you know that I am really bad with dates and times" does not remove the warranty (assurance of truth) from the statement that Tony was with me at the time of the murder, in which case I *can* still count this example as a case of lying. If the original warranty of truth is very strong, then saying "you know I am really bad with dates and times" does not cancel the warranty of truth. If the person says this as a witness in court, he might still warrant the truth of what he says despite the disclaimer. Of course, this disclaimer removes any claim to certainty, but a person can lie without claiming that he is certain that what he is saying is true. Warranting comes in degrees of strength; a *moderately strong* assurance of truth is all that is required for lying. The second possibility is that saying "you know I am really bad with dates and times" cancels even a moderately strong assurance of the truth of the statement about Tony. In that case, the second part of the utterance seems to undermine the first part, and the utterance is no longer a straightforward statement or assertion about Tony. At most, it implies something like "I *believe* that Tony was with me at the time of the murder . . . ." Given the second possibility, the speaker is not lying about having been with Tony at the time of the murder and my definition yields this result.

In this case, the speaker wants to both (1) give an assurance of truth (and go on the record as having given an assurance of truth), and (2) not be held responsible or blamed if the statement turns out to be false. This is a very fine line to walk. The qualification that he gives in order to avoid being blamed is likely to cancel any warranty of truth for his statement (if it does, then his utterance is not a straightforward statement or assertion about Tony and it is not a lie and my definition is correct not to count it as a lie). If his qualification does not cancel the warranty of truth (as in a case of testimony in court) then his statement is a lie, and my definition counts it as a lie.

L7 allows me to give a very similar answer to Fallis's second objection. Provided that the witness intends to give some, on balance, warrantee or assurance that what he is saying is true, then my revised definition counts his statement that he was with Tony at the time of the murder as a lie. If the proviso "you know that I am bad with dates" is intended to weaken, but not remove, the assurance of truth, then my revised definition counts this statement as a case of lying. On the other hand, if the proviso is intended to completely remove or nullify any assurance of truth then the statement is not a lie.[32]

CONCLUSIONS

Standard definitions of lying are correct in that they include a requirement to the effect that the liar must believe that what she says is false (or not believe that it is true). In addition, the arguments of this chapter show that (1) lying does not require the intent to deceive, and (2) lying involves warranting or intending to warrant the truth of what one says. This chapter identifies a distinct range or "space" of plausible definitions of lying:

L5. A person S tells a lie to another person S1 iff: 1. S makes a false statement X to S1, 2. S believes that X is false or probably false (or, alternatively, S does not believe that X is true), 3. S states X in a context in which S thereby warrants the truth of X to S1, and 4. S does not take herself to be not warranting the truth of what she says to S1.

L5'. A person S tells a lie to another person S1 iff: 1. S makes a statement X to S1, 2. S believes that X is false or probably false (or, alternatively, S does not believe that X is true), 3. S states X in a context in which S thereby warrants the truth of X to S1, and 4. S does not take herself to be not warranting the truth of what she says to S1.

L7. A person S tells a lie to another person S1 iff: 1. S makes a false statement X to S1, 2. S believes that X is false or probably false (or, alternatively, S does not believe that X is true), and 3. S intends to warrant the truth of X to S1.

L7'. A person S tells a lie to another person S1 iff: 1. S makes a statement X to S1, 2. S believes that X is false or probably false (or, alternatively, S does not believe that X is true), and 3. S intends to warrant the truth of X to S1.

Since condition 2 presents two alternatives, these four definitions are really eight distinct definitions. Note that L5 includes two requirements for lying that are "external" to the agent's beliefs and intentions—the statement must be false and the liar must succeed in warranting the truth of what she says to the other person(s). L7' does not include either of these requirements.[33] For my own part, I endorse these external requirements; therefore, I prefer L5 and think that L5 is the true or correct definition of lying. To the extent that one prefers a more "internalist" definition of lying, one will prefer L7 or L7' to L5 and L5'.

Any of these definitions is perfectly adequate for my purposes in this book. *Nothing* I say in the rest of the book turns on the differences between these definitions. Clearly, the requirement that a lie must be a false statement, which is included in L5 and L7 but not L5′ or L7′, will make a difference as to whether or not a statement counts as a lie in some cases. However, this difference is not relevant to any of the claims I make in this book. The difference between L5/L5′ and L7/L7′ is relevant to whether some of the cases of bluffing I discuss in Chapter 10 count as lies. However, nothing I say about the morality of bluffing requires me to choose between these four definitions of lying. The difference between L5/L5′ and L7/L7′ matters in certain variations on Kant's example of the would-be murderer the door. Some versions of this case count as lies according to L7/L7′, but not according to L5/L5′ (see Chapter 3.II.4). However, nothing I say about Kant's example commits me to choosing between L5, L5′, L7, and L7′. The difference between L5/L5′ and L7/L7′ does not matter for any of the other examples I discuss in Chapters 8–14; none of these other examples is a case in which one intends to warrant the truth of a statement but fails to do so. Cases in which one warrants the truth of what one says without intending to are already ruled out as lies by condition 4 of L5 and L5′, so L5/L5′ and L7/L7′ do not differ in what they say about those cases.

ENDNOTES

1. I owe this example to Bruce Russell.
2. Manison (1969, p. 134) also criticizes standard dictionary definitions on these grounds.
3. Chapter 2 gives a much more careful definition of deception. Linda Coleman and Paul Kay argue that these three conditions give us an account of central or paradigm cases of lying. According to Coleman and Kay (1981), anything that satisfies all three conditions is clearly a lie. However, when a statement satisfies only two of the three conditions, it is not clear whether or not it counts as a case of lying. Arnold Isenberg (1964) defines a lie as a statement that one believes to be false and is intended to deceive others. Isenberg's definition is equivalent to L1 without the stipulation of condition 1 that statement X is false. Bernard Williams (2002) proposes a definition of lying very similar to Isenberg's. Williams's definition is as follows: "I take a lie to be an assertion, the content of which the speaker believes to be false, which is made with the intention to deceive the hearer with regard to its content" (p. 98).

   Unlike Isenberg, Williams stipulates that the liar must intend to deceive others about the content of the statement in question. Isenberg's and Williams's definitions are very similar to the following definition that Sissela Bok attributes to Augustine: "having one thing in one's heart and uttering another with the intention to deceive," Bok (1979, p. 33). Kant also defends a similar definition—see Chapter 3.II.2. Bok herself defines a lie as "any intentionally deceptive message which is stated" (p. 13).

4. Grotius holds that in order to count as a "falsehood" (lie), a statement must conflict with the rights of the person(s) to whom it is addressed (the person's right to know the truth), bk. 3, chapter 1. (This passage is reprinted in the appendix to Bok, 1979, pp. 263–267.)

5. Bernard Williams also argues against attempts to construe the concept of lying very narrowly in order to make plausible the view the lying is always wrong no matter what the consequences, see B. Williams (2002, p. 105).

6. These examples of lying without the intent to deceive refute the definition endorsed in Mahon (2008). Mahon endorses a version of the intent to deceive requirement. He says that the liar must intend that the "other person believe the statement to be true" or else intend "that the other person believe that the statement is believed to be true" (or must intend both).

   In a paper presented at the University of Arizona in April 2009, Mahon suggested the following objection to my cheating student example. The student must keep his knowledge of the Dean's policy secret from the Dean and deceive the Dean about this. He cannot succeed in his aims and avoid punishment if the Dean knows that he knows the Dean's policy. However, we can imagine ways in which it would be possible for the student to avoid punishment even if the Dean knows that he (the student) knows the Dean's policy. Suppose that the Dean's policy is that he will not fail the student unless the student makes a written confession. In that case, the student can achieve his aims as long as he does not sign the written confession; he does not need to conceal his knowledge of the Dean's policy from the Dean.

7. Traditional "just war theory" makes much of the distinction between what is intended and what is merely foreseen. This distinction also has a very important place in scholastic ethics and is central to the "doctrine of the double effect."

8. Franklin Roosevelt and American military leaders were acting in exactly this way when they ordered massive precision daylight bombing attacks on German armaments factories and other military targets during WWII.

9. The British night-time attacks on German cities and the American fire-bombing and nuclear attacks on Japanese cities at the end of WWII aimed at killing innocent civilians as a means to demoralizing the enemy and thereby diminishing their will to continue fighting. In this sense, it is arguable that Churchill, Roosevelt, and Truman were all "terrorists."

10. I do not claim that this is an analysis of our "ordinary language" concept of an intentional action—on this point see Knobe (2003).

11. Chisholm and Feehan (1977) note that their definition is "essentially the same as that proposed by Frege," and quote the following definition of lying from Frege: "In 'A lied in saying that he had seen B', the subordinate clause designates a thought which is said (1) to have been asserted by A (2) while A was convinced of its falsity." Fried (1978) defends a very similar definition (he acknowledges his debt to Chisholm and Feehan): "A person lies when

he asserts a proposition which he believes to be false" (p. 55, also see p. 59). He claims that in order to assert a proposition one must intend that it be believed (pp. 56–57). His definition implies that the intent to deceive others is a necessary condition of lying and is, therefore, open to the sort of objection presented above.

12. Chisholm and Feehan's (1977) definition implies that one can lie without making a false statement. I argue against this in 1.I.1. However, since my argument there appeals to disputed intuitions, I do not rest my criticisms of Chisholm and Feehan on this point.

13. Ross claims that all moral duties can be reduced to six basic types. The first class of duties on his list is duties derived from one's own past actions. He makes a further division within this class. First, there are duties to make reparations for one's own previous wrongful acts. The other kinds of duties that rest on one's own previous actions are: "those resting on a promise or what may fairly be called an implicit promise, such as the implicit undertaking not to tell lies which seems to be implied in the act of entering into conversation (at any rate by civilized men), or writing books that purport to be history and not fiction" (Ross, 1930, p. 21). Hartman (1975) also defends the view that lying violates an implicit promise to tell the truth (volume II, p. 286). See also Fried (1978): "Every lie is a broken promise, and the only reason that this seems strained is that in lying the promise is made and broken at the same moment. Every lie necessarily implies—as does every assertion—an assurance, a warranty of its truth" (p. 67).

14. I am not sure that I agree with Ross that an *implicit* promise is broken whenever someone lies. Sometimes lying involves breaking an explicit promise to tell the truth.

15. The default warranty of truth is an example of what Paul Grice calls a "conversational implicature." Like other conversational implicatures, it is governed by rules and expectations understood by language users. See Grice (1989, chapters 2 and 3).

16. J. A. Barnes describes a case that is arguably a counterexample to the claim that there is a default warranty of truth for statements in *every* linguistic community. Barnes (1993) gives the following description of a village in Lebanon:

In this community liars are typically young men or children. Lies are told for fun, to trick one's friends. Success in lying depends on skill, but the final triumph comes when the liar reveals his lie to the dupe and claims victory . . . There is thus an attitude of playful competition towards lying, somewhat similar to the attitude towards tricks played on the first of April in some countries. Lying is indulged in sometimes for its own sake, without an instrumental motive . . . It is not surprising that in an environment of this kind there are special devices to indicate that what is about to be said is true, and not a lie. These markers for code switching are phrases such as "seriously", "will you believe me", "without joking", "by your life", and "by your father's life".   (pp. 70–71)

The last part of this quotation provides an indirect confirmation of my view. The fact that, in ordinary contexts, we (and most other linguistic communities) *do not need* special markers to indicate that what is about to be said is true, confirms the idea that in those communities there is a default presumption that what is said is warranted to be true. Given my definition of lying, many of the cases that Barnes describes as cases of "playful lying" are not genuine instances of lying, because the false statements in question are not warranted to be true. This, I would suggest, is a virtue of my definition. The villagers Barnes describes have different understandings about when statements are warranted to be true than people in most other societies. This is the salient difference between their society and most other societies.

17. It might be argued that the notion of warranting makes an implicit appeal to the notion of intention. It has been suggested to me that "to warrant the truth of a statement is to make an utterance under conditions where *normally* the speaker intends that others believe him." This suggests that I have removed the notion of the intention to deceive from the concept of lying only to smuggle it back in under the rubric of the concept of warranting. Normally we intend that others believe our statements. It is difficult to imagine how it could be the case that the use of language involves the default warranty of truth if this were not the case. There would be no *point* in warranting the truth of what we say unless we sometimes intended that others believe what we say. There would be no point in having a *default* presumption that any given statement is warranted to be true unless we usually intended that others believe what we say. (The (or a) purpose of having such a warranty is to make it more likely that people will believe what we say.) I accept all of this, but it leaves untouched my earlier objection to the standard dictionary definitions of lying. According to these definitions, *a particular statement on a particular occasion* cannot constitute a lie unless the person who makes it intends thereby to mislead others. I believe that I have shown that this is untenable.

18. It might not be possible for the student to lie to the Dean with the intention of causing him to *disbelieve* what he says by accompanying his statement with a series of winks and nods. The winks and nods may remove the default warranty of truth. For my purposes, I do not need to deny this. I only need to claim that it is *possible* to lie without any intention of deceiving others (about the truth of what one is saying, or about one's own sincerity, or anything else).

19. J. A. Barnes gives numerous examples of this (see J. A. Barnes, 1993, p. 114 and elsewhere).

20. Alternatively, we could say that in order to lie one must believe that one is warranting the truth of what one says. I believe that my condition 4 is preferable to this alternative condition, because there are many cases of lying in which the liar has no conscious beliefs about whether or not s/he is warranting what s/he says.

21. Chisholm and Feehan (1977) also relativize the concept of lying in this way. Their definition is a definition of what it is for one to lie *to a particular person*. Although they do not explicitly say this, their definition allows for the possibility that one and the same statement could be a case of lying to one person but not a case of lying to the other.

22. Those who do not share my view that a lie must be a false statement might wish to modify L5 as follows:

L5′. A person S tells a lie to another person S1 iff: 1. S makes a statement X to S1, 2. S believes that X is false or probably false (or, alternatively, S does not believe that X is true), 3. S states X in a context in which S thereby warrants the truth of X to S1, and 4. S does not take herself to be not warranting the truth of what she says to S1.

23. Bill Tolhurst is the first of several who made this suggestion to me.

24. J. A. Barnes (1993) defends this claim at length and gives numerous examples.

25. Barnes gives numerous examples of this (see J. A. Barnes, 1993, p. 114 and elsewhere).

26. If so, this may be due to the fact that the more strongly a statement is warranted as true, the more likely it is that others will rely on it and be deceived by it.

27. Cf. Chisholm and Feehan (1977):

The liar would have his victim believe that, at the moment at least, the liar is someone in whom he may place his faith. Thus we may say, with St. Augustine: "No liar preserves faith in that about which he lies. He wishes that he to whom he lies have faith in him, but he does not preserve faith by lying to him." (p. 152).

Also see Fried (1978, p. 57), "A lie invites belief in an assertion which the speaker knows to be false."

28. Sorensen (2007) defines lying as follows: "Lying is just asserting what one does not believe" (p. 256).

29. Sorensen (2007) explains this concept on pp. 255–257.

30. Fallis is beginning to do such work himself; he is conducting empirical tests of people's linguistic intuitions about cases in which his definition, my definition, and other definitions yield conflicting results.

31. This definition can be modified to drop the requirement that a lie must be a false statement.

32. Fallis (2009) defines lying as follows: "You lie to X if and only if: 1. You state that p to X, 2. You believe that you make this statement in a context

where the following norm of conversation is in effect *do not make statements that you believe to be false*, 3. You believe that p is false" (p. 34).

33. L7′ is very similar to Sorensen's (2007) definition, provided that he gives a plausible definition of "assertion." I would argue that adopting L7′ is a more promising line for him than trying to supplement his definition of lying with an analysis of assertion.

2

Deception and Related Concepts

INTRODUCTION

Roughly, deception is intentionally causing someone to have a false belief that the deceiver believes to be false. This definition needs to be qualified to deal with cases such as the following. I intentionally cause you to believe statement X and X is false, but I neither believe that X is true nor believe that X is false. I discuss several other cases that may require modifications of this definition and formulate several revised versions of the definition; I count cases in which people intentionally cause others to persist in false beliefs as cases of deception.

Section 2.II explains the difference between deception and preventing others from learning the truth and offers a definition of "keeping someone in the dark." Section 2.III examines the relationship between lying, deception, keeping someone in the dark, withholding information, and concealing information. There are two main differences between lying and deception. First, unlike "lying," "deception" implies success. An act must actually cause someone to have (or persist in) false beliefs in order to count as a case of deception. Intentional false statements need not succeed in deceiving others in order to count as lies. Second, although a lie must be a false statement, deception need not involve making a false statement; true statements can be deceptive, and many forms of deception do not involve making statements. Thus, many instances of deception do not constitute lying. Generally, withholding information is not a case of deception (*causing* someone to have or persist in false beliefs); it is merely a case of failing to correct false beliefs or incomplete information. On the other hand, actively concealing information, e.g., painting over rust on a used car, often constitutes deception. Section 2.IV offers a brief account of the concepts of "spin" and "half-truths" and the relationship between these concepts and lying and deception.

Section 2.V discusses Frankfurt's claims about the relationship between lying, deception, and bullshit. Frankfurt claims that bullshit requires the intention to deceive and that bullshit does not constitute lying (bullshit is a kind of misrepresentation "short of lying"). I argue that both claims are mistaken—bullshit need not be intended to deceive others, and one can produce bullshit while lying. I also argue that Frankfurt's famous claim that bullshitters, unlike liars, are unconcerned with the truth is mistaken; there are clear cases of bullshit in which bullshitters are very concerned to say what's true.

Section 2.VI is a brief account of the concept of honesty. I distinguish between "honesty in the negative sense" and "honesty in the positive sense."

2.I. DECEPTION

2.I.1. My Definition

As a first approximation, we might say that to deceive someone is to cause her to have false beliefs. *The New Shorter Oxford English Dictionary* (1993) defines the verb "deceive" as to "cause to believe what is false."[1] This definition is too broad. If a perfectly clear and truthful statement is misinterpreted by others and causes them to have false beliefs, it is not necessarily a case of deception. An automobile salesperson does not necessarily deceive her customers if her clear and accurate description of a car, which includes the claim that the car has side and front air bags, causes a buyer to believe falsely that the car is safe in case of high-speed collisions with large vehicles.

The salesperson's statement is not a case of deception because she has no *intention* of causing the customer to have false beliefs. Deception requires some kind of intention to cause others to have false beliefs. I take it to be self-contradictory to say that someone deceived another person unintentionally. Consider the following case. Suppose that I am told something that is false. I believe what I am told and repeat it to you, thereby causing you to believe it. (In reporting this to you, I am not trying to bring it about that you believe anything that I do not believe to be true.) Some people think that it makes sense to describe this as a case in which I deceived you "albeit without intending to do so."[2] Here people's linguistic intuitions conflict; no definition can be consistent with everyone's linguistic intuitions about the word "deception." There are pragmatic reasons to accept the view that deception must be intentional. The words "deception" and "deceive" are typically terms of reproach or condemnation. (The word "mislead" does not imply the same kind of negative evaluation as the word "deceive.") The negative evaluative connotations of the term "deception" are inappropriate if we hold that there can be completely unintentional deception (for which people are often blameless). There *is* an important distinction to be drawn between intentionally and unintentionally causing others to have false beliefs. Rather than coin new words, we can use the terms "deceive" and "mislead" (or "inadvertently mislead") to mark this distinction. Roughly, to mislead someone is to cause her to have a false belief. It is not self-contradictory to say that someone *misled* another person unintentionally or inadvertently.

In order to deceive you, I must intentionally mislead you or intentionally cause you to have false beliefs. However, this is ambiguous. It is not deception if

I intentionally cause you to believe X where X is false, but I myself believe that X is true. Intentionally causing you to believe X where X is false is not sufficient for deception. We might say that in order for there to be deception it is necessary that the deceiver believes that what she causes the other person(s) to believe is false. Consider the following definition of deception:

D1. A person S deceives another person S1 if, and only if, S intentionally causes S1 to believe X, where X is false and S knows or believes that X is false.

This is much closer to the mark than the previous definition, but several questions remain. What if I intentionally cause you to believe that X where X is false and I neither believe that X is true nor believe that X is false? For example, suppose that I want you to believe X where X is false and I have not given any thought to the question of whether X is true or false. (Such statements are characteristic of bullshit.³) If we want to count this as a case of deception, we should reject D1 in favor of something like the following:

D2. A person S deceives another person S1 if, and only if, S intentionally causes S1 to believe X, where X is false and S does not believe that X is true.⁴

Clearly, a modified version of D1 gives sufficient conditions for deception. A person who intentionally causes another person to believe X, where X is false and s/he knows or believes that X is false, has clearly deceived the other person. A modified version of D2 gives necessary conditions for deception; a necessary condition of my deceiving you is that I intentionally cause you to believe (or persist in believing) something false that I do not believe to be true.

Ordinary language does not give us a clear basis for choosing between D1 and D2. The kinds of cases in which D1 and D2 give conflicting results, e.g., cases in which S intentionally causes S1 to believe X, X is false, and S has not given any thought to the question of whether X is true or false, are borderline for the concept of deception. I do not know of any decisive reasons for preferring D1 to D2 or D2 to D1. Rather than claim that one of the definitions is the correct account of deception (or is closer to being correct than the other), we should simply say that there are broader and narrower concepts of deception. D1 defines deception in the narrow sense. D2 defines deception in the broader or looser sense.

Often the distinction between deceiving you about one thing and deceiving you about something else is morally relevant. For moral purposes, we want more than just a definition of deception simpliciter—we want a definition of what it is to deceive someone about something in particular. I propose the following:

D1′. S deceives S1 about (proposition) X iff S intentionally causes S1 to believe X, X is false, and S knows or believes that X is false.

D2′. S deceives S1 about (proposition) X iff S intentionally causes S1 to believe X, X is false, and S 'doesn't believe that X is true.

Is all deception propositional in this sense? Is all deception, deception about the truth of some particular proposition (in the sense articulated by D1′ and D2′)? Suppose that I intend to bring it about that you are confused and have certain false beliefs. I know that what I am doing will cause you to have a number of false beliefs, but I do not have a very clear idea of which false beliefs I am likely to cause you. So, there is no particular false proposition that I intend to cause you to believe. Should we count this as deception? I propose the following. When deception occurs it must be possible to specify what the deception is *about* (the deceiver must have some idea about what he is deceiving the other person about), but it is not necessary that the deceiver intentionally causes the deceived to falsely believe some particular false proposition. So, for example, it is (or can be) deception if I intentionally bring it about that you have false beliefs about Lincoln's attitudes about slavery (without having any idea of which false beliefs about Lincoln's attitudes about slavery I am causing you to have). However, it is not deception if I intend to bring it about that you have many false beliefs so that you will be confused and unable to act in a certain situation but have no idea of what those false beliefs are about. In such a case, I intentionally *confuse* you and cause you to have false beliefs, but I do not deceive you because there is nothing I deceive you *about*. This is *a proposal*. I am assuming that either most people share my linguistic intuitions about these cases, or else that people have conflicting intuitions about these cases (but that many share my intuitions). If I were shown that I am mistaken about this, I would withdraw this proposal.

My definition comes fairly close to capturing how most people use the word "deception." Since people disagree in their linguistic intuitions about the word "deception," no definition of deception can be consistent with everyone's linguistic intuitions about all cases. There are good pragmatic reasons to accept the definition I propose here. The concepts of lying and deception are important from the moral point of view because they help us pick out morally salient features of actions and classify different types of actions. It is helpful to classify or categorize different types of actions *before* we assess them morally. It is not helpful to assess the moral status of deception or any other class of actions without first clearly delineating that class of actions. The morally salient feature of deception is that it involves intentionally causing others to have false beliefs that one believes to be false or does not believe to be true. My concepts of misleading others (causing others to have false beliefs) and deceiving others (intentionally causing others to have false beliefs that one believes to be false or does not believe to be true) pick out morally salient features of actions and help facilitate normative assessments of action. We should mark this distinction in some way.

2.1.2. Several Objections and Modified Versions of My Definition

Suppose that I intentionally tamper with the relevant evidence in order to try to cause you to believe X when I know that X is false. Unbeknownst to me, you already believe X. I do not cause you to believe X, but I strengthen your belief that X. At a later date, you acquire *prima facie* evidence for thinking that X is false. You persist in believing X but you would have ceased to believe X, were it not for my past action. Is this deception? Have I deceived you about X? Consider a similar case. I know that X is false. I also know that you believe X. I want you to continue to believe X, but I am worried that you will discover evidence that X is false. I give you bogus evidence for X that reinforces your belief that X and has the result that you persist in believing X; you would have ceased to believe X, were it not for my actions. Have I deceived you about X? I am inclined to think that this is deception. On this point, I follow Mahon (2007, pp. 189–190) and agree with him that causing someone to persist in a false belief can constitute deception. Therefore, I think that the following are preferable to D1 and D2:

D1a. A person S deceives another person S1 if, and only if, S intentionally causes S1 to believe X (or persist in believing X), where X is false and S knows or believes that X is false.

D2a. A person S deceives another person S1 if, and only if, S intentionally causes S1 to believe X (or persist in believing X), where X is false and S does not believe that X is true.

Mahon considers what he calls the standard dictionary definition of lying, "To deceive = def. to cause to believe what is false." He offers the following case as a counterexample to this definition:

it is possible to (intentionally) cause a person to have a false belief by, for example, stimulating the other person's cerebral cortex, or hypnotizing or drugging the other person. These are ways of causing the other person to have a false belief that bypass the other person's agency. However, the majority of philosophers hold that deceiving must involve the deceived person's agency, and that cases of causing another person to have a false belief by stimulating the other person's cortex, or hypnotizing or drugging the other person, are not cases of deceiving . . . if "Christopher gets Peter to believe that there are vampires in England by operating on Peter's brain," then Christopher does not deceive Peter.   (p. 185)

Mahon (2007, pp. 189–190) defends the following definition of deception: "To deceive = df. to intentionally cause another person to have or continue to have a false belief that is known or truly believed to be false by bringing about evidence on the basis of what the person continues to have the false belief."

I do not share Mahon's intuition that this is not a case of deception. This is an odd case that stretches our concept of deception; it's not a clear paradigm case of deception or non-deception. At present, we cannot directly cause other people to have beliefs; few people consider such cases and apply or fail to apply the word "deception" to them, so there is not a basis for saying that ordinary language has clear rules and understandings about what to say about such cases. We should not use this case as a test for the adequacy of definitions of deception. The fact that D1, D2, D1a, and D2a are simpler than Mahon's definition is a reason in their favor. Mahon offers no evidence in support of his claim that "the majority of philosophers hold that deceiving must involve the deceived person's agency, and that cases of causing another person to have a false belief by stimulating the other person's cortex, or hypnotizing or drugging the other person, are not cases of deceiving." My guess is that this is a case about which people have conflicting intuitions. If it could be shown that most people (Should I say most philosophers? Whose intuitions matter?) have the strong intuition that the case in question is not a case of deception and regard this as a paradigm case of nondeception, then I would concede this objection and modify D1 and D2 by adding Mahon's requirement to the effect that the deceiver causes the deceived to have the false belief by means of altering the evidence available to the deceived. So modified D1a and D2a read as follows:

D1b. A person S deceives another person S1 if, and only if, S intentionally causes S1 to believe X (or persist in believing X) by bringing about evidence on the basis of which the person believes (or continues to believe) X and X is false and S knows or believes that X is false.

D2b. A person S deceives another person S1 if, and only if, S intentionally causes S1 to believe X (or persist in believing X) by bringing about evidence on the basis of which the person believes (or continues to believe) X and X is false and S does not believe that X is true.

D1b and D2b closely resemble Mahon's preferred definition of deception.

Consider the following case. I intend to bring about some result. The result I intend has nothing to do with your having any false beliefs; however, I reliably foresee that it will cause you to believe that X and X is false and I believe X is false (or do not believe that X is true). Is this a case of deception (deceiving you about X)? D1, D2, D1a, D2a, D1b, and D2b do not count this as a case of deception because in this case I do not intend to cause you to believe anything that is false. (Although I know that X is false (or do not believe that X is true), I do not intend to cause you to believe X either as an end or as a means to the end of my action—refer to the distinction between what is intended and what is foreseen in Chapter 1.I.5.) I would describe this as a case in which I knowingly mislead you (as opposed to inadvertently mislead you), but do not deceive you. (The following analogous examples of unintentional actions are instructive here. Suppose that someone causes an explosion as part of a mining operation. He takes care to avoid harming anyone but through bad luck someone is killed by the explosion. This is a case of unintentional and inadvertent killing. If a leader who orders the aerial bombing of an unoccupied factory surrounded by a crowded residential neighborhood knows that it is almost certain that some of the bombs will miss their target and kill civilians, then he kills the people knowingly, but not intentionally. The killing is unintentional, but not inadvertent; he expects it to result from his actions.) I do not have a strong intuition that this is or is not an instance of deception. It seems to me to be a borderline case. If we want to call this a case of deception we could do this by modifying the definition of deception by stipulating that the relevant belief that the deceived person acquires (or retains) is one that the deceiver intentionally causes the deceived person to acquire (or retain), *or else* a belief that the deceiver *foresees* that the deceived person will acquire (or retain) the belief as a result of something else that he intentionally brings about.

Annette Barnes (1997) rejects the view that a necessary condition of deception is that what the deceived comes to believe is false. She presents the following case:

> I falsely believe that your friend is honest, but . . . I want you to believe that he is dishonest. I invent examples of his dishonesty and intentionally get you to believe that he is dishonest. While I have deceived you into believing that he is dishonest, I did not know or truly believe that it was false that your friend was dishonest. For it was true that your friend was dishonest.   (p. 8)

Barnes's argument trades on the ambiguity of the expression "A deceives B into thinking X." This is a confusing and (for present purposes) misleading locution. As she uses this expression, to deceive someone into believing X is a case of using deception about something (other than X itself) as a means to causing her/him to believe X. I am not deceiving you about the fact that your friend is dishonest (you are not deceived into thinking that your friend is dishonest). Rather, I am deceiving you about other things—I cause you to have very specific false beliefs about things that your friend has done and this causes you to acquire the true belief that he was dishonest. There can't be any deception at all in this case unless I intentionally cause you to believe something that is false that I believe to be false (or do not believe to be true), e.g., that your friend acted dishonestly in such and such cases. The only reason we can say that I deceived you into believing something that is true is that I perform other acts of deception (acts that satisfy the conditions of my definition of deception).

2.1.3. Some Considerations Relevant to Later Parts of the Book

My definition of lying helps to reveal and highlight an important kind of deception (or attempted deception) short of lying. Suppose that I believe that X is true, even though I am aware of serious reasons for doubting the truth of X. I assert the truth of X on a solemn occasion in which reliance on my statement will be used as a justification for an important decision (such as the decision to start a war), and I intend to cause others to believe X. I give *prima facie* evidence for the truth of X but make no mention of the reasons for doubting the truth of X. My statement is strongly warranted to be true—in this case my statement implies a strong assurance of its own truth. My statement is not a lie because I believe that X is true. Since I believe that X is true, my intending to cause others to believe X is not a case of attempted deception. However, my statement still intends to deceive in virtue of giving/implying a strong assurance of its truth—an assurance that I hope others will rely on. I intend to cause others to (falsely) believe that there is strong, unambiguous evidence for the truth of X. Although I believe that X is true, I believe that it is false that there is clear unambiguous evidence for thinking that X is true. In this case, withholding information about the counter-evidence constitutes deception. It is arguable that some members of the Bush administration were guilty of this kind of deception in their claims to the effect that it was certain that Iraq possessed "weapons of mass destruction" (see 12.III.4). One of the advertising cases (the Vioxx case) that I discuss in 9.I also involves this kind of deception.

Another kind of case that is important for our purposes is this. Suppose that I have made an honest mistake and intentionally cause you to believe that X where X is a false statement, but I believe that X is true. I do this because I want you to do A. This is not a case of lying or deception. Suppose, however, that I later acquire strong evidence that X is false and still want you to do A. My failure to report my earlier mistake to you counts as deception. When I realize my mistake and fail to take advantage of my opportunity to correct it, I am intentionally causing you to persist in believing something that is false.

Suppose that a physician urges her patient to have surgery in order to prevent a possible problem in the future. The patient rejects this suggestion. Then the physician makes an honest mistake and misreads an X-ray. She claims that there is an urgent need for surgery. The patient relents and schedules the surgery. Before the surgery, the physician discovers her error but fails to report it to the patient and performs surgery on him. By failing to correct her error, she is intentionally causing the patient to persist in believing falsely that there is an urgent need for the surgery. In this example, she uses deception to manipulate the patient to do what she wants him to do. It is likely that Bush was guilty of this kind of deception in connection with the claims he made as a rationale for beginning the Iraq War of 2003 (see 12.II.4).

2.II. KEEPING SOMEONE IN THE DARK

Cases in which we try to prevent people from discovering the truth raise interesting questions about the concept of deception. First, consider cases in which we try to prevent people from learning things that we do not want them to know by distracting their attention. Suppose that we are trying to close a business deal, and you are reading the contract that describes the terms of a loan I am offering you. I do not want you to read it carefully because I fear that you will be distressed by provisions that call for you to surrender collateral in case of default. You begin to read the contract but I distract you from doing this by discussing the fortunes of our favorite baseball team or engaging you in a political argument. Because you have only a limited amount of time to look at the contract, you don't read it carefully. You know that there are penalties in case of default, but your true beliefs about this are vague and incomplete. In this case, I have prevented you from gaining certain information. However, I have not caused you to acquire or retain any false beliefs, and, therefore, I have not deceived you about anything. Preventing someone from learning the truth about X is not the same as causing her to have or retain false beliefs about X.

We need a term other than "deception" to describe cases of preventing others from learning the truth. The English expression that most closely describes this is "keeping someone in the dark." Intentionally and actively preventing someone from learning something counts as keeping him/her in the dark. Sometimes withholding information or failing to correct someone's false beliefs counts as keeping that person in the dark. A lawyer keeps her client in the dark if she fails to inform him that a certain course of action she is advising him to take is likely to result in his being the subject of a lawsuit. However, not every case of failing to correct another person's false beliefs or remove his ignorance about something one knows about counts as "keeping someone in dark." (I am not keeping my neighbor in the dark if I fail to inform her about my past membership in the Cub Scouts.)

Here is a first stab at a definition of "keeping someone in the dark" (this is both a proposal and an attempt to fit with ordinary language):

A person S keeps another person S1 in the dark about X (where X is something that S knows and S1 doesn't know) if, and only if, either: 1. S actively and intentionally prevents S1 from learning about X, or 2. S fails to inform S1 about X when either: (i) S knows that S1 wants the information in question and S can easily give it to S1, or (ii) S occupies a role or position in which he is expected to provide S1 with the sort of information in question.

It is possible to keep someone in the dark by means of lying and/or deception. One can intentionally prevent someone from learning X by means of lying to him and/or deceiving him (this can be done either by lying and/or deceiving him about X or lying to him and/or deceiving him about something else). Suppose that I attempt to prevent you from discovering the truth by causing you to be less diligent in your pursuit of evidence or by temporarily diminishing your cognitive functioning. For example, suppose that you are a detective working on a murder case. I know that my daughter Astrid is guilty of the crime. However, there is strong *prima facie* evidence that John committed the murder and no one suspects Astrid. Unless you are diligent and alert, you will not suspect Astrid and will probably come to believe that John is the murderer. I might try to cause you to believe that John is guilty by impairing you in some way. Suppose that I induce you to get drunk with me and make noise during the night to cause you to have a very bad night's sleep. The next day you are hung over and very tired. As a result, you overlook essential clues about Astrid and come to believe that John is guilty. You would have discovered the truth were it not for my actions.

In this case, I have deceived you (in a very indirect way) about John's guilt and Astrid's innocence. My actions intend and bring it about that you believe falsely that John is guilty and Astrid is innocent.

Briefly, consider a variation on this case. I do not try to cause you to have false beliefs about Astrid but just try to prevent you from acquiring true beliefs about her. Suppose that you are unaware of Astrid's existence. I want to prevent you from learning the truth (that she is guilty), but I am not trying to cause you to have any false beliefs about Astrid (that she is innocent), because my purposes are served equally well if you remain unaware of her existence. If I cause you to believe that John is guilty in order to protect Astrid, I am deceiving you about John's guilt and keeping you in the dark about Astrid's guilt, but I am not deceiving you about her guilt.

2.III. THE RELATIONSHIP BETWEEN LYING, DECEPTION, KEEPING SOMEONE IN THE DARK, CONCEALING INFORMATION, AND WITHHOLDING INFORMATION

2.III.1. The Difference between Lying and Deception

Lying differs from deception in two important respects. First, in order to lie, one must make a false statement. Deception does not require that one make a false statement or make any statement at all. True statements can be deceptive and some forms of deception do not involve making statements. Consider the following case: I am selling a used car that frequently overheats, and I am aware of the problem. You are a prospective buyer and ask me whether the car overheats. If I say "no," I am lying. If I answer by making the true statement "I drove the car across the Mojave Desert on a very hot day and had no problems," I am not lying. Even though this statement is true and I believe that it is true, it might still be deceptive—perhaps I drove the car across the desert four years ago and have had lots of trouble with it overheating since then. Since my statement is true, I do not deceive you about the fact that I once drove the car across the desert. Rather, I deceive you about whether the car is now prone to overheating. (Given the debate about whether a lie must be a false statement, this example is contentious. Examples in which we deceive others without using language to make a statement are clearer cases of deception without lying. It is not a matter of debate that making a statement is necessary for lying.) Second, unlike "lying," the word "deception" connotes success. An act must actually mislead someone (cause someone to have false beliefs) if it is to count as a case of deception. Many lies are not believed and do not succeed in deceiving anyone.[5] The relationship between lying, deception, and attempted deception is represented in Figure 2.1.

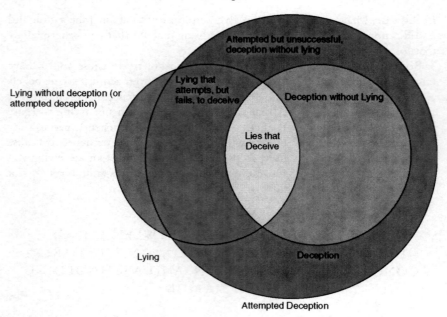

Figure 2.1.

2.III.2. Deception Versus Withholding Information

There is a clear distinction between withholding information and deception (or attempted deception). To withhold information is to fail to offer information that would help someone acquire true beliefs and/or correct false beliefs. Not all cases of withholding information constitute deception. A business person who withholds from his clients information about how much a product he is selling costs him does not thereby deceive (or attempt to deceive) them about his costs. However, withholding information can constitute deception if there is a clear expectation, promise, and/or professional obligation that such information will be provided. If a tax adviser is aware of a legitimate tax exemption her client can claim that would allow the client to achieve considerable tax savings, her failure to inform the client about it constitutes deception. She thereby intentionally causes her client to believe falsely that there is no way for him to save more money on his taxes.

2.III.3. Concealing Information, Withholding Information, and Deception

To conceal information is to do things to hide information from someone—to prevent someone from discovering it. Often, concealing information constitutes deception or attempted deception. Consider the following example. I am selling a used car that has extensive body rust. I smooth out the rust (but do not remove it) and paint over it, taking care to match the original color. I am trying to cause you to believe falsely that the body is free of rust or relatively free of rust. If my action causes you to believe that the car has no rust, then I have deceived you. However, it is possible to conceal information successfully without deceiving anyone. Suppose that I successfully conceal rust on my car from careful inspection. It doesn't follow that I have caused you to have any false beliefs. It might be the case that the rust on the car was not obvious to casual inspection and that you would not have noticed it anyway. If that is the case, then my concealing the rust is not the cause of your false belief that my car has no rust and is not a case of deception, but this is still a case of attempted deception.

The following case illustrates the difference between concealing information and withholding information. I am selling a used car that does not start well in the cold. You are interested in buying the car and come to look at it on a warm day. You don't ask me any questions about the car or how it starts, and I don't mention anything about how the car starts in cold weather. The car starts well when you try it out and you conclude that the car starts well in all conditions. This is a case of withholding information but not a case of deception. On the other hand, suppose that you look at my car on a very cold day. I start it up and run it for an hour before you look at it to make sure that it has warmed up before you see it. Shortly before you come to look at the car, I place it out in the cold and cover it with snow to make it look as though it has not run for several days. You start it without any difficulty and conclude that the car starts very well in cold weather. This is deception. (I intentionally cause you to believe falsely that my car starts well in the cold.)

2.IV. TWO RELATED NOTIONS: "SPIN" AND "HALF-TRUTHS"

"Spinning a story" or "putting spin on a story" involves putting an interpretation on events or facts which, themselves, are not in dispute. People spin stories/events when they place a particular interpretation on them. Political candidates often spin stories in such a way as to make themselves and their policies look good and make their opponents look bad. Ideologues of all stripes often spin their interpretation of events so that those events seem consistent with their ideological commitments. Sometimes the interpretations they spin are correct, but sometimes not. If someone spins the interpretation of an event, then his interpretation is biased and unreliable but not necessarily incorrect.

One common way of spinning events involves stating "half-truths." Half-truths are true statements or sets of true statements that selectively emphasize facts that tend to support a particular interpretation or assessment of an issue and selectively ignore or minimize other relevant facts that tend to support contrary assessments. For example, a politician spins the interpretation of recent events to support the claim that his policies were successful if he describes the good consequences of those policies in great and vivid detail and omits any mention of the bad consequences of his policies. A man's description of his marriage to a friend (or the description he gives to himself) is a half-truth if it contains a long and accurate account of unkind and hurtful things that his wife has said and done to him but mentions only a few of the equal (or greater) number of unkind and hurtful things he has said and done to her.

Interpretations that involve spin can be misleading if they advance unreasonable interpretations of events and incline other people to accept those interpretations. Misleading spin counts as deception if the "spinner" knows or believes that the interpretation he defends is unreasonable/implausible. If spin involves making deliberate false claims about one's state of mind (false statements about how one thinks that events should be interpreted), it usually involves lying. Even when there is no lying or deception involved, spinning often calls into question one's intellectual honesty. Often we spin evidence to protect our cherished beliefs when that evidence ought to cause us to question those beliefs. (See Chapter 13.III for a discussion of examples of half-truths and 13.IV for a discussion of intellectual honesty.)

2.V. BULLSHIT

Harry Frankfurt (2005) claims that: (1) bullshit requires the intention to deceive; (2) bullshit does not constitute lying (bullshit is a kind of misrepresentation "short of lying"); and (3) bullshitters are unlike liars in that they are unconcerned with the truth of what they say. I argue that these three claims are all mistaken.

2.V.1. Frankfurt on Bullshit, Deception, and Lying

According to Frankfurt (2005), bullshit necessarily involves deception or the intention to deceive others. Bullshitters do not necessarily attempt to deceive others about the content of what they say, rather they deceive or attempt to deceive others about themselves.

The bullshitter may not deceive us, or even intend to do so, either about the facts or what he takes the facts to be. What he does *necessarily* [my emphasis] deceive[6] us about is his enterprise. His only indispensably distinctive characteristic is that in a certain way he misrepresents what he is up to (Frankfurt, 2005, p. 54).

Frankfurt's (2005, pp. 17–18) example of the "Fourth of July" speech illustrates his idea of misrepresenting what one "is up to."

Consider a Fourth of July orator, who goes on bombastically about "our great and blessed country, whose Founding Fathers under divine guidance created a new beginning for mankind ... " It is clear that what makes the Fourth of July oration hum-bug is not fundamentally that the speaker regards his statements as false. Rather ... the orator intends these statements to convey a certain impression of himself. He is not trying to deceive anyone concerning American history. What he cares about is what people think of *him*. He wants them to think of him as a patriot, as some-one who has deep thoughts and feelings about the origins and the mission of our country ... [7]

Frankfurt (2005, p. 19) says that bullshit falls "short of lying." He claims that bullshitters are unconcerned with the truth of what they say, whereas liars know that what they say is false and are "guided by the truth" (see below). This commits him to the view that bullshit cannot constitute lying.

2.V.2. Bullshit and Lack of Concern with the Truth

Frankfurt (2005) famously claims that the essence of bullshit is unconcern with the truth (how things are) and that bullshitters are greater enemies of the truth than liars (who are concerned with knowing how things are).

It is just this lack of connection to a concern with truth—this indifference to how things are—that I regard as the essence of bullshit. (pp. 33–34)

This points to a similar and fundamental aspect of the essential nature of bullshit: although it is produced without concern with the truth, it need not be false. (pp. 47–48)

The fact about himself that the bullshitter hides, on the other hand, is that the truth values of his statements are of no central concern to him ... the motive guiding and controlling it is unconcerned with how the things about which he speaks truly are. (p. 55)

Someone who lies ... is guided by the authority of the truth ... The bullshitter ignores these demands altogether. He does not reject the authority of the truth, as the liar does, and oppose himself to it. He pays no attention to it at all. By virtue of this, bullshit is a greater enemy of the truth than lies are. (pp. 60–61)[8]

In a very illuminating passage, Frankfurt (2005) observes that:

Bullshit is unavoidable whenever circumstances require someone to talk without knowing what he is talking about. Thus, the production of bullshit is stimulated whenever a person's obligations or opportunities to speak about some topic exceed his knowledge of the facts that are relevant to that topic. This discrepancy is common in public life, where people are frequently impelled—whether by their own propensities or by the demands of others—to speak extensively about matters of which they are to some degree ignorant. (p. 63)

One important kind of bullshit involves trying to convey a certain impression of oneself to others. For example, one might bullshit someone in order to convey the impression of knowledge, intelligence, piety, or patriotism, as in Frankfurt's example of the "Fourth of July" speech. Another important kind of bullshit (that Frankfurt does not say much about) involves evasion. Sometimes we are pressured to answer questions that we do not want to answer. When asked such questions, people often produce bullshit responses that do not directly answer the questions. Here is an example of this kind of bullshit. In a televised presidential debate, a candidate is asked the following question: "I want to ask you about your criteria for nominating people to the US Supreme Court. Would you be willing to nominate anyone who supports the Roe v. Wade decision? Or, will you make opposition to abortion and Roe v. Wade a requirement for anyone you nominate?" The answer is that the candidate is not willing to nominate anyone who supports Roe v. Wade. He firmly intends to nominate only people who oppose abortion and the Roe v. Wade decision and has privately promised some antiabortion leaders that he will do this. Answering the question truthfully is likely to cost him the votes of many people who support abortion. Lying and saying that he would be willing to nominate someone who supports abortion and Roe v. Wade would cost him the votes of many people who oppose abortion. The candidate wishes that the question had not been asked and gives the following bullshit reply that completely fails to answer or address the question that was asked: "Look, there are lots of things to be taken into account when nominating someone for the Supreme Court. This isn't the only relevant consideration. I want someone with a good legal mind and judicial experience who supports my judicial philosophy of following the constitution as it is written." (Note that the question does not ask whether a potential nominee's views about abortion are the *only* relevant considerations. Rather, it asks whether the candidate will make opposition to abortion and Roe v. Wade a *necessary* condition for nominating someone for the court.)

Similar examples of evasion by means of bullshit occur when people are asked to testify in court or other semi-legal proceedings. Suppose that I am a witness in court and am asked a question about a friend who committed a crime that I witnessed. An honest answer will incriminate him; lying will make me guilty of perjury. Refusing to testify will make me guilty of contempt of court. In this situation, resorting to evasive bullshit is an attractive option for me.

2.V.3. Bullshit Does Not Require the Intention to Deceive

Some cases of evasive bullshit do not involve the intention to deceive others. In cases of evasion, we often want to deceive others and make them think we are answering or trying to answer their questions. Witnesses and politicians who engage in evasive bullshitting typically intend that others (mistakenly) believe that they are trying to answer their questions. However, not all cases of evasion by means of bullshit involve the intent to deceive in this way. There are cases in which one is rewarded for making a performance in response to a question; in some of these cases one will be rewarded for saying *almost anything* rather than saying nothing. There are cases in which one knows that one can obtain rewards for bullshit responses to questions without deceiving other people about anything (including the fact that what one says is pure bullshit). Consider the following example. I am a student who needs to receive a good grade in a class. I am assigned to write a short essay on a very clearly and precisely defined topic. I know nothing about the topic and cannot write on it at all. Despite this, I know that my instructor will give me partial credit for turning in something, however incompetent and far off the topic. The worst grade I can receive for writing something that is completely incompetent and off the topic is an F—60%. If I write nothing I will receive a zero—0%. In producing a bullshit answer, I am not attempting to mislead my teacher about my level of knowledge or about what I am up to (namely bullshitting her). I don't care about any of these things; I just want to receive 60 points instead of zero points. I might even want my bullshitting to be transparent to the teacher in order to amuse or annoy her. Here is an example of such an answer. A student is asked the following question in an exam for an applied ethics class: "Briefly describe the facts of the case of Dodge v. Ford and answer the following question: Was Henry Ford morally justified in his actions in this case? Defend your answer." The student has not read the case nor was she in class when it was discussed so she cannot describe the facts of the case. Since she does not know what Henry Ford did in this case, she cannot possibly formulate a coherent argument for thinking that he was or was not morally justified in what he did. She gives the following bullshit answer:

In today's society there are many important ethical questions about the role of business in the larger society. These are important questions since business and its actions play such a large role in today's society. We have addressed these questions in our class. Milton Friedman holds that the only obligation of business is to make money for the shareholders, provided that it avoids fraud, deception, and unfair competition. Others say that corporations should be run for the benefit of all their "stakeholders." Utilitarians hold that corporations should promote the social good. The Ford Motor company had many obligations in this case. In this case, I think that the obligation to society was the most important obligation. The company failed to live up to this obligation, to an extent, but this is not a black or white issue. In any case, Henry Ford didn't adequately fulfill his duty to the public.[9]

In the sort of case that I have described, a student could produce this kind of bullshit answer without intending to deceive anyone.

2.V.4. Lying Can Constitute Producing Bullshit

Contrary to what Frankfurt says, one can tell a lie while producing bullshit. One can tell a lie as a part of an evasive bullshit answer to a question. Suppose that I teach at a university that is very intolerant of atheists. I am asked by an administrator whether a friend and colleague is an atheist. I know that he is an atheist and that it will harm him if I reveal this. I do not want to harm my friend nor do I want to lie and say that he is not an atheist as I fear that I am likely to be found out if I lie about this. I give an evasive bullshit answer. I say "as a boy he always went to church and loved singing Christmas Carols" even though I know this to be false. (I am not worried that I will be caught or found out if I lie about this.) My answer is evasive bullshit, but because I say what I know to be false in a context in which I know that I am warranting the truth of what I say, my answer is also a lie.

2.V.5. Bullshitters Can be Concerned with the Truth of What they Say

A student who gives a bullshit answer to a question in an exam might be concerned with the truth of what he says. Suppose that she knows that the teacher will bend over backwards to give her partial credit if he thinks that she may have misunderstood the question, but she also knows that if the things she writes are false she will be marked down. In that case, she will be very careful to write only things that are true and accurate, although she knows that what she writes is not an answer to the question.

A politician who gives evasive bullshit answers to difficult questions might still be concerned with the truth of what he says. Suppose that he fears that the media will dissect his every public word and catch him in false and inaccurate statements. In that case, he will care very much about whether what he says is true. Not only will he carefully craft evasive bullshit statements and answers, he will be careful to make sure that what he says is true.

Similarly, the witness in court who gives evasive bullshit answers may be very concerned to say only things that are true so that he can avoid charges of perjury. Contrary to Frankfurt's (2005, pp. 55–56) claim that bullshitters are not concerned with whether the statements they make are true or false, the bullshitting witness may be very concerned with the truth value of his statements.

Some bullshit deceives others and much bullshit is intended to deceive others, but contrary to what Frankfurt says, some bullshit is not intended to deceive others. One can bullshit even if one knows that one's bullshitting is completely transparent to others. One can lie without bullshitting and most bullshitting does not involve lying, but, Frankfurt to the contrary, one can produce bullshit while lying. Although Frankfurt's claim that bullshitters are unconcerned with the truth of what they say is an apt and insightful description of much bullshit, some bullshitters are concerned with the truth of what they say. Therefore, Frankfurt's claim that unconcern with the truth of what one says is the essence of bullshit is mistaken. I do not have a better alternative definition of bullshit that I am prepared to defend. I suspect that the concept of bullshit is too loose and amorphous to admit of a definition in terms of necessary and sufficient conditions. Frankfurt (2005, p. 2), himself, says as much. To paraphrase Frankfurt's own hopes for his account of bullshit, it is "helpful" (very helpful indeed) but not "decisive" (definitive).

2.VI. A VERY BRIEF NOTE ON HONESTY

The terms "honest" and "dishonest" ("honesty" and "dishonesty") are often used to refer to global traits of character as opposed features of individual actions. In Chapter 14, I ask whether honesty is a virtue. My answer appeals to the distinction between what I call honesty in a positive sense and honesty in a negative sense. It will help to have a brief account of honesty on the table earlier in the book. So, here goes.

I want to *stipulate* that "honesty" and "dishonesty" as I will use the terms in this book have to do only with lying, deception, withholding information, and the like. In ordinary language, the terms "honesty" and "dishonesty" are used more broadly. In this broader sense, whether a person is honest or dishonest is partly a function of whether she keeps her promises and refrains from stealing and bribery. We take the fact that someone is a thief to be incompatible with his being an honest person. My purpose here is not to capture the ordinary language meaning of the words "honesty" and "dishonesty," but to assess whether honesty/dishonesty in my narrow sense (a character trait that is directly related to lying, deception, and withholding/providing information) is a virtue/vice. It is useful to distinguish between "honesty in a negative sense" (having a strong principled disinclination to tell lies or deceive others) and "honesty in a positive sense," which (in addition to involving being disinclined to tell lies or deceive others) involves being candid, open, and willing to reveal information.

ENDNOTES

1. I used this definition of deception in the first definitions of lying that I considered in Chapter 1, L1 (p. 18) and L2 (p. 19).
2. Al Mele, for one, claims that it is possible to deceive others unintentionally; see Mele (2001, pp. 8–9).
3. Frankfurt claims that lack of concern for the truth and falsity is one of the most salient features of bullshitters; see Frankfurt (2005, pp. 33–34, 47–48, and 56–57).
4. The distinction between D1 and D2 closely parallels the distinction discussed earlier (Chapter 1.I.2, p. 17) between the view that a necessary condition of telling a lie is that one makes a false statement that one believes is false (or believes is probably false) and the view that a necessary condition of telling a lie is that one makes a false statement that one does not believe to be true.
5. For a qualified defense of the moral relevance of the distinction between lying and deception (the view that lying is worse than deception), see Adler (1997).

6. Here, Frankfurt's view would more plausible if he said "*intends* to deceive us about" instead of "deceives us about." Succeeding in deceiving others is not a necessary condition for bullshit. One can bullshit others even if the fact that one is bullshitting is apparent to them.

7. Frankfurt describes bullshit as a form of bluffing. He says that bluffing is a mode "of misrepresentation or deception" (p. 46). Also, see pp. 12 and 14.

8. Also, see pp. 47–48.

9. I have suffered through numerous answers of this sort.

II

MORAL THEORY

IIA NORMATIVE ETHICAL THEORY

Chapters 3–5 examine the implications of Kant's moral theory, act-utilitarianism, Ross's theory, and rule-consequentialism for questions about the morality of lying and deception. (The historical figures in question have much more to say about lying than deception, though this book is equally concerned with deception.) I argue that Kant's theory does not commit him to the view that there is an absolute moral prohibition against lying. I also present a Rossian argument for thinking that lying is sometimes permissible. Many critics contend that utilitarianism often permits lying when lying is, in fact, wrong. Mill attempts to answer this objection in *Utilitarianism* where he claims that lying always has indirect bad consequences (lying makes people less honest and undermines trust between people). Mill claims that, therefore, utilitarianism implies that there is a strong moral presumption against lying. Ross and rule-consequentialists argue that act-utilitarianism is too permissive about the morality of lying and present cases in which they claim that the theory conflicts with our moral intuitions or "considered moral judgments" about the wrongness of lying. I argue that the standard debate between act-utilitarians, Rossians, and rule-consequentialists is inconclusive because it involves an appeal to disputed moral intuitions or disputed "considered moral judgments." Each of the parties appeals to his/her own moral intuitions or considered moral judgments, without doing enough to justify them. Similarly, though I share the intuitions of those who find Kant's absolutism about lying untenable, we cannot settle this issue by appeal to moral intuitions, because the intuitions of ostensibly rational people conflict.

3

Kant and the Absolute Prohibition against Lying

INTRODUCTION

Kant's moral theory is one of the most important theories of moral obligation in the history of philosophy. In several of his published works, Kant claims that lying is always wrong, no matter what the consequences. He is probably the most well known defender of an absolute prohibition against lying in the history of Western philosophy.[1]

In Section 3.I, I explain the three versions of Kant's basic moral principle, the categorical imperative (hereafter CI), and Kant's distinction between perfect and imperfect duties. Section 3.II surveys what Kant says about lying in *Grounding for the Metaphysics of Morals* (hereafter *GW*), *The Metaphysics of Morals* (hereafter *MM*), "On a Supposed Right to Lie Because of Philanthropic Concerns," (hereafter *SR*) and *Lectures on Ethics* (hereafter *LE*). In one discussion of lying in *LE*, Kant rejects the absolute prohibition against lying. I pay special attention to the various definitions of lying that Kant employs in these writings; he defines lying differently in different works. Sections 3.III and 3.IV address the question of whether Kant's moral theory really commits him to the view that lying is always wrong, no matter what. Kant never explicitly appeals to the CI in any of his arguments to show that lying is always wrong. In Section 3.III, I argue that the universal law version of the CI does not imply that lying is always wrong—one can will that everyone follows maxims or principles that sometimes permit lying. In Section 3.IV, I argue that, Korsgaard to the contrary, the second version of the CI does not imply that lying is always wrong. In Section 3.V, I present a Rossian argument for thinking that lying is sometimes morally permissible. The duty not to lie can conflict with other moral duties. If lying is always wrong no matter what, then the duty not to lie must *always* be more important than any conflicting duties. However, it seems unreasonable to hold that the duty not to lie is *always* more important than any conflicting duties. Kant's own example of a case in which lying is necessary to thwart the plans of a would-be murderer is one of the best illustrations of this.

3.1. KANT'S CATEGORICAL IMPERATIVE

Kant calls CI "the supreme principle of the doctrine of morals" (*MM*, p. 226).[2] He states three versions of the CI.

3.1.1. The Universal Law Formulation of the Categorical Imperative

Kant's first formulation of the CI in *GW* is as follows: "Act only according to that maxim whereby you can at the same time will that it should become a universal law. . . . Act as if the maxim of your action were to become through your will a universal law of nature" (p. 421).[3] Maxims are general principles that prescribe actions, e.g., "don't lie," "Never sacrifice your queen for the sake of taking a knight," and "don't bet on a lame horse." The maxim of a particular action is the principle that the person actually follows in performing that act—Kant calls it the "subjective principle of action" (*GW*, p. 421 n. 9). Kant seems to think that every action has just one maxim; in his illustrations of the CI, he repeatedly refers to "the [singular] maxim of the action" (*GW*, pp. 422–423).[4] A maxim can be a universal law of nature provided that it is possible that all rational beings always follow it or comply with it. Therefore, the first version of the CI is roughly equivalent to the following: "Act only on maxims/principles that you *can will* that every rational being in the universe follows, i.e., act only on maxims that it is possible for you to will that every rational being follows." Kant's examples of maxims typically mention both the means and ends of actions, e.g., "let me do act X in order to achieve end Y." One test of whether such a maxim can be a universal law of nature is whether universal adherence to that maxim would make it impossible for one to achieve the end by means of the action in question. Korsgaard writes: "On my reading . . . the universalized maxim contradicts itself if the efficacy of the action for achieving its end would be undermined by its being a universal practice . . . Thus the test question will be: Could this action be a universal method of achieving this purpose?" (Korsgaard, 1996, p. 135).

3.1.2. Perfect and Imperfect Duties

Kant claims that certain maxims are such that they cannot be universal laws of nature; it is not just that we *cannot will* that they be universal laws of nature, these maxims cannot *be* universal laws of nature. When people act on such maxims they violate perfect duties. "Some actions are so constituted that their maxims cannot without contradiction even be thought as a universal law of nature, much less be willed as what should become one . . . [this] kind of action conflicts with strict or narrow perfect (irremissible) duty . . ." (*GW*, p. 424). A perfect duty is a duty such that in order to violate it one must act on a maxim that cannot be a universal law of nature, i.e., it is impossible that everyone follows the maxim. The maxim of an action that violates an imperfect duty can be a universal law of nature (i.e., it is possible that everyone follows the maxim), but one cannot *will* that it be a universal law of nature. An imperfect duty is a duty such that the maxim of an action that violates it can be a universal law of nature, but the maxim cannot be willed to be a universal law of nature.

According to Kant, there is a perfect duty not to make a "lying promise" (a promise that one knows one cannot keep) in order to obtain a loan. Not only is it impossible to *will* that everyone else follows maxims that permit making lying promises in order to borrow money, everyone's following maxims that permit this is an *impossible* state of affairs. Universal adherence to such maxims would destroy the background of honesty and trust necessary for the existence of the *institution* or *practice* of lending money on the strength of promises to repay. If everyone followed such maxims, no one would be willing to rely on the promises to repay loans and no one could succeed in borrowing money by means of making such promises.

Another man in need finds himself forced to borrow money. He knows well that he won't be able to repay, but sees also that he will not get any loan unless he firmly promises to repay within a fixed time. . . . The maxim of his action would then be expressed as follows: when I believe myself to be in need of money, I will borrow money and promise to pay it back, although I know that I can never do so . . . such a maxim could never hold as a universal law of nature and be consistent with itself, but must necessarily be self-contradictory. For the universality of a law which says that anyone believing himself to be in difficulty could promise whatever he pleases with the intention of not keeping it would make promising itself and the end to be attained thereby quite impossible, inasmuch as no one would believe what was promised him but would merely laugh at all such utterances as being vain pretenses.[5]

GW (p. 422)

3.1.3. The Second and Third Versions of the Categorical Imperative

Kant formulates the second version of the CI as follows: "Act in such a way that you treat humanity, whether in your own person or in the person of another, always at the same time as an end and never *simply* [my emphasis] as a means" (*GW*, p. 429). Kant does not say that it is wrong to treat other persons as means. Rather, he says that it is wrong to treat others *simply* as means. The view that it is always wrong to treat another person (even partly) as a means to fulfilling one's own ends implies that it would be wrong for me to hire a plumber to fix my shower or ask a stranger for directions when I am lost. Intuitively, it seems that it *is* permissible to treat another person *partly* as a means to one's own ends, but not permissible to treat another person *simply* as a means, as one might a treat a tool or an inanimate object.

Presumably, Kant takes "treating persons as ends" to mean more than not treating them as *mere means*. Not treating someone as a *mere means* is such a weak requirement (a requirement that most people satisfy in their treatment of their pets) that it cannot be all that Kant means by this. The positive requirement to treat other persons *as ends* requires us to treat other people in a way that befits and respects their status as ends in themselves and rational autonomous agents. It is unclear what *this* means; I examine Korsgaard's interpretation of this requirement later in Section 3.IV.

Kant formulates the third version of the CI in the following:

> A rational being must always regard himself as a legislator in a kingdom of ends . . . Reason, therefore, relates every maxim of the will as legislating universal laws to every other will and also to every action toward oneself: it does so not on account of any other practical motive or future advantage but rather from the idea of the dignity of a rational being who obeys no law except what he at the same time enacts himself.
>
> *GW* (p. 434)

This is roughly equivalent to the first version of the CI. Acting as if you were legislating universal laws to which all rational beings (including yourself) are subject, is the same as acting in such a way that you can will that it be the case that everyone else follows the maxims that you follow. Therefore, I will focus on the first two formulations of the CI here.

Kant claims that the three formulations of the CI are "at bottom merely so many formulations of the same law . . . " (*GW*, p. 436), but he stops short of saying that they are equivalent.[6] Kant gives priority to the first version of the CI. After discussing the relationship among the three versions of the CI, he writes:

> But one does better if in moral judgment he follows the rigorous method and takes as his basis the universal formula of the categorical imperative: Act according to that maxim which can at the same time make itself a universal law. . . . We can now end where we started in the beginning, viz., the concept of an unconditionally good will . . . . This principle is therefore also its supreme law: Act always according to that maxim whose universality as a law you can at the same time will.
>
> *GW* (p. 437)

In *MM* Kant writes: "The supreme principle of the doctrine of morals is, therefore, act on a maxim which can also hold as a universal law. Any maxim which does not so qualify is contrary to morals" (*MM*, p. 226).

In the *Critique of Practical Reason* Kant writes: "The rule of judgment under laws of pure practical reason is this: ask yourself whether, if the action you propose were to take place by a law of nature of which you were yourself a part, you could indeed regard it as possible through your will" (5: 69) (these numbers refer to volume and page numbers of the standard Prussian Academy German edition of Kant's works).

3.II. WHAT KANT SAYS ABOUT THE MORALITY OF LYING

3.II.1. The *Grounding for the Metaphysics of Morals* (1785)

In *GW*, there are three discussions of "lying promises" or "false promises" (pp. 402–403, 422, and 429–430). Kant says that lying promises violate perfect duties and the second version of the CI. He claims that lying promises are always wrong, but in these passages he neither says nor implies that lying is always wrong. Kant does say that the command "thou shall not lie" holds not only for men, but all rational beings (*GW*, p. 389), but from the context, it is unclear whether or not he means that "thou shall not lie" means "thou shall *never* lie." The only other reference to lying in the *GW* is in a discussion of the difference between hypothetical and CIs. Kant writes: "The former [hypothetical imperative] says that I ought not to lie if I would maintain my reputation; the latter [categorical imperative] says that I ought not to lie even though lying were to bring me not the slightest discredit" (*GW*, p. 441). Perhaps Kant means to say that lying is always wrong no matter what, but that is unclear from this passage alone. In this passage, he discusses lying in cases in which lying will not harm one's reputation; he is not talking about all cases of lying.

3.II.2. *Metaphysics of Morals* (1797)

In a discussion of lying in *MM* (pp. 429–431) Kant writes:

> The greatest violation of man's duty to himself regarded merely as a moral being (the humanity in his own person) is the contrary of truthfulness, *lying* (*aliud lingua promptum, alid pecotore inclusum genere*) (To have one thing in one's heart and another ready on one's tongue). . . . [T]he dishonor (being an object of moral contempt) that accompanies the lie also accompanies the liar like a shadow.   (p. 429)

In *MM* Kant distinguishes between two different kinds of moral duties, duties of right or juridical duties (which Kant also calls "duties in accordance with rightful law giving") and ethical duties or duties of virtue (*MM*, pp. 218–219 and 239–240).[7] Duties of right or juridical duties are duties that one can be rightfully compelled to fulfill. The duty to keep promises is a duty of right, since one can be [rightfully] coerced to keep one's promises. Ethical duties or duties of virtue are moral duties that one cannot be [rightfully] coerced to fulfill (*MM*, pp. 219–220). Kant thinks that lying sometimes violates duties of right and sometimes violates ethical duties or duties of virtue. He distinguishes between two different senses of lying—lying in the juridical sense or the sense bearing on duties of right and lying in the ethical sense of the term: "In the doctrine of the Right an intentional untruth is called a lie only if it violates another's right; but in ethics, where no authorization is derived from harmlessness, it is clear of itself that no intentional untruth in the expression of one's thoughts can refuse this harsh name" (*MM*, p. 429). By "untruth" Kant does not mean "a false statement" but rather "a statement that one believes to be false." A true statement that one believes to be false can count as a lie.[8] Kant qualifies his definition of lying a few paragraphs later by adding that a lie must be intended to deceive another person: "a lie requires a second person whom one intends to deceive" (*MM*, p. 430). With this qualification, Kant's definition of lying (in the ethical sense) is that a lie is an intentional untruthful statement (an intentional statement that one believes to be false) that purports to "express one's thoughts" and is intended to deceive another person. [Lying in the sense bearing on right requires an additional condition — the intentional untruthful statement (that purports to express one's thoughts and is intended to deceive another person) must violate another person's right.]

In this same passage, Kant argues that lying (in the ethical sense) is (or can be) wrong even if it does not harm others:

Lying (in the ethical sense of the word), intentional untruth as such, need not be *harmful* to others in order to be repudiated; for it would then be a violation of the rights of others. It may be done merely out of frivolity or even good nature; the speaker may even intend to achieve a really good end by it. But this way of pursuing his end is, by its mere form, a crime of a man against his own person and a worthlessness that must make him contemptible in his own eyes.

MM (p. 430)

I take this passage to imply that lying in the ethical sense is always wrong no matter what—"this way of pursuing" our ends (lying) "is a crime" and is [always] wrong. Because Kant thinks that lying in the juridical sense is wrong for all the same reasons (as lying in the ethical sense) and wrong for other reasons as well, what he says here commits him to the view that all lies in either sense of the term are wrong. In this passage, Kant does not appeal to the CI, nor does he offer any argument for the view that pursuing one's ends by means of lying is (always) a crime or always wrong.

The *MM* includes "A Fragment of a Moral Catechism" (pp. 480–484). The fragment includes a dialogue between a teacher and pupil. Both the teacher and pupil (and, it also seems, Kant) endorse the view that lying is always wrong no matter what:

Teacher: . . . Suppose . . . that a situation arises in which you could get a great benefit for yourself or your friend by making up a subtle *lie* that would harm no one: What would your reason say about it?

Pupil: That I ought not lie, no matter how great the benefits to myself and my friend might be. Lying is *mean* and makes a man *unworthy* of happiness. Here is an unconditional necessitation through a command (or prohibition) of reason, which I must obey; and in the face of it all my inclinations must be silent.

MM (pp. 481–482)

In this catechism Kant makes no appeal to the CI. He offers no argument for his view that I "ought not lie, no matter how great the benefits to myself" or others "might be," and he gives no argument for thinking that it would be wrong to lie if it were necessary in order to avoid great harm to oneself or others, e.g., to save the life of an innocent person (or many innocent persons).

3.II.3. "On a Supposed Right to Lie from Philanthropic Concerns"

In this essay written near the end of his life (1797), Kant holds that lying is always wrong no matter what, even if lying is necessary in order to save the life of an innocent person: "To be truthful in all declarations is, therefore, a sacred and unconditionally commanding law of reason which admits of no expediency whatever" (*SR*, p. 427).[9] *SR* defends the following definition of lying: a lie is "an intentionally untruthful declaration to another man" (an intentional declaration/statement that one believes to be false to another person) (*SR*, p. 426). Kant makes it clear here that he thinks that a lie/untruth can be a true statement. He says that it would be a lie if one says that someone is not in one's house when one believes this to be false but (unbeknownst to one) the person in question has left the house and one's statement (that the person is not there) is actually true (*SR*, p. 427).

Kant asks us to imagine the following case. Someone who fears that he will be murdered has taken refuge in my home. The person he is hiding from comes to my door and asks whether his intended victim is in the house. I cannot avoid answering "yes" or "no" to the question. The person at the door demands to know whether his intended victim is in my house—yes or no. Kant claims that I ought to answer the person truthfully.

This essay is a reply to Benjamin Constant who criticized Kant's absolutism. According to Constant, one has a duty to tell the truth only to those who have a right to know the truth. More generally, Constant claims that if someone has a duty to do something for you, then you have a right that they do it. Because the potential murderer does not have a right to know the information in question, I do not have a moral obligation to tell him the truth.[10] Kant concedes that often the people to whom we speak have no right to the truth. He also concedes that by lying we do no wrong to those who would use the truth for bad purposes. However, Kant argues that in such cases lying is, nonetheless, wrong because it harms "humanity in general."

And even though by telling an untruth I do no wrong to him who unjustly compels me to make a statement, yet this falsification, which as such can be called a lie (though not in a juridical sense), I do wrong to duty in general in a most essential point. That is, as far as in me lies, I bring it about that statements (declarations) in general find no credence, and hence also that all rights based on contracts become void and lose their force, and this is a wrong done to mankind in general. Hence a lie defined merely as an intentionally untruthful declaration to another man does not require the additional condition that it must do harm to another . . . For a lie always harms another; if not some other human being, then it nevertheless does harm to humanity in general, inasmuch as it vitiates the very source of right.[11]

SR (p. 426)

Kant claims that contracts would be rendered uncertain and useless if even the "slightest exception" to rules forbidding lying were permitted, "truthfulness is a duty that must be regarded as the basis of all duties founded on contract, and the laws of such duties would be rendered uncertain and useless if even the slightest exception to them were admitted" (*SR*, p. 427).

The foregoing arguments are quite unconvincing and curiously utilitarian. Kant argues that every lie "harms humanity" by undermining trust between people. This is very doubtful. Only those lies that are discovered by others can make people less trusting of others. It is debatable that the kind of lie in question harms humanity. It may be a good thing if murderers and criminals cannot trust or rely on the statements of others. However, for the sake of argument, let us grant Kant the claim that all lying harms humanity by diminishing trust or veracity. This alone would not show that lying is always wrong. Sometimes it is permissible to do things that harm others. The harm to individuals that can be *prevented* by lying in cases in which lying saves the lives of innocent people far outweighs any indirect harm to society that such lies would cause. Kant's claim that language and contracts would be rendered useless if we allowed the slightest exceptions to the rule against lying is patently false. In our world, many lies are told, and most people endorse moral principles that sometimes permit lying. However, the trust necessary for the viability of language exists almost everywhere, and in many/most societies there exists a level of trust sufficient to sustain the viability of contracts and promise-keeping.

In *SR* Kant makes no mention of the CI, nor does he attempt to show that the CI commits us to the view that lying is always wrong.

3.II.4. Allan Wood's Alternative Reading of "On a Supposed Right . . . "

Wood lays great stress on Kant's definition of lying in *SR*—a lie is "an intentionally untruthful declaration to another man." According to Wood (2008), Kant takes declarations to be statements that others are warranted or authorized to rely on.

we need to understand yet another crucial piece of technical terminology—the term "declaration" (*Aussage, Deklaration*, Latin *declaratio*). All these terms, in Kant's vocabulary, refer to statements that occur in a context where others are warranted or authorized (*befugt*) in relying on the truthfulness of what is said, and make the speaker liable by right, and thus typically subject to criminal penalties or civil damages, if what is said is knowingly false.   (p. 241)

Wood cites passages in which Kant uses the term "declaration" and says that the correctness of his interpretation of Kant's concept of a declaration is clear from what Kant says but does not cite any passages in which Kant defines "declaration" (pp. 241–242). (Wood says that if the person who answers the door in Kant's example is forced to answer, his statement cannot be a declaration, because the would-be murderer would not be authorized to rely on the answer (p. 246).) If the would-be murderer extorts an answer from the person at the door—and intends to use it for unjust purposes—then answering falsely would be a case of "a necessary lie" and hence permissible (Wood, 2008, pp. 246, 248). (Here, Wood appeals to an argument Kant gives in *LE*, which I discuss later in 3.II.5; Wood does not explain what he and Kant mean by "extort" in this context.) According to Wood, Kant holds that speaking falsely to the person at the door is a case of wrongful lying only if the declaration is neither coerced nor extorted and is still somehow necessary in the situation (p. 248). Wood says that Kant's description of the example is very implausible; it is implausible to think that all of the conditions Kant ascribes to it apply to any possible case: (1) the speaker is not coerced into answering; (2) the person at the door does not extort an answer that he intends to use for unjust purposes; and, nonetheless, (3) answering the question is unavoidable so that the person who comes to the door does not have the option of not answering the question.

There are serious problems with Wood's reading of the passage in *LE* in which Kant defends "necessary lies." Kant describes the necessary lie as a case in which someone is both coerced and extorted to tell the truth (see later in 3.II.5). According to Wood, Kant's definition of lying in *SR* does not count this as a case of lying. Therefore, it seems that either Wood is mistaken in his interpretation of Kant's use of the term "declaration," or else Kant is employing different definitions of lying in these two works and Wood's strategy of interpreting *SR* in terms of *LE* is called into question.

Wood thinks that Kant's ethical theory properly understood permits one to speak falsely intentionally to the would-be murderer in certain variations of this in this case (cases in which the answer is coerced), but that doing so would not be a case of lying according to Kant's definition of lying. Wood also thinks that there are other variations on this case (cases in which the would-be murderer extorts but not does not coerce the person at the door) that Kant would regard as cases of justifiable lying (see later).

In his interpretation of *SR* Wood appeals to Kant's discussion of "necessary lies" in *LE*; however, it is very doubtful that Kant still endorsed the view that "necessary lies" are permissible when he wrote *SR*, which was written 12–13 years later in 1797. *SR* was written roughly the same time he wrote the *MM*, 1797/1798 (a work in which he claims that lying is never permissible). Wood (2008) dismisses Kant's absolutism in the *MM* as "rhetorical exaggeration of truths which, as moral philosopher, he should have recognized (and even does recognize) some important limitations and exceptions" (p. 253), which is justified by people's tendency "to make exceptions to rules in their own interest when they should not, and this makes the speech act of asserting the unexceptionableness of moral rules morally justified even when it is in error theoretically" (pp. 253–254).

The definition of lying that Wood attributes to Kant in *SR* is inconsistent with Kant's definition of lying (in the ethical sense) in *MM*. In *MM*, Kant says that one can lie in the "ethical sense" without violating anyone's rights. According to Wood (2008), however, when one makes a declaration, others are justified in relying on the truth of what one says. Therefore, any untruthful declaration violates the rights of others (pp. 241–243). The definition of lying that Wood attributes to Kant in *SR* also seems to be inconsistent with Kant's understanding of lying in the passage in *LE* by which Wood sets so much store. In *LE*, Kant describes the "necessary lie" as a case in which one is coerced ("I am constrained by force used against me" (p. 204)) to answer the question (see 3.II.5). Others are not warranted in relying on statements that are coerced, and thus, Wood to the contrary, Kant's definition of lying in *SR* cannot count this crucial example as a case of lying.

[My first definition of lying, L5 (see Chapter 1.I.12, p. 30), which employs a concept of warranting similar to Kant's notion of a declaration, also implies that, when one is compelled to answer the would-be murderer at the door, answering falsely would not be lying. According to L5, the statement in question is not a lie, as one does not warrant the truth of what one says. However, my alternative definition, L7 (see Chapter 1.II.2, p. 37) leaves open the possibility that when the person is compelled to speak his statement is a lie, because he still might intend to warrant the truth of what he says in this situation. The standard dictionary definition of the English word "lying" (an intentional false statement intended to deceive others) counts this as a case of lying. L1 (from Chapter 1, p. 17) also counts this as a case of lying.]

Wood (2008) also explicitly rejects my criticism of Kant's argument in *SR* (my criticism of Kant's argument about how lying undermines trust and contracts) and claims that it is based on a misinterpretation of Kant.

The claim here is *not* that some particular lie might *in fact* shake people's confidence in trials and contracts (as if it by itself would cause them no longer to believe anyone, or had no other reason to mistrust what people say). It is rather that the system of right is constituted by a set of laws that are universally valid—actions are right only if they can coexist with everyone's freedom under this system according to a universal law. . . . Hence it is contrary to the very concept of right that it could be right to make an untruthful declaration when the truthfulness of that declaration is required by rational laws of right. By making such a declaration, I am in that way acting in a way that if its permissibility were generally allowed, would deprive all declarations of their validity, whether or not I intend that result and whether or not it actually occurs. Kant also puts it this way: "It cannot hold with universality of law of nature that declarations should be allowed as proof and yet be intentionally untrue."   (p. 243)

If we read the passage at issue in *SR* very literally, Kant seems to hold the views I attribute to him. He talks about what lying in this case would cause or bring about. To be more charitable to Kant, however, let us suppose that Wood's interpretation of this passage is correct. Wood gives no reason why we cannot allow very rare exceptions to the rules against lying. Lying when doing so is absolutely necessary in order to save an innocent person's life is a very rare and unusual kind of case (very few of us have ever told such lies); allowing this as a justifiable exception to rules against lying would not "deprive all declarations of their validity." (I say much more about this matter later in 3.III).

3.II.5. Lectures on Ethics

In an extended discussion of lying in *LE* (taken from lectures delivered during 1784–85, 12–13 years before he published *MM* and *SR*), Kant rejects the view that lying is always wrong (pp. 201–205). In this same passage, Kant defines a lie as an untruthful statement (a statement that one believes to be false) intended to deceive others that is made in a context in which one expressly declares that one is speaking truthfully. He explicitly rejects the broad definition of lying that he defends in *MM* and *SR*:

> If an enemy, for example takes me by the throat and demands to know where my money is kept, I can hide the information here, since he means to misuse the truth. This is still no *mendacium* [a lie with intent to deceive], for the other knows that I shall withhold the information, and that he also has no right whatever to demand the truth of me. Suppose, however, that I actually state that I mean to speak my mind . . . Am I a liar? If the other has cheated, and I cheat him in return, I have certainly done this fellow no wrong . . . yet I am a liar nonetheless . . .
> . . . Not every untruth is a lie; it is so only if there is an express declaration of my willingness to inform the other of my thought.
>
> *LE* (p. 203)

Kant goes on to claim that there is one (and only one) situation in which lying (so defined) is morally permissible:

> we often court danger by punctilious observance of the truth, and hence has arisen the concept of the necessary lie, which is a very critical point for the moral philosopher. . . . For example, somebody, who knows that I have money, asks me: Do you have money at home? If I keep silent, the other concludes that I do. If I say yes, he takes it away from me; if I say no I tell a lie; so what am I to do? So far as I am constrained by force used against me, to make an admission, and a wrongful use is made of my statement, and I am unable to save myself by silence, the lie is a weapon of self-defense; the declaration is extorted, and is then misused, permits me to defend myself, for whether my admission or my money is extracted, is all the same. Hence there is no case in which a necessary lie should occur, save when the declaration is wrung from me, and I am also convinced that the other means to make wrongful use of it.
>
> *LE* (p. 204)

Note that Kant describes this "necessary lie" as a case in which one is coerced ("constrained by force") to answer the question. Wood's description of this as a case in which an answer is extorted but not coerced is incorrect. According to Wood's account, Kant cannot call this a case of lying if he consistently applies his definition of lying from *SR*.

It seriously understates the extent to which Kant changed his views between the time he delivered these lectures and the time he wrote *MM* and *SR* if we say that Kant once thought that lying was *wrong in all but one kind of case* and then later came to hold that lying is *always wrong*. This overlooks the fact that Kant also changed his definition of lying. He moved from a narrow definition (a lie is a deliberate statement that one believes to be false that is intended to deceive others and is made in a context in which one has explicitly stated that one will speak truthfully) to a broader definition (a lie is any deliberate declaration that one believes to be false). Relatively few deliberate untruthful declarations are made in contexts in which one explicitly tells others that one is speaking truthfully. We rarely preface statements/declarations we make by making *explicit* assurances or promises that we are telling the truth. Kant's earlier definition from *LE* implies that the great majority of the untruthful statements that we ordinarily regard as lies are not, in fact, genuine lies. In this passage from *LE*, Kant gives no indication that he thinks that there is anything wrong with making untruthful statements (statements that one believes to be false) in contexts in which one has not *explicitly* given others to think that one intends to tell the truth. Thus, many (perhaps most) of the statements Kant calls lies and claims to be wrong in *SR* are not claimed to be wrong in passages in question in *LE*.

Kant takes a rather permissive view about the morality of deception (deception without lying) in these same passages in *LE*. He justifies both equivocation (ambiguous deceptive statements that are true—and that one believes to be true—in at least one sense and therefore are not lies) and statements made with "mental reservation" (statements that one believes to be true only in virtue of qualifications that one silently thinks to oneself but does not express to others)[12] in situations in which one has not expressly declared that one is speaking what one believes to be the case (pp. 204–205). He also says that it can be permissible to deceive another about one's beliefs short of lying (p. 426).

There are several other brief discussions of lying in *LE*. Kant writes: "*Joking* lies, if they are not taken to be *true*, are not immoral. But if it be that the other is *ever* meant to believe it, then, even though no harm is done, it is a lie, since at least there is always deception" (p. 28).[13] In the first sentence, Kant says that joking lies that are not intended to be taken as true (not intended to be believed) are permissible. In the next sentence he says that when a "joking liar" intends that others believe what he says, his statement is a lie—this suggests that when joking lies are not intended to be believed (and are thus permissible), they are not really lies. It is unclear whether he takes "joking lies" that the joker does not intend others to believe to be genuine cases of lying, and thus it is unclear whether, in this passage, Kant is claiming that lying is sometimes permissible.[14]

In two other brief discussions of lying in *LE* Kant says things that imply that lying is always wrong no matter what. Both of these passages date from 1793–94.

Lying, in the ethical sense at any rate, is viewed as the transgression of a duty to oneself . . . . In the ethical sense it comprises every intentional untruth, or every intentional false statement of my disposition, and is blameworthy in and for itself . . . (pp. 350–351)

In ethics, though, every *falsiloquium*,[15] every knowing deception, is impermissible, even though it be not immediately coupled with injury. (p. 427)

It seems that Kant changed his views about the morality of lying some time between 1784–85 and 1793–94.

3.III. DOES THE FIRST VERSION OF THE CATEGORICAL IMPERATIVE IMPLY THAT LYING IS ALWAYS WRONG?

The first version of the CI gives two tests for the maxims of our actions: (1) Can the maxim of the action be a universal law of nature? (Is it possible that every rational being follows the maxim?), and (2) Can we will that the maxim of the action be a universal law of nature? (Is it possible for us to will that every rational being follows the maxim?) In *LE* Kant asks us to consider the maxim "tell a lie or untruth whenever [you can] thereby gain a great advantage" (p. 264).[16] Arguably, it is impossible that everyone follows this maxim, because if *everyone* lied whenever s/he thought s/he could gain an advantage, dishonesty would be so rife that people would not trust or rely on the assertions of others, and one could not gain an advantage by means of lying. However, this does not show that the first version of the CI commits us to an absolute prohibition against lying. This is not the only maxim that sometimes permits lying. Consider the following maxims:

M1. Let me lie in order to prevent someone from being murdered.

M2. Let me lie when doing so is necessary in order to prevent an innocent person from being killed and lying does not produce any other consequences as bad as (or nearly as bad as) the death of an innocent person.[17]

Universal adherence to M1 and M2 would not threaten the institution of language or make it impossible for people to communicate and advance their interests by using language. (The great majority of people have never told a single lie that was sanctioned by M1 or M2 during their entire lives.) Further, many/most people are *willing* to have everyone else follow the policy of lying when it is necessary in order to save the lives of innocent people, and, therefore, they *can will* that everyone else makes it a policy to lie whenever it is necessary to save the lives of innocent people.

Wood (2008) claims that Kantian ethics or Kant's moral theory, properly understood, implies that certain kinds of lies or untruthful declarations are always wrong.

> Suppose that you are a witness under oath in a court of law. You are asked by the prosecutor a question the truthful answer to which will predictably result in the conviction of your friend (or in Kant's example, your brother), who you know to be innocent, on a charge of murder . . .
>
> No one should deny that this would be a deeply troubling predicament to be in . . . And my own considered view about it is the Kantian one: Unless I think that the legal process is illegitimate, or a sham, I think that I had better tell the truth and be prepared to live with the consequences. Otherwise (as Kant himself suggests), *I* am the one turning that process into a sham, by behaving according to a principle which if universally followed would bring all solemn testimony and all legitimate legal processes into discredit.
>
> (p. 249)

Wood stops short of saying that the first version of the CI implies that it is always wrong to lie under oath. However, if we accept what Wood says here, then no one who is unwilling to bring it about that all testimony and all legitimate legal processes be brought into discredit can accept maxims that justify lying in this case. We should not accept Wood's argument. Consider very narrow maxims/principles such as "let me lie under oath if I know *for certain* that doing so is necessary in order to prevent someone who I know for certain to be innocent from being unjustly executed for murder." Because in reasonably just societies (the sorts of societies in which we could not/would not will that "testimony and all legitimate legal processes be brought into discredit") the circumstances described are very rare, everyone acknowledging and behaving in accordance with that principle would not "bring all solemn testimony and all legitimate legal processes into discredit." I am willing to grant that the law should not allow exemptions to perjury law for cases of the sort in question. Therefore, I grant that committing perjury in order to save the life of an innocent person violates a just law, but there seems to be no reason why it cannot be morally right to do so. It might be the case that there are certain actions that the law should not allow which could still be morally permissible in very unusual cases. It is not an a priori truth that it is always morally wrong to violate a just law. If he thinks otherwise, Wood has the burden of proof.

3.IV. DOES THE SECOND VERSION OF THE CATEGORICAL IMPERATIVE IMPLY THAT LYING IS ALWAYS WRONG?

Lying for the good of others is consistent with treating them as ends in themselves and respecting their humanity. Suppose that a man has just had open-heart surgery and is temporarily in a precarious state. His surgeon says that he must be shielded from any stress or emotional distress for the next few days. Unbeknown to the patient, his only child, Bob, has been killed in an automobile accident. When the patient awakens after the surgery, he is surprised that Bob is not there and he asks, "Where is Bob?" You fear that in his condition, the shock of learning about Bob's death might cause him to die. So you lie and say that his son has been delayed. Doing this does not necessarily involve treating the patient as a mere means; indeed, it is consistent with loving him very much. Korsgaard strongly disagrees; I now turn to Korsgaard's reading of the second version of the CI.

Korsgaard claims that the second version of the CI implies that lying is always wrong but that the first version of the CI does not.[18] Korsgaard appeals to a passage in *GW* in which Kant derives perfect duties to others from the second formulation of the CI. In this passage, Kant invokes the idea that sometimes people do things to others that they cannot possibly assent to—in certain cases, "one cannot possibly assent to my mode of acting toward him" (Korsgaard, 1996, p. 138). The passage from Kant reads as follows:

the man who intends to make a false promise will immediately see that he intends to make use of another man merely as a means to an end which the latter does not likewise hold. For the man whom I want to use for my own purposes by such a promise cannot possibly concur with my way of acting toward him and hence cannot hold himself the end of the action (*GW* 429–430).[19]

Korsgaard (1996, p. 138)

Korsgaard (1996) says that the second version of the CI requires that we never act toward others in ways that it is impossible for them to assent to.

The question whether another can assent to your way of action can serve as a criterion for judging whether you are treating her as a mere means. We will say that knowledge of what is going on and some power over the proceedings are the conditions of possible assent; without these, the concept of assent does not apply. This gives us another way to formulate the test for treating someone as a mere means: suppose that it is the case that if the other person knows what you are trying to do and has the power to stop you, then what you are trying to do cannot be what is really happening. If this is the case the action is one that by its very nature is impossible for the other to assent to. (p. 139)

[Quite apart from its merits as an interpretation of Kant, Korsgaard's test for treating someone as a mere means is flawed. She says that if another person is trying to do X to me and I know this and have the ability to stop him then it cannot be the case that the other person is really Xing me. The following case is a clear counter-example to this. A woman knows that a man is trying to rape her and she has the ability to stop him, but she can stop him only if she kills him. She does not stop him because she thinks that killing is wrong no matter what. The man rapes her, even though she has the ability to stop him.] Korsgaard (1996) is at pains to stress that the test is not whether others *do* assent to the way we treat them, nor is the test whether they *would* assent to the way we treat them in certain hypothetical circumstances; rather, the test is whether it is *possible* for them to assent to how we treat them (p. 138). Korsgaard claims that it is not possible for someone to assent to being deceived or coerced. All deception and coercion violate the second version of the CI, "According to the Formula of Humanity, coercion and deception are the most fundamental forms of wrongdoing to others—the roots of all evil. Coercion and deception violate the conditions of possible assent, and all actions which depend for their nature and efficacy on their coercive or deceptive character are ones that others cannot assent to" (p. 140).

The argument that Korsgaard attributes to Kant is remarkably subtle and elegant. Nonetheless, it is not clear that this is *Kant's* argument rather than Korsgaard's. The idea of it being possible for someone to assent to "another's mode of treating her" is ambiguous between (1) it being possible for her to assent to a particular action with a particular end in particular circumstances, and (2) it being possible for her to assent to other people following *policies or principles* that permit them to treat her in the mode or manner that she is treated in the case in question. Suppose that I lie to you in an attempt to deceive you into thinking that I am at least 21 years of age, when in fact I am not. I cannot both lie and deceive you about this *and* at the same time obtain your assent to my doing this to you in the present circumstances. If you assented to my doing this, then I could not deceive you about my age. However, you *can* assent to others acting on principles that sometimes permit them to tell you lies that are intended to deceive you. (Many of us in fact *do assent* to others acting on such principles.) It is possible for you to assent to the idea that physicians should lie to you to protect your health in cases in which not lying would cause great harm to your health; you can assent to this as a general principle.[20] However, it is not possible for a physician who lies to you and deceives you in order to protect your health to have obtained your consent to being lied to and deceived in this particular situation and time and place. If you give your consent, then you know what is going on, and you cannot be deceived. (My preferred definition of lying (L5, see p. 30) implies that the statement the physician makes cannot be a lie. The physician cannot affirm/warrant its truth to you after having told you that what he is about to say is false.)

Korsgaard anticipates this objection and argues that in such a case the sort of lie that the person consents to being told cannot succeed in deceiving her, because after having given her consent, she will no longer trust the other person to whom she has given the consent, and she will not be deceived by the lies she has consented to being told (her example is consenting to having a physician lie to one if one is fatally ill). If this is correct, it follows that one cannot consent to another person lying to one *and* deceiving one, because if one consents to being lied to one cannot be deceived by the lies one has consented to being told.

Sometimes it is objected that someone could assent to being lied to in advance of the actual occasion of the lie, and that in such a case the deception might still succeed . . . I can certainly agree to remain uninformed about something, but this is not the same as agreeing to be deceived. For example, I could say to my doctor: "Don't tell me if I am fatally ill, even if I ask." But if I then do ask the doctor whether I am fatally ill, I cannot be certain whether she will answer me truthfully. Perhaps what's being envisioned is that I simply agree to be lied to, but not about anything in particular. Will I then trust the person with whom I have made this odd agreement?

Korsgaard (1996, pp. 155–156)

No doubt, this argument succeeds in many cases. Suppose that a gravely ill elderly woman has just undergone surgery for a deadly and fast-growing form of cancer. She knows that she has had cancer surgery, but has not been informed about the gravity of her condition. If she has consented to being lied to in this way by her doctor, she is unlikely to trust her doctor's answers to her questions about the gravity of her illness. However, suppose that a healthy 20-year-old who reasonably expects to live to be 85 consents to her physician lying to her about a fatal illness. In that case, she will for many years think it very unlikely that she is fatally ill and trust her doctor's reports, as she will think it very unlikely that the conditions under which she has consented to be lied to actually obtain. If she develops a fatal illness when she is 30 years of age and her physician lies to her about it, she will trust him and believe what he says.

There is no compelling reason to accept Korsgaard's interpretation of the idea of its being possible for someone to "assent to my mode of acting toward him" over the alternative interpretation that I have sketched here. Indeed, Kant's use of the expression "mode of acting" strongly favors my interpretation; it suggests that he is talking about a type of action (that falls under the scope of general policies or principles) rather than a particular act at a particular time and place. The fact that on her reading the second formulation of the CI *clearly implies* that all forms of coercion are impermissible argues against her interpretation. Kant clearly believes that coercion is sometimes morally permissible.[21] He also believes that criminal punishment and capital punishment (which are inherently coercive) are sometimes morally permissible (*MM*, pp. 472–477).

Korsgaard (1996) also gives another argument for her view that the second version of the CI implies that lying and deception are always wrong, no matter what. She claims that all cases of coercion and deception involve treating others as mere means.

The idea of deciding for yourself whether you will contribute to a given end can be represented as a decision to initiate a causal chain which constitutes your contribution. Any action which prevents or diverts you from making this decision is one that treats you as a mediate rather than a first cause; hence as a mere means, a thing, a tool. Coercion and deception both do this. And deception treats you as a mediate cause in a specific way: it treats your reason as a mediate cause. The false promiser thinks: if I tell her I will pay her back next week, then she will choose to give me the money. Your reason is worked, like a machine: the deceiver tries to determine what levers to pull to get the desired results from you.   (pp. 140–141)

To treat others as ends in themselves is always to address and deal with them as rational beings. Every rational being gets to reason out, for herself, what she is to think, choose, or do. So if you need someone's contribution to your end, you must put the facts before her and ask for her contribution. (p. 142)

Any attempt to control the actions and reactions of another by any means except an appeal to reason treats her as a mere means, because it attempts to reduce her to a mediate cause. (p. 142)

In support of her interpretation, she appeals to the following passage from the *Critique of Pure Reason*: "Reason depends on this freedom for its very existence. For reason has no dictatorial authority; its verdict is always simply the agreement of free citizens, of whom each one must be permitted to express, without hindrance, his objections, or even his veto" (A738–739/B766–767, Korsgaard, 1996, p. 142). This passage does not provide grounds for Korsgaard's claim that Kant takes the second version of the CI to imply that *any attempt* to control the actions or reactions of another person (or any case in which one treats another person "as a mediate rather than a first cause") involves treating the other person as "a mere means" or "a mere tool." Kant is clearly endorsing freedom of inquiry or freedom of expression and the view that citizens should be free from dictatorial authority. It is not clear what Kant means when he says that each person must be permitted to "express his veto," nor is it clear what things Kant thinks each person must be permitted to express his veto *about*. Thus, it is far from clear that Kant intends this passage to imply that all cases of coercion and deception are wrong, even when they are necessary to prevent people from being killed. Further, Kant does not mention the second version of the CI. Therefore, this passage does not entitle us to conclude that the second version of the CI implies that one cannot ever be justified in "taking a decision out of someone else's hands" (Korsgaard, 1996, p. 142).

To treat someone as *mere means* or a *mere tool* means treating her as if she had no interests, completely disregarding considerations of how one's actions harm or benefit her. We sometimes deceive or coerce people we *love* and whose interests we care about deeply. Here, Korsgaard might reply that coercion and deception involve not treating others as *rational persons*. To coerce or deceive others is to fail "to address and deal with them as rational beings." If I treat you as a "mediate cause" of my actions by means of coercion or deception, I am not treating you as a rational, autonomous person. However, this claim is too strong. I can recognize and respect you as a rational person while following policies that *sometimes* permit deception or coercion. Regarding oneself as a rational person is compatible with agreeing to be deceived or coerced under certain circumstances. It is *rational* to agree to be coerced or deceived under certain circumstances. For example, it is rational for one to agree to be deceived if one finds oneself in the position of a desperately ill patient who is likely to die unless others deceive him about recent bad news. Also, it is rational for one to agree to be coerced and forcibly prevented from killing oneself if (unbeknownst to one) someone gives one a drug that causes one to become suicidally depressed. Recognizing and respecting you as an autonomous agent is compatible with recognizing that coercing or deceiving you might be appropriate in certain circumstances.

3.V. A ROSSIAN ARGUMENT FOR THINKING THAT LYING IS SOMETIMES MORALLY PERMISSIBLE

The duty not to lie can conflict with other moral duties such as the duty to help others, the duty to keep promises, and the duty not to harm others. If we say that lying is always wrong no matter what, then we are claiming that the duty not to lie is *always* more important than any conflicting duties. However, on reflection, this claim is very dubious. There is no good reason to think that the duty not to lie is *always* and *necessarily* more important than the duty to prevent harm to others. Kant's own example of lying to thwart the plans of a would-be murderer is a very good illustration of this. Sidgwick (1966) speaks convincingly to this issue: "so if we may even kill in defense of ourselves and others, it seems strange if we may not lie, if lying will defend us better against a palpable invasion of our rights: and common sense does not seem to prohibit this decisively" (p. 315).

To see just how unreasonable it is to claim that the duty not to lie is always more important than any other conflicting duties consider the following example of a woman who lied to save the lives of at least twelve people:

In a little frame cottage just off Milwaukee Avenue, the Jewish community on Friday knocked a tiny bit off its debt to Zofia Kukla, Chicago's version of Oscar Schindler.

. . . During the Holocaust, she hid several Jewish families as Nazis herded Poland's Jews to the gas chambers of Auschwitz and Treblinka. Her own family, of course, was imperiled by her actions.

"What I did, I did only because I couldn't live with the thought that someone else's death could be on my hands," Kukla said. "They still come to me in the night, the people I couldn't save."

When the Nazis occupied Poland during World War II, Jews were rounded up in the rural areas and distributed as slave-laborers to local peasants. . . . But in mid-war, having established the extermination camps, the Nazis issued new orders that Jewish farmhands were to be surrendered.

Many of Kukla's neighbors in a tiny village near the city of Bialystok complied, but not Zofia and her husband, Franceszek. At gunpoint, they rescued a Jewish family from another farmer, warning him he faced death at their hands if he breathed word to the Nazis. Other refugees showed up at the Kukla's small farm, until they were sheltering about a dozen in space hastily dug under the floor of their dairy barn.

The Germans suspected as much, and a Polish collaborator brought Nazi troops to Kukla's house, even as two additional refugees were crouching in the attic. A German officer put a gun to Zofia's head, but she denied hiding Jews. Then he took a crucifix from the wall and told her to swear upon it.

"I know it's a sin to lie upon a cross," Kukla said. "But I know that human life is more important."

. . . several of her guests had died from privation and disease bred in their cramped quarters. But others survived . . .

Grossman (1995)

It gets even worse than this for the absolutist. In principle, absolutistism is committed to the view that it would be wrong to lie, even if lying were necessary in order save the lives of millions or billions of people. Paul Griffiths, who also defends an absolute prohibition against lying, goes out of his way to underscore the counter-intuitiveness of the absolutist view. He says that it would be wrong to lie if lying were necessary in order to prevent the pilot of a warplane from dropping a nuclear bomb on a city and killing a million people (Griffiths, 2004, p. 230). Griffiths's view rests on an appeal to claims about God's will and the idea that language/speech is a gift from God and that our use of it must respect God's will and purposes (pp. 85–86). I assume that Griffiths is mistaken about God's will in some way or other (I assume that either God's will or purposes are not served by refusing to lie to save the lives of a million people or that there is no God who is concerned with human affairs). I grant that there are some theological assumptions, which, if true, would make the absolutist view plausible. However, unless these theological assumptions are true, it seems that Griffiths's absolutism is mistaken.

Conclusions

This Rossian argument shows that Kant's absolutism is *extremely* counterintuitive and probably will persuade most readers. However, for reasons that will be given in much more detail at the end of Chapter 5, we should not be satisfied with this and other arguments that are based simply on appeals to moral intuitions. The problem is that ostensibly reasonable people often have conflicting moral intuitions. If we try to defend our moral judgments by appealing to our moral intuitions, we need to give some explanation of why our own intuitions are correct and the intuitions of those who disagree with us incorrect. In Chapter 7.II, I offer a much stronger argument against the view that there is an absolute prohibition against lying (and deception)—this argument appeals to the golden rule.

ENDNOTES

1. Augustine and Aquinas also defend an absolute prohibition against lying. See Augustine and Aquinas, *Summa Theologica* II-II, Question 110, Article, 3 ("Whether Every Lie is a Sin").
2. All *MM* references include the page numbers from the Prussian Academy Edition.
3. All *GW* references include the page numbers from the Prussian Academy Edition.
4. This seems oversimplified in that sometimes people act on more than one maxim. Sometimes we justify our actions by appeal to several different principles. A possible solution for Kant would be to say that one must be able to will that it be the case that *all* of the maxims one acts on are universal laws of nature.
5. Also see *GW* (p. 403).
6. Kant goes on to say "Nevertheless, there is a difference in them, which is subjectively rather than objectively practical, viz., it is intended to bring an idea of reason closer to intuition (in accordance with a certain analogy) and thereby closer to feeling" (*GW*, p. 436). On this point, see Wood (2008, *Kantian Ethics*, pp. 79–82).
7. On this see Baron (1995, p. 31):

   Ethical duties do not entail corresponding rights to exercise compulsion; juridical duties or duties of right do (*MM* 383). Ethical duties whether perfect or imperfect, imply no corresponding right to coerce us to fulfill them; indeed, it is impossible, since the constraint entailed by an ethical duty is *self*-constraint (*MM* 380), and has to be self-constraint because otherwise one would not, in acting morally, act freely.

8. On this point, see the passage cited above, "*lying (aliud lingua promptum, alid pecotore inclusum genere)* (To have one thing in one's heart and another ready on one's tongue)" (*MM*, p. 429). Also see the discussion of Kant's definition of lying in *SR* below and "On the miscarriage of all philosophical trials in theodicy" 8: 267–268 (p. 34).) On this point, I am indebted to Mahon (2009).
9. All *SR* references include the page numbers from the Prussian Academy Edition.
10. Grotius would deny that this statement constitutes a lie, since the other person does not have a right to know the truth. See Chapter 1, endnote 4.
11. Also, see *LE* (p. 193) where Kant also says that lying wrongs humanity, even if it does not wrong any particular person. (Page numbers refer to the pages in this translation of *LE* (1997).)

12. For an example, suppose that I say "I have never been arrested" and under my breath say "except after the brawl in Texarkana in August of 1970".

13. What if as part of a joke, I want you to believe something false for several minutes and then after that time I want you to realize that I am joking? I take it that, given what Kant says here, this counts as a case of lying.

14. Also, see *LE* (p. 427) for a reference to "tall stories". He says that telling "tall stories" can "only pass as jest if the judgment of others about the content of their truth cannot be in doubt."

15. The translator renders this as "false statement."

16. "For suppose that someone were to have the maxim, that he might tell an untruth whenever he could thereby gain a great advantage. . . ."

17. Cf. Paul Dietrichson (1969, p. 201) who says that "attempting to deceive for the sake of preventing a murder from taking place" can be willed to be a universal law of nature. Herman (1993, p. 152) says that "the restricted maxim 'to deceive to save a life' " can be willed to be a universal law of Nature.

18. I will not bother to explain Korsgaard's (1996) argument that the first version of the CI permits lying on occasion, as this point is not in dispute.

19. Quoted from Lewis White Beck's (1959) translation of *Foundations of the Metaphysics of Morals*.

20. Also, see Mahon (2006). Mahon says that it is possible for me to obtain your consent to lie to you under certain circumstances in the future. I can for example obtain your consent to this by asking you "May I lie to you in the future, for the sake of throwing a surprise party for you?" (pp. 682–683).

21. See *MM*, Introduction to the Doctrine of Right, Section D "Right is Connected with an Authorization to Use Coercion" and Section E "A Strict Right can also be Represented as the Possibility of a Fully Reciprocal Use of Coercion that is Consistent With Everyone's Freedom in Accordance with Universal Laws."

4

Act-Utilitarianism

INTRODUCTION

There is a strong consensus among both philosophers and non-philosophers that Kant's absolute prohibition against lying is too strict. On the other hand, many contend that utilitarianism is too permissive about the morality of lying. Mill attempts to answer this objection in chapter 2 of *Utilitarianism*, where he claims that lying always has indirect bad consequences, and that, therefore, utilitarianism implies that there is a strong moral presumption against lying. Mill argues that utilitarianism supports a strong presumption against lying. I defend Mill's argument, and note several ways in which it can be extended and strengthened. I address other objections to act-utilitarianism (AU) in Chapter 5. My ultimate view is that the standard objections to the act-utilitarian view about the morality of lying and deception do not succeed and that AU is *a* reasonable theory about the morality of lying and deception, but not the only one. AU marks the weakest acceptable prohibition against lying and deception—the prohibition against lying and deception is at least as strong as that endorsed by AU (see Chapter 7).

4.I. THE DEFINITION OF (ACT) UTILITARIANISM

Sidgwick (1966) defines utilitarianism in the following passages from *The Methods of Ethics*:

By utilitarianism is here meant the ethical theory, that the conduct which, under any given circumstances is objectively right, is that which will produce the greatest amount of happiness on the whole; that is taking into account all whose happiness is affected by the conduct.   (p. 411)

We shall understand, then, that by the greatest happiness is meant the greatest possible surplus of pleasure over pain, the pain being conceived as balanced against an equal amount of pleasure so that the two amounts annihilate each other for the purposes of ethical calculation.   (p. 413)

Mill offers the following definition in *Utilitarianism* (p. 7): "The creed which accepts as the foundation of morals 'utility' or the 'greatest happiness principle' holds that actions are right in proportion as they tend to promote happiness; wrong as they tend to promote the reverse of happiness. By happiness is intended pleasure and the absence of pain; by unhappiness, pain and the privation of pleasure."

Sidgwick and Mill define utilitarianism as a hedonistic consequentialist theory of right and wrong. Consequentialism or act-consequentialism is the view that (1) an act is morally right provided that it results in the best consequences (overall) of all the possible alternative courses of action open to the agent, and (2) an act is morally wrong if it fails to result in the best consequences of all the possible alternative courses of action open to the agent. According to the hedonistic theory of value, pleasure (and pleasure alone) is intrinsically good, and pain (and pain alone) is intrinsically bad.

The classical utilitarian philosophers, Bentham, Mill, and Sidgwick, were hedonists. However, contemporary philosophers tend to use the term "utilitarianism" in a broader sense to mean roughly "consequentialism." Richard Brandt (1997) defends a broader definition of AU in the following: "the thesis that a particular act is right, if and only if, no other act the agent could perform at the time would have, or probably would have on the agent's evidence better consequences" (p. 373).[1] In this broader sense, AU is the view that one should always do what will have the best possible results, or more precisely: "An act is morally right if and only if there is no other possible alternative act open to the agent that would result in a better balance of good consequences relative to bad consequences."

Many contemporary philosophers who describe themselves as utilitarians reject hedonism and endorse the "desire-satisfaction" theory of value. The desire-satisfaction theory holds the following: (1) the welfare of human beings (and other sentient creatures?) is the only thing that is intrinsically good, and (2) a person's welfare (what is good or bad *for* a person) is determined solely by the satisfaction or non-satisfaction of her/his desires (or by the satisfaction or non-satisfaction of her/his *rational* desires or *the desires s/he would have if s/he were fully informed and fully rational*). According to desire-satisfaction versions of utilitarianism, we should act so as to maximize the satisfaction of people's desires (or the desires they would have were they rational and informed). There are also "objectivist" theories of value. According to these theories, some things such as knowledge, beauty, love, and/or moral virtue, are intrinsically good independently of whether they give anyone pleasure and independently of whether anyone desires them or would desire them under ideal conditions. Moore, Rashdall, Brentano, and Hurka all defend consequentialist theories of right and wrong and objectivist theories of value (see Rashdall, 1928; Brentano, 1969, 1973; Hurka, 1993).

Act and Rule Utilitarianism/Consequentialism

With the possible exception of Mill, the classical utilitarians endorse "AU" — they hold that the rightness or wrongness of a particular action is determined solely by the consequences of *that particular act*. Rule-utilitarianism or rule-consequentialism (RC) holds that an act is right provided that it is in accordance with the rule or set of rules the general acceptance of which would have the best consequences. According to RC, we should not judge the rightness or wrongness of individual actions directly by their consequences. Rather, we should judge the rightness or wrongness of actions by reference to moral codes, which in turn are justified by the consequences of their general acceptance. According to RC, the rightness or wrongness of actions is determined by the moral code, the general acceptance of which would produce better consequences than the general acceptance of any other moral code. For reasons that will be clear in Chapter 5, I discuss RC in connection with Ross's theory. I read Mill as an act-utilitarian, but, for my purposes in this chapter, nothing hangs on this, and I will not address the scholarly debate about whether Mill is an act-utilitarian or rule-utilitarian/consequentialist. Mill's arguments about lying in chapter 2 of *Utilitarianism* can be plausibly understood to be consistent with AU (see 4.III).[2]

4.II. GUIDE TO ACTION VERSUS CRITERION OF RIGHT AND WRONG

Act-utilitarians defend their theory as the *ultimate criterion* of right and wrong. According to AU, what *makes* an action right is that it results in the best consequences. AU does not imply that all moral agents should always use AU to decide what they ought to do.[3] Often people need to make very quick decisions and do not have the time to directly apply the principle of utility which requires estimating all the good and bad consequences of all the different courses of action open to one. Mill notes this problem in chapter 2 of *Utilitarianism* (p. 23): "defenders of utility often find themselves called upon to reply to such objections as this—that there is not time, previous to action, for calculating and weighing the effects of any line of conduct on the general happiness." Mill concedes that moral agents often lack the time to do direct utilitarian calculations. However, he says that, even when we have very little time, we can have knowledge of the probable consequences of our actions. Mill writes:

The answer to the objection is there has been ample time, namely, the whole past duration of the human species. During all that time mankind have been learning by experience the tendencies of actions; on which experience all the prudence as well as all the morality of life are dependent. People talk as if the commencement of this course of experience had been put off . . . and as if . . . he had to begin considering for the first time whether murder and theft are injurious to human happiness . . . mankind must by this time have acquired positive beliefs as to the effect of some actions on their happiness; and the beliefs which have thus come down are the rules of morality for the multitude, and thus for the philosopher until he has succeeded in finding better.

Utilitarianism (pp. 23–24)

Humanity's knowledge of the tendencies of certain kinds of actions is embodied in (conventional) "secondary" or "subordinate" moral principles. When there is no time for calculation, we can act on secondary moral principles. Mill gives the example of the very simple rule prohibiting lying as a secondary moral principle (*Utilitarianism*, pp. 22–25). He endorses this rule as a secondary moral principle. He recommends that people make it a policy to follow this rule. According to Mill, it is necessary to appeal to secondary moral principles when we do not have time to directly apply the principle of utility. He also says that such principles help us to guard against rationalizing immoral conduct; we should violate them only with great reluctance and compunction.[4]

Hare's version of AU is similar to Mill's in that he rejects the idea that people should always try to directly apply and follow the principle of utility. Like Mill, Hare recognizes the need for secondary moral principles (what he calls "intuitive moral principles") because of the limitations of human knowledge and the propensity of people to rationalize wrong conduct when it benefits them personally. According to Hare, we all need to engage in "intuitive moral thinking." A person operating at the intuitive level applies fairly simple principles and attitudes. Intuitive moral thinking is needed for everyday ethical choices and judgments in which it is inappropriate or impossible to take the time and effort for protracted reflection on the issue at hand. Intuitive moral thinking also helps to free us from the "constant temptation to special pleading" (*Moral Thinking*, p. 38).

For example, it is only too easy to persuade ourselves that the act of telling a lie in order to get ourselves out of a hole does a great deal of good to ourselves at relatively small cost to anybody else; whereas in fact, if we view the situation impartially, the indirect costs are much greater than the total gains. It is partly to avoid such cooking that we have intuitions or dispositions firmly built into our characters and motivations.

> *Moral Thinking* (p. 38; cf. Smart and Williams, 1973, p. 43)

According to Hare, intuitive moral principles should not be regarded as mere "rules of thumb;" they are not just time-saving devices whose breach should excite "no compunction" (*Moral Thinking*, p. 38). There are good utilitarian reasons for bringing up children to feel guilty for violating intuitive moral principles, even when violating those principles produces the best consequences and is justified on act-utilitarian grounds (*Moral Thinking*, p. 49). In addition, there is a third reason why we need secondary moral principles, a reason that Mill and Hare do not mention. Many decisions are not important enough to warrant lengthy deliberation, even if one has time for it. It is a waste of time to reflect carefully on the morality of lying every time one is tempted to lie.

Even the best secondary moral principles are fallible and admit of exceptions—following them does not guarantee that one acts rightly. Further, as Mill and Hare both note, secondary moral principles can conflict. However, good or plausible secondary moral principles are such that by following them we do what is right much more often than not.

All of us frequently face moral questions about lying and deception. Because of this, and because of time constraints and our frequent temptation to rationalize lying and deception (even when they have bad consequences on balance), AU implies that we should accept and internalize secondary moral principles about lying and deception. According to AU, secondary moral principles should be such that their adoption maximizes utility. What are the ideal secondary moral principles governing lying and deception? We need to distinguish the following questions:

1. What are the secondary moral principles concerning lying and deception, the general acceptance and internalization of which (as secondary moral principles) by *humanity as a whole*, would produce the best consequences?
2. What are the secondary moral principles concerning lying and deception, the general acceptance and internalization of which by *members of my society*, would produce the best consequences?
3. What are the secondary moral principles concerning lying and deception, the general acceptance and internalization of which by *the members of my profession*, would produce the best consequences?
4. What are the secondary moral principles concerning lying and deception, the acceptance and internalization of which by *me*, would produce the best consequences?

These are different questions for which it is likely that there are different answers.

Rule-utilitarians/rule-consequentialists, such as Hooker and Brandt, address these questions, albeit for different purposes than act-utilitarians. Hooker asks a question very similar to question 1. He asks "which moral code is such that its acceptance by the overwhelming majority of everyone everywhere would produce better consequences than the general acceptance of any other moral code?" He thinks that the optimal moral code for everyone would include Rossian *prima facie* moral prohibitions (see 5.VI.1). [Note that act-utilitarians and Hooker assign a very different status to this code. According to Hooker, this code is the ultimate basis for determining the rightness or wrongness of actions, whereas act-utilitarians would say that this code is a (good) secondary moral principle.] Brandt asks a question very similar to question 2. He asks "which moral code is such that its general acceptance by most of the members of our society would produce the best consequences?" Brandt claims that the optimal moral code for our society would include Rossian *prima facie* moral principles (see Chapter 5 endnote 11).

Regarding question 3, I conjecture that the codes of ethics for many professions should include a nearly absolute prohibition against lying to and deceiving rational adult clients (for whom paternalistic lying/deception is inappropriate). Such rules are likely to prohibit justifiable lying and deception in certain cases, but less

stringent prohibitions are likely to result in self-serving rationalizations for lying
and deception on the part of professionals. In constructing codes of ethics for
professions, we should not try to make allowances for every conceivable case in
which lying and deception would be justified. More salient is the worry that
such rules invite abuse and self-serving rationalizations of impermissible lying
and deception.[5]

4.III. THE IMPLICATIONS OF ACT-UTILITARIANISM FOR ISSUES OF LYING AND DECEPTION

Let us move on from talking about the secondary moral principles concerning
lying and deception that a utilitarian would endorse to talking about how to
directly apply AU to questions about lying and deception. According to AU,
lying and deception are morally right when (and only when) they have better
consequences than not lying. When assessing the rightness or wrongness of an
action, act-utilitarians would ask whether there was a better alternative course
of action that the agent could have performed instead. If there was a better
alternative, then the act was wrong; if there was not a better alternative, then the
act was right; if the act had better consequences than any possible alternative,
then the act was obligatory. In principle, AU implies that any act can be
morally right (or obligatory) if it results in the best consequences. According to
AU, any means can be justified if it is necessary in order to bring about the
best consequences. Some people regard this implication of AU as unacceptable.
They claim that some acts are wrong no matter what the consequences. For
example, some critics of utilitarianism claim that killing "innocent" human
beings is always wrong no matter what. Others claim that knowingly punishing
an innocent person is always wrong, regardless of the consequences.[6] These issues
are beyond the scope of the present book. For our purposes, it is important
for us to assess the following two claims: "It is always morally wrong to
deceive another person, no matter what," and "It is always morally wrong
to tell a lie, no matter what." Each of these statements is inconsistent with
AU. AU clearly implies that lying and deception are sometimes permissible.
There are cases in which lying that involves deception has better consequences
than not lying. If lying so as to deceive someone else is necessary in order
to save the life of an innocent person, then presumably it has much better
consequences than not lying. Consider again the example of Zofia Kukla who
saved the lives of several Jewish families hiding in her barn by lying to the Nazis
(Chapter 3.V).

Lying and deception *can* be justified if they are necessary in order to save lives or
avert a catastrophe (for a defense of this see Chapters 3.V and 7.II). Hardly anyone
finds this consequence of utilitarianism objectionable. However, utilitarianism
also implies that lying and deception can be justified if they produce *slightly better*

consequences than not lying and deceiving others; lying and deception can be justified if they produce small or even trivial net benefits. The objection is not that utilitarianism *sometimes* permits lying and deception, but that it permits lying, deception, and other violations of common sense moral prohibitions *much too often*. To put this another way, the objection is that utilitarianism is too permissive about the morality of lying and deception.

In chapter 2 of *Utilitarianism*, Mill attempts to answer this objection. He considers the objection that utilitarianism is a doctrine of "expediency" as opposed to "principle." In this discussion, he makes particular reference to lying, "Thus, it would often be expedient, for the purpose of getting over some momentary embarrassment, or attaining some object immediately useful to ourselves and others, to tell a lie" (p. 22). Mill begins his reply by saying that usually, when we talk about lying for reasons of expediency, we mean lying for the sake of "that which is expedient for the particular interest of the agent himself" (p. 22). He gives the example of a government official who lies and does something harmful to his country in order to save his own position. In this case, lying benefits the liar but does not have the best consequences overall. Utilitarians, therefore, are not committed to the view that what the official does is right.

Mill continues by posing what he takes to be a more serious objection: "When it means anything better than this, it means that which is expedient for some immediate object, some temporary purpose, but which violates a rule whose observance is expedient in a much higher degree" (p. 22). Mill is talking about cases in which lying has temporary benefits. He does not give an example of such a case, but here is one. A father is tempted to lie to his children so that they will not cause a fuss. The children ask if they can have candy to eat. The father does not think that they should eat any candy at this time. However, he knows that if he tells his children that they are not permitted to eat any candy they will complain and give him trouble. He lies and says that there is no candy in the house. Mill claims that the short-run benefits of lying in such cases are outweighed by the bad consequences caused by violating the very beneficial (expedient) rule against lying.

Mill then continues with the following long tortuous sentence:

But inasmuch as the cultivation in ourselves of a sensitive feeling on the subject of veracity is one of the most useful, and the enfeeblement of that feeling one of the most hurtful, things to which our conduct can be instrumental; and inasmuch as any, even unintentional, deviation from truth does that much toward weakening the trustworthiness of human assertion, which is not only the principal support of all present social well-being, but the insufficiency of which does more than any one thing that can be named to keep back civilization, virtue, everything on which human happiness on the largest scale depends—we feel that the violation, for present advantage, of a rule of such transcendent expediency is not expedient, and that he who, for the sake of convenience to himself or to some other individual, does what depends on him to deprive mankind of the good, and inflict upon them an evil, involved in the greater or less reliance which they can place in each other's word, acts the part of one of their worst enemies.

Utilitarianism (pp. 22–23)

In this passage Mill notes that lying has short-term benefits in many cases, but he says that he is *not* committed to the view that we should always do what will have the best consequences in the short run. Other things equal, consequences in the distant future are no less important than immediate consequences. When Mill talks about doing something that is expedient in certain respects in the short run, but that also "violates a rule whose observance is expedient in a much higher degree," he is claiming that the indirect long-term bad consequences of lying in such cases (the bad consequences of violating the very useful rule against lying) outweigh the short-term benefits of lying. According to Mill, any lie (or almost any lie) one tells has two indirect bad consequences: (1) it weakens one's honesty or veracity (it enfeebles one's "sensitive feeling on the subject of veracity"), and (2) it diminishes the trust and reliance that we can have in each other's assertions.

In his discussion of lying on pp. 22–23 of *Utilitarianism* Mill appeals to the indirect *bad consequences of particular acts of lying*. He also claims that lying is wrong because it tends to destroy trust ("confidence") between people (see his essay "Bentham," 1969, p. 112). Whether or not Mill is a rule-utilitarian/consequentialist, and whether or not he says things that commit him to RC, his argument about lying *in this passage* is one act-utilitarians can consistently make. I want to stress again that I am not attempting to answer the scholarly question of whether Mill is an act-utilitarian or rule-utilitarian/rule-consequentialist.

Mill's argument is that lying always (or almost always) has bad indirect consequences that outweigh the (relatively trivial) good consequences of lying in cases in which people lie for reasons of expediency. This argument works in the example of the father who is tempted to lie to his children. In this case lying will cause considerable harm if he is caught in his lie and his children come to distrust him. Children need to be able to trust their parents. Parents who frequently resort to lying in cases of this sort are certain to be discovered by their children who are likely to carry away the very harmful lesson that lying can be justified for the sake of fairly trivial benefits to oneself. (See Sissela Bok's (1979) *Lying* for a very detailed account of the indirect bad consequences of lying.) Many of the examples in Chapters 8–13 testify to the indirect bad consequences of lying.

Mill continues by saying that the "sacred rule" against lying admits of exceptions:

Yet that even this rule, sacred as it is admits of possible exceptions is acknowledged by all moralists; the chief of which is when the withholding of some fact (as of information from a malefactor, or of bad news from a person dangerously ill) would save an individual (especially an individual other than oneself[7]) from great and unmerited evil, and when the withholding can only be effected by denial [i.e. a lie].

Utilitarianism (p. 23)

To make this more concrete, recall an example used earlier. Suppose that a man has just had open heart surgery and is temporarily in a precarious state of health. His surgeon says that he must be shielded from any emotional distress for the next few days. Unbeknownst to the patient, his only child, Bob, has been killed in an automobile accident. When the patient awakens after the surgery, he is surprised that Bob is not there, and he asks, "Where is Bob?" The surgeon fears that, in his condition, the shock of learning about Bob's death might cause the patient to die. So she lies and says that his son has been delayed.

Mill concludes his discussion of lying by saying that "if the principle of utility is good for anything" it should be able to define when there are and are not legitimate exceptions to the rule against lying and "weigh these conflicting utilities against one another." He says that our way of distinguishing between legitimate and illegitimate exceptions to the rule against lying should "have the least possible effect in weakening reliance on veracity" (*Utilitarianism*, p. 23). However, to the best of my knowledge, there is no place in his writings in which Mill, himself, attempts to do this by giving a general account of when there are and are not legitimate exceptions to the rule against lying.

Mill's arguments about the indirect bad consequences of lying are largely, but not entirely, successful. Inasmuch as not being disposed to tell lies is a good or desirable character trait (I defend this assumption with qualifications in Chapter 14), and becoming less honest or more inclined to lie is a bad thing. It is much less clear that every lie diminishes trust. Often people lie successfully without arousing the distrust of others. However, any lie still runs the *risk* of being found out and diminishing trust between people. This last point needs to be tempered. If someone is a dishonest person, it is not a good thing that others trust her. Distrust is not always a bad thing. However, it *is* desirable that others can reasonably trust and rely on what one says.

Mill's arguments about the indirect bad consequences of lying can be considerably strengthened by noting several prudential considerations that weigh strongly against lying. Almost all of us have prudential reasons to want to be regarded as honest people. To be regarded as a dishonest and untrustworthy person is very disadvantageous for one. This means that when one lies, one almost always needs to avoid being found out. Our lies are often found out despite our best efforts to conceal them. People frequently underestimate the likelihood of being caught in telling lies. Often, lies are discovered long after they are told. More often than not, hiding or concealing a lie requires that one remember the lie and remember to whom one told it and to whom one did not tell it. One also needs to consider whether the people one lies to are likely to repeat what they have been told. Many of us have had the unpleasant experience of having told two people different things and then having them compare notes. All of this greatly complicates one's life. Here, it is apt to remember Lincoln's quip: "No man has a good enough memory to be a liar." Roy Sorensen makes this point well: "The proverb 'Lies have no legs' alludes to their lack of support from reality. Lies tend to collapse without the assistance of secondary lies. These secondary lies are also legless and so often must be propped up with another round of lies. Lying is mentally taxing because you cannot depend on reality to be your memory bank" (Sorensen, 2007, p. 253).

Even when we can succeed in hiding our lies, telling lies greatly complicates our lives—the price of maintaining deception and the pretense of not having lied can be great. We need to be on guard and not let our dishonesty slip out. Sometimes we need to suppress our spontaneous emotional reactions to events in order for us to maintain the pretense of not having lied. According to AU, these prudential considerations are morally relevant and weigh against lying. The good and bad consequences of lying include the serious problems that lying often creates for the liar.[8]

Because lying is often imprudent as well as morally wrong, it frequently involves weakness of will. People often lie against their better moral and prudential judgment because it is easier in the short run and avoids immediate unpleasant consequences for the liar. I ask the reader to reflect on her own experience.

Direct Bad Consequences of Lying and Deception

We are generally harmed when we are deceived because we cannot effectively pursue our ends and interests if we act on the basis of false beliefs. Of course, someone could be deceived about matters that are not relevant to any of her concerns or decisions. I am not harmed if someone deceives me about the economic situation of Ethiopia in the seventeenth century. However, ordinarily, when we lie or attempt to deceive others, we do so in order to influence their attitudes or behavior. Thus, generally, when we deceive others, we deceive them about matters of interest and concern to *them* and we try to influence them to do things (or have attitudes) that they would not do (or have) if they were not deceived, and ordinarily we *harm* them. This simple point is developed in greater detail in Chapter 7 and illustrated over and over again in many of the examples in Chapters 8–13.

CONCLUSIONS AND TRANSITION TO CHAPTER 5

AU supports the view that there is a strong moral presumption against lying and deception. It also seems more reasonable than Kant's absolutism, to the extent that it permits people to lie to save someone's life. However, even if we grant all of Mill's arguments and the additional arguments I have proposed in this chapter, there remains a serious objection to the act-utilitarian view about the morality of lying. AU views lying as morally neutral or indifferent, *other things equal* (apart from its consequences). Speaking with reference to moral rules such as the rule against killing, Frankena (1973) writes: "Even though I think that no such rules are absolute . . . I do still believe . . . that some kinds of actions are intrinsically wrong, for example, killing people and lying to them" (p. 55). Ross gives the classic statement of this argument. Ross's theory is an important alternative to both AU and Kant's absolutism; it is arguably closer to our common sense moral beliefs than either AU or Kant's absolutism.

ENDNOTES

1. Smart and Williams (1973) define utilitarianism somewhat more broadly than Mill, and Sidgwick (1966), and more narrowly than Brandt. They define utilitarianism as the view that the rightness or wrongness of an action is determined solely by its effect on the happiness or welfare of human beings and/or sentient beings. They leave open the question of whether happiness/welfare should be defined hedonistically (see Smart and Williams, 1973, pp. 4, 79).
2. For good discussions of the question whether Mill is a rule-utilitarian/rule-consequentialist, see Brandt (1992, pp. 128–130), Lyons (1994, pp. 47–65), and West (2004, chapter 4). The main textual evidence given for thinking that Mill is rule-utilitarian is found in chapter 5 of *Utilitarianism* and Mill's definition of utilitarianism at the beginning of chapter 2.
3. Cf. Sidgwick (1966):

   [A] utilitarian may reasonably desire, on Utilitarian principles, that some of his conclusions should be rejected by mankind generally; or even that the vulgar should be kept aloof from his system as a whole, in so far as the inevitable indefiniteness and complexity of its calculations render it likely to lead to bad consequences in their hands (p. 490).

4. Mill describes the prohibition against lying as a "sacred rule." Mill writes: "that even this rule, sacred as it is, admits of possible exceptions . . . " (*Utilitarianism*, p. 23).
5. Again, this is a conjecture that I will not attempt to defend here. I defend a narrower version of this claim (the claim that codes of ethics for business executives should include an absolute or nearly absolute prohibition against lying and deception) in my paper "Side Constraints and the Levels of Moral Discourse: A Modified Shareholder Theory," presented at the American Philosophical Association, Central Division Meeting, February 2009.
6. Elizabeth Anscombe claims that deliberately executing an innocent person through a dishonest legal proceeding is wrong no matter what the

consequences. She writes: "But if someone really thinks, *in advance*, that it is open to question whether such an action as procuring the judicial execution of the innocent should be quite excluded from consideration—I do not want to argue with him, he shows a corrupt mind" (Anscombe, 1997, pp. 257–258).

7. Comment: it is not consistent for a utilitarian to place so much emphasis on the distinction between what benefits others and what benefits oneself.

8. We can make analogous prudential arguments against deception. Like lying, deception is likely to be discovered and resented by others. Often deception can be effected in subtle indirect ways so that the deceiver can plausibly deny any intention to mislead others (and often deny any intent to influence others' beliefs). By contrast, telling a lie involves making a false statement. While it is often possible for liars to plausibly deny that they knew or believed that their statements were false, they cannot deny having made false statements that they invited others to rely on. In this respect, it seems that often the prudential considerations that weigh against deception are not as strong as those that weigh against lying. Another reason why prudential arguments against deception are often weaker than those against lying is that many people do not seem to resent deception as much as lying. Frankfurt thinks that people are more tolerant of bullshit (which according to him requires the intention to deceive others) than lying. He makes much of the following passage in Eric Ambler's novel, *Dirty Story*: "Although I was only seven when my father was killed, I still remember him very well and some of the things he used to say . . . One of the first things he taught me was, '*Never tell a lie when you can bullshit your way though*' " (Frankfurt, 2005, p. 48).

The father's advice is based on the assumption that people are more tolerant of bullshit than lying (Frankfurt, 2005, p. 50). Frankfurt endorses this assumption, though it is doubtful that he agrees that we *should be* more tolerant of bullshit than we are of lying (his claim that bullshitters are worse enemies of the truth than liars suggests that he does not agree)—see Chapter 2.V.2.

5

Ross and Rule-Consequentialism

INTRODUCTION

Ross's theory is an important alternative to act-utilitarianism (AU) and Kant's absolutism. Many philosophers think that it constitutes a reasonable middle ground in ethics between these other two theories. Ross gives the classic statement of the objection that utilitarianism is too permissive about the morality of lying.

I explain Ross's theory and his argument that utilitarianism is too permissive about lying. Ross claims that it is "self-evident" that there is a *prima facie* duty not to lie (even when lying does not harm anyone) and likens our knowledge of this and other basic moral principles to our knowledge of the axioms and postulates of mathematics. He also claims that his theory squares much better with "the moral convictions of thoughtful and well-educated people" than AU.

However, Ross's criticisms of utilitarianism and his defense of his own theory are unsuccessful because he fails to deal adequately with objections arising from the pervasive phenomenon of moral disagreement. Many thoughtful and well-educated people do not find his principles self-evident. Indeed, some utilitarians claim that it is self-evident that we should always do whatever will have the best consequences. Our knowledge of morality and basic moral principles is not comparable to our knowledge of the postulates and axioms of mathematics. Ross's appeal to the "data" constituted by the moral convictions of thoughtful and well-educated people also fails because of the existence of very extensive moral disagreement. Thoughtful and well-educated people do not all side with Ross on the moral questions concerning which Ross and utilitarians disagree.

The last section of this chapter examines Brad Hooker's well-known version of rule-utilitarianism or (as he prefers) "rule-consequentialism" (hereafter RC). Roughly, RC holds that an act is morally right provided that it is consistent with the moral code, the general acceptance of which would produce the best consequences. Hooker claims that the ideal moral code that determines the rightness and wrongness of our actions includes rules about lying and deception very similar to Ross's *prima facie* duties. Hooker appeals to the method of reflective equilibrium. He claims that his theory matches better with "*our* considered moral judgments" than AU. The success of Hooker's arguments against AU depends entirely on the reliability of the considered moral judgments to which he appeals. (He has no argument against AU other than its inconsistency with these judgments.) However, some ostensibly reasonable people disagree with the considered moral judgments to which he appeals, and he does not do enough to show that his considered moral judgments are correct/reliable and that the judgments of those who disagree with him are incorrect/unreliable. In the absence of some convincing defense of the reliability of these judgments, Hooker's arguments are unsuccessful.

5.I. ROSS'S THEORY

5.I.1. The Concept of a *Prima Facie* Duty

Ross's theory of right and wrong is based on his concept of a "*prima facie* duty" or "*prima facie* obligation." He (1930) defines this notion in the following passages:

I suggest "*prima facie* duty" or "conditional duty" as a brief way of referring to the characteristic (quite distinct from that of being a duty proper) which an act has, in virtue of being of a certain kind (e.g., the keeping of a promise), of being an act which would be a duty proper if it were not at the same time of another kind which is morally significant. (pp. 19–20, also see p. 28)

Ross defines "*prima facie* duty" in terms of the concept of one's actual duty or "duty proper." One's *actual duty* is what one ought to do, all things considered. A *prima facie* duty is one's actual duty, other things being equal.[1] We could also put this by saying that a *prima facie* duty is an actual moral duty in the absence of countervailing reasons/considerations (cf. Ewing, 1959, p. 110, and Kagan, 1998, pp. 180–181). Ross (1930) uses the term "*prima facie* duty" interchangeably with the term "conditional duty" (p. 19). A *prima facie* duty is one's actual duty on the condition that it does not conflict with another *prima facie* duty of equal or greater importance.

Ross says that there is a *prima facie* duty not to lie. He allows that lying is sometimes morally permissible, even obligatory. Lying is morally permissible when, and only when, the duty not to lie conflicts with a more important or equally important *prima facie* duty. More precisely, lying is morally permissible (morally right) when, and only when, the duty not to lie conflicts with another duty, X, such that X, taken together with other duties that are fulfilled by doing X, is as important as (or more important than) the duty not to lie together with any other duties that are fulfilled by not lying. Lying is morally obligatory when, and only when, the duty not to lie conflicts with another *prima facie* duty, X, such that the duty to do X, together with the other duties fulfilled by doing X, are more important than the duty not to lie together with the other *prima facie* duties that are fulfilled by not lying. In order to determine whether an action is morally right or morally permissible (all things considered), we need to consider all of the respects in which it is *prima facie* right and *prima facie* wrong. In order to be morally right, an act must be such that: "of all acts possible for the agent in the circumstances, it is that whose *prima facie* rightness in the respects which it is *prima facie* right most outweighs" its *prima facie* wrongness in any respects in which it is *prima facie* wrong" (Ross, 1930, p. 46).

5.1.2. Ross's List of *Prima Facie* Duties

Ross proposes a list of eight *prima facie* duties on pp. 20–21 of *The Right and the Good*. He (1930) does not claim "completeness or finality" for his list (pp. 20, 23). Ross's list is as follows:

1. *The duty to keep promises.* The act of making a promise creates duties that would otherwise not exist. Ross writes "To make a promise is to put oneself in a relation to one person in particular, a relation which creates a specifically new *prima facie* obligation to him . . ." (p. 38)
2. *The duty not to lie.* According to Ross, the duty not to lie is a special case of the duty to keep promises. He claims that one makes an implicit promise not to lie whenever one uses language to communicate with another person (p. 21). According to Ross, there is a duty to refrain from lying but no duty to tell the truth or reveal information. Being silent and refusing to answer questions are not violations of the duty not to lie. Ross does not define lying, but his discussion of lying has affinities with the definition I defended in Chapter 1 (see Chapter 1.1.7).
3. *The duty to make reparations to people one has harmed.*
4. *Duties of gratitude.* If someone has done something that helped you, then you have a special obligation to help him.
5. *The duty to distribute happiness according to merit.* Whenever the actual distribution of happiness in the world is not according to merit (moral goodness), "there arises a duty to upset or prevent such a distribution" (p. 21). If good people are unhappy and bad people are happy, then the distribution of happiness is not according to merit and we have a *prima facie* duty to upset this distribution.
6. *The duty to do things that benefit others.* According to Ross, there are three ways in which one can help another person: one can give her pleasure, give her knowledge, or improve her moral character.
7. *The duty to improve one's own intellect and moral character.*
8. *The duty not to harm others.*

Ross does not say that there is a *prima facie* duty not to deceive others. Note the asymmetry between items 6 and 7. Ross thinks that we have a *prima facie* duty to give other people pleasure but no duty to give ourselves pleasure (Ross, 1930, pp. 24–25).

5.1.3. Applying Ross's Theory to Cases

All of our voluntary actions involve choices between alternative courses of action. Whenever one chooses between different (incompatible) courses of action, one of the following must be the case:

1. None of the alternative courses of actions is a *prima facie* duty in any respect.
2. One and only one of the alternative courses of actions is a *prima facie* duty in some respect.
3. More than one of the alternative courses of actions is a *prima facie* duty in some respect.

Most of our everyday choices are of the first sort. One chooses between options, none of which are *prima facie* duties. For example, when I choose between wearing my blue socks, my brown socks, or my black socks, none of my options either fulfills or violates a *prima facie* duty. In such cases, any choice one makes is morally permissible, and one is free to do whatever one wants. According to Ross, in cases of type 2, cases in which I have a *prima facie* duty to do X and I have no conflicting duty (no duty that requires me to not do X), then I clearly ought to do X (doing X is clearly my actual duty).

Most, if not all, controversial moral questions involve what Ross calls conflicts of duties. In order to apply Ross's theory to cases involving conflicts of duty we need to determine when one *prima facie* duty is more important than another one. Ross (1930) says that the duty not to harm others is more stringent than the duty to help others (p. 21). Ross also says that the "duties of 'perfect obligation'" (promise keeping, gratitude, and reparations) are very stringent—quoting Aristotle, he says, "For the rest, the decision rests with perception" (pp. 41–42). Ross does not claim that perfect duties are always more important than other conflicting duties; he explicitly denies this in a passage in which he says that it would be permissible to break a trivial promise in order to help the victims of an accident.[2] Ross does not provide any general guidelines for determining what one ought to do in cases of conflicts of duty. According to him, each case must be judged on its own merits. Any attempt to formulate general rules or guidelines for resolving conflicts of duties would oversimplify things. Judgments to the effect that one duty is more (or less) important than another (in a concrete case) are a matter of perception, they involve "moral risk" and are neither certain nor self-evident (Ross, 1930, p. 30). Another reason why Ross thinks that moral judgments about the rightness or wrongness of particular actions are very fallible is that any act may have indirect good and bad consequences in the future that we cannot know about. Any act that I perform might harm or benefit other people in ways that I cannot know about at the time I act (Ross, 1930, p. 31).

5.I.4. How Strong is the Moral Presumption against Lying?

Ross says that telling lies is *prima facie* wrong. This means that there is a moral presumption against telling a lie. How strong is this presumption? Ross says that duties of fidelity (which include the duty not to lie or break promises) are "stringent" (see Ross, 1930, pp. 41–42). He clearly thinks that it is wrong to tell a lie in order to bring about a very small amount of good or prevent a very small amount of bad. For example, I would not be justified in telling a lie to spare you momentary distress or embarrassment. On the other hand, Ross is not an absolutist. He thinks that lying can be justified if it is necessary to produce a great good or avoid a great evil. Ross never gives a clear explanation of the *threshold* of benefit provided or harm avoided that is necessary in order to justify telling a lie. Perhaps Ross would reject the idea that there is a single threshold that applies to all cases of lying; perhaps he would say that this threshold varies according to the gravity of the lie (how "big" or "small" the lie is) (cf. Hooker, 2000, pp. 131–132). On this reading, Ross holds that the duty not to lie and the duty to keep promises admit of different degrees of stringency.

5.II. ROSS'S CRITICISMS OF ACT-UTILITARIANISM

5.II.1. Ross and Utilitarianism on Promise Keeping

Utilitarians hold that, *other things being equal*, it is a matter of indifference whether one breaks a promise or keeps it. If breaking a promise will have exactly the same consequences as keeping it, then it does not matter whether one breaks it or keeps it. Ross (1930) says that, other things being equal, it is a duty to keep promises, "If, so far as I can see, I could bring equal amounts of good into being by fulfilling my promise and by helping someone to whom I had made no promise, I should not hesitate to regard the former as my duty" (p. 18). Ross also argues that utilitarianism mistakenly implies that breaking a promise is morally right whenever breaking a promise produces slightly better consequences than keeping it. He asks us to consider a case in which by keeping a promise I will bring about 1000 units of good and by breaking the promise I will bring about 1001 units of good (I assume that he means "net" units of good) (pp. 34–35, 38–39). Utilitarians are committed to the view that I ought to break my promise in cases in which breaking the promise would result in slightly better consequences than keeping it. Ross thinks it *obvious* that I should not break my promise in such a case.

Ross does not explain what the units in question are supposed to represent, but I take it that he wants this example to describe a case in which lying has *slightly better* consequences than not lying. I do not think that we can measure/quantify goodness and badness in the very precise way that Ross suggests. However, for Ross's purposes it would be enough to talk about cases in which lying has slightly better consequences than not lying. Further, one cannot defend utilitarianism against Ross's objections by raising questions about the quantifiability of goodness and badness, since utilitarians are committed to the view that goodness and badness are fairly precisely quantifiable.

5.II.2. Ross's Arguments about Promise-Keeping Modified to Apply to Cases of Lying

Ross's first argument about promise-keeping can be easily modified to apply to the issue of lying. (This is clearly in the spirit of Ross's view, as he holds that all lies are cases of promise-breaking.[3]) The argument would go roughly as follows:

Sometimes lying will result in *exactly* the same consequences (or *exactly* the same amount of good and bad) as not lying. In such cases, utilitarians must say that it doesn't matter whether one lies or tells the truth. But surely this is unacceptable. *Other things being equal*, it is wrong to tell a lie. There is a presumption against lying.

On the face of it, this is a very strong argument. However, it is very difficult to find an example of a case in which lying and not lying will have *exactly* the same consequences. The best examples I can think of involve lying to a total stranger one will probably never see again about a very trivial or insignificant matter that the other person is completely uninterested in. Suppose that I lie about my age to a stranger on a train—I tell her that I am 45 years old, when, in fact, I am 48 years old. It is hard to see how being misinformed about my age could possibly harm her or anyone else. Since I will never see her again, and since she is almost certain to forget what I say to her, my lying will not undermine trust between us. However, my lying to the stranger is likely to harm *my* character by making me less honest. (Utilitarians can say that it is bad to be prone to telling lies, because lying usually has worse consequences than not lying (cf. Mill, *Utilitarianism*, pp. 22–23; see Chapter 14.II for a qualification).) Given this, utilitarians can claim that, because lying almost always harms one's character, there is almost always a moral presumption against lying. If successful, this line of argument would allow utilitarians to explain the apparent moral presumption against lying while maintaining that the rightness or wrongness of an action is determined solely by its consequences.

Ross can avoid these complications by considering the following kind of case. Suppose that the quantity of good that lying produces is equal to the quantity of bad that it causes by harming the liar's character. Suppose also that there are no other good or bad consequences that result from lying or not lying and that no other *prima facie* duties are involved. In this case, lying and not lying produce the same net amount of good (bad).[4] To make this more concrete, suppose that someone asks you how you like a house that she helped design. She asks you the question in such a way that you cannot evade it without being very rude. You do not like the house at all, but you lie to spare her feelings. In this case, the slight harm to your character from lying might be exactly counterbalanced by the slight benefit she receives if you spare her feelings. Ross would claim that it is clearly wrong to lie in such cases. If we imagine that a slightly greater bad is avoided by telling the lie, we have a case in which lying has slightly better consequences than not lying. Ross would say that it is clearly wrong to lie in such cases.

5.III. ROSS ON THE BASIS OF OUR KNOWLEDGE OF FUNDAMENTAL MORAL PRINCIPLES

5.III.1. Self-Evidence

Ross claims that his *prima facie* principles are "self-evident." Ross (1930) says that it is self-evident that there is a *prima facie* duty not to lie and a *prima facie* duty to keep promises.

That an act, *qua* fulfilling a promise, or *qua* effecting a just distribution of good . . . is *prima facie* right, is self-evident; not in the sense that it is evident from the beginning of our lives, or as soon as we attend to the proposition for the first time, but in the sense that when we have reached sufficient mental maturity and have given sufficient attention to the proposition it is evident without any need of proof, or evidence beyond itself. It is self-evident just as a mathematical axiom or the validity of an inference, is self-evident. The moral order expressed in these propositions is just as much part of the fundamental nature of the universe (and, we may add, of any possible universe in which there were moral agents at all) as is the spatial or numerical structure expressed in the axioms of geometry or arithmetic. In our confidence that these propositions are true there is involved the same trust in our reason that is involved in our confidence in mathematics; and we should have no justification for trusting it in the latter sphere and distrusting it in the former. In both cases we are dealing with propositions that cannot be proved, but that just as certainly need no proof.   (pp. 29–30; also see pp. 20–21)

Ross does not define "self-evident," but his use of the term implies both of the following: (1) self-evident knowledge is non-inferential knowledge, something that one knows without having inferred or deduced it from anything else one knows, and (2) when one has self-evident knowledge, adequately understanding or attending to the proposition in question is sufficient to give one knowledge of its truth. To paraphrase Ross, in the case of self-evident knowledge, there is no need of proof (or inference), and the proposition is evident if one has reached sufficient mental maturity and given sufficient attention to it.

Ross claims that some of the basic axioms of mathematics and logic are self-evident. These principles or axioms cannot be proven or deduced from anything else we know; nonetheless, we know that they are true. (The principle "all three-sided plane closed figures must have three angles" is an example of the sort of principle he has in mind.) In Euclidean geometry, theorems can be proven on the basis of certain axioms or postulates, but those axioms and postulates themselves cannot be proven.[5] Some claim that we have non-inferential knowledge of our own immediate experience. They claim, for example, that I can know without inference that I am not now in pain—it is self-evident to me that I am not in pain now.

5.III.2. The Data of Ethics

Ross argues that his theory is preferable to utilitarianism because it squares better with what he calls "the moral convictions of thoughtful and well-educated people." According to Ross (1930), the moral convictions of thoughtful and well-educated people constitute a kind of data against which moral theories must be tested.

> What we are apt to describe as "what we think" about moral questions contains a considerable amount that we do not think but know ... this forms the standard by reference to which the truth of any moral theory has to be tested ... the moral convictions of thoughtful and well-educated people are the data of ethics just as sense-perceptions are the data of a natural science. Just as some of the latter have to be rejected as illusory, so have some of the former; but as the latter are rejected only when they conflict with more accurate sense perceptions, the former are rejected only when they are in conflict with other convictions which stand better the test of reflection. The existing body of moral convictions of the best people is the cumulative product of the moral reflection of many generations, which has developed an extremely delicate power of appreciation of moral distinctions; and this the theorist cannot afford to treat with anything other than the greatest respect. The verdicts of the moral consciousness of the best people are the foundation on which he must build; though he must first compare them with one another and eliminate any contradictions they may contain.   (pp. 40–41)

Ross makes an analogy between moral theories and scientific theories. Our experience of the world constitutes the "data" for testing scientific theories. Similarly, the moral convictions of thoughtful and well-educated people are the data against which moral theories must be tested. Moral theories must yield results consistent with the moral convictions of thoughtful and well-educated people. Utilitarianism must be rejected because it implies things that we know to be false. Here it is fair to ask whether Ross includes Mill, Sidgwick, Brentano, and Moore among those he regards as the "best people," and, if not, why not? (Apparently, Ross thinks that the "best people" are to be found at Oxford, not Cambridge, Vienna, or the British East India Company.)

5.IV. CRITICISMS OF ROSS'S VIEW ABOUT THE BASIS OF MORAL KNOWLEDGE

5.IV.1. Self-Evident Knowledge

Moral disagreement raises serious problems for Ross's claim that we have "self-evident" knowledge of basic moral principles. Certain moral principles claimed to be self-evident by some people are rejected by others. Disagreement alone does not undermine Ross's claims, but disagreement among competent or "expert" moral appraisers creates serious problems for him. Agreement among competent and expert judges makes possible much of our knowledge. Without this agreement, we could not fully trust our own intellectual and sensory capacities. There is nearly unanimous agreement among intelligent people and expert logicians about the validity of certain forms of inference and argument, e.g., *modus ponens*. This is at least a negative condition of our having knowledge (or self-evident knowledge) of the validity of those forms of inference and argument. To take a different example, our knowledge of the external world is dependent on the extent of inter-subjective agreement in reports about the external world by those with properly functioning sensory organs. If our observations of the world were frequently contradicted by the observations of others, we could not rely on them to nearly the extent that we are able to. The observations and testimony of *other people* that form the basis of our knowledge of astronomy, e.g., observations relevant to the occurrence or nonoccurrence of solar eclipses (temporary darkening of the skies and observations of the moon blocking the light from the sun), give us knowledge only because we know that these observations and testimony are not seriously disputed by other reliable sources.

There is no comparable consensus about the truth of moral principles among those who might qualify as "experts" or authorities about moral questions. Ross, Moore, Brentano, and Sidgwick arguably count as "experts" about morality. However, they do not agree about the truth of such principles as "lying is *prima facie* wrong." Ross claims that this principle is self-evidently true, but its truth is not self-evident to Sidgwick and Moore—indeed, Moore would say that it is self-evidently false. Moore says that it is self-evident that consequentialism is true. He writes: "It seems to me to be self-evident that knowingly to do an action which would make the world, on the whole, really and truly *worse* than if we had acted differently, must always be wrong" (*Ethics*, 1965, p. 77).[6] Ross's claim that it is self-evident that lying is *prima facie* wrong is flatly inconsistent with this. Ross claims that lying can be wrong, even if not lying results in slightly worse consequences than lying. It is not plausible to claim that Moore lacks "mental maturity" or that he does not adequately attend to or understand the propositions in dispute between him and Ross. It would be question-begging for Ross to disqualify people with utilitarian intuitions as moral experts on the grounds that they have utilitarian intuitions.[7]

Intellectual honesty and humility require that we not automatically assume that we are correct and others are mistaken when we disagree with them. Sidgwick (1966) writes:

> Since it is implied in the very notion of Truth that it is essentially the same for all minds, the denial by another of a proposition that I have affirmed has a tendency to impair my confidence in its validity. . . . the absence of such disagreement must remain an indispensable negative condition of the certainty of our beliefs. For if I find any of my judgments, intuitive or inferential, in direct conflict with a judgment of some other mind, there must be error somewhere: and I have no more reason to suspect error in the other mind than in my own.   (pp. 341–342)

Ross does not adequately address the problem of disagreement. In the absence of some reason for thinking that Moore and other act-utilitarians are mistaken in denying that lying is *prima facie* wrong, Ross has no warrant for his claim that it is self-evident that lying is *prima facie* wrong. In this case, it is implausible to suggest that the disagreement stems from the failure of one or both of the parties to understand adequately the judgments and propositions in question (cf. Gaut, 2002, p. 144). Principles such as "there is a *prima facie* duty to keep promises" are not knowable simply on the basis of understanding them.

Our knowledge of basic moral principles is not comparable to our knowledge of axioms and postulates of mathematics (and our knowledge of the validity of certain forms of argument).

5.IV.2. The Moral Convictions of Thoughtful and Well-Educated People

Ross notes that the moral convictions of thoughtful and well-educated people can conflict. For instance, your moral convictions may tell you that it is morally permissible to lie in order to spare someone mild embarrassment, whereas other people's moral convictions tell them that it is wrong to lie simply for that reason. There is no single comprehensive set of moral beliefs that is accepted by all thoughtful and well-educated people. Ross is aware of this problem and notes that we must find some way to eliminate the conflict between different people's moral beliefs. He says that we must reject those moral beliefs that conflict with other moral beliefs that better stand the test of reflection, but he does not spell out what this involves or give any examples of how this might be done.

There is a great deal of disagreement about the moral convictions to which Ross appeals in his arguments about promise breaking and lying. I have discussed cases in which lying and not lying have the same consequences (or produce the same net amount of good/bad) to numerous groups of students over many years.

My students are not unanimous in sharing Ross's intuitions about these cases. Many of them express puzzlement that anyone would object to lying when it does not have worse consequences than not lying. In response to these examples, many say such things as "What's the harm of lying?" or "What's the big deal?" Many of them think that it is morally permissible to tell lies in order to bring about slightly better consequences than not lying; for example, saving someone from mild embarrassment. In the face of such sharply conflicting moral intuitions, Ross's argument is inconclusive (at best, he needs to add a subsidiary argument to show that the intuitions of my students and others who disagree with him are mistaken).

No doubt, Ross would claim that people's moral convictions must be consistent with our knowledge of self-evident *prima facie* moral principles, but, to the extent that Ross's claims about our knowledge of self-evident principles are undermined by disagreements between ostensible "moral experts," his argument about the moral convictions of thoughtful and well-educated people is also seriously undermined. Barring appeal to self-evident moral principles, Ross gives us no grounds for thinking that reflective tests can resolve disagreements between thoughtful and well-educated people.

In science, there is often a strong consensus about what the data are. For example, in astronomy there is strong agreement about the exact times and places in which the skies have darkened during normal daylight (and moonlight) hours. This agreement strongly corroborates conventional scientific theories about solar and lunar eclipses. It is not nearly as clear what the data of ethics are. The expression "*the* convictions of thoughtful and well-educated people" suggests a single common or shared set of beliefs about morality. However, there is no single consistent and comprehensive set of moral beliefs accepted by all thoughtful and well-educated people. Most societies throughout human history have granted women rights and freedoms far less extensive than those accorded to men. Many (most) human societies have practiced slavery (or something like it—serfdom or rigid social castes) at times in the past. Further, these practices were *thought to be* morally acceptable. (Serious controversy about the morality of slavery and conscientious opposition to slavery among non-slaves have been extremely rare in the great majority of human societies.) Slavery existed in the US until 1865. Serfdom was abolished in Russia in 1861. Ethiopia abolished serfdom/slavery around 1940. Slavery was abolished in Saudi Arabia in 1960. Mauritania passed laws outlawing the institution of slavery in the 1980s. Slavery persists in many countries, most notably Mauritania, Haiti, The Sudan, Niger, and Mali.[8] Many moral codes of other times and places now seem to us to be seriously mistaken. In light of this, we should not be too confident of the common sense moral beliefs of our own time and place. Thoughtful and well-educated people in our own place and time might be (and likely are) seriously mistaken in their views about many important moral issues.

5.IV.3. A Possible Reply for Ross

Susan Hurley gives a very unapologetic defense of epistemological intuitionism. She says that the appropriate response for the intuitionist to make to objections about disagreement is to claim that certain individuals may be deficient in their ability to discern moral properties. According to Hurley, moral properties are objective properties of things constituted by natural properties in the same way that the parts of a physical object constitute a pattern. Hurley (1989) likens the ability to see moral properties to the ability to recognize someone's face (pp. 292–293).

Hurley is committed to the view that many people are deficient in their ability to discern moral properties. She acknowledges this:

What can be supposed . . . to be necessary for some person's belief to constitute knowledge . . . is *not* that a range of investigators would reasonably and unconstrainedly come to converge on it . . . but rather that if the proposition believed weren't true the person in question wouldn't believe it (and, perhaps we should add, that if it were he would). . . . The failure of these convergence conditions does not *per se* undermine the knowledge of those who possess it. . . . To ignore this is to assume (optimistically? or on political grounds?) too great a uniformity, or potential uniformity among persons and their situations; one person's knowledge does not depend on another's capacity for it. . . .

Some people might simply be better at discovering truths about what should be done, all things considered, than others (who might be better at discovering other kinds of truth). . . .

For example, some people have very specific agnosias, or recognitional disabilities. Perhaps the most familiar is prosopagnosia, or inability to recognize faces, on the part of someone whose vision is otherwise unimpaired.

(1989, pp. 292–293)

It is possible that many otherwise normal and intelligent people are deficient in their ability to discern moral truths. However, in order to show that some people are actually deficient, Hurley needs to give a convincing account of the difference between correct and incorrect perception of moral truths. She and other intuitionists have failed to do this. The ability to recognize faces is a way of finding one's way around in the world. Those with the ability to recognize faces can make discriminations that others cannot. A person who can recognize faces can identify particular people in a crowd without difficulty. There are non-controversial and non-question-begging ways of determining whether or not someone has the ability to recognize faces. If someone's competence in recognizing faces is called into question, we can test her ability to do so without relying on *anyone's* ability to recognize faces. There are *independent* ways of identifying people, e.g., fingerprints. There is nothing comparable to this in the case of morality (at least not on Hurley's view). Suppose that you and

I disagree about the moral properties of an action, although we agree about all of its natural properties. Each of us claims that the other is deficient in his/her ability to perceive normative properties. Given Hurley's view, there is no non-question-begging way for us to determine whose perceptions are deficient and whose are not. If her theory is true and moral properties are patterns that we perceive, then the only way that I can test someone else's moral perceptions is to appeal to my own moral perceptions. Hurley fails to show that there are any non-question-begging ways to resolve disputes about the veracity of people's moral perceptions.

This same problem arises for Ross. He needs to provide independent tests of the veracity of reports of self-evident moral knowledge (tests independent of disputed appeals to self-evident moral knowledge). He needs to give us grounds for distinguishing between reliable and unreliable reports of self-evident knowledge of moral principles. The burden of proof falls on Ross, and it is a burden that he fails to meet.

5.IV.4. Two Other Possible Lines for Ross to Take

Perhaps we should say that ideal moral judges must be paragons of moral goodness and moral virtue, e.g., the people of La Chambonne who sheltered and cared for many intended victims of the Holocaust, rather than intellectuals such as Ross and Moore. Alternatively, and more plausibly, we might require that ideal moral judges be both intellectually and morally virtuous.[9] Given such a view, Ross could say that people differ markedly in their ability to discern moral truths, and Hurley's conjecture might be plausible. This view has much to recommend it, but for Ross's purposes, it has a very serious problem that I cannot see any way around. The problem is that our characterization of the moral virtues of an ideal moral judge seems to presuppose certain first-order moral views. It is doubtful that we can use the notion of a morally virtuous ideal moral judge to settle controversial first-order moral questions. This is because if we seriously disagree about the answers to first-order moral questions, then it is likely that we will also disagree about the moral virtues we ascribe to ideal moral judges and about the ways in which we should define or characterize those virtues. It is also likely that we will be unable to agree on a list of moral paragons.

Another option for Ross would be to appeal to more conventional notions of a cognitively or intellectually ideal observer or ideal moral judge and say that *ideally rational* moral judges would agree that Ross's *prima facie* principles are self-evident. However, I think it very unlikely that all ideal observers would agree in endorsing the judgments to which Ross appeals in his arguments against utilitarianism.[10]

5.V. HOOKER'S RULE-CONSEQUENTIALISM

5.V.1. Hooker's Theory

In light of the foregoing, it is appropriate to examine Hooker's RC. Hooker claims that, in practice, RC is nearly equivalent to Ross's theory for issues of lying and deception.[11] However, Hooker claims that his theory provides a better foundation and justification for Rossian *prima facie* rules than Ross himself gives.

Hooker's book *Ideal Code, Real World* gives the definitive statement of RC. Hooker (2000) states his preferred version of RC in the following passage:

An act is wrong if and only if it is forbidden by the code of rules whose internalization by the overwhelming majority of everyone everywhere in each new generation has maximum expected value in terms of well-being (with some priority for the worst off). The calculation of a code's expected value includes all the costs of getting the code internalized. If in terms of expected value two or more codes are better than the rest but equal to one another, the one closest to conventional morality determines what acts are wrong.   (p. 32)

Several features of Hooker's view should be noted.

1. Hooker formulates his theory in terms of the "expected value" of rules rather than "*consequences that would actually result*" from their adoption (pp. 72–74).
2. Hooker states his theory in terms of the set of rules, the (general) *acceptance* of which, can be expected to produce the best consequences, rather than the set of rules the (general) *compliance* with which has the best expected consequences (pp. 75–80).
3. Hooker says that the rightness or wrongness of an action is determined by the moral code, the general acceptance of which by everyone everywhere (90% of everyone everywhere), can be expected to produce the best results.

By contrast, some rule-consequentialists, such as Richard Brandt, relativize the rightness or wrongness of actions to the moral codes whose general acceptance by the agent's society would produce the best consequences. Hooker gives plausible and interesting arguments for each of these features of his view, but the details of these arguments are not important for our present purposes.

Hooker says that the ideal moral code (the code whose acceptance by the great majority of people everywhere would have the best consequences) consists largely of rules very similar to Ross's list of *prima facie* duties and includes prohibitions against lying and promise-breaking and general duties of beneficence and non-malevolence. Such rules can conflict. The ideal moral code must include higher-level rules for resolving conflicts of duties. What should the ideal moral code tell us to do in cases of conflicts between conflicting *prima facie* moral rules? Some versions of RC tell us to resolve conflicts by directly applying AU to the case. Hooker (2000) rejects this on the grounds that it would have bad "expectation effects." If everyone resolved conflicts of duties by directly applying AU, "How much confidence would you have in others to keep their promises and tell the truth, if you knew that they would abandon promises or the truth whenever a conflict with beneficence appeared?" (p. 89). In addition, the policy of resolving conflicts of duties by direct appeal to AU would commit Hooker to too many of what he regards as the deeply counterintuitive consequences of AU (p. 89). Another way to resolve conflicts of duties would be to build many exceptions into the rules so that they will not conflict. Hooker rejects this on the grounds that this would make the code so complex that its internalization costs would be unacceptably high (p. 90).

Hooker (2000) says that the ideal moral code includes a rule enjoining people to "prevent disasters." This rule tells one to violate any of the other (*prima facie*) moral rules if doing so is necessary to prevent a disaster or avoid very bad consequences (p. 99). This prompts the question "What counts as a disaster?"—someone dying, many people dying, friends or spouses becoming estranged, someone losing his job, someone losing a promotion, my co-workers being angry with me? Hooker rejects the idea that we can state a simple threshold level of bad consequences that constitutes a "disaster." He proposes a "sliding scale" method for applying the "prevent disaster rule." Whether we should apply the prevent disaster rule depends on how big the disaster is and how big the violation of the rules is. "The more important the rule, the larger the disaster in question would have to be to justify breaking the rule" (p. 135).

The prevent disaster rule will resolve only a relatively small number of the conflicts of duties that occur in practice (most conflicts of duties do not involve potential disasters). In principle, there are an infinite number of ways in which moral rules can conflict. Hooker says that when duties conflict we determine which duty is most important by determining which acts would be permitted by "the set of motivations whose internalization would be reasonably expected to have consequences as good as those of any other set we can identify" (p. 131). I take it that by this he means the motivations whose internalization by *everyone* would have the best consequences, i.e., better consequences than the consequences of everyone internalizing any other set of motivations.

Hooker (2000) claims that:

people with a good rule-consequentialist training would have an enormously strong aversion to killing others, a very strong aversion to doing serious bodily harm to others, but a much weaker aversion to doing very small harms to others. Likewise, they would have a very strong aversion to telling huge lies under oath and breaking solemn promises about important matters, but a much weaker aversion to telling small lies or breaking little promises . . . rule-consequentialism holds that when rules (and thus aversions) conflict, the stronger aversion determines what action is right . . .   (pp. 131–132)

This is plausible as far as it goes, but Hooker needs to explain what he means by "big" and "small" lies/promises. In addition, it is unclear how these motivations not to lie will weigh against optimal motivations to fulfill other duties, e.g., the duty to not harm others. To put this another way, how does the strength of the optimal motivation to refrain from lying compare with the strength of the optimal motivations to fulfill other *prima facie* duties?

Hooker (2000) says that the ideal moral code includes Rossian *prima facie* rules prohibiting physical attack, torture, theft, promise-breaking, and lying, because it would be best if we internalized (*prima facie*) rules against these actions (p. 126). Hooker agrees with Ross that lying is *prima facie* wrong. Hooker never mentions deception, and I take it that, like Ross, he does not think that deception is *prima facie* wrong. According to Hooker, there is no absolute prohibition against lying, because it is sometimes permissible to lie to save lives (p. 127).

5.V.2. Hooker's Arguments for Rule-Consequentialism

Hooker's arguments make use of Rawls' method of reflective equilibrium. Hooker (2000) says that moral theories must cohere with and systematize the moral convictions that we have confidence in after careful reflection (pp. 4, 12). Rawls conceives of reflective equilibrium as a state one reaches after a process of reflection involving a mutual adjustment between general moral theories one finds appealing and one's "considered moral judgments" about particular cases. Considered moral judgments are: (1) judgments that one makes with confidence; (2) judgments that one does not make as a consequence of being frightened, angry, or ill; and (3) judgments that one does not stand to gain by in one way or another (Rawls, 1971, p. 47). We might reject or revise certain kinds of moral theories if we see that they conflict with some of our considered moral judgments. According to Rawls, when engaging in the process that leads to reflective equilibrium, one will reject or modify some of one's considered moral judgments if they conflict with moral theories one finds appealing. If one is presented with an intuitively appealing theory that accounts for some of our considered moral judgments, one may revise or reject those judgments that are inconsistent with the theory (Rawls, 1971, p. 47).

Rawls distinguishes between narrow and wide reflective equilibrium. Hooker (2000) characterizes the difference between them as follows: "Narrow reflective equilibrium is obtained when we find a set of principles that economically systematizes our considered moral convictions. Wide reflective equilibrium is narrow reflective equilibrium *plus* consistency with 'background conditions.' These background conditions are composed of theories of personal identity, human flourishing, rationality, and everything else" (p. 15). Hooker claims that, in practice, there is very little difference between narrow and wide reflective equilibrium, "Of course, rule-consequentialism should be consistent with other things we believe (or ought to believe), including the background conditions. But it is. And so are its main rivals" (p. 16).[12]

Hooker summarizes the main considered moral judgments to which he appeals in a section entitled "Moral Convictions We Share." He writes:

Reflective equilibrium starts with moral beliefs about which we confidently agree. What are these? Most of us confidently agree morality can require us to help others, even if we have no special connection to them. Suppose that at no cost to yourself, you could save thousands of innocent people from some horrible fate . . . Obviously, when you can save many innocent people at *no* cost to yourself or to others, morality requires you to save them . . . Helping the needy can be morally required, even if it does involve self-sacrifice . . . Yet morality does not require you to be *constantly* making *huge* self-sacrifices for the sake of other people to whom you have no special connection.   (p. 16)

Most of us also believe that we owe more altruism to certain people than to others. Other things being roughly equal, your allocation of your own resources should favor your own parent, or child, or friend, or those to whom you have a debt of gratitude over those who do not have any special relationship to you.   (pp. 16–17)

We also share confident beliefs about the moral impermissibility of certain kinds of act. Morality prohibits physically attacking innocent people or their property. It prohibits taking the property of others, lying, breaking one's promises, and so on.   (p. 17)

Hooker says that there is wide, but not unanimous, agreement about these matters.

The success of Hooker's argument for RC over AU depends entirely on his appeal to his initial considered moral judgments. His reflective equilibrium argument moves directly from his considered moral judgments to his rejection of AU and then to his argument that RC accounts for and systematizes these considered judgments better than Ross's theory. He has no other arguments for RC over AU other than AU's inconsistency (and RC's consistency) with his ("our") considered moral judgments.[13] Hooker stresses three objections in his arguments against AU: (1) AU is too demanding; (2) AU does not adequately justify moral prohibitions such as the prohibition against lying; and (3) AU does not adequately account for the special obligations we have to certain people. In his discussion of the issue of demandingness, Hooker focuses on the obligation of affluent people to aid those who are very poor. He notes that in a world in which millions of destitute people die of hunger each year, relatively small donations to the "best charities" save lives (p. 149), "Given these facts, we must accept that good would be maximized if I gave away most of my material goods to the appropriate charities" (p. 150). He claims that this level of self-sacrifice is supererogatory, "But many of us may on reflection think that it would be *morally unreasonable* to demand this level of self-sacrifice for the sake of others . . . But, however praiseworthy such self-sacrifice may be, most of us are quite confident that perpetual self-impoverishment for the sake of those outside of one's circle of family and friends is supererogatory . . ." (pp. 150–151).

Hooker's arguments about moral prohibitions focus on promise keeping and lying. He rejects the AU view that it is always right to lie or break promises whenever doing so produces slightly better consequences than not (pp. 131, 145–146). He appeals to Ross's example of a case in which keeping a promise will produce 1000 total units of good and breaking the promise will produce 1001 units of good (pp. 145–146).

> Most of us would agree with Ross that keeping the promise is morally right when the total good produced by breaking the promise is only slightly greater than the total good produced by keeping the promise. Act-consequentialism, of course, disagrees.
> . . . Act-consequentialism of course accepts that it is right to break promises, take or harm the possessions of others, lie, or harm innocent people *when doing so is necessary to prevent a disaster*. But act-consequentialism also holds that it is right to do these things *when doing them would produce only slightly greater good* than not doing them would.
>
> Hooker (2000, p. 146)

Hooker (2000) claims that AU cannot give an adequate explanation of our special obligations to certain people:

> most of us think you should give your (at least close) friends and family some priority over others in the distribution of your own private resources . . . you are broadly allowed and indeed required to give special consideration to those to with whom you have special connections. Suppose you have only enough money to buy a meal for your own hungry child, or a meal for some equally hungry stranger. There would be something perverse about devoting your private resources to securing benefits for a stranger when you could have used them to provide your own child with equally large benefits. The same could be said even if the benefits to your own child would be somewhat smaller than the benefits to the stranger.   (pp. 136–137)

In addition, those who follow AU must forgo the great good of deep friendship.

> Why is deep friendship incompatible with constant impartiality? Jonathan Dancy writes: "To want to treat all impartially is to love nobody." Why? Because of the conjunction of two facts . . . deep friendships necessarily contain strong affection and concern. The second is the empirical fact that human beings cannot have strong concern for any and equal concern for all.
>
> Hooker (2000, p. 139)

> The cost of having equal concern for all is that there would be no more than weak concern for any. To have but weak concern for others would preclude the obtaining of deep personal attachments. To lack deep personal attachments would itself be a loss. In addition, it would deprive us of much pleasure and of much of our sense of security.
>
> Hooker (2000, p. 141)

In practice, Hooker's theory is nearly equivalent to Ross's theory. (At least this is how Hooker puts it. However, it is not clear that Ross speaks directly to questions about the extent our obligations to sacrifice ourselves to help others.)

Hooker grants that Ross's theory (or what he calls "Ross-style pluralism") coheres as well with our considered moral judgments as RC. However, he contends that his theory gives a better and more systematic explanation and rationale for Rossian rules than Ross himself does. For all its intuitive appeal, Ross's theory looks like a "heap of unconnected duties." Hooker's theory provides a principle that underlies and explains the various *prima facie* duties that Ross identifies. Ross, by contrast, has no underlying theory or rationale for the duties he identifies, just a list (Hooker, 2000, pp. 21–22 and 104–107).[14]

5.V.3. Problems with Hooker's Arguments

As noted earlier, Hooker's argument against AU is completely dependent on his appeal to his ("our") considered moral judgments about the three matters in question. AU is able to give a coherent and systematic justification and explanation of all the other considered moral judgments to which he appeals. However, there are reasons to question the reliability of the first two kinds of considered moral judgments and there are other serious problems with Hooker's arguments about special obligations.

Some ostensibly rational and reflective people reject the claim that lying and promise breaking are wrong in cases in which they have the same (or nearly the same) consequences as lying. Hooker's appeal to Ross's example of a case in which keeping a promise will produce 1000 total units of good and breaking the promise will produce 1001 units of good is unpersuasive for reasons that we saw earlier in 5.IV.2. Not all reasonable people share Ross's firm intuition that it is wrong to lie or break a promise to produce *slightly* better consequences than one would produce by not lying or keeping the promise. Twentieth-century and contemporary utilitarian philosophers who *have* reflected carefully about this matter and who are aware of Ross's arguments do not share his view that it is wrong to lie or break a promise in such cases, much less have confidence in the truth of this view.

Many people do not share the considered moral judgments Hooker invokes to show that act-consequentialism is too demanding. There are philosophers and others who accept AU despite being aware of the objection that it is "too demanding"—they think that affluent people are obligated to make very large sacrifices for poor and destitute people in distant lands. In addition, many religious people unfamiliar with utilitarianism accept very demanding moral codes. Christian morality is just as demanding as AU. "Love your neighbor as yourself," the fundamental moral principle espoused by Jesus in the *New Testament*, commands impartial benevolence (cf. Mill, *Utilitarianism*, p. 17 and Outka, 1972, p. 299). Christians cannot be confident of the judgments that Hooker appeals to in his discussion of the demands of morality. Many Christians take their failure to live up to the stringent moral demands of their faith to be morally wrong and to require repentance and forgiveness by God. Given the self-interested reasons that relatively privileged people have for regarding morality as less demanding, their judgments to the effect that morality is much less demanding are highly suspect and not reliable bases for moral theorizing. Rawls's third requirement for considered moral judgments (c) should exclude these judgments, since we stand to gain or benefit from the judgment that we are not obligated to make large sacrifices for poor people in distant lands. Hooker needs to show why act-utilitarians' considered moral judgments (and the considered moral judgments of many Christians) are mistaken if he is to claim plausibly that his arguments give us good reasons reject AU and accept RC.

Here, one might object that we can be much more confident of (many of) our considered moral judgments than we can be of any epistemic/metaethical principles that call them into question. Michael DePaul (1993, pp. 122–124, 128–135) and Noah Lemos (2004, pp. 168–179) have developed this argument in considerable detail. Hooker (2000, p. 104) hints at it himself. Even if we grant that some of our considered moral judgments are very credible, this does not rescue Hooker's argument. I think that we can be very confident of *some* of our considered moral judgments; for example, the judgment that there is a strong presumption against harming others, telling lies, and breaking promises. We can also be confident that we have obligations to help others and that we are sometimes obligated to make sacrifices for them. Arguably, we can be more confident about many of these judgments and many judgments about particular cases than we can be about any full-blown normative or metaethical theories such as AU or the ideal observer theory. I agree with Lemos (2004) that we can be very confident in many of his judgments about particular cases, including his judgment that "it would now be wrong for me to rape and kill my secretary and that it would be wrong for me to now torture my father to death" (p. 158). However, we cannot attach a high level of initial credibility to the fine-grained controversial judgments that Hooker appeals to in his arguments against AU.[15] The kinds of intuitive moral judgments that Lemos appeals to are not judgments about issues that divide proponents of Ross's theory and proponents of AU. Further, we can have considerable confidence in the non-controversial metaethical and epistemic principles to which I am appealing here (and later in Chapters 6 and 7): the universalizability principle, the view that moral judgments need to be "adequately informed," and the view that the fact that other reasonable people disagree with one should (substantially) lower one's confidence in one's initial considered moral judgments.

Further, even if we allow that *Hooker* is justified in attaching high credibility to *his* initial considered moral judgments, he still needs to give reasons why people whose initial considered moral judgments conflict sharply with his are not justified in attaching high credibility to *their* initial considered moral judgments. If he does not do this, it seems that his version of reflective equilibrium will yield us a kind of relativism. When he reaches equilibrium after a process of reflection, he will endorse RC. However, not every reasonable person who reflects and reaches reflective equilibrium will converge on the same theory; it is likely that some people will endorse AU in reflective equilibrium.

There is a strong consensus that we have special duties to certain people. However, Hooker does not show that AU cannot give an adequate account of such duties. Hooker's argument about choosing between feeding one's own hungry child and feeding an equally hungry stranger is unconvincing because the actions in question do not have the same consequences. Failing to feed one's own child has bad consequences—causing emotional harm to the child and weakening family ties—that failing to feed the stranger will not have. Love and friendship are great goods without which human life is hardly worth living. If, as Hooker says, we lose these great goods by always trying to directly follow AU as our decision procedure, then AU implies that we should *not* always try to be impartial and always use AU as a decision procedure. AU is a standard or criterion of right and wrong that says that we should act so as to do the best we can. If (as Hooker himself suggests) trying to always directly follow AU will lead to disastrous consequences, then AU will say that we should not adopt the policy of always trying to follow AU.[16] Clearly AU permits people to do the things that they need to do to have close friendships and preserve loving family ties.

Hooker's argument that AU requires that we be equally concerned with everyone (and thus only weakly concerned with anyone) also overlooks the distinction between AU as a standard of right and wrong and using AU as a decision procedure. (By having "concern" for someone I take Hooker to mean being emotionally attached to and taking practical efforts to help/benefit that person.) Since suppressing special affections to certain people and trying to have equal concern for all will lead (in Sidgwick's words) to " 'but a watery kindness' and feeble counter poise to self-love" (Sidgwick, 1966, p.434), AU recommends against trying to have equal concern for all. AU allows me to have special emotions and practical commitments to certain people, because by having these emotions and commitments I bring about much better consequences than by trying to concern myself equally with everyone.

Conclusions

In the case of special obligations to others, Hooker does not show that AU has the very counterintuitive consequences that he alleges. In the case of the arguments about moral prohibitions and demandingness, there are ostensibly reasonable people who reject many of the considered moral judgments to which Hooker appeals. Hooker needs to give further subsidiary arguments to show that his considered moral judgments are true/reliable and that the considered moral judgments of those who disagree with him about the issues to which he appeals in his arguments against AU are mistaken/unreliable. Without further arguments for these considered moral judgments, his overall case for RC is inconclusive. Hooker might want to avail himself of my golden-rule arguments in Chapter 6. Alternatively, he might want to incorporate some version of the ideal observer theory or the suggestion that ideal moral judges must be morally virtuous considered earlier (see 5.IV.4). Later (Chapter 7.III), I propose an improved version of reflective equilibrium that uses the rationality/golden rule tests in Chapter 6 as tests for considered moral judgments. I argue that this version of reflective equilibrium yields a substantial convergence among reasonable views, but still does not resolve the disagreements between Ross, Hooker, and AU.[17]

5.VI. CONCLUSIONS TO CHAPTERS 3–5 AND TRANSITION TO CHAPTER 6

It seems obvious to many people that lying is morally permissible when it is necessary to save the life of an innocent person. Kant and at least some others disagree. They are completely unmoved by this appeal to moral intuitions. Ross claims it is "self-evident" that it is wrong to lie, other things being equal. He thinks that it is obvious that it is wrong to lie when lying produces only slightly better consequences than not lying. Other philosophers contend that this is not self-evident. Moore claims that it is self-evident that we should always do whatever has the best consequences. Moore's claim is flatly inconsistent with what Ross says about the case in which lying produces slightly better consequences than not lying. Neither Ross nor Moore gives convincing reasons for thinking that his own moral intuitions are correct and the other is mistaken. Ross and Moore largely ignore the phenomenon of moral disagreement and the attendant problems of moral skepticism and relativism. Standard debates between act-utilitarians and anti-utilitarians about lying and other moral prohibitions are inconclusive because both parties appeal to intuitions disputed by ostensibly reasonable and consistent people. Appeals to moral intuitions are not adequate to justify judgments about the issues discussed in this book.

Hooker's more restrained appeal to "independently credible moral judgments" and "considered moral judgments" does not succeed either. He claims that "our considered moral judgments" conflict sharply with act-consequentialism. However, many ostensibly reasonable people disagree with many of the specific considered moral judgments Hooker appeals to in his arguments against AU. Without independent arguments for the controversial considered judgments to which he appeals, Hooker's defense of RC is ultimately unconvincing.

Because ostensibly reasonable people disagree in their moral intuitions and considered moral judgments, arguments for moral theories that rely solely on appeals to intuitions or considered moral judgments reach a dialectical impasse.

ENDNOTES

1. Cf. Ewing (1959): "to say that we have a *prima facie* duty to produce something is the same as a saying that it ought to be produced for its own sake, other things being equal" (p. 104). Frankena (1973) gives essentially the same definition: "Something is a *prima facie* duty if it is a duty other things being equal . . ." (p. 27).

2. Ross (1930) writes: "If I have promised to meet a friend at a particular time for some trivial purpose, I should certainly think myself justified in breaking my engagement if by doing so I could prevent a serious accident or bring relief to the victims of one" (p. 18).

3. I think that Ross (1930) is correct in claiming that all cases of lying involve breaking an implicit promise or guarantee that what one says is true (see Chapter 1.I.7 and 1.I.12, this book).

4. Ross (1930) proposes something similar to this to handle utilitarian replies to his second example of a case in which utilitarianism seems too permissive about breaking promises (p. 38).

5. Given the existence of non-Euclidean geometries, which according to some scientists describe physical reality, and given debates about the foundations of mathematics, this example is questionable. Ross's claim that we have self-evident knowledge of the validity of certain forms of inference, e.g., *modus ponens*, seems better for his purposes.

6. Also, see Brentano (1973):

   It is self-contradictory to say that it could be morally better to choose a lesser good over a greater. For choice is a sort of preference, and "better" means nothing other than "preferable". No one can appeal to the disrepute of the dictum that the end justifies the means, for it deserves to be condemned only when it is used with reference to a certain end without regard to all the circumstances or to the consequences that would flow from its realization. If we subsume under the end the totality of foreseeable consequences, then it is morally right to use means not desirable in themselves for the sake of a better end.   (pp. 81–82)

7. Here, one could object that Moore might have changed his view if he had been aware of Ross's arguments. Moore wrote *Ethics* long before Ross wrote *The Right and the Good*. (I owe this objection to Brad Hooker.) This objection is well taken. However, later, Moore did read Ross (he makes several references to Ross and Ross's concept of a *prima facie* duty in his "A Reply to My Critics." Moore was apparently unmoved by Ross's arguments. He still makes strong claims about the necessary connection between the concepts of value and rightness. He says that from the proposition that "The total subsequent effects of this action would be intrinsically better than those of any other action I could do instead" it "necessarily" follows that "I ought to do this action" ("A Reply to my

Critics," p. 562). Moore does not explicitly respond to the arguments (of Ross) presently under discussion, but it is safe to assume that he was aware of them.

Moore and many other act-utilitarians who are familiar with Ross's arguments do not find it self-evident that there is a *prima facie* duty to keep promises and not to lie.

8. Slavery existed on large scale through the twentieth century and persists to the present day. *Time Magazine* (March 5 2001, pp. 50), reports that there are presently 300 000 child slaves in Haiti. On slavery in Mauritania, see Finnegan (2000) and Sawyer (1986). On slavery in The Sudan, see Sawyer (1986) and Finnegan (1999). On Slavery in Niger and Mali, see Polgreen (2008).

9. For views of this sort, see Kawall (2002) and Zagzebski (2004). Zagzebski defends what she calls "exemplarism." She claims that we should make lists of moral exemplars the foundation of ethical theories (see Zagzebski, 2004, pp. 40–50).

10. I have argued elsewhere that standard versions of the ideal observer theory commit us to moral relativism and at most allow for a minimal version of moral objectivism, according to which relatively few moral judgments, e.g., "the Holocaust was morally wrong," are objectively true. See Carson (1984, chapter 2; 1989).

11. The other leading rule-utilitarian, Richard Brandt, also thinks the ideal moral code that determines the rightness or wrongness of actions includes Rossian *prima facie* duties, such as the *prima facie* duty not to lie.

12. What Hooker says needs to be qualified in at least one respect. The truth about theories of welfare can force one to adjust one's preferred moral theories. For example, hedonistic utilitarian is plausible only if hedonism is the correct theory of human welfare.

13. There are other versions of reflective equilibrium that do not attach so much weight to one's initial considered moral judgments. These other versions of reflective equilibrium allow for the possibility that one will come to reject most of one's initial considered moral judgments. See DePaul (1993, pp. 32–33, 43). According to DePaul, it is possible that one will come to reject all of one's initial considered moral judgments.

14. For a criticism of the view that Ross's theory is "an unconnected heap of duties," see McNaughton (1996).

15. Lemos (2004) does not claim that moral judgments about particular cases support any particular theory of right and wrong. His concern is to answer moral skepticism.

16. This distinction between the principle of utility as a decision procedure and the principle of utility as a criterion of right and wrong is firmly rooted in

the utilitarian tradition. Act-utilitarians, such as Sidgwick (1966) and Hare, reject the principle of utility as a decision procedure.

17. There are many other versions of utilitarianism that I have not discussed. David Lyons (1994), Donald Regan, and others have formulated alternative versions of rule-utilitarianism. In *Ethics*, Moore sketches, but does not endorse, an alternative version of AU according to which the rightness or wrongness of an action is determined by its likely or predictable consequences, rather than its actual consequences.

Mendola (2006) formulates a highly original version of utilitarianism that does not fit neatly into the traditional act/rule utilitarian categories. He proposes what he calls "multiple-act-consequentialism" (MAC). He contends that, like RC, MAC avoids the objectionable counterintuitive consequences of AU, but that there is a much better theoretical rationale for MAC than RC. According to Mendola, MAC has four key tenants:

(1) There are group agents of which we are constituents. (2) Direct consequentialist evaluation of the options of group agents is appropriate. (3) Sometimes we should follow our roles in a group act even at the cost of the overall good we could achieve by defection from those roles . . . one should defect from a group act with good consequences only if one can achieve better consequences by the defecting act alone than the entire group act achieves. (4) When different beneficent group agents, of which one is a part, specify roles that conflict for one, one should follow the role in the group act with the more valuable consequences. (p. 23)

Mendola claims that:

According to MAC . . . we have a general cooperative practice that is a group agent generally forbidding lies though with various exceptions, and that does allow a certain amount of misleading speech. Roughly speaking, you should lie in a way forbidden by that practice only when you can gain as much value by that defection from our general group act as that whole vast cooperative practice creates. (p. 84)

Group acts of refraining from lying produce enormous amounts of good (viable human societies are not possible apart from the existence of such practices). The actions of individuals almost never produce amounts of good that approach the amounts created by the practices of large groups that forbid lying. Zofia Kukla (see Chapter 3.V) did a great deal of good by lying to the Nazis, but the good of the lives she saved is still less than the good produced by practices that forbid lying in large societies. If this were the only grounds on which Mendola's theory permitted lying/deception it would, for all practical purposes, be an absolutist theory. However, the actual group practices Mendola appeals to allow for exceptions to rules against lying and deception. The group acts and social practices (of Polish Catholics) in which Zofia Kukla participated permitted lying in order to save lives. However,

Mendola's theory implies that if one is part of a social group whose norms never permit lying or deception, e.g., the pietist Lutherans of Kant's time and place, then one is never permitted to lie or deceive others unless the net good produced by an individual act of lying/deception exceeds the entire good produced by practices/group acts. This seems objectionable. Mendola attaches too much weight to the actual practices of which we are a part and that often contain arbitrary and harmful rules.

IIB MORAL REASONING

In order to avoid the dialectical impasse of appealing to moral intuitions (or considered moral judgments) that are rejected by ostensibly rational and competent people, I defend a version of the golden rule and a broadly Kantian theory of moral reasoning in Chapter 6. My theory enables me to justify and defend moral judgments about a wide range of cases without appealing to disputed moral intuitions.

That which is hateful to you, do not do to your neighbor: that is the whole of the Torah, while the rest is commentary thereon; go and learn it.

Rabbi Hillel (quoted in Wattles, 1996, p. 48)

All things therefore which you want/wish/will that people do to you do thus to them for this is the law and the prophets.

Jesus Christ (*Matthew*, 7:12)

As I would not be a *slave* so I would not be a *master*. This expresses my idea of democracy—Whatever differs from this, to the extent of the difference, is no democracy.

Abraham Lincoln, "On Slavery and Democracy," 1858, in Lincoln (volume I, p. 484)

He who would *be* no slave, must consent to *have* no slave. Those who deny freedom to others, deserve it not for themselves; and, under a just God, cannot long retain it.

Abraham Lincoln, "Letter to H. L. Pierce and others," in Lincoln (volume II, p. 19)

6

The Golden Rule and a Theory of Moral Reasoning

INTRODUCTION

In order to avoid the dialectical impasse noted in Chapter 5, we need to address metaethical questions about the justification of moral judgments. This chapter proposes a theory of moral reasoning in the form of rationality conditions for moral judgments. I argue that moral judges must be: (1) consistent; (2) adequately informed by knowledge of relevant facts (this requires vividly understanding relevant considerations, including the feelings of others); and (3) able to reason properly and have properly functioning cognitive abilities. This chapter focuses on the first requirement, consistency.

My three requirements are at least *necessary* conditions for (ideally) rational moral judgments. I do not claim that my list of rationality requirements is complete. Even if my list is incomplete, we can use my theory to answer many moral questions. There are certain moral judgments that would be accepted by every moral judge who satisfies my three requirements. Since, at a minimum, my three rationality requirements are necessary for being an ideally rational moral judge; all ideally rational judges satisfy my three requirements. Therefore, if there were a moral judgment that would be accepted by all judges who satisfy my requirements, then that judgment would be accepted by all ideally rational moral judges.

Sections 6.II and 6.III defend several different versions of the golden rule. Section 6.IV defends those versions against several well-known objections to the golden rule. Section 6.V applies my theory to several moral issues (the Holocaust and fraud and deception by members of professions) and argues that all rational and consistent moral judges who venture to make moral judgments about those issues must agree that the actions in question are morally wrong. My theory also provides a basis for disproving ethical egoism. Egoists cannot be consistent, because ethical egoism requires that individuals sometimes harm others in ways that almost everyone objects to being harmed. In Section 6.VI, I venture an answer to the question "Why should I be consistent?"

The consistency arguments I offer in this chapter have the following limitation. They apply only to people who make moral judgments; they do not provide any basis for arguing against moral nihilists who refuse to make any moral judgments. In Section 6.VII, I offer reasons not to be a moral nihilist. My consistency arguments resemble those of R. M. Hare, but, as I explain in Section 6.VIII, my theory differs from Hare's in a number of important respects and avoids Hare's most serious mistakes. Among other things, my theory does not require me to accept Hare's account of what it is to accept a moral principle—an account that commits him to rejecting the possibility of moral weakness.

6.I. RATIONALITY CONDITIONS FOR MORAL JUDGMENTS AND MORAL JUDGES

What are the features of a rational or ideally-rational moral judge?

6.I.1. Consistency

Rational moral judges must be consistent. There are two generic consistency requirements for moral judgments: (1) moral judgments are universalizable (whatever moral judgments we make must be consistent with the judgments we make about relevantly similar cases), and (2) our attitudes and actions must be consistent with the moral judgments that we make. Together these principles commit us to several versions of the golden rule (see later in 6.II).

6.I.2. Being Adequately Informed

Rational moral judges must be informed about relevant facts concerning the actions they judge. To make a fully rational moral judgment about a particular action, I must have adequate information about the action in question, including: (1) the reasons for which the agent performed the act; (2) the consequences of the act; and (3) how the consequences of the act compare with the consequences of alternative courses of action. Being ignorant of, or mistaken about, relevant facts disqualifies one as a reliable moral judge. For example, suppose that I am making a judgment about the permissibility of the bombing of a city during a war. If I mistakenly believe that only combatants will be killed, when in fact thousands of civilians will be killed, then I am not in a position to make a reliable judgment about this case.[1] Ideal moral judges must be *vividly aware* of relevant information. Among other things, an ideal moral judge must have a vivid understanding of the experiences of other people. If an action causes someone to experience certain kinds of feelings, then knowing what it is like to experience those feelings is relevant to assessing the morality of that action. Lack of empathy often constitutes ignorance about relevant matters. For example, if I do not know (in vivid and excruciating detail) what it feels like to be burned to death, then I lack crucial knowledge relevant to assessing the morality of firebombing a city during a war.

6.I.3. Proper Cognitive Functioning

Being an ideal moral judge requires proper cognitive functioning concerning relevant matters. Moral judges must be capable of making correct inferences and avoiding fallacious inferences in moral arguments. They must also be able to understand and appreciate the logical implications of all the moral principles that they accept or consider. For example, a person who says that any substance that is both addictive and harmful to people's health should be illegal must realize that this implies not only that narcotics should be illegal but that tobacco, alcohol, and potato chips should also be illegal. Ideal moral judges would be free of logical and conceptual confusions and would not make incorrect inferences. Here are examples of the kinds of confusions I have in mind. Sometimes, people mistakenly assume that because an action is morally wrong the law should prohibit it. Many people are confused about the distinction between an actual duty and a *prima facie* duty. (I could add many other examples.) My aim here is to underscore the extent to which many of the moral judgments people actually endorse depend on cognitive failings and errors. These considerations make it easier for us to claim that one or more of the parties to an apparently intractable moral dispute is mistaken and, thus, make it easier to show that there are any objectively correct answers to some disputed moral questions.

6.II. THE GOLDEN RULE

6.II.1. Proofs of the Golden Rule

Here is a "proof" of a version of the golden rule:

1. Consistency requires that I judge acts done to me or to people I love in the same way that I judge acts done to others, unless the acts differ in some morally relevant respect.
2. Our attitudes must be consistent with our moral judgments. Among other things, this means that if I think that it is morally permissible for someone to do something to me (or someone I love), then I must not object to her doing it to me (or someone I love).

Therefore:

GR. Consistency requires that if I think it would be morally permissible for someone to do a certain act to another person, then I must not object to someone doing the same act to me (or someone I love) in relevantly similar circumstances. [I am inconsistent if I think that it would be morally permissible for someone to do something to another person but object to someone doing the same act to me or someone I love in relevantly similar circumstances.][2]

Here is a proof of another version of the golden rule:

1a. If I am consistent and think that, on balance, it is morally wrong for person (S) to do act X, then I will think that, on balance, it would be wrong for me to do X in relevantly similar circumstances.

2a. If I think that (on balance) it is morally wrong for me to do X, and I am able to refrain from doing X, then I am inconsistent if I do X.

Therefore,

GRa. Consistency requires that if I think that it is morally wrong for someone to do X and I am able to refrain from doing X, then I must refrain from doing X if I find myself in relevantly similar circumstances. [I am inconsistent if I think that it would be morally wrong for someone to do X, but still do X in (what I recognize are) relevantly similar circumstances when I am able to refrain from doing X.][3]

These two arguments are valid; if we accept the premises, we must accept the conclusions. The premises are consistency requirements. Premises 1 and 1a address the consistency of a person's different moral beliefs. Premises 2 and 2a address the consistency of a person's moral beliefs and her attitudes and actions.

6.II.2. Defense of Premises 1, 1a, 1b, and 1c.

Premises 1, 1a, 1b, and 1c (for 1b and 1c see endnote 3) are narrower versions of the universalizability principle (UP) and follow from the UP. The UP can be stated as follows:

UP. If one makes a moral judgment about a particular case, then one must make the same moral judgment about any similar case, unless there is a morally relevant difference between the cases. (Cf. Gensler, 1996, p. 70, 1998, p. 205; also see Sidgwick, 1966, pp. 209, 380.)

Universalizability *is* a feature of our conventional moral concepts. When using conventional moral concepts, any moral judgment we make commits us to making the same judgment about relevantly similar cases. Statements of the following sort are self-contradictory:

Act A is morally permissible. Act B is exactly like A in all morally relevant respects, however, B is not morally permissible.

Granting this, one still might object that conventional moral concepts should be dropped in favor of alternative normative concepts that do not have the feature of universalizability (cf. Blackburn, 1984, pp. 220–221; Hare, 1997, pp. 99, 101, 124, 134). I have two replies to this objection.

First, there is a strong presumption in favor of wielding conventional normative concepts rather than alternative concepts. Doing so enables us to discuss and debate normative questions with others; it also enables us to benefit from the insights of our philosophical and religious traditions. Adopting alternative concepts of right and wrong and good and bad would put us in the position of having to continually reinvent the wheel and continually explain our concepts to others. Most of our acquaintances are simply not willing to wield alternative normative concepts. We want to use our normative concepts to offer and receive criticism of each other's actions and to try to justify our actions to each other. This requires that we use the same concepts as other people. If I employ an idiosyncratic notion of right and wrong and try to show that an action I performed was morally right in that idiosyncratic sense of "right," other people will not take this to be a serious justification of my action.

Second, it is doubtful that alternative normative concepts that lack the feature of universalizability could serve the purposes we want our normative concepts to serve, even if we could persuade our interlocutors to employ them. We are interested in questions about what others ought to do (largely) because we take those questions to have implications for what we ought to do in relevantly similar situations. We also take questions about what fictional characters should do to be relevant to questions about what we should do. Without universalizability, moral discourse would lose much of its point and many people would become almost completely indifferent to moral questions about what others should or should not do.

A person could dispense with conventional normative concepts, but doing so has a high cost.

6.II.3. Defense of Premises 2, 2a, 2b, and 2c

(For 2b and 2c see endnote 3.) Premises 2 and 2b say that my attitudes must be consistent with the moral judgments I make; if I say that it is morally permissible for you to do something, I must not object to your doing it. My thinking that it is morally permissible for you to beat me at chess does not commit me to desiring that you beat me, or to playing so as to allow you to beat me. However, it commits me to refraining from objecting to your beating me (cf. Gensler, 1996, pp. 63–64). Of course, it is consistent to object to actions that one takes to be morally permissible because they are rude, imprudent, uncool, or produce something ugly. However, one cannot consistently *resent* or feel aggrieved by an action that one takes to be morally permissible, nor can one consistently hold that others should feel guilty for doing something that one takes to be morally permissible. Certain characteristic ways of objecting to what others do to us (the strongest ways of objecting) are inconsistent with judging that the act in question is permissible. (For reasons why we should care about making our moral judgments consistent with our attitudes and actions, see Section 6.VI.)

Premises 2a and 2c are true because moral judgments about what is morally right and wrong, all things considered, are "overriding." To say that moral judgments are overriding means that a person who makes moral judgments thinks that the prescriptions expressed by them ought to be followed even if they conflict with other sorts of prescriptions; for example, conflicts between morality and considerations of prudence, etiquette, and the law. To assert that S's doing X is morally wrong *all-things-considered* (as opposed to *prima facie* wrong) is to prescribe that S not do X and hold that the wrongness of S's doing X overrides all other countervailing considerations and reasons.[4] Statements of the form "it would be morally wrong all-things-considered for you to do X, but still you would be justified in doing X," and "your doing X would be morally wrong, all-things-considered, but the balance of reasons favors your doing X" are self-contradictory. Moral judgments would not be action-guiding in the way we take them to be unless they were overriding. Questions about what is morally right and wrong are practical questions about what we should do, on balance.

Moral duties are, by definition, "higher duties." The common use of the term "higher law" to refer to moral duties is very revealing and strongly supports the view that moral duties are, by definition, overriding. If moral duties were not overriding, then moral judgments would not even purport to give definitive answers to practical questions about what to do, and, of course, all-things-considered moral judgments *do* purport to give definitive answers to such questions. By contrast, *prima facie* moral duties are overridible.

To accept the moral judgment that it is morally obligatory/wrong on balance for one to do X is to believe that one has overriding reasons to do/not do X. Often, people are not strongly motivated to do what they believe is morally obligatory (on balance) or refrain from doing what they believe is morally wrong (on balance). Being motivated to follow one's (on balance) moral judgments is not a necessary condition of one's sincerely accepting them. On this point, I differ sharply with Hare. Hare rejects the possibility of moral weakness. Suppose that I claim to believe that, on balance, I ought to do X; I also know that I am able to do X. According to Hare, if I don't do X, this shows that I don't really believe that I ought to do it.[5] My argument for 2a and 2c does not commit me to endorsing Hare's view. I only claim that people who fail to do what they believe they ought to do (when they are able to do it) are *inconsistent*—their actions are inconsistent with their moral beliefs.

Suppose that someone rejects the overridingness of moral judgments and makes non-overriding normative judgments about the rightness or wrongness of actions. Let us call this person's normative system "shmorality."[6] It is misleading to use conventional moral language to state shmoral judgments. To avoid confusion and misunderstanding, the proponent of shmorality must coin different normative terms. If the proponent of shmorality insists on using conventional moral terms, then she uses what Charles Stevenson calls "persuasive definitions." She wants her shmoral judgments to have the aura of importance that moral judgments have, but this aura of importance rests on a confusion, since shmoral judgments have been emptied of the crucial feature that gives moral judgments their (overriding) weight and importance. This is similar to what an atheist does if he continues to use theological language to gain the sort of comfort that people who really believe in God obtain from their (genuine) religious beliefs.[7] We have no good reasons to give up morality for shmorality. Suppose someone tells me that I am doing something that is shmorally wrong. It makes perfect sense for me to ask "why should I care if what I am doing is shmorally wrong?" Shmorality does not even try to answer our practical questions about what we should do and care about (on balance).

6.III. THE FORCE OF GOLDEN RULE ARGUMENTS

According to GR, if I claim that it is permissible for someone to do something to another person, then, on pain of inconsistency, I cannot object if someone else does the same thing to me (or someone I love) in relevantly similar circumstances. (I use the term "object" as shorthand for "morally object," which involves resenting others and thinking that they should feel guilty.) The force of this version of the golden rule derives from the fact that since we *do object* to other people doing certain things to us or our loved ones (we resent their actions and think that they should feel guilty on account of them), we cannot consistently say that it would be morally permissible for us to do these same things to them in relevantly similar circumstances. Because of our concern for others, there are actions we object to being done to them. We are inconsistent if we claim that it is permissible for anyone to perform these same actions to others in relevantly similar circumstances.

Suppose that I judge that it would be morally right for me to do X, but object when someone else does X to me in relevantly similar circumstances. My judgment about this case is inconsistent with my attitudes about relevantly similar cases. To be consistent, I must either (1) change my moral judgments, or (2) change my attitudes about the action in question.

An Example

I am a plumber and often lie to my customers—I claim that they need expensive repairs when they do not. I claim that it is morally right for me to do this. Yet, I object very strongly when I discover that my auto mechanic lies to me and claims that I need a $2000 engine overhaul when, in fact, I only need a $200 tune-up. On the face of it, there is no morally relevant difference between what I do and what my mechanic does. To be consistent, I must either (1) change my moral judgment about my own lying and say that it is wrong for me to lie to my customers, or (2) change my *judgment and attitudes* about what the mechanic does to me, and hold that his lying to me about my engine is morally permissible and no longer resent it or object to it. (Note that the first option, changing my judgment about the moral permissibility of lying to my customers, imposes other consistency demands on me. If I judge that it is wrong for me to lie to my customers, then I am inconsistent if I continue to lie to them (my lying to my customers is inconsistent with the belief that it is wrong for me to lie to them).)

Here, we surely want to say that (1), *not* (2), is the appropriate response. However, (2) is equally consistent. The real force and power of golden rule arguments consist in the fact that often responses of type (2) are not a serious option. We object to some things being done to us because of our concern for our own welfare. The present example is such a case. Because most of us *do object* to being lied to and harmed in this way because of our concern for our own interests, we cannot consistently hold that it is morally right for anyone to tell such lies. Our concern for the welfare of others also lends force to consistency arguments. I object to your defrauding my mother, and, therefore, I cannot claim that it is permissible for anyone to perform relevantly similar actions.

6.IV. OBJECTIONS TO THE GOLDEN RULE

6.IV.1. When are Differences Morally Relevant?

People often disagree about whether or not certain differences are morally relevant. For example, people disagree about the moral relevance of the difference between killing people and allowing people to die and the relevance of the difference between abortion and infanticide. Some conclude that the UP and golden rule are useless as principles of moral reasoning because any application of the UP or the golden rule presupposes controversial claims about what sorts of differences are and are not morally relevant. In turn, claims about which differences are and are not morally relevant presuppose answers to disputed moral questions. No two actual cases are ever exactly alike, and it is always debatable whether the differences between them are morally relevant.

This objection does not succeed. We can effectively use the UP and GR in moral arguments without making any *controversial* or problematic assumptions about which differences are morally relevant and which are not. The only assumption we need to make is that one's own personal place in the universe is not morally relevant, e.g., it is not a morally relevant fact about the universe that *I* am Tom Carson instead of someone else. If two cases differ only in that two individual people reverse their positions and all of the universal properties remain the same, then there is no morally relevant difference between them.[8]

Two actual cases never, or almost never, have exactly the same universal properties. However, thought experiments about *hypothetical cases* in which people switch places are cases in which different actions have exactly the same universal properties. This gives us a way to determine which differences are and are not morally relevant. Dubious claims to the effect that certain differences are or are not morally relevant can be tested and refuted by these kinds of thought experiments. For example, suppose that I say that the fact that my father was born in Ohio and yours was not makes it permissible for me to defraud you in our business dealings, but impermissible for you to defraud me. I cannot consistently endorse this view, because it commits me to saying that it would be permissible for you to defraud me and impermissible for me to defraud you if our positions were reversed. It also commits me to saying that it would be permissible for anyone whose father was born in Ohio to defraud my friends and family members whose fathers were not born in Ohio. (For a more detailed discussion of cases of special pleading and dubious claims about morally relevant differences, see Chapter 8.I.2—"An Objection.")

For any moral judgment involving two people, we can imagine a *hypothetical* case *exactly* like it, except that the positions or personal identities of the two individuals are reversed. For any case in which I claim that it is morally right for me to do something to you, we can ask if I think that it would be right for you to do the same thing to me were our positions reversed. For example, suppose that I am a white slave owner in the *ante bellum* American south. I claim that it is morally permissible for me to own my black slave, Robert. This commits me to the view that it would be permissible for Robert to own me as a slave if our positions were reversed (cf. Hare, 1963, pp. 106–107; 1981, pp. 62–64).

My theory does not provide a surefire way to distinguish between relevant and nonrelevant differences in difficult controversial cases, such as abortion and infanticide, but it does enable us to determine the moral relevance of differences in many cases.

6.IV.2. Masochists and People with Unusual Preferences

A standard objection to the golden rule is that it permits people with unusual preferences to perform wrong actions. For example, the golden rule permits, or perhaps even requires, masochists to inflict pain on non-masochists because masochists would like others to inflict pain on them. This objection takes the golden rule to be roughly equivalent to the following: do unto others, as you (with your present desires) would want others to do to you. However, a masochist who inflicts pain on non-masochists violates GR because he objects to this being done to him *in relevantly similar circumstances*. Relevantly similar circumstances would be circumstances in which he is a non-masochist who finds having pain inflicted on him very distressing and objects to others inflicting pain on him. (The people the masochist is causing pain are non-masochists who object to having pain inflicted on them.) A masochist who adequately imagines the position of non-masochists having pain inflicted on them against their will will object to having pain inflicted on him in cases in which he is not a consenting masochist (see Gensler, 1996, p. 99; 1998, pp. 110–12).

The foregoing argument works for "garden variety masochists" who desire pain as a means to pleasure and, in some sense, enjoy pain. It might be objected that there are other sorts of masochists who neither enjoy pain nor desire pain as a means to pleasure. Consider the following case. Person A desires to suffer pain because he wants to punish himself and believes that he deserves to suffer; he inflicts similar pain on others he judges to be equally deserving of suffering. Person A can honestly say that he does not object to other people inflicting severe pain on him (and he thinks that it would be permissible for others to do this to him). Person A thinks that others should inflict severe pain on him because he deserves to suffer. If he can rationally and consistently hold this view, then he can also rationally and consistently hold that it would be permissible for him to inflict severe pain on other people who deserve it. Can rational, informed, and consistent moral judges hold such views? The answer is that it depends on whether all of the following are true: (1) certain people deserve to suffer pain; (2) some people can accurately ascertain the fact that others deserve to suffer pain with sufficient certainty to be justified in inflicting pain on them through extra-judicial means; (3) there is no reliable mechanism, such as a principle of Karma or the existence of a just God, that ensures that people suffer their just deserts; and (4) there is no compelling reason independent of 1–3 for people to refrain from giving others their just deserts. Note that Christians are committed to rejecting 4. They hold that, in some sense, people deserve to suffer or be punished but God forgives us anyway and wants us to show this same gratuitous grace to our fellows—"forgive us our trespasses as we forgive those who trespass against us." I do not think that 1–4 are all true. However, if 1–4 were all true, then person A's view would be reasonable. Either way, this case does not seem to constitute an objection to GR-GRc. (Either my view does not commit me to saying that person A's views are rational and consistent, or else my view commits me to saying this, but 1, 2, 3, and 4 are all true, and the truth of 1–4 provides independent reasons for thinking that A's views are defensible.)

I have not considered all possible types of masochism. Thus, for all that I have shown here, certain kinds of masochists could be rational and consistent in holding that it is permissible for them to inflict severe pain on others against their will, independently of the truth of 1–4. However, even if we grant this, it is clearly rational and consistent for me and many/most other people to claim that the actions in question are morally wrong. Rational and consistent moral judges can reject the masochist's view that it is permissible for him to inflict severe pain on others. Thus, my view does not commit us to the view that the masochist's moral judgments are objectively true (correct). At worst, my view fails to provide an objective justification for the view that we *want* to hold about this matter. This does not detract from the fact that my theory successfully justifies many other moral judgments.

6.IV.3. Punishing People and Doing Things that they Do Not Want One to Do

The golden rule is sometimes taken to mean that I must do to others what I would *want* done to me were I in their position with their desires. On this interpretation, judges or jurors who punish a murderer who is not willing to be punished violate the golden rule, because if they were in the murderer's place with the murderer's desires they would not be willing to be punished. Kant raises this as an objection to the golden rule.[9] My GR avoids this result. We are not willing to have society make it a policy that murder goes unpunished. Because we recognize the consistency demands of the UP, many of us (who are consistent) do not object to it being the case that the rules for punishing murderers are invoked against us and our loved ones if we commit murder (see Gensler, 1996, p. 98; 1998, pp. 108–109). Criminals and murderers who claim that it is wrong for others to punish them for their crimes are inconsistent. They desire security for their own property and persons and are not willing to have it be the case that those who commit crimes against *them* should go unpunished.

Granted that murderers who object to being punished for their crimes are inconsistent, and granted that many of us are consistent in claiming that we should be punished if we commit murder, aren't I still doing something that I would not want done to me were I in the murderer's position, and thus violating GR, if I vote to convict and punish the murderer? This objection assumes that GR commits us to the following:

A. If I claim that someone's doing act X to person S is morally permissible, then, on pain of inconsistency, it must be the case that I would not object to someone doing X to me were I in S's position with S's desires.

However, GR does not imply A; it only implies the following:

B. If I claim that someone's doing act X to person S is morally permissible, then, on pain of inconsistency, I must *now* not object to someone's doing X to me in a relevantly similar situation (among other things, I must now not object to someone's doing X to me in the hypothetical situation in which S and I switch places and I have all of S's properties).[10]

The difference between A and B depends on the difference between: (1) *the preferences I would have in a hypothetical situation* in which I switch places with another person and actually *have* his preferences and aversions, and (2) my *present preferences for a hypothetical situation* in which I switch places with another person and acquire his wants and aversions. Suppose that I take a mind-altering drug that causes me to become so severely depressed that I want to kill myself. I *now* prefer that if I were to take such a drug and become suicidal, others should forcibly intervene to prevent me from taking my own life. However, if I were determined to commit suicide, I would strongly prefer that others not try to stop me and would strongly object to their doing so. B (but not A) is consistent with the view that it would be permissible for others to intervene to stop me from killing myself in such a case.

Also contrast the differences between A and B in cases in which someone tries to act on immoral desires. Suppose that a Hutu member of the Interahamwe wants to murder his Tutsi neighbors. According to A, you cannot consistently hold that it would be right for you to use force to stop him from killing his neighbors, because if you were in his position and had the motivations of a fanatical member of the Interahamwe, then you would object to being forcibly restrained from killing. B, however, allows for the possibility that you could be consistent in holding that it would be morally right for you to stop him from killing his neighbors. You might (now) be willing to be coerced should you acquire and try to act on immoral desires. B gives intuitively more plausible results than A for these cases and a wide range of other cases.

6.IV.4. People Who are Depressed and Do Not Care What Happens to them

Our regard for our own interests and our unwillingness to be harmed and abused by others does much of the work in golden rule arguments. Because there are certain things I object to being done to me, I cannot claim that it is permissible for me or others to perform relevantly similar actions. Our concern for the welfare of loved ones also lends force to golden rule arguments. As there are certain things I object to being done to my loved ones, I cannot claim that it is permissible for me or others to perform relevantly similar actions. Suppose, however, that someone is depressed and indifferent to what happens to him and his loved ones; he is willing to have anything be done to him and those he loves. Such a person could do *anything* without violating GR. For anything he does to another person, he does not object to it being done to him and his loved ones.

This is a very serious problem. What can be said by way of reply? First, we should note that even clinical depression seldom involves complete indifference to what happens to oneself and one's loved ones. Depression usually involves being liable to be distressed by misfortunes that befall oneself and one's loved ones. (Wallowing in distress about such matters is characteristic of depression.) The great majority of depressed persons would be saddened by personal misfortunes such as the loss of a job and the misfortunes of loved ones such as the death or injury of a child or spouse. Such people are not sufficiently depressed for this objection to arise in their case.

A person so profoundly depressed that she is *completely indifferent* to what happens to her and her loved ones would be nearly catatonic. Imagine this kind of case more concretely. The person in question is utterly lacking in self-concern and concern for her loved ones. She is totally apathetic. Not only is she dispirited about her present state, she does not prefer that her depression lift nor does she wish that she had not become depressed. She is completely indifferent to what happens to her. In her depressed state there is no act that she objects to be being done to her, her loved ones, or anyone else. Thus, she can do anything to another person without violating GR-GRc. However, such a person fails *other rationality conditions* for moral judgments. Her depression is incompatible with her being able to vividly imagine the joys of life or correctly judge the probable consequences of actions or the significance of events. (A person so depressed that she is indifferent to her own child being tortured cannot imagine vividly the suffering of others.) Profound depression and the lassitude that characterizes it result in a general diminishment of cognitive powers of reasoning and imagination.

6.V. APPLICATIONS: RATIONAL CONSISTENT MORAL JUDGES WILL ALL AGREE IN THEIR JUDGMENTS ABOUT CERTAIN ISSUES

6.V.1. Nazis

Suppose that a Nazi claims that it is morally permissible for him to help bring about the extermination of the Jewish people. In order to be consistent, the Nazi must say that it would be permissible for others to kill him, his friends, and his family if they are Jewish. He must not object to his being killed (and his friends and family being killed) if it can be established that they are of Jewish ancestry.[11]

It is possible to be a consistent Nazi. One might so hate Jews that one does not object to being killed if one is Jewish (or object to one's friends and loved ones being killed if they are Jewish). The obvious question to ask here is whether such hatred is rational, and it seems that it is not. Such hatred depends on numerous false beliefs about the characteristics of Jews and their responsibility for the ills of the world. Only someone who had false beliefs and/or irrational attitudes about Jews could be a consistent Nazi. A Nazi could be consistent, but a Nazi could not be *both* consistent and adequately informed about matters relevant to her moral convictions.

Not only do Nazis have false beliefs about the moral depravity of Jews, they do not have an adequate understanding of the feelings and sufferings of the people they victimize, e.g., being vividly aware of what it is like to be forcibly separated from one's family or to see one's children led off to the gas chambers. Nazis fail to comprehend the humanity of their victims, i.e., the fact that their victims have just the same kinds of loves, hates, hopes, and fears that other human beings have. (On this point, see Glover, 1999.) In order to be fully informed, a Nazi would have to reflect vividly on the extent of the suffering prevented by the invention of polio vaccine by the Jewish doctor, Jonas Salk (the Nazi would also have to reflect on the likelihood that s/he or people s/he cares about would have suffered polio were it not for the invention of the vaccine). In order to be adequately informed Nazis would need to be vividly aware of the fact that many Jews have attributes, abilities, and character traits that they greatly admire in non-Jews.

The relevance of empathy and understanding the experiences of other people for moral issues is also illustrated by the debate about American slavery. Few, if any, defenders of American style slavery were vividly aware of the fact that many African slaves had attributes, abilities, and character traits that they greatly admired in other people. Defenders of slavery also lacked knowledge and vivid awareness of the fact that slaves' feelings about their children and family were much like their own and that the slaves were grieved as much by forced separation of their families as the slave owners would have been if they were forcibly separated from their families. Their failure to appreciate this stemmed from obtuseness and lack of empathy. This is wonderfully illustrated in the following dialogue from Harriet Beecher Stowe's *Uncle Tom's Cabin*:

A. "The most dreadful part of slavery to my mind, is its outrages on the feelings and affections—the separating of families, for example."

B. "That is a bad thing certainly," said the other lady . . . ; "but then, I fancy, it don't occur often."

A. "O, it does," said the first lady, eagerly; "I've lived many years in Kentucky and Virginia both, and I've seen enough to make any one's heart sick. Suppose, ma'am your two children, there, should be taken from you, and sold?"

B. "We can't reason from our feelings to those of another class of persons," said the other lady.

Stowe (1965, p. 125; Gensler, 1996, pp. 164–165 cites this passage)

6.V.2. Fraud

It is wrong for professionals who have no urgent financial needs to deceive and defraud clients in ways that cause great harm to their clients in order to enrich themselves. Suppose that I am the wealthy owner of an auto repair shop. I routinely lie to my customers to inflate their bills. One day a customer, Sue, brings her car to me. I quickly diagnose the problem; I lie and say that she needs a $2000 engine overhaul, when all that she needs is a simple adjustment that normally costs $100. (I know that she is a single mother of three who has many creditors and is in danger of becoming homeless.) She indicates that she will need to borrow the money from a loan shark to pay the bill and asks me if there is a cheaper way to fix the car. I harden my heart to her plight, and lie and say "no."

Most people who do this sort of thing are clearly inconsistent; they object bitterly to other professionals lying to them to make more money. I would strongly object if I were to learn that my plumber overcharged me or my elderly parents by $2000. Therefore, I cannot honestly say that I do not object to this being done to me, and I cannot consistently say that it would be morally right for anyone to do this. However, the question is whether it is *possible* for a reasonable and consistent person to claim that fraud of this sort is morally permissible. Suppose that I see my inconsistency and try to be consistent by no longer judging it to be wrong (and no longer objecting) when other professionals lie to their customers for the sake of gains less than $10 000. For the sake of consistency, I no longer object to being the victim of small-scale fraud but still object to being the victim of large-scale fraud that would cost me my retirement savings or my home. I have not succeeded in becoming consistent by modifying my judgments and attitudes in this way. I object to fraud that would harm me to the extent that my fraud harms Sue. I am also inconsistent in that I have a number of relatively poor friends and relatives who I care about. I object to their being defrauded (of sums less than $10 000) if that would put them in danger of becoming homeless. Unless I lack even minimal concern for my own welfare and the welfare of others, I cannot consistently hold that it is morally permissible for me to lie to Sue in this case.

In this case, the victim of the deception and fraud is poor, and the perpetrator is well-to-do. This feature of the case makes it easier to show that lying and deception are wrong because the harm they cause in this case is much greater than the harm that similar lying and deception would cause an affluent person. Further, since the perpetrator is rich, the benefit produced by the lying and deception is much less than it would be if the perpetrator were poor. The extent to which lying and deception harm others is relevant to their moral assessment. There is nothing absurd or counterintuitive about this result. I am using this case to show that my theory gives clear answers to certain moral questions. For a discussion of more difficult cases in which the perpetrators of fraud and deception have pressing financial needs, see 8.II.1, 9.I.2, and 9.III.2.

6.V.3. Another Case of Fraud

I am a heart surgeon and earn a great deal of money. To increase my income, I regularly perform unneeded surgery on patients. A 56-year-old man named Ray comes to me complaining of chest pains. It is clear that he has no serious problems that warrant surgery. However, I tell Ray that he needs open heart surgery to replace a defective heart valve. I tell him that he needs the surgery immediately and that he has only a 20% chance of surviving the next two months without the surgery. In fact, I know the following:

1. Ray has a 10% chance of dying during the surgery or shortly after.
2. The surgery will shorten his life expectancy by about ten years.
3. He has a 40% chance of suffering a debilitating stroke during the next ten years as a result of his surgery.

4. Even if the surgery turns out as well as possible, their knowledge of the risks of the valve replacement surgery will cause Ray and his wife great anxiety for the rest of Ray's life.
5. The surgery will cost Ray's insurance company $250 000 and cost Ray $30 000 out of pocket.
6. I will earn $20 000 for performing the surgery.
7. I will not lose a minute of sleep by feeling guilt or compunction for what I do to Ray.

Surely no one with even minimal concern for her own welfare or the welfare of those to whom she is attached could fail to object to this being done to her or to people to whom she is attached in relevantly similar circumstances. We *do object* to being grievously harmed by dishonesty and fraud for the sake of such relatively trivial benefits for others. We *do object* when those we care about are grievously harmed by deception and fraud to enrich others.

6.V.4. Ethical Egoism

An important test of the implications of my theory for first-order moral questions is whether an ethical egoist can satisfy the demands of GR-GRc and the other rationality principles I have defended here. Ethical egoism is the view that each person should always act to promote his/her own self-interest. Can a person consistently endorse ethical egoism? No doubt, some people are sincere when they say that they are willing to have others always act in their own self-interest. They say this without lying. However, they could not say this on reflection if they considered all of the implications of egoism and vividly imagined all of the sorts of actions that ethical egoism permits and requires. Ethical egoists would say that one never has an obligation to help others unless doing so benefits oneself. Ethical egoism implies that we are not obligated to make very small sacrifices to help others, even if the benefits to them would be enormous. Those comfortably positioned might say that they are willing to pay for the help they need from others and never have others sacrifice themselves to help them. This line of thought is consistent as far as it goes, but the egoist overlooks the fact that, however wealthy s/he might be, s/he might need the benevolence of strangers in emergencies. Suppose that a person is stranded on the highway without large amounts of cash during a hurricane evacuation and is in need of shelter and assistance. We can easily imagine cases in which a consistent ethical egoist must refuse to render life-saving assistance to a stranger in an emergency because doing so would result in a small loss of welfare. An egoist cannot honestly say that s/he does not object to others failing to help her/him and her/his loved ones in such cases.

Even more problematically, ethical egoism allows people to cause great harm to others for the sake of relatively trivial benefits for themselves. If defrauding you and leaving you destitute, or killing you, or slandering you so as to destroy your reputation and livelihood would be in my self-interest (we can easily imagine cases in which such actions would be in my self-interest), then, according to ethical egoism, I ought to defraud you, slander you, or kill you. The case of medical fraud described above is such a case (or *could be* such a case, given appropriate stipulations). Here are two other examples that illustrate this point. Suppose that a very wealthy person is guilty of serious mistakes that make her liable to lose a bonus of several thousand dollars, but she can avoid losing the bonus by telling plausible lies to the effect that you are guilty of fraud. If she tells these lies your career will be ruined and there is almost no chance that she will be caught in her lie. If you are an ethical egoist, you must say that she ought to do this. It might be in a criminal's self-interest to murder your mother in order to prevent her from testifying against him in court and sending him to prison. If you are an egoist, you must say that the criminal ought to murder your mother. We cannot honestly say that we do not object to these things being done to us or our loved ones.

6.VI. WHY BE CONSISTENT?

One might respond by saying "Granted that consistency requires that I accept the golden-rule, I don't care because I don't see any reason why I should be consistent." This is a serious question. It is really two distinct questions:

1. Why care whether or not the moral judgments one makes are consistent?
2. Why care about whether or not one's actions and attitudes are consistent with the moral judgments one makes?

Question 1

Consistency in one's beliefs or judgments is a minimal condition of rationality. Requirements of consistency are presupposed in all discussions and debates. Agreeing or disagreeing with someone presupposes the principle of non-contradiction. To see this, imagine the following exchange (cf. Gensler, 1996, pp. 30–31, 36–37):

I say, "Lying is always wrong no matter what."

You say, "No, lying is not wrong if it saves someone from being killed."

I reply, "We agree, lying is not wrong if it saves someone from being killed, and lying is always wrong no matter what."

Holding inconsistent normative judgments is likely to impede us in the pursuit of our goals and cause us to be inefficient in finding the best means to our ends. Suppose that I accept two inconsistent normative principles, P1 and P2. P1 implies that I ought to bring about X and P2 entails that I ought to bring about not-X. If I am unaware of the conflict between P1 and P2, then I am likely to try to follow both principles and waste my efforts doing things that tend to both bring about X and prevent X. When we become aware of the inconsistencies in our normative views, we generally want to modify them to avoid acting at cross purposes and wasting our efforts. Suppose that I become aware of the conflict between P1 and P2. On reflection, I discover that I strongly prefer X to not-X, and strongly prefer that I bring about X to my not bringing it about. On reflection, I will probably want to modify my normative views in some way to make them consistent; I will want to modify P2 so that it no longer implies that I ought to bring about not-X in preference to X.

Universalizability is a feature of *our* shared moral language. When we use the concepts of good and bad and right and wrong, we are making universalizable moral judgments. If I say that something is good (bad), I am saying that anything like it in relevant respects is also good (bad). Those who reject universalizability must stop using the fundamental moral/normative concepts of our language (good and bad and right and wrong). As I argued earlier (6.II.2), there is a great cost involved in giving up these concepts.

Question 2

Why care if our attitudes and actions are inconsistent with our moral judgments and our value judgments? Imagine vividly and concretely what it would be like to be inconsistent in this way. When we fill in the details, this does not seem attractive at all. Suppose that someone:

1. dislikes and shuns things that he thinks are good and good for him (for example, he prefers and chooses what he judges to be a bad job to what he judges to be a good job; and he chooses to marry someone he judges would be a very bad wife who would make his life miserable in preference to someone he believes would be a good wife who would make him very happy);
2. likes and desires things that he believes are bad or bad for him;
3. hates and despises other people he thinks are good and loves and admires other people he thinks are evil;
4. feels proud for doing what he thinks is morally wrong; and
5. feels guilty for doing what he thinks is morally right.

We are describing a kind of schizophrenia or split personality. One of the things that makes this kind of inconsistency so problematic is that moral standards and standards of value are norms for how we should act and feel and for what things we should desire. To say that something is good *means* (or at least implies) that it is worthy of desire (see Carson, 2000, chapter 6). Therefore, the person who shuns and dislikes something she judges to be good shuns and dislikes something she thinks is worthy of desire (something she thinks that she should desire and should pursue). To accept a moral judgment upon due reflection is to endorse reflectively the attitudes and actions that are consistent with it and to reject reflectively those attitudes and actions that are inconsistent with it. To be inconsistent in this way is to have many attitudes and perform many actions that one does not reflectively endorse.

Given the precarious nature of human life and human fortunes, losing normative control of one's behavior only briefly can be disastrous. If I *totally ignore* normative considerations and do not make any attempt to govern my attitudes and actions by the normative judgments that I endorse for even a brief period of time, the consequences are likely to be disastrous (for example, if I act contrary to my judgment that it would be a bad idea for me to follow my impulse to jump off a tall building or my impulse to wager my life savings at a gambling casino). On reflection, no rational person would want to completely lose normative control of her actions even briefly.

When we vividly and concretely imagine what it would be like to be the sort of person who is not concerned about being consistent, it seems quite unattractive. There are good reasons to want to be consistent.

An Objection

Granted that, on reflection, every reasonable person will want her attitudes and actions to be consistent with her well-considered normative judgments about what is good and bad *for her*, why should one care if one's *moral judgments* about right and wrong are inconsistent with one's attitudes and actions? We need norms for the good life and we need to take them seriously, but why do we need *moral norms* and why do we need to conform our actions and attitudes in accordance with them?

Suppose that someone accepts moral judgments about what it is morally right or wrong for her to do, on balance, but asks why she should care about making her attitudes and actions consistent with them. The question, I contend, is illegitimate. The question "Why should I do X?" asks for reasons for me to do X. If I ask "why should I care about whether I do X?" I am asking for reasons for me to care about my doing X. If I grant that I have overriding reasons to do X, then I must grant that I have adequate reasons to care about my doing X. If I have overriding reasons to do something, then I have reasons to want my motivations to respond appropriately to those reasons. Therefore, if I grant that I have overriding reasons to do something, then it does not make sense for me to ask why I should care about my doing it.

Some people only pay lip service to the idea that moral considerations are overriding. They use conventional moral language but do not take moral judgments to be overriding. Others selectively refuse to treat *certain* moral judgments (judgments that require them or others to sacrifice themselves) as overriding.

A person whose attitudes and actions are inconsistent with her moral judgments has attitudes and performs actions that she does not reflectively endorse. A person who endorses this kind of inconsistency endorses the policy of doing things and having attitudes that she does not reflectively endorse. That is quite bizarre.

6.VII. MORAL NIHILISM/AMORALISM (OPTING OUT OF MORAL DISCOURSE)

6.VII.1. Consistency Arguments Only Apply to People Who Make Moral Judgments

A limitation of my consistency arguments is that they apply only to people who make moral judgments. Hare also acknowledges that his consistency arguments have no force against those who completely refrain from making moral judgments. So now, we have the question. "Why shouldn't we opt out of morality?" For reasons given above, the option of rejecting normative standards altogether is quite unattractive. However, there is still the question of why we should employ moral norms. Why shouldn't we operate only with non-moral norms for welfare and prudence and/or something like the code of honor of a warrior society? Amoralists and moral nihilists are invulnerable to consistency arguments. Can I offer any kind of argument against moral nihilism?

6.VII.2. Reasons to Accept Morality

For reasons of prudence, most of us need to give the appearance of making moral judgments and taking them seriously. We are all in the position of commenting on the actions of others and justifying our actions to them. All of us need to confide in others and seek their advice. Similarly, others confide in us and seek our advice. Prudence requires that when nihilists speak with others in these circumstances, they use moral discourse, pretend to make moral judgments, and pretend to take them seriously. This involves a systematic attempt to deceive others on several levels, and the costs of being vigilant in this deception are high. To bring off this deception successfully, we must feign beliefs and attitudes that we do not have. We can easily betray ourselves in actions, expressions of feeling, and slips of tongue that reveal our motives. We need to monitor carefully our own emotional expressions, which rob life of spontaneity and joy.[12] In addition, actually accepting and being moved by moral considerations often saves us from committing moral violations and getting caught in them in ways that would be disastrous for our own welfare. We tend to underestimate the difficulty of concealing moral violations from others and overestimate the benefits we derive from moral violations, e.g., wealth, worldly success, and status. A parent who was solely concerned with promoting the welfare of his child would want the child to be moral and accept moral beliefs (cf. R. M. Hare, 1981, pp. 190–196).

Even if one accepts the foregoing argument, it will leave many readers very uncomfortable. My argument makes our reasons to be moral contingent on the fact that most other people accept moral norms, enforce them, and take them seriously. On this understanding, our reasons to be moral are created *ex-nihilo*—other people adopt moral norms and take them seriously without reason in some kind of state of nature, and then lo and behold this gives *us* reasons to adopt them. This makes morality dependent on all-too-contingent features of human life that might have been otherwise.

To begin my reply, we need to distinguish sharply between the following questions:

1. Given that most other people accept moral norms and will strongly disapprove of me if I do not give the appearance of accepting them also, do I have reasons to accept moral norms?
2. Is it a good thing that people and societies accept moral norms?

My earlier arguments address question (1) and give reasons for thinking that the answer is "yes." The answer to question (2) is clearly "yes." To see this, reflect on what human life would be like if human beings did not accept any moral norms to control and limit their conduct. Suppose that there were no moral norms and that all we had to control human behavior was the law and "nonmoral" social pressure (social pressure that does not derive in any way from moral considerations). The following would result from this:

1. The restraints against our impulses to assault, kill, rape, and rob others would be greatly diminished. (It is a mistake to think that the law alone protects us against the violence of others. In stable societies, the law effectively protects individuals only because most people voluntarily restrain their violent impulses, in part, for moral reasons. Without the restraints provided by moral norms, violent acts would be so common that the law would not be able to constrain them effectively.)
2. Many/most people would be willing to lie and break promises whenever doing so seemed to be to their advantage and doing so harmed only people outside of their own circle of friends and family. (To the extent that people are not willing to do these things, it is largely because they accept moral norms.) Business and commerce as we know them would not be possible. Most economic transactions depend on the trust and confidence that others will live up to the spirit as well as the letter of agreements. The law works well in fostering commerce only because most people adhere to it for moral reasons. Authorities can focus on the relatively small number of people who break the law. In modern commercial societies, the courts have resources to deal with only a small percentage of the contracts that are entered into. If every commercial contract were contested in the courts, the legal system would quickly grind to a halt. The law is effective in the commercial sphere only because the great majority of people do not call upon its services.

The human condition is such that we do not flourish without moral norms to curb the harmful impulses we all have. Economic systems never function well where dishonesty is rampant.

The existence of a "moral order of the universe" constituted by the will of a benevolent moral God or the operation of something like a principle of "Karma" would also give us very powerful reasons to accept moral judgments and take them seriously. Christians, Muslims, and Jews believe that God exists and wants us to be moved by moral considerations and care for the welfare of our fellow creatures. According to them, morality and moral actions play an important role in fulfilling divine purposes and ends. The existence of a God who has such ends would give everyone reasons to be moral and be moved by moral considerations. (These reasons need not be purely prudential or self-interested. A person might desire to please God or promote God's purposes independently of wanting to be rewarded by God.) Moral nihilism is not an attractive option for anyone on the assumption that there exists a God who wants us to be moral. Any serious argument for moral nihilism must assume that there exists nothing like a moral order of the universe constituted by the will of a benevolent God or the operation of a Karma-like principle. Given the existence of such a moral order of the universe, we clearly have good reasons to be moral. Absent such a moral order of the universe, the considerations noted above give us very strong, albeit contestable, reasons to be accept morality.

6.VII.3. A Reservation

One might reject morality as I have defined it, but still endorse some other sort of code of values for people to live by. Morality as I have defined it is just one of many possible sorts of normative standards. Those who reject morality (so defined) are not committed to dispensing with norms all together. The relative attractiveness or unattractiveness of moral nihilism depends on what sorts of *alternative* norms one can adopt *in place of morality*. I cannot even begin to survey the possibilities here; this is a serious limitation of my arguments. One alternative to morality would be to live by the code of honor of a warrior society, e.g., the code of honor followed by Ghengis Khan's warriors.[13]

6.VIII. A NOTE ON R. M. HARE

I am indebted to the work of R. M. Hare. Hare's theory is generally acknowledged to be a powerful and sophisticated theory of moral reasoning and moral argument. He gives clear expression to the fundamental insights of the universal law version of Kant's categorical imperative without Kant's difficult writing style and dubious casuistry. However, the merits of Hare's theory are not adequately appreciated by most philosophers because he makes unwise and implausible claims about what his theory can and cannot show and because his position rests on several dubious assumptions.

In *Freedom and Reason*, Hare relies exclusively on consistency arguments. In his treatment of Nazi genocide, he is disarmingly candid about the limitations of his arguments (Hare, 1963, pp. 171–185). Hare famously grants the possibility of a consistent Nazi. He shows why it is very difficult to be a consistent Nazi, but grants that people who are willing to have Nazi principles applied against themselves and those they love could be consistent Nazis. He calls such people "fanatics" but concedes that his consistency arguments cannot force fanatical Nazis to abandon their views (Hare, 1963, pp. 174, 184–185). Hare ignores the easy and obvious move of saying that consistent Nazis are not (and cannot be) adequately informed.[14]

In *Moral Thinking*, Hare makes much more ambitious claims; he says that facts and logic so constrain us, that we are compelled to make the same moral judgments about *all* cases concerning which we make any moral judgments at all. According to Hare, the moral judgments we must make, if we make any moral judgments, are the same judgments that are endorsed by preference maximizing versions of act-utilitarianism. The theory in *Moral Thinking* resembles the view I am defending here in that it combines Hare's consistency principles with other rationality requirements such as those that I have defended here. (Hare describes his theory as a version of the ideal observer theory; Hare, 1981, pp. 44–46.) His "proof" of utilitarianism has not convinced many philosophers. I do not believe that Hare has given a successful "proof" of utilitarianism, nor do I think that his principles for moral reasoning can give rational answers to all moral questions (for criticisms of Hare's proof see Carson, 1986, and Feldman, 1984). Hare's "proof" of utilitarianism depends on his very implausible denial of the possibility of moral weakness (see endnote 5). The main argument of *Moral Thinking* depends on two other controversial/dubious assumptions. It presupposes a very strong impartiality condition. Hare contends that if I say that an act is morally obligatory, then it must be the case that I would prefer that the act be performed if I had an equal chance of being in the position of any of the people affected by the action. More problematically, Hare's argument assumes that when we place ourselves in another person's position and ask whether we can still accept the prescriptions that we make, we must have taken on his desires and preferences, at least conditionally; we must have a desire that the other person's desires be satisfied if we find ourselves in his situation with his desires and preferences, etc. Hare (1982) claims that one cannot *understand* what another person's position is like *for him* (with his preferences), unless one now has a preference that if one were in the position of the other person (with his preferences) those preferences that one would have should be satisfied (pp. 94–95, 99). This seems to be false. Sometimes, I can understand what it is like to be in another person's position, even if I do not have her desires/preferences, even the conditional desire/preference that, other things equal, if I find myself in her position, things should go as she wants them to go. Suppose that you have preferences that I deem to be immoral. I can understand perfectly well what it is like to be in your position and have the preferences you have without my *now* having the preference that if I should find myself in your position (with your preferences) those preferences should be satisfied. For example, suppose that you desire to kill someone who defeated you in an election. It is possible for me to understand what it is like to be in your position quite adequately, even if I *now* desire/prefer that if I were to find myself in your position (with your desire to kill the other candidate) the desire I would have to kill the other person should be thwarted.[15]

Despite the failure of Hare's most ambitious claims and arguments, the modified version of his theory that I have defended here enables us to justify many moral judgments. In particular, Hare-type consistency arguments can justify strong moral prohibitions against lying and deception. All people can be harmed by the lying and deception of others. No fully rational person is willing to endorse permissive rules about lying and deception; e.g., the view that it is permissible to lie or deceive others whenever doing so promotes one's own self-interest. (See Chapter 7 for more on these points.)

6.IX. LIMITATIONS/CAVEATS

My three rationality conditions (consistency, full information, and proper cognitive functioning) are *necessary conditions* for rational moral judgments. We cannot say that every moral judgment that satisfies these three conditions is true or acceptable, but we can say that any moral judgment that fails to satisfy these three conditions is false or unacceptable. For example, the Nazi's judgment that the Holocaust was morally permissible and the surgeon's judgment that it is permissible for him to defraud his patient (in the examples from 6.V) are both false/unacceptable. Moral judgments that contradict these false/incorrect moral judgments are true/correct. It is true/correct that the Holocaust was morally wrong, and it is true/correct that it is wrong for the physician in this example to defraud his patient.

I would welcome reasons for thinking that my theory is incomplete and that there are other requirements for rational moral judgments, because, with the addition of other rationality conditions (perhaps some kind of impartiality requirement), my theory would support a stronger, more robust version of moral objectivism. Additional conditions would allow us to rule out certain views as true/acceptable and narrow, perhaps considerably narrow, the range of acceptable moral judgments that a rational consistent moral judge can make.

My view leaves open metaethical questions about the ultimate nature of moral truth. In particular, it leaves open the question of whether there are independent moral facts of the sort that moral realists postulate. *Moral realism* is the view that there are moral facts in virtue of which moral judgments are objectively true or false and that these facts are logically independent of the beliefs, attitudes, emotions, or preferences of rational beings and logically independent of the beliefs, attitudes, emotions, or preferences that rational beings would have in hypothetical situations (e.g., the moral beliefs that someone would have if s/he were fully informed about relevant facts).[16] Moral non-realism is the view that there are no independent moral facts. If realism is false, there might still be moral facts that are constituted by the agreement of rational and consistent moral judges. Hare is a non-realist and thinks that there are moral facts/truths (or things that closely resemble moral facts/truths) that are constituted by the ways in which "facts and logic" constrain us to make certain moral judgments rather than others, if we make any moral judgments at all. My theory fits best with non-realism, because, given the truth of non-realism, it is reasonable to hold that moral facts are identical with facts about what sorts of moral judgments rational consistent moral judges could accept. However, my theory is consistent with realism and does not presuppose the falsity of moral realism. Whatever the ultimate nature of moral facts, they can be discerned though rational procedures of the sort that I have explained here. Even if realist moral facts exist, there is no way to recognize them apart from our best epistemological ways of finding them (cf. Putnam, 2002, p. 32).[17]

ENDNOTES

1. This leaves open some difficult questions about the notion of "relevant information." Some contend that claims to the effect that certain information is or is not relevant to a given moral question presuppose answers to controversial first-order moral questions. For example, the moral relevance of the fact that human fetuses are members of the species *homo sapiens* is hotly disputed by those who debate the morality of abortion. [On the difficulty of distinguishing between relevant and non-relevant information, see Brandt (1954, p. 410), Firth (1954, p. 417), Carson (1984, pp. 56–58), and Carson (2000, pp. 234–236).] I think that we can avoid these problems by appealing to the notions of being "adequately informed" and having "better or worse information." (I develop and defend these notions at length elsewhere—see Carson, 2000, pp. 230–239.)

2. This argument follows Gensler's defense of the golden rule in Gensler (1986, pp. 89–90), but my arguments for the two premises are substantially different from Gensler's. Gensler gives no argument for premise 1 (the universalizability principle). He follows Sidgwick in claiming that the universalizability principle is self-evident; see Gensler (1996, p. 180) and Sidgwick (1966, pp. 379–380). Gensler (1996, pp. 93–95; 1998, pp. 104–106) presents similar versions of this argument.

    The arguments for GRa-GRc (below and endnote 3) are entirely my own.

3. There are several other versions of this argument. Among them are the following:

1b. Consistency requires that I judge acts performed by me or people I love in the same way I judge acts performed by other people, unless there are morally relevant differences between the actions in question.

2b. Our attitudes must be consistent with our moral judgments. Among other things, this means that if I think it is morally permissible (or morally wrong) for someone to do something, then I must not object (must object) to her doing it.

Therefore:

GRb. Consistency requires that if I think that it is morally permissible for me or someone I love to do something, then I must not object to anyone else doing the same act in relevantly similar circumstances. Consistency also requires that if I think that it is wrong for someone to do something, then I must object if I (or someone I love) do (does) the same act in relevantly similar circumstances.

1c. If I am consistent and think that, on balance, it is morally obligatory for someone (S) to do X, then I will think that, on balance, it would be morally obligatory for me to do X in relevantly similar circumstances.

2c. If I think that, on balance, it is morally obligatory for me to do X, and I am able to do X, then I am inconsistent if I do not do X.

Therefore,

GRc. Consistency requires that if I think that it is morally obligatory for someone to do X and I am able to do X, then I must do X if I find myself in relevantly similar circumstances. [I am inconsistent if I think that it would be morally obligatory for someone to do X, but fail to do X when I am able to in (what I realize are) relevantly similar circumstances.]

4. It is not clear that judgments about good and bad are overriding. For the record, I am inclined to think that they are not. However, we need not worry about this here. For my purposes, it is only necessary to claim that (all things considered) moral judgments about the rightness and wrongness of actions are overriding.

5. According to Hare, accepting a moral judgment (such as "killing is wrong") entails assenting to a prescription ("do not kill"). Hare says that in order for one to be said to "assent to" a prescription (or an overriding prescription) it is necessary that one follow it whenever possible, Hare (1963 p. 79; 1981, pp. 57–58). According to Hare, if a person fails to do something that he professes to believe he ought to do, then it follows that either he was unable to do it or that he did not really believe that he ought to do it. This is tantamount to

a denial of the existence of moral weakness. Hare defends his view of moral weakness at length in all of his major works (1952, pp. 166–170; 1963, chapter 5; 1981, pp. 57–60). Although Hare's discussion of moral weakness merits careful study, in the end, he does not give us adequate reasons for denying what seems to be one of the most obvious features of the moral life. I have discussed this issue elsewhere and will not pursue it further here (see Carson, 1986, pp. 97–115, in particular, pp. 108–109).

My defense of GR-GRc does *not require* that we endorse Hare's views about what it is to accept a moral judgment. Hare's denial of the possibility of moral weakness is dispensable for *my* purposes, but it is *not* dispensable for Hare's purposes. It is a crucial premise in his proof of utilitarianism (see Carson, 1986, pp. 98–99, 104–106, 108–109).

6. I take this term from Blackburn (1993, pp. 149 ff.). Blackburn uses the term "shmorality" to refer to a system of norms that lacks the feature of universalizability. I am using the term "shmorality" to refer to a system of norms that lack the feature of overridingness, but otherwise resemble moral norms.

7. Arguably (contentiously) this is a description of Paul Tillich. (Stevenson, 1945, chapter IX.)

8. Note the following passage from Hare (1981):

   Our present argument has no need of a definition of universalizability in terms of relevant similarity. In this book we shall be appealing, in our account of critical thinking, only to *exact similarity* [my emphasis], and shall not need, therefore to say, before the argument begins, what is and what is not relevantly similar. . . . therefore we can use hypothetical cases exactly similar in their universal properties, and differing only in the roles played by individuals . . . (pp. 62–63)

   Also see Hare (1963, pp. 93–111, in particular, pp. 106–107; Hare, 1981, p. 64).

9. Kant writes "the criminal would on this ground be able to dispute with the judges who punish him" (*Grounding for the Metaphysics of Morals*, pp. 27, 421 — Prussian Academy Edition).

10. Hare clearly accepts B and rejects A; see Hare (1963, p. 108); cf. Gensler (1996, p. 98).

11. Wole Soyinka recounts an analogous case from the 1994 Rwandan genocide. An official of the Hutu dominated Rwandan government visited a small Rwandan town to stir up hatred against the Tutsi people. He accused the citizens of being lax in a "bush clear" (a euphemism for the "task" of eliminating the Tutsi people). After he left, a Hutu man who was married to a Tutsi woman killed his wife. Soyinka describes this case as follows:

   [The man speaks to a group of villagers.] But that was only a first step, he said. It was not enough to kill off all Tutsi, they must eliminate every vestige of Tutsi blood that contaminated the purity of the breed. In earnest of which, he announced, I publicly set you all a further example. And with one stroke of his machete, he lopped off the head of his eldest son. One by one, his three other sons were led out of the hut in which he had kept them, and slaughtered. And with that, yet another village that, until then, had withstood the hate rhetoric of the Interahamwe dived headfirst in the sump of bloodletting.

The Interahamwe are a Hutu hate group who were the main perpetrators of the Rwandan genocide.

12. Here, I draw on an argument from Foot's "Moral Beliefs," in Foot (1978, pp. 110–131).

13. Gibbard attempts to give an answer to this objection. He asks about the value of morality (narrowly construed)—would we be better off with a normative code in which norms for guilt and anger did not play a central role? Gibbard offers an answer to Nietzschean criticisms about the value of morality. He says that moral norms help co-ordinate guilt and anger. Guilt assuages anger and thereby helps promote peace between human beings. Normative codes that do not include norms for guilt will not be able to assuage anger and promote reconciliation between human beings (Gibbard, 1990, pp. 294–302).

14. Hare hints at this answer near the end of Hare (1963, p. 214), but he does not revisit the issue of the overall success or failure of his theory of moral reasoning for dealing with the Nazis. In *Freedom and Reason* he never retracts what he says about the limits of moral argument for dealing with the case of the Nazis on pp. 184–185.

15. For more on this point, see my paper (Carson, 1986, p. 107).

16. See, Arrington (1989, p. 179), Hare (1989, p. 84), Brink (1989, p. 17; also see p. 7), and Platts (1980, p. 69). For the record, I think that realism is false; see Carson (2000, chapter 7). Also for the record, I defend a divine preference theory of moral truth in Carson (2000). I take my divine preference theory to be a non-realist theory. I am still inclined to endorse this theory of moral truth, but in any case, I am not presupposing it here. I think that the views I am defending in this chapter and this book are consistent with my earlier views.

17. Some versions of moral realism imply that our most well thought out rationally justified moral judgments could be *radically* mistaken. For example, consider versions of moral realism according to which there are ultimate irreducible moral facts that (1) people with red hair ought to be the masters of those who do not have red hair, and (2) the happiness of people with curly hair is much much more valuable than that of people who do not have curly hair. I am assuming that *such versions* of moral realism are false. There are no good reasons to think that such theories are true or that there are extensive realist moral facts that sharply conflict with our best and most rationally defensible moral judgments.

IIC THE IMPLICATIONS OF PARTS IIA AND IIB FOR QUESTIONS ABOUT LYING AND DECEPTION

My theory implies that there is a strong moral presumption against lying and deception *when they cause harm*, a presumption that is at least as strong as that endorsed by act-utilitarianism. At a minimum, lying and deception are wrong in those cases in which act-utilitarianism implies that they are wrong. My view leaves open the possibility that lying and deception are wrong in a broader range of cases as well; it leaves open the possibility that the correct account of the morality of lying and deception is something like the account given by Ross or rule-consequentialism. I argue that lying and deception are sometimes permissible, and thus (though I appeal to a Kantian theory of moral reasoning) Kant's absolutism is not a reasonable view about the morality of lying. Although my theory leaves some questions open, it enables me to justify moral judgments about lying and deception in a broad range of cases and provides a basis for answering the practical moral questions addressed in Part III.

7

The Partial Overlap/Convergence of Reasonable Views

INTRODUCTION

The rationality and consistency tests defended in Chapter 6 can be used to discredit and rule out certain moral principles and moral judgments. We must reject principles and judgments that we cannot consistently accept if we are rational and informed. Because there is a substantial overlap or convergence in the judgments that pass rationality and consistency tests, these tests can indirectly establish the truth or correctness of certain moral judgments and moral principles.

There is a *large* overlap or convergence in the moral judgments about lying and deception of people whose judgments satisfy rationality/consistency requirements and, therefore, there is a large and important class of moral judgments about lying and deception that is true or justified. With some qualifications, we can claim the following:

The moral principles and moral judgments about lying and deception that survive consistency and rationality tests support a moral presumption against harmful lying and deception that is at least as strong as that endorsed by (welfare maximizing versions of) act-utilitarianism. Moral principles and moral judgments that claim or imply that lying or deception is permissible in cases in which it harms others and the harm it causes outweighs the benefits it produces fail rationality/consistency tests. In addition, the view that lying and/or deception are always wrong no matter what does not survive consistency and rationality tests.

I also propose an improved version of Rawls's and Hooker's reflective equilibrium; on my view, acceptable initial moral judgments must pass rationality and consistency tests. This improved version of reflective-equilibrium yields roughly the same results for the issues of lying and deception as the direct application of consistency tests. It does not permit us to say that there is a single correct view about the morality of lying and deception, but there is a large convergence in the reasonable views that can be held in reflective equilibrium. All such views imply that there is a presumption against harmful lying and deception that is at least as strong as that endorsed by act-utilitarianism (AU). Ross's theory, several modified versions of Ross's theory, and rule-consequentialism are also consistent with this result and, thus, they are also reasonable views about the morality of lying and deception. My improved version of reflective equilibrium also implies that the view that lying/deception are wrong no matter what is not a reasonable view.

These results enable me to justify moral judgments about lying and deception in a broad range of cases and provide a basis for answering most of the practical moral questions I address in Chapters 8–13. However, my theory also leaves some questions open—rational consistent moral judges can (and sometimes do) disagree about questions of lying and deception. They can disagree about the questions that divide the proponents of AU, rule-consequentialism, and Ross's theory.

7.1. WHAT RATIONALITY/CONSISTENCY TESTS CAN AND CANNOT SHOW

The rationality and consistency tests defended in Chapter 6 cannot directly establish the truth of moral judgments and moral principles. The fact that a moral judgment/principle passes such tests does not show that it is true, because it is possible that conflicting judgments/principles pass those tests. It is possible that some people are rational and consistent in holding certain moral judgments/principles and that other people are rational and consistent in holding conflicting moral judgments/principles. In particular, it is possible to be a rational and consistent act-utilitarian, rule-consequentialist, or Rossian. It is also possible to be a rational and consistent proponent of either of the following modified versions of Ross's theory: the view that deception but not lying is *prima facie* wrong (I will call this "Ross2") and the view that both lying and deception are *prima facie* wrong (I will call this "Ross3"). The thin rationality conditions and consistency tests of Chapter 6 leave these possibilities open. Satisfying these conditions/tests *underdetermines* one's moral judgments and attitudes about the moral issues concerning which these theories disagree. My rationality/consistency requirements cannot discredit or disprove any of these views. AU, Rossianism, and rule-consequentialism have many adherents among contemporary philosophers who have thought about the implications of their views and seem to be completely consistent in endorsing them. Thus, for all that these consistency/rationality tests can establish, there is more than one reasonable view about the morality of lying and deception.

However, the rationality/consistency tests of Chapter 6 rule out many principles and judgments. There are many principles and judgments that we cannot consistently endorse on due reflection. Among the principles and judgments that are ruled out are ethical egoism, moral judgments to the effect that very egregious and harmful fraud, which enriches people who are well-to-do, is permissible, and the distinctive moral judgments of Nazis and members of the Interahamwe. Thus, my theory also enables us to defend a modest version of moral objectivism according to which at least some moral judgments are objectively true. The partial overlap/convergence of the moral judgments/principles of reasonable, consistent people allows us to say that certain moral judgments are true/correct. There is, in fact, a *large* overlap or convergence in the moral judgments about lying and deception of people whose judgments satisfy rationality/consistency requirements. Thus, there is a large and important class of moral judgments about lying and deception that is true or justified. The relatively minimal assumptions of Chapter 6 enable us to defend a robust version of moral objectivism about the issues of lying and deception. With some qualifications (see below), we can claim the following:

The moral principles and moral judgments about lying and deception that survive consistency and rationality tests support a moral presumption against harmful lying and deception that is at least as strong as that endorsed by (welfare maximizing versions of) act-utilitarianism. Moral principles and moral judgments that claim or imply that lying or deception is permissible in cases in which it harms others and the harm it causes outweighs the benefits it produces fail rationality/consistency tests.

Given their concern for their own welfare and the welfare of those they care about, people who make moral judgments about lying and deception must accept the view that lying and deception are wrong when they harm others and the harm they cause outweighs the benefits they produce. Rational consistent people who make moral judgments about lying and deception must agree that harmful lying and deception are wrong in all cases in which AU implies that they are wrong. Sometimes people claim that acts of lying and deception that they know harm others and cause more harm than benefit are morally permissible. However, in those cases, changing positions tests will show that they cannot consistently endorse such views. In such cases, they will find that they disapprove of and object to the harmful acts of lying/deception in question if they imagine themselves or their loved ones in the place of the person(s) who is (are) harmed by it. At the very least, they will have difficulty holding such views consistently and thus cannot be confident about the truth/correctness of their views.

An objection

Why can't we say that certain non-utilitarian reasons justify lying and deception? For example, why can't I say that I should lie to protect members of my own family from harm even if it has bad consequences on balance? More generally, why cannot we say that the special duties we have to certain people permit us to engage in harmful deception/lying in order to promote their interests? There may be special duties to others (e.g., duties of gratitude and duties to help protect members of one's own family) over and above those that AU recognizes. Many people think that such duties exist, and one can be consistent in holding this view. However, if such duties exist, it is reasonable to think that they are constrained by rules against harming others. (For more on this point, see Chapter 8.I.2.) It would be very difficult to be consistent in claiming that people have special duties to help certain people that sometimes require them to engage in lying or deception that causes more harm than good on balance. Anyone who claims this will have to consider possible cases in which she or her loved ones are greatly harmed by lying that brings about a lesser benefit for someone to whom the liar owes special obligations. We cannot honestly say that we do not object to this. For example, some of us might be able to be consistent in saying that it is morally permissible to lie to help a loved one escape from some kind of official punishment (when doing so does not harm anyone else). However, we cannot say that it is permissible to help a loved one escape punishment if it requires that one falsely accuse someone else and thereby cause the other person to be subject to the same punishment because we object to this being done to ourselves or our loved ones. This is particularly clear if the harm produced by deception/lying is much greater than the benefit it produces.[1]

7.II. ABSOLUTISM

My view clearly requires some exceptions to rules against lying and deception. If one says that lying/deception is always wrong, then one must object to lying/deception, even when it is necessary to save one's own life or the lives of one's loved ones. However, on reflection, no one can consistently say that. Here, one might object that, although it is very difficult to be consistent in holding that there is an absolute prohibition against lying/deception, this is still *possible*. Kant and Paul Griffiths hold that lying is always wrong no matter what. Are they not rational and consistent? However, as we have seen, if Kant believes that the absolute prohibition against lying follows from either the first or second version of the categorical imperative, then he is mistaken about this (see Chapter 3.III and 3.IV), and his view about the morality of lying is not fully reasonable. On the other hand, if Kant does not think that the categorical imperative commits him to the view that lying is always wrong and he rests his absolutism about lying on the sorts of arguments he gives in "On a Supposed Right to Lie . . . ," then the glaring weakness of those arguments (see Chapter 3.II.3 and 3.II.4) gives us other reasons for thinking his views about the morality of lying are less than fully rational. Griffiths thinks that it would be wrong to tell a lie, even if doing so were necessary in order to prevent someone from killing a million people (see Chapter 3.V). Griffiths's view rests on claims about God's will and the idea that language/speech is a gift from God and that our use of it must respect God's will and purposes. I assume that Griffiths is mistaken about God's will in some way or other. I assume that either God's will or purposes are not served by refusing to lie to save the lives of a million people or that there does not exist a God who is concerned with human affairs. I grant that there are some theological assumptions, which, if true, would make the absolutist view plausible. However, unless these theological assumptions are true, it seems that Griffiths's absolutism is mistaken. More generally, there are special assumptions, e.g., "God disapproves of people doing (not doing) X" that make it possible to be consistent in holding almost any view about the permissibility of an action. However, this is not a serious limitation of golden rule arguments or my argument against absolutism, because there is no good reason for us to make the sorts of theological assumptions we need to make in order to render the view that there is an absolute prohibition against lying/deception reasonable. The best defenses of absolutism are seriously flawed, and there are good reasons to think that absolutism is false.

7.III. REFLECTIVE EQUILIBRIUM

We cannot be confident about the moral judgments we endorse on reflection if we find that reasonable, consistent people disagree with us (see Chapter 5.V and 5.VI and the Conclusions of Chapter 5). Several of the considered moral judgments to which Hooker appeals in his arguments against AU are disputed by ostensibly reasonable people. Without some further independent support for these judgments, Hooker cannot plausibly claim that the fact that AU is inconsistent with these judgments is a decisive objection to AU. Analogous reflective equilibrium arguments in favor of AU also fail since ostensibly reasonable people, such as Hooker, endorse considered moral judgments that conflict strongly with AU and can be better accounted for by other moral theories.

Moral disagreements are far more extensive than the disagreements between Ross/Hooker and act-utilitarians. Not everyone thinks that it is *prima facie* wrong to cause great harm to others. For example, Ghengis Khan and members of other warrior societies had few, if any, moral scruples about killing and enslaving others. Ghengis Khan's moral outlook is starkly revealed in the following statement that is attributed to him: "Happiness lies in conquering one's enemies, in driving them in front of oneself, in taking their property, in savoring their despair, in outraging their wives and daughters" (Rodzinski, 1979, pp. 164–165).[2] Note that we are talking about the moral beliefs of entire societies and cultures, not just the beliefs of isolated individuals (lunatics). Unlike Nazis, American slave owners, and Bolsheviks, the Mongols, and Vikings, etc., did not find it necessary to dream up all kinds of wildly false beliefs about their victims in order to justify killing and enslaving them. To take another example, not everyone thinks that it is wrong to lie in cases in which lying causes great harm to others for the sake of small benefits for oneself. Some people have a very casual attitude about acts of fraud that causes great harm to others. When presented with egregious cases of fraud that cause great harm to others for the sake of fairly trivial benefits to oneself, at least some people are very reluctant to say that such actions are wrong. Some are inclined to say of the victims of such fraud "if they are so stupid that they believe the other person, then they deserve what happens to them."[3]

Unless we can rule out these kinds of judgments as acceptable initial considered moral judgments it is very unlikely that the method of reflective equilibrium will yield anything other than a very extreme version of moral relativism according to which few, if any, moral judgments are objectively correct. The rationality/consistency tests of Chapter 6 can serve as a test for acceptable initial considered moral judgments. Moral judgments that fail such tests do not have a strong claim to reliability (indeed they are false) and should not count as considered moral judgments that moral principles must be consistent with. This rules out the moral judgments of members of warrior societies who take there to be little, if any, moral presumption against killing or enslaving others and the judgments of those who casually condone fraud that causes great harm to others. (*Note*. We need to distinguish between people who say that the actions of Ghengis Khan and the like are morally permissible and amoralists who reject judgments to the effect that those acts are morally wrong because they reject all moral judgments. Arguments that appeal to considerations about the consistency of one's moral judgments have no force against amoralists who refrain from making any moral judgments. See Chapter 6.VII for my suggestions about how to respond to amoralists.)

Suppose that different people adjust their initial considered moral judgments in light of rationality/consistency tests—they count as considered moral judgments only moral judgments that pass rationality/consistency tests. It is doubtful that their views in reflective equilibrium will all converge on a single moral theory or a single set of moral judgments about cases of lying and deception. It is possible that some people will start out with considered moral judgments almost all of which are consistent with AU. They will not need to modify their initial considered moral judgments very much in light of rationality/consistency tests. If they engage in the process leading to reflective equilibrium, they will likely endorse AU in reflective equilibrium. It is also possible that some people will start out with the sorts of considered moral judgments that Hooker appeals to. They will not need to modify their initial considered moral judgments very much in light of rationality/consistency tests. If they engage in the process leading to reflective equilibrium, it is likely that they will endorse RC in reflective equilibrium. However, it seems clear that, in reflective equilibrium, there will be a very significant overlap in people's views about cases of lying and deception. All will endorse a strong presumption against lying and deception that harm others—a presumption that is at least as strong as that endorsed by (welfare maximizing versions of) AU (with some possible exceptions in cases in which lying and deception enable one to fulfill special obligations to others). Hooker is overly optimistic in claiming that reflective equilibrium will justify a single comprehensive moral theory. However, those moral theories that can be endorsed in reflective equilibrium all agree on a wide range of issues concerning lying and deception and there are objective moral truths about those issues.

7.IV. THE IMPLICATIONS OF THESE RESULTS FOR THE REST OF THE BOOK

In most of the cases I discuss in the remaining chapters of the book, it is clear that lying and deception cause more harm than good. Thus (given the success of the foregoing arguments) the appeal to consequentialist considerations alone is sufficient to justify the claim that these actions are wrong. I directly apply rationality/consistency tests to some of the cases in Chapter 8, but in most cases, the appeal to consequentialist considerations suffices. In many of the cases it is clear that lying and deception cause much more harm than good—in these cases it is *clear that* lying and deception are morally wrong.

In a large class of issues/cases, roughly those in which AU, RC, Ross's theory, Ross2, and Ross3 disagree, my view does not yield definite answers (in those cases it seems that rational and consistent people could disagree about the morality of lying/deception). Some will find this unsatisfactory and complain that I give answers to obvious issues/cases (to which they already knew the answers) and fail to give answers or guidance in difficult issues/cases. I do not claim to be defending surprising results or giving answers to difficult cases that involve serious moral dilemmas. Rather, I am trying to answer many practical moral questions without appealing to disputed moral intuitions or inadequately grounded principles (whose truth is the subject of ongoing reasonable debate in contemporary moral philosophy). All too much work in applied ethics ignores the problems created by (ostensibly) reasonable moral disagreement. I am answering skeptical, egoistic, and relativist challenges to conventional moral beliefs about issues of lying and deception and vindicating the core of most people's common sense moral beliefs about lying and deception.

The objection that I do not answer difficult cases is question-begging in that it assumes that there *are answers* or objective moral truths about these difficult cases that are accessible to us. It assumes the falsity of relativism and skepticism. However, the truth about metaethics might be (and likely is) the kind of moderate relativism or skepticism according to which there are objectively correct and knowable answers to some moral questions but not others. It is possible that there is no single comprehensive theory of right and wrong, such as AU, that is objectively true (true for everyone) and that we can know is objectively true. Therefore, it is possible that there is more than one reasonable view about the morality of lying and deception.[4] However, all reasonable views about lying and deception have this much in common: they agree that lying and deception are wrong when they produce more harm than benefit.

Although I think it likely that relativism is true, I *hope* that my rather minimal/thin theory of rationality can be augmented by other rationality/consistency requirements. I also hope that the augmented theory of rationality yields a version of moral objectivism according to which every moral judgment is objectively true or false. At any rate, these possibilities are consistent with everything I say in this book.

ENDNOTES

1. In my discussion of deceptive advertising (Chapter 9.III.1) I consider an objection that concerns cases in which acts of deception cause small amounts of harm to many people. I answer this objection, but if successful, the objection is also an objection to my claim that my theory shows that deception is wrong whenever it causes more harm than benefit. If my reply in Chapter 9 is not adequate to answer the objection, then I need to qualify this claim.

2. Strictly speaking, this statement about the nature of happiness is not a moral judgment. However, as it is clear that Ghengis Khan approves of seeking happiness in this way, the statement does reveal important features of his moral views.

3. All too many of my students say this sort of thing.

4. This view (which I think *might* be true) resembles the view defended in Nussbaum. Nussbaum says that there is more than one reasonable view about the nature of justice—but some views about justice are unreasonable/untenable.

III

APPLICATIONS

Chapters 8–14 apply the definitions of Part I and the conclusions reached in Part II to a wide range of practical moral issues: deception and withholding information in sales, deception in advertising, bluffing and deception in negotiations, the duty of professionals to inform their clients, lying and deception by leaders as a pretext for fighting wars (or avoiding wars), intentionally or unintentionally distorting the historical record, and spinning the facts or telling half-truths to support theories/interpretations that one accepts (or to justify one's own actions or the actions of groups or nations with which one identifies).

Chapters 8–11 address questions about lying, deception, and information disclosure in business and professional practice. Because lying and deception in commercial transactions tend to be harmful to the other party, there is a strong presumption that lying and deception in commerce are wrong. An exception is deception in negotiations as a means of "self-defense," when the other party is engaging in deception. I argue that professionals often have fiduciary obligations to provide information that go well beyond the negative obligation to refrain from lying and deception. Even when there are no fiduciary obligations to others, as in the case of salespeople, one still has the duty to warn others of dangers—refraining from lying and deception is not enough.

Chapter 12 examines cases in which political leaders and public figures told lies or engaged in deception in order to justify wars, with particular attention to the case of Bush and Cheney. I also discuss cases in which leaders may have engaged in lying and deception in order to *avoid* war. Lying by public officials is a terrible betrayal of trust and *prima facie* very wrong, but I argue that it was justified in at least some of these cases. Chapter 13 illustrates the ways in which deception and dishonesty can create or aggravate conflicts. I give a detailed account of one particularly important and calamitous case of this, the myth of the "stab in the back" (*Dolchstosslegende*) and Germany's defeat in WWI. In Chapter 14 I distinguish between "honesty in a negative sense" (having a strong principled disinclination to tell lies or deceive others) and "honesty in a positive sense" (which, in addition to involving being disinclined to tell lies or deceive others, involves being candid, open, and willing to reveal information). I argue that honesty in the negative sense (or something that closely resembles it) is a cardinal virtue in ordinary circumstances, but that honesty in the positive sense often is not a virtue. I also identify spheres of activity in which candor and openness are virtues.

8

Deception and Withholding Information in Sales

INTRODUCTION

This chapter addresses issues that are of practical concern for many people. A large percentage of the US work force is involved in sales. In addition, most members of our society occasionally sell major holdings such as used cars and real estate.

In the first section, I formulate a theory about the duties of salespeople concerning issues of deception and withholding information. I argue that salespeople have *prima facie* duties to: (1) warn customers of potential hazards; (2) refrain from lying and deception; (3) fully and honestly answer questions about what they are selling (insofar as their knowledge and time constraints permit); and (4) refrain from steering customers toward purchases they have reason to think will be harmful to their customers. I defend this theory by appealing to the version of the golden rule and the strong presumption against harmful lying and deception established in Chapters 6 and 7. Section 8.II analyzes cases of deception and withholding information in sales.

Caveat emptor

According to the common-law principle of *caveat emptor* ("buyer beware"), sellers are not legally obligated to inform prospective buyers about the properties of the goods they sell. Under *caveat emptor*, sales and contracts to sell are legally enforceable even if the seller fails to inform the buyer of serious defects in the goods he sells. Under *caveat emptor*, buyers themselves are responsible for determining the quality of the goods they purchase.

Currently, all US states operate under the Uniform Commercial Code of 1968. Section 2-313 of the Code defines the notion of sellers' warranties (see Preston, 1975, p. 52). The Code provides that all factual affirmations or statements about the goods being sold are warranties. This means that sales are not valid or legally enforceable if the seller makes false statements about the features of the goods s/he is selling. The American legal system has developed the concept of an "implied" warranty. Implied warranties are a significant limitation on the principle of *caveat emptor*. According to the Uniform Commercial Code, any transaction carries with it the following implied warranties: (1) that the seller owns the goods he is selling, and (2) that the goods are "merchantable," i.e., suitable for the purposes for which they are sold (see Preston, 1975, pp. 56–57). The implied warranty of merchantability does not apply to defects when the buyer inspects the goods and reasonable inspection ought to have revealed the defects. However, a buyer's failure to inspect does not negate implied warranties unless the buyer refuses the seller's demand that she inspect. Implied warranties can be expressly disclaimed by saying such things as "all warranties express or implied are hereby disclaimed." Such disclaimers of warranties are often made by used car dealers (see Preston, 1975, pp. 59–60). Many local ordinances require that people who sell real estate inform buyers about all known serious defects of the property they sell. These ordinances are also a significant limitation on the traditional principle of *caveat emptor*.[1] Many salespeople take the law to be an acceptable moral standard for their conduct and claim that they have no moral duty to provide buyers with information about the goods they sell, except when the law requires them to do so.

8.I. THE OBLIGATIONS OF SALESPEOPLE

8.I.1. My view

Salespeople have the following moral duties when dealing with *rational adult consumers*:[2]

1. Salespeople should provide buyers with safety warnings and precautions regarding the goods and services they sell. Sometimes it is enough for salespeople to call attention to written warnings and precautions that come with goods and services. These warnings are unnecessary if it is clear that the buyers already understand the dangers or precautions in question.
2. Salespeople should refrain from lying and deception in their dealings with customers.
3. As much as their knowledge and time constraints permit, salespeople should fully answer customers' questions about the products and services they sell. They should answer questions forthrightly and not evade questions or withhold information that has been asked for (even if this makes it less likely that they will make a successful sale). However, they are not obligated to answer questions about competing goods and services or give information about other sellers, e.g., the price that something sells for at other stores.
4. Salespeople should not try to "steer" customers toward purchases that they have reason to think will cause harm to customers (without a compensating benefit) or toward purchases they have reason to believe that customers will later regret.

Duties 1–4 are *prima facie* duties that can conflict with other duties and are sometimes overridden by other duties. (*Note*: in calling these *prima facie* duties, I am not claiming that they are ultimate indefeasible moral obligations of the sort that Ross posits in his moral theory. Rather, I am merely claiming that, *in ordinary circumstances*, salespeople have a moral obligation to fulfill them in the absence of weighty conflicting obligations.)

1–4 is a minimal list of the duties of salespeople concerning deception and the disclosure of information. I am inclined to think that the following are also *prima facie* duties of salespeople, but I am much less confident that these duties can be justified:

5. Salespeople should not sell customers goods or services they have reason to think will be harmful to customers (financial harm counts) or that the customers will come to regret later, without giving the customers their reasons for thinking that this is the case.
6. Salespeople should not sell items they know to be defective or of poor quality without alerting customers to this.

8.1.2. A Justification for My View

Any rational and consistent moral judge who makes judgments about the moral obligations of salespeople must accept 1–4 as *prima facie* duties.

- *(Duty) 1.* All of us have reason to fear the hazards about us in the world; we depend on others to warn us of hazards. Few people would survive to adulthood were it not for the warnings of others about such things as oncoming cars and electrified rails. No one who values her own life and health can say that she does not object to others failing to warn her of the dangers of products they sell her. The reader should imagine her reaction to the following case. Your child or loved one is about to cross a very busy street and is unaware of the dangers involved. A stranger standing by understands the dangerousness of the situation but does not attempt to warn your loved one who then crosses the street and is killed or seriously injured.
- *(Duty) 2.* Like everyone else, a salesperson needs correct information in order to act effectively to achieve her goals and advance her interests. She objects to others deceiving her or lying to her about matters relevant to her decisions in the marketplace in order to enrich themselves.
- *(Duty) 3.* All salespeople represent themselves as sources of information and as people to whom questions should be addressed. Salespeople have questions about the goods and services they themselves buy. They object to others who represent themselves as being available to answer questions evading or refusing to answer *their* questions. (Duty 3 permits salespeople to refuse to answer questions that would force them to provide information about their competitors. Why not say instead that salespeople are obligated to answer *all*

questions that customers ask? The answer is that we cannot consistently say this if we imagine ourselves in the position of the salesperson's employer. In applying the golden rule to this issue one cannot simply consider the position of the customers, one must also take into account one's obligations to one's employer. The role of being an advocate or agent for someone who is selling things is legitimate within certain limits.) This duty can probably be improved upon, but it is a decent first approximation. Explicit promises or disclaimers can expand or narrow the scope of this duty. Duty 3 represents the default understanding between salespeople and customers in contemporary America; salespeople represent themselves as being willing and able to answer customers' questions.

- *(Duty) 4.* All of us are capable of being manipulated by others into doing things that harm us, especially in cases in which others are more knowledgeable than we are. We object to others manipulating us into doing things that significantly harm us whenever doing so is to their own advantage.

Salespeople who claim that it is permissible to make it a policy to deceive customers, fail to warn them about dangers, evade their questions, or manipulate them into doing things that are harmful to them whenever doing so is advantageous for themselves are inconsistent because they object to others doing the same to them (or their loved ones). They must allow that 1–4 are *prima facie* moral duties.

A Qualification

Duties 1–4 can be overridden by other more important duties. It would be permissible to violate 1–4 if doing so were necessary in order to save the life of an innocent person. In practice, violating 1, 2, 3, or 4 is permissible only in unusual cases. The financial interests of salespeople seldom justify this. The fact that a salesperson can make more money by violating 1, 2, 3, or 4 would not justify her in violating 1, 2, 3, or 4 unless she has very pressing financial obligations that she cannot meet otherwise. Often salespeople need to meet certain minimum sales quotas to avoid being fired (on this see Oakes, 1990, p. 86). Suppose that a salesperson needs to make it a policy to violate 1–4 in order to meet her sales quota and keep her job. In order for this to justify her in violating 1–4, the following conditions would have to be met: (a) she has important moral obligations such as feeding and housing her family that require her to be employed (needing money to keep one's family in an expensive house or take them to Disneyworld does not justify violating 1–4); (b) the harm that she causes her customers is not so great as to outweigh the benefits that she and her family derive from her violations of 1–4; and (c) she cannot find another job that would enable her to meet her obligations without violating 1–4 (or other equally important duties). Those salespeople who cannot keep their jobs or make an adequate income without violating 1–4 should seek other lines of employment.

Any proposed justification for violating 1–4 in order to fulfill another more important conflicting obligation must be subjected to golden rule consistency tests. One must ask if one objects to this being done to oneself in hypothetical cases in which the positions are reversed. (We also need to imagine ourselves in the positions of the parties to whom the other conflicting obligations are owed.) If done honestly, such tests will limit illegitimate justifications for violations of 1–4. However, it seems likely that reasonable people who are informed and consistent will sometimes disagree about the importance of conflicting duties. In such cases it is unclear that there is any ultimate moral truth about the matter that we can know or discover—at least my theory of moral reasoning does not enable us to find it.

This is not as troubling as it seems, because salespeople's duties to make sales for their employers do not conflict with 1–4. The duty to serve the interests of employers is not a *prima facie* duty to *do anything whatever* that promotes the interests of the employer. Rather, it is a *prima facie* duty to promote the interests of the employer within certain limits—respecting other moral and legal duties (including 1–4). Similarly, one cannot create a *prima facie* duty to do something that is morally wrong by promising to do it. Promising to murder someone does not give one a *prima facie* duty to kill the person. This has important implications for our understanding of the duties of salespeople. Consider a case in which a salesperson can make a sale (and thereby promote the interests of her employer) only if she deceives her customers. We should *not* count this as a case in which a salesperson has a conflict between her duty not to deceive customers and her duty to benefit her employer. She has a duty to act for the benefit of her employer *only within* the constraints of other moral and legal duties such as the duty not to deceive customers.

An Objection

No one can consistently hold that it is permissible for *everyone* (or members of *every profession*) to make it a policy to fail to warn others of hazards, deceive others, evade their questions, or steer or manipulate them into doing things that will significantly harm them, whenever doing so is advantageous to them. (We and our loved ones would suffer greatly at the hands of doctors, lawyers, accountants, and financial advisors if they acted on this policy.) No reasonable person can say that she does not object to others harming her or her loved ones in this way. However, why can't a salesperson consistently hold that, while members of *other professions* ought to follow rules 1–4, she and other *salespeople* have no moral obligation to obey 1–4? She might say something like the following:

I do not object to other *salespeople* failing to give warnings or deceiving others, etc. I am willing to have other *salespeople* lie to or deceive others. Even though I don't *want* others to deceive me, fail to warn me of hazards, evade my questions, or manipulate me, I prefer a world in which salespeople routinely do all of these things to a world in which all salespeople follow 1–4. I am willing to have this be the case, because, on balance, I would be better off if this were the case. (I myself profit from violations of 1–4.) In such a world, I would need to be very wary of other salespeople and I would occasionally be harmed by them, but this would be more than counterbalanced by the benefit that I would obtain by violating 1–4 in my dealings with my own customers. I maintain that I and other salespeople have no duty to follow 1–4 and my position is perfectly consistent.

Even more narrowly, couldn't a shoe (or car) salesperson be consistent in saying that he is willing for other *shoe* (*car*) salespeople to violate 1–4?

Reply

This is just special pleading on behalf of oneself or one's own profession. The proponent of this argument needs to show that there is a morally relevant difference between violations of 1–4 by salespeople and violations of 1–4 by members of other professions. There plainly *is* no morally relevant difference. The only reason that the salesperson is willing to allow salespeople (but not others) to violate 1–4 is because he knows that he is a salesperson. We can use Hare-type switching places thought experiments to test the salesperson's claim that there are morally relevant differences between violations of 1–4 by salespeople (or shoe salespeople) and violations of 1–4 by members of other professions (such as physicians and attorneys). We can ask her to consider carefully all kinds of hypothetical cases in which she and her loved ones are in the position of people who are greatly harmed by salespeople's violations of 1–4. If she gives adequate consideration to such cases, she cannot honestly say (as her avowed principles commit her to saying) that she does not object to her and loved ones being harmed in such cases. (On this, see Chapter 6.IV.1.)

The Justification of Duties 5 and 6

I would like to claim that 5 and 6 are also *prima facie* duties of salespeople, but I am not sure that 5 and 6 can be justified by appeal to the version of the golden rule defended in Chapter 6. I object to salespeople violating 5 and 6 and am confident that I satisfy the relevant consistency tests in so objecting. However, it would seem to be *possible* for a rational person to be consistent in holding that it is permissible for salespeople not to follow 5 and 6. Suppose that someone endorses a kind of "rugged individualism." She believes that competent adults should be self-reliant and, as much as possible, make their own decisions without asking for the help and advice of others. It is open to question whether those who hold this sort of view adequately consider and represent to themselves the position of people who are vulnerable, ill-informed, and/or unintelligent.

However, without further argument that I will not attempt to provide here, this does not show that the views of those who reject 5 and 6 are inconsistent or unreasonable.

8.II. CASE STUDIES

8.II.1. Deception in Sales

Case 1: The Sales Tactics of the Holland Furnace Company

This is an actual case. I quote from Christopher Stone's (1975) description of the case:

A Holland salesman would make his way into a house by claiming himself to be an inspector from the gas company or the city, or claim he was making a "survey" of furnaces. Once inside, he would use his ostensible authority to dismantle the furnace, then flatly refuse to reassemble it on the grounds that to do so would involve grave dangers of an explosion. If the furnace was that of a Holland competitor, the salesman would inform the homeowner that it had passed its useful life, was not worth the expense involved in repairing it, or that the manufacturer had "gone out of business" and necessary replacement parts were unattainable. At this moment, though, the solution presented itself miraculously at the door: A Holland furnace man (the "inspector's" buddy who had been waiting around the corner) rang the bell and made the sale.   (pp. 175–176)

Case 2: Falsifying an Odometer

A used car salesperson is trying to sell a car on which the odometer has been turned back. A prospective customer asks whether the odometer reading on the car is correct. The salesperson replies by saying that it is illegal to alter odometer readings (this case comes from Holley, 1993, p. 465).

Case 3: College Admissions

The Director of Admissions for a private university that desperately wants to increase its enrollments speaks to a group of prospective undergraduate students and their parents. She extols the virtues of her university. A parent who is concerned about the extent to which courses are taught by part-time faculty and graduate students raises this issue. The Admissions Director replies that 90% of the courses taught at the university are taught by full-time faculty. In fact, she knows the following: only 70% of all the class sections in the university are taught by full-time faculty members and the course sections counted in this 70% figure include graduate courses and courses in the Law School and Medical School. Only 50% of the undergraduate course sections are taught by full-time faculty and, excluding small upper division courses, the figure is 25%. In Freshman level courses, only 15% of students are taught by full-time faculty members.

Case 4: Shoe Sales

A customer in a shoe store wants to purchase a certain kind of shoe, but the store does not have any in her size (size 7). The salesperson tries to trick the customer into purchasing the shoe in a larger size (7 1/2). While in the stock room he lifts up the inner sole of the 7 1/2 and inserts a foam "tap." This gives more cushion under the ball of the foot and takes up the extra space. He brings out several shoes, including a pair of 6 1/2 shoes and the altered 7 1/2. The customer asks for a size 7, but he puts the 6 1/2 on her without telling her what size it is (as she asked to see a size 7, she assumes that the shoe is a size 7). The customer reports that the shoe is too tight at which point the salesman replies, "They all cut them a little differently, let's try the 7 1/2." He puts the 7 1/2 on her. It feels fine and the customer purchases the shoes. The shoes will feel fine for a while. However, in few weeks, the foam tap will become flattened out and the shoes will fit too loosely and cause blisters. In order to wear the shoes, the customer will need to purchase several more foam taps/insoles.[3]

Cases 1 and 3 involve lying and deception (or attempted deception); cases 2 and 4 involve deception (or attempted deception) without lying. There is a strong moral presumption against deception in sales because of the harm it is likely to cause potential buyers. Such deception is likely to harm buyers by causing them to have false beliefs about the nature of the products in question and thereby cause some consumers to make different purchasing decisions than they would have otherwise made. In case 1, those who are deceived by this fraud are likely to be greatly harmed. Those who allow their furnace to be disassembled will need to either purchase a new furnace that they do not need, or else pay someone to reassemble the furnace. In addition, they are likely to be harmed by the inconvenience of not having a working furnace for a period of time. Suppose that in case 2 the salesperson's deceptive statements cause someone to believe that the car's mileage is 50 000 when, in fact, it is 97 000. Acting on this belief, she purchases the car for a certain price. It is likely that she would have been unwilling to purchase the car for the same price if she had known the true mileage. She might not have been willing to purchase the car at all in that case. The deception in case 3 is potentially very harmful to the student and his family. The decisions in question are very important and involve very large amounts of money (tens or even hundreds of thousands of dollars). This is a very serious case of fraud. It is difficult to imagine even remotely likely circumstances in which the Admissions Director's actions would be morally permissible. In case 4, the customer is harmed because she purchases a pair of shoes that are quite unsuitable for her needs.

We strongly object to being harmed and deceived in these ways; we also object to this being done to our loved ones. Barring very unusual circumstances, such acts are wrong. It is *not* above and beyond the call of duty for salespeople to refrain from lying and deception, even when that means forgoing opportunities to make more money. The legitimate pursuit of one's own self-interest and the interests of one's employer are constrained by rules against lying and deception.

The fact that deception in sales harms consumers (or is likely to harm them) gives us a presumption for thinking that it is wrong for salespeople to deceive customers. Are there any conceivable justifications for harmful deception in sales that might override this presumption? What about the benefits to the salesperson? Can a salesperson justify deception because it benefits her or those who are dependent on her? This is *possible*—we can imagine cases in which the salesperson's family is in dire straights and the customer is very rich and unlikely to be significantly harmed by the deception. However, such cases are rare. In any given case, it is unlikely that the benefits derived by the seller outweigh the harms to others; deception not only harms the customer, it also harms competing sellers. In addition, lying and deception have indirect bad consequences. Lying and deception harm the social fabric and background of trust essential for a flourishing society and economy. The law alone cannot ensure the level of trust that people need in order to be willing and able to enter into mutually beneficial transactions. No legal system can effectively police and deter rampant and universal dishonesty in the economic sphere. The enforcement mechanisms of the law can only work in a background in which most people are generally adhering to norms of honesty for moral reasons independently of the fear of getting caught (see Chapter 6.VII.2 for more on this point). Lying and deception also harm the salesperson's character by making her less honest. If a salesperson needs to practice deception in order to get by, she should look for a different kind of job—her talents could probably be put to better use in some other line of work.

What about Cases in Which a Person Benefits by Being Deceived?

It is possible that some of the people who purchased Holland furnaces actually owned very dangerous furnaces. Some people may have benefited as result of being deceived; this deception may have even saved their lives. It is also easy to imagine how the customers in cases such as 2 and 3 might have benefited as a result of being deceived. Should we say that there is nothing morally wrong with deception in such cases?

Here, it must be noted that the Holland salespeople had no reason to think that they were helping the people in question; they had reason to think that they were harming them. (It is much more likely that they were causing serious safety problems by disassembling people's furnaces.) In any case, from the point of view of an agent deciding what to do, such considerations are *irrelevant* and give no justification whatever for deceptive practices in sales. From the prospective point of view, the fact that there is a remote possibility that a certain action that is very likely to harm others might actually help them instead is no justification for doing it. Similarly, the fact that it is remotely possible that driving while intoxicated might benefit others (one's erratic driving might frighten a motorist who is nodding off to sleep and cause her to pull off the road) is no justification whatever for choosing to drive while intoxicated.

What about cases in which salespeople claim that deception is antecedently likely to benefit customers? Consider the following case.

Case 5: Paternalistic Deception

A tire salesperson exaggerates the risks of driving on inexpensive tires and thereby deceives a customer and manipulates her into purchasing a higher grade of tires than she intended to buy. He claims that his actions are justified because the customer is better off with the more expensive tires. (Very conveniently, this deception also benefits him by earning him a higher commission on the sale.) To claim to know better than a well-informed customer what is in the customer's best interests is presumptuous. Whether or not a purchase will benefit someone depends on facts about his personal situation, including his finances that salespeople are seldom privy to. If the more expensive tires really are better for the customer, then the salesperson ought to be able to persuade her of this without resorting to deception. No doubt, there are cases in which this kind of paternalistic (or allegedly paternalistic) deception helps others; however, there are still reasons to think that paternalistic deception by salespeople is a harmful *practice*. It is harmful, in part, because it tempts one to deceive oneself about what is really in the best interests of customers in order to promote one's own self-interest. In cases in which paternalistic deception actually benefits people, my consistency arguments about the wrongness of harmful deception cannot show that this deception is wrong. Inasmuch as it seems possible to be consistent in either condoning or condemning such actions, my view leaves this issue open. Ostensibly rational, consistent, and informed political philosophers disagree strongly about questions of paternalism; my version of the golden rule does not help to resolve this debate.

8.II.2. Withholding Information in Sales

Case 1: Health Insurance [4]

I once received a one-year fellowship from the National Endowment for the Humanities. The fellowship paid for my salary but not my fringe benefits. I had the option of continuing my health insurance through the university if I paid for the premiums out of my own pocket, but the premiums seemed very high. I went to the office of Prudential Insurance agent Mr. A. O. "Ed" Mokarem. I told him that I was looking for a one-year medical insurance policy to cover me during the period of the fellowship, and that I planned to resume my university policy when I returned to teaching. He showed me a comparable Prudential policy that cost about half as much as the university's policy and explained it to me. I asked him to fill out the forms so that I could purchase the policy. He then told me that there was a potential problem I should consider. He said roughly the following:

You will want to return to your free university policy next year . . . The Prudential policy is a one-year terminal policy. If you develop any serious medical problems during the next year, Prudential will probably consider you "uninsurable" and will not be willing to sell you health insurance in the future. If you buy the Prudential policy, you may encounter the same problems with your university policy. Since you will be dropping this policy *voluntarily*, they will have the right to underwrite your application for re-enrollment. If you develop a serious health problem during the next year, their underwriting decision could be "Total Rejection," imposing some waivers and/or exclusions, or (at best) subjecting your coverage to the "pre-existing conditions clause," which would not cover any pre-existing conditions until you have been covered under the new policy for at least a year.

If I left my current health insurance for a year, I risked developing a costly medical condition for which no one would be willing to insure me. That would have been a very foolish risk to take, so I thanked him and renewed my health insurance coverage through the university.

I have discussed this case with numerous classes through the years. Most of my students regard Mr. Mokarem's actions as supererogatory or above and beyond the call of duty. Many of them endorse the following argument: "The potential buyer should have asked about (or known about) the possibility of being turned down for medical insurance on account of pre-existing health problems. The buyer was foolish and imprudent." Therefore, "The insurance agent had no duty to inform the buyer of the potential harm he might suffer, even though it is likely that the buyer would have been seriously harmed by his purchase. The fault or blame for this harm would lie with the *buyer*, not the insurance agent." This argument presupposes something like the following principle: "If a person is about to harm himself through his own foolishness and rashness, others are not obligated to warn him about the harm he is likely to suffer."[5] On examination, this principle is untenable. Surely, we are sometimes obligated to warn other people about potential harms they might suffer as the result of their own folly. For example, suppose that a drunken man wanders out on to a subway track. He is careful to avoid oncoming trains but he is unaware of the fact that the third rail will electrocute him if he touches it. Onlookers would be obligated to warn him about the dangers posed by the third rail. When we reflect that we and those we love and care for often do rash and foolish things, the principle in question seems even harder to consistently endorse. Some of my students also endorse the following view: "if the buyer is so stupid as to believe what s/he is told then s/he deserves what happens to her." On this view, it is morally permissible to take advantage of people who are imprudent, foolish, unintelligent, or naive. On reflection, almost no one can consistently endorse this view, because people one loves and cares for (including one's future and past self, one's descendants, and one's elderly friends and relatives) are, *or might be*, among those who are rash, imprudent, unintelligent, and/or naive.

My View about this Case

If 1–4 are a salesperson's only duties concerning the disclosure of information, then Mr. Mokarem was not obligated to inform me as he did. In this case, the information in question was information about a *competing product*—the university's health insurance policy. If 5 is a *prima facie* duty of salespeople, then (assuming that he had no conflicting moral duties of greater or equal importance) it was his duty, all things considered, to inform me as he did. This case illustrates part of what is at stake in the question of whether 5 is a *prima facie* duty of salespeople.

Case 2: Steering Customers

Suppose that I am a salesperson in a large hardware store. A customer wants to purchase a propane-driven electrical generator to keep his furnace operating during power outages. We sell a rather inexpensive 1000-watt generator that is very reliable and runs for a long time without refueling. It will only drive the furnace—not any other electrical appliances—but this is what the customer is seeking, and this model is ideal for his purposes. We also sell a more expensive 6000-watt generator that is less reliable and does not run for as long a time, but will run other electrical items in the house. The cheaper model would be much better for his purposes than the more expensive model. The customer tells me what he is looking for, and I show him the 6000-watt generator, stressing how many other items in the house this generator will power. He purchases the 6000-watt generator. I do not mention the 1000-watt generator or show it to him, even though it is out on the floor. Consider the following variation on this case. Scenario 2: the customer tells me about what he needs. He sees both models on the floor and asks me for a recommendation. I tell him that the 6000-watt model is more reliable and better for his purposes than the cheaper model.

In the first scenario, I violate duties 4 and 5. In the second scenario, I violate duties 2, 4, and 5. In the absence of conflicting obligations that are at least as important as 4 (or 2 and 4), my actions in these two scenarios are wrong.

Case 3: Withholding Information about Defects

I am selling a used car that starts very poorly in cold weather. Based on our conversations, I know that you need a car that starts well in the cold to get to work. When you look at the car, the weather is warm, and it starts well. You do not ask me any questions to which a candid answer would require me to divulge this information. I sell you the car without informing you of the problem.

In this case, I violate duty 5. My observations about case 1 apply here. If duties 1–4 are a salesperson's only duties concerning the disclosure of information, then my actions are morally permissible. If 5 is a *prima facie* duty of salespeople, then (assuming that I have no conflicting moral duties of greater or equal importance) it is my duty, all things considered, to inform you about the problem.

Golden rule arguments enable us to defend duties 1–4. Duties 1–4 give us reasonable guidance for many cases, but my view leaves open whether 5 and 6 are duties and also leaves open how to weigh 1–4 against conflicting duties. It implies that there are no determinate knowable answers to these questions in many cases, because it seems possible for informed, consistent, and rational people to disagree about these matters. Cases in which being honest substantially harms one's interests because one's competitors are succeeding through dishonesty are particularly troubling. (See Chapter 9.III.2 for a discussion of such cases.)

ENDNOTES

1. Deceptive sales practices also fall under the purview of the Federal Trade Commission (FTC). The FTC prohibits deceptive sales practices. FTC Policy Statement on Deception (1983—still current). Available online at: http://www.ftc.gov/bcp/guides/guides.htm then click on FTC Policy Statement on Deception.
2. Cases involving children or adults who are not fully rational raise special problems that I will not try to deal with here. There are also questions about whether salespeople can always identify irrational adult consumers.
3. Case 4 is an actual case that I present in greater detail in Carson (1998).
4. A true story. I present this case in greater detail in Carson (1998).
5. Alternatively, one might appeal to the following principle: "If the buyer is at fault in a case that caused him/her harm, then the seller is not at fault and cannot be blamed or faulted for the harm that the buyer suffers." This principle is untenable, as it is at least possible that both the buyer and seller are at fault.

9

Deception in Advertising

INTRODUCTION

Deceptive advertising harms people in much the same ways as deception in sales and tends to be wrong for the same reasons. Deceptive ads harm consumers by causing them to have false beliefs about the nature of the products being advertised and thereby causing them to make different purchasing decisions than they would have made otherwise (and purchase things unsuitable for their needs). In Section 9.I, I present some examples of deceptive ads that harm consumers and argue that running such ads is morally wrong. My arguments appeal to the presumption against harmful deception established in Chapters 6–8. Section 9.II examines US laws regarding deceptive advertising. The law prohibits deceptive advertising, but it defines "deceptive advertising" too narrowly and frequently permits what is, in fact, deceptive advertising. Thus, following US laws is not an adequate ethical standard for advertisers. Section 9.III addresses the objection that deceptive advertising is permissible if one's competitors are putting one at a disadvantage by means of their own deceptive practices.

9.I. DECEPTIVE ADVERTISING

9.I.1. The Harmfulness of Deceptive Advertising: Case Studies

Sears Dishwasher

Many consumers were harmed by ads for Sears' Kenmore dishwasher that falsely claimed that it could completely clean dishes, pots, and pans "without prior rinsing or scraping" and that its "extra hot final rinse" destroyed all harmful microorganisms (Federal Trade Commission (*FTC*) *Decisions* 95, 1980). The Sears ads were successful, because the Kenmore dishwasher gained an increased market share (*FTC Decisions* 95, 1980, p. 489). Thus, the ad harmed Sears's competitors (the FTC found this to be the case, *FTC Decisions* 95, 1980, p. 494). The FTC found that this deception caused a "substantial number" of people to purchase Sears dishwashers (*FTC Decisions* 95, 1980, p. 494). Since they acted on the basis of false claims, many who purchased the Kenmore dishwasher presumably would have preferred not to purchase it, had they not been deceived.

The harm was considerable, since the dishwashers cost hundreds of dollars. Sears clearly knew that the claims made by these ads were false. Tests that Sears ran indicated that the dishwasher would not clean the dishes unless they were first rinsed and scraped. The owner's manual instructed people to rinse and scrape the dishes before putting them in the dishwasher (Preston, 1994, pp. 16–18)! Further, Sears continued to run these ads after its own consumer satisfaction surveys revealed that most purchasers of the dishwasher did not think that the dishwasher performed as advertised (*FTC Decisions* 95, 1980, p. 451). The false claims about killing all microorganisms might have been very harmful to anyone who relied on the dishwasher to sterilize baby bottles or jars for home canning. Sears ran one ad that claimed the final rinse would make baby bottles "hygienically clean" (*FTC Decisions* 95, 1980, p. 489).

Listerine

Listerine mouthwash was long advertised as a strong (bad tasting) mouthwash "that kills millions of germs which can cause colds on contact." This ad was deceptive. Listerine does kill bacteria, but bacteria do not cause colds (colds are caused by viruses). These ads harmed many consumers. Many consumers were led to spend more money for Listerine than they otherwise would have spent on a different mouthwash and many who spent money on Listerine and endured its bad taste would not have chosen to use mouthwash at all (or as often as they did) had they not been deceived by the ads. The ads also harmed Listerine's competitors who lost market share (Beauchamp, 1983, pp. 65–74).

Vioxx

Vioxx, an arthritis pain medication, was aggressively marketed by Merck. Gastrointestinal problems are a common side effect of such drugs. In 2000, Merck completed a large-scale study (VIGOR, the Vioxx Gastrointestinal Outcomes Research study) involving 8000 people. Merck hoped to demonstrate that Vioxx was less likely to cause gastrointestinal problems than its competitor Aleve. The VIGOR study supported this claim. However, the study also revealed that Vioxx users thought to be at high risk for heart problems were five times more likely to suffer serious heart damage due to coronary blockages than users of Aleve. Low-dose aspirin is a recommended treatment for such patients, but the aspirin was withheld from the patients for the purposes of the study. The result disturbed scientists at Merck, but they attributed the results not to the harmful effects of Vioxx, but to the heart-protective effects of Aleve (they claimed that Aleve had heart-protective effects similar to aspirin). Merck offered this explanation of the VIGOR findings in a press release issued in 2000. Merck's marketing department attempted to quell concerns among physicians raised by the VIGOR study. It created brochures for salespeople to show physicians; these brochures made very strong claims based on short-term studies of limited scientific value. Among other things, the brochures claimed that patients using Vioxx were eight times less likely to die of strokes and heart attacks, half as likely to die of heart attacks as people using a placebo, and no more likely to die of heart attacks than users of other anti-inflammatory drugs. At this time, Merck was struggling with the US FDA, which wanted Merck to give stronger warnings of cardiovascular risks for Vioxx. In 2002, Merck sponsored a long-term clinical trial involving 2600 subjects to test the risks of Vioxx. The study ended abruptly 18 months later in 2004 when a Merck safety monitoring board found that Vioxx users had a significantly "increased relative risk for confirmed cardiovascular events, such as heart attack and stroke . . . compared to those taking a placebo" (Green, 2006, p. 756).[1] Merck withdrew Vioxx from the market and has not reintroduced it.

It is not obvious that people at Merck were guilty of deliberate deception in this case. Those involved may have believed Merck's explanation of the VIGOR results; some who have examined the case incline toward this view (see Green, 2006, p. 757). However, at a minimum, it seems clear that the people at Merck made false and misleading claims about the safety of Vioxx in its brochures for physicians on the basis of flimsy evidence and wishful thinking. Long after there was strong reason to question the safety of Vioxx, these claims together with Merck's direct marketing to consumers meant that many users of Vioxx had a greatly increased risk of heart attacks and strokes. Many people at Merck were aware of the reasons for questioning these claims. In September 2001, Thomas Abrams (Quoted in Green, 2006), head of the FDA's division of Drug Marketing, Advertising and Communications wrote to Merck saying:

Although the exact reason for the increased rate of MI's [myocardial infarctions—irreversible heart damage resulting from coronary blockages] observed in the Vioxx treatment group is unknown, your promotional campaign selectively presents the following hypothetical explanation for observed increase in MI's. You assert that Vioxx does not increase the risk of MI's and that the VIGOR finding is consistent with naproxen's [Aleve's] ability to block platelet aggregation like aspirin. That is a possible explanation, but you fail to disclose that your explanation is hypothetical, has not been demonstrated by substantial evidence, and that there is another explanation, namely that Vioxx may have pro-thrombotic properties.   (p. 758)

Some of the people at Merck who asserted that the use of Vioxx did not increase people's risk of heart attacks and strokes may have believed what they said. (If so, their saying *this* did not constitute lying or attempted deception.) However, the Merck marketing campaign to physicians was still deceptive in that it invited reliance on the claims that those involved knew were open to serious question and in need of much further support. Inviting confident reliance on claims about such serious matters without revealing the weakness of its evidence and revealing that Merck's account of the VIGOR study was merely an untested hypothesis constitutes deception or attempted deception. It is a case of knowingly and intentionally providing a strong assurance of truth for claims that one knows are open to serious question. (In giving this assurance, the people at Merck intended to cause people to falsely believe that there was little basis for doubting the truth of the claims in question.)

R. J. Reynolds

R. J. Reynolds ran a print ad entitled "Of Cigarettes and Science." This ad cited a large-scale medical experiment (MR FIT) that studied 12 000 men who were thought to have a high risk of heart disease; smoking was one of the three risk factors studied. Half of the men received no medical treatment; the other half received medical treatments that reduced the risk factors. According to the ad: "It was assumed that the group with lower risk factors would, over time, suffer significantly fewer deaths from heart disease than the higher risk factor group. But this was not the way it turned out" (*FTC Decisions* 113, 1990, p. 346). The ad concluded:

We at R. J. Reynolds do not claim that this study proves that smoking doesn't cause heart disease. . . .

Despite the results of MR FIT and other experiments like it, many scientists have not abandoned or modified their original theory . . .

They continue to believe that these factors cause heart disease. But it is important to label their belief accurately. It is an opinion. A judgment. But *not* scientific fact.

. . . Science is science. Proof is proof. That is why the controversy over smoking and health remains an open one.

FTC Decisions 113 (1990, p. 346)

The FTC found this ad deceptive for a number of reasons: (1) it falsely implied that the medical study in question was designed to test whether smoking causes heart disease; (2) it falsely implied that the study seriously undermined the view that smoking causes cancer; and (3) it failed to disclose that the study showed that men who quit smoking had a significantly lower incidence of coronary disease and death than those who continued to smoke (*FTC Decisions* 113, 1990, p. 348). The potential for grave harm to the public is clear in this case. Any smoker who believed this ad and questioned the need to endure the difficulties involved in quitting smoking might have suffered dire consequences.

9.1.2. The Wrongness of Deceptive Advertising

Are there any conceivable justifications for deceptive advertising that might override the general presumption against harmful deception established in Chapters 6–8? What about the benefits to the advertiser? Can a company justify deceptive advertising on the grounds that the company and its shareholders and employees benefit from it? This is *possible*, but such cases are very rare. In any given case, it is unlikely that the benefits derived by the seller outweigh the harms to other people. Consider a case in which deception provides great benefits to a corporation and its employees and shareholders. A company that is on the verge of bankruptcy might be able to stay in business only by deceiving the public about its products. "Economic necessity" is very rarely, if ever, an adequate moral justification for deceptive practices. A firm that needs to deceive the public about the nature of its goods or services in order to stay in business is of doubtful value to society—the resources it utilizes could be put to better use in some other way. In the normal course of things, the benefit to the advertiser is likely to be counterbalanced by the harm to (honest) competitors and their employees and shareholders—to say nothing about harm to consumers and the social fabric. We should remember that, ordinarily, in such cases the alternative (or an alternative) is a *mutually beneficial* transaction between the buyer and some other seller who does not deceive the buyer.

Advertisers who practice deception violate the golden rule. They, themselves, are consumers who object to others deceiving them in the marketplace and causing them to base their own economic decisions on false beliefs. They object to being harmed by deception in the marketplace. They also object to their loved ones being harmed by deception.

9.II. WHY FOLLOWING THE LAW IS NOT ENOUGH

9.II.1. The FTC's Definition of Deceptive Advertising

In the US, the laws concerning deceptive advertising are administered by the FTC and state consumer protection agencies (most states follow the FTC standards) (Preston, 1994, p. 176). The FTC prohibits deceptive advertising and defines the deceptiveness of an ad in terms of the likelihood of it misleading reasonable consumers (misleading consumers who act *reasonably*; FTC Policy Statement on Deception). The FTC rules do not specify exactly what it is for an ad to be "likely to mislead customers." In practice, the FTC looks to see whether ads convey false claims about the products in question (a claim is conveyed if consumers take the ad to be making or implying that claim). The FTC usually judges an ad to be deceptive if it conveys a false claim to 20–25% or more of the target audience and usually judges ads to be non-deceptive if they do not convey any false claims to 20–25% or more of the target audience (Preston, 1994, p. 13). Note that it is possible for an ad to convey a false claim to someone without misleading her. Suppose that I take an ad to be claiming that X, where X is a false statement. The ad conveys to me the claim that X is true, but I am not misled unless I believe that X is true. I am not misled by the ad if I think that X is false. Ordinarily, when it finds that deception has occurred the FTC will ask advertisers to stop the deception and does not impose penalties unless the advertiser continues the deceptive ads, but the FTC sometimes fines advertisers for ads that contain explicit falsities when the falsity is judged to be obvious and deliberate (Preston, 1994, pp. 10, 41).

Several features of the FTC definition of deception stand out.

1. The FTC regards an ad as deceptive only if it is likely to affect the behavior of reasonable consumers (FTC Policy Statement on Deception). An ad that caused many reasonable consumers to have false beliefs would not be considered deceptive if the FTC judged that it was unlikely to affect their behavior.
2. Statements in an ad that are literally true might be considered deceptive in virtue of implying false claims. For example, an ad for Black Flag Roach Killer presented a demonstration in which Black Flag killed roaches while "the other leading brand" failed to kill them. The claims made in the ad were true, but this ad was very deceptive because the demonstration used roaches that had been bred to be resistant to the type of poison used by the competitor (Preston, 1994, p. 41).
3. Deception as defined by the FTC does not require that the advertiser intends to mislead consumers. It is a "no fault concept"—intention and blameworthiness are not assumed, and, ordinarily, advertisers are not subject to any punishment for their first violation of the law (Preston, 1994, p. 133). In this respect, the FTC's definition of deception differs from the ordinary language concept of deception according to which the intent to mislead others is necessary for deception (see Chapter 2.I).
4. If an ad is directed at a specific audience or group, the FTC judges the deceptiveness or non-deceptiveness of the ad relative to that audience. Ads targeted at children are judged to be deceptive if they are likely to mislead and convey false beliefs to children (FTC Policy Statement on Deception, part III; Preston, 1994, pp. 13, 131–133).

In addition, The Federal Lanham Trademark Act allows businesses that have been harmed by the misrepresentations of other sellers to sue for damages (see Preston, 1994, pp. 4, 9, 47, 97). Lanham courts tend to apply stricter criteria for deceptiveness. Ads that convey false claims to 15% or more of the target audience are usually found to be deceptive by Lanham courts (Preston, 1994, p. 13).

9.II.2. Why It's not Enough to Follow the Law

In practice, the FTC condones and regards as non-deceptive ads that convey false claims to up to 20–25% of their target audiences. Although they are permitted or tolerated by the law, such ads can be deceptive and morally wrong. Suppose that an ad conveys false claims to 12% of its target audience and seriously misleads 10% of its target audience. Such ads are permitted by the FTC and are unlikely to be the basis for successful lawsuits in Lanham courts, even though they have the potential to cause significant harm. It is wrong to run such ads, even if they only tend to mislead people who are gullible, unintelligent, and/or ill informed. We cannot consistently hold that it is permissible to deceive the gullible, unintelligent, and/or ill-informed in commercial transactions—to hold this is to hold that it is permissible for others to deceive and harm us and our loved ones (see Chapter 8.II).

9.III. TWO OBJECTIONS

9.III.1. Cases of Small Harms to Many People

The golden rule applies most naturally in cases involving small numbers of people. Certain kinds of actions cause small amounts of harm to large numbers of people and substantially benefit much smaller numbers of people. Often, ads for brand name products falsely imply that those products are better than cheaper generic products and induce consumers to pay more for them (on this point see Preston, 1994, pp. 58, 207; Preston, 1998, pp. 80–81, 96–98). If the item in question is inexpensive, the harm suffered by any individual is very small. Consider a case of deceptive advertising that causes a very small amount of harm to 2 000 000 consumers and substantially benefits 5000 people (the employees and owners of the businesses). The total harm created by the ad exceeds the total benefit it produces. Such cases raise questions about my claim (in Chapter 7) that my theory supports a prohibition against lying and deception at least as strong as that endorsed by welfare maximizing versions of act-utilitarianism. In such a case, why can't an advertiser be consistent in justifying deceptive practices that (in the aggregate) cause more harm than good? Why can't the advertiser consent to deception that inflicts very small harms on him and many other people in various hypothetical situations, provided that the deception affords considerable benefits to a much smaller number of people?

In order for this permissive view about the morality of deceptive advertising to be fully informed and consistent, it must be the case that the advertiser could persist in it, even if she did all kinds of switching places thought experiences and vividly imagined cases in which she and those she cares for are harmed by these actions. She must adequately grasp the full magnitude of the harm she causes and imagine herself in the place of all who are harmed, including her competitors. In addition, she must hold that deceptive advertising is morally permissible in all relevantly similar cases. Deceptive advertising that causes small amounts of harm to many people is very common. The cumulative effect of many small harms on a single person is sometimes very substantial. Therefore, the defender of this permissive view about deceptive advertising cannot now object to being substantially harmed by deceptive advertising in such cases. That is not a tenable view. This last consideration about the cumulative effect of many small harms undercuts the point of the objection. Granting the permissibility of deceptive ads that cause small amounts of harm to individuals, in principle, commits one to not objecting to general practices that cumulatively cause one (or people one loves) great harm.

I do not accept this objection, but, for my purposes, how damaging would it be if the objection succeeded? The objection casts doubt on my claim about the wrongness of deception that causes more harm than good in cases in which there is a small harm to many people. However, it does not lend any support to the contrary view that some acts of deception that cause more harm than good are permissible. At most, the objection shows that reasonable people can disagree about such cases. (Surely the view that deception of the sort in question is impermissible is reasonable and consistent—the only question is whether a reasonable consistent person could reject it.) The objection casts doubt on what I say about the Listerine case, but it does not raise problems for what I say about the other cases of deceptive advertising that involve very substantial harm to particular individuals. The objection is not a problem for my arguments in Chapters 8 and 10–13. In the cases considered there (cases of lying and deception in sales, lying and deception in negotiations, lying and deception as a means to starting wars, and lying about history) the harm to particular affected individuals is very substantial and is as great or greater than the benefits to any individual from the lying or deception.

9.III.2. What if Being Honest gives Dishonest Competitors an Advantage?

Another objection is that my theory is too strict in competitive situations in which dishonesty is widespread and one's competitors are gaining an advantage over one by means of lying and deception. According to Roy Sorensen (pers. comm.), there is a perverse kind of "invisible hand" that will harm and drive out honest businesses that follow the dictates of my theory. Suppose that the competitors of a business that sells to the public are all running successful deceptive ads that increase their business. Refraining from running deceptive ads might result in one being driven out of business.

As Sorensen notes, this problem arises in many other types of cases. When construction firms bid on projects it might be to their advantage to project dishonest and unrealistic estimates of costs and time for completion (clients are "locked in" once contracts are signed and often have little recourse in such cases). In countries in which cheating on corporate income taxes is a common practice, corporations that honestly report their earnings will be at a disadvantage. Scrupulously honest politicians who give accurate estimates of the costs of the policies they favor may be less likely to be elected than politicians who give deceptively optimistic accounts of the costs and pros and cons of their policies.

I have several replies and comments. First, if we accept what Sorensen says about these cases, it is likely that these are cases in which lying and deception by the parties in question do not cause more harm than good. If dishonesty is rampant, then in these cases being honest oneself does not protect people from being harmed by the dishonesty of others. Consider deceptive advertising. If a business will lose out to its dishonest competitors unless it practices deception, then deceiving its customers probably does not make their customers worse off than they would have been if they had not deceived them. This is because by hypothesis customers will be deceived by some other party whatever the business in question does. In such cases, at least one reasonable view (act-utilitarianism) will not object to the deception (unless there are serious indirect bad consequences of the deception). This is the kind of case about which reasonable people will disagree. Must businesses be honest if that means that they will lose market share to dishonest competitors? Reasonable people will disagree. Is it reasonable to demand honesty of business if that means that they will go out of business? Here, again, I think that reasonable people may differ; though, if the consequences of refraining from dishonesty are sufficiently bad, then it is very difficult to hold that it is wrong to be dishonest/deceptive. Sorensen's argument may be an objection to some of my applications of my theory in Chapters 8–9. However, since everything he says is consistent with act-utilitarianism, it is not an objection to the theory I defend in Chapters 6 and 7. (My theory is also consistent with act-utilitarianism.)

In cases of the sort that Sorensen raises, one often has the option of trying to expose the dishonesty of others and touting the truth or honesty of one's own claims. If this can be successful, it seems preferable to deception. In the US, businesses that are harmed by the dishonest advertising of their competitors can seek damages in Lanham courts. (If one does not have a strong case in Lanham courts, it is doubtful that one can claim to know that one is being harmed by the dishonest advertising of one's competitors.)

Sorensen's view may be true, but it is a dangerous view and is likely to be seriously abused in practice. A person who follows it is likely to rationalize dishonesty when she suspects (but lacks solid evidence for) the dishonesty of others.

The sort of deception that Sorensen advocates is not "self-defense" (and he does not claim that it is). In these cases, one deceives innocent parties (not one's competitors) in order to avoid being harmed by the actions of the competitors. For a justification of lying and deception in self-defense see Chapter 10, to which we now turn.

ENDNOTES

1. My account of this case is taken from Green's (2006) paper.

10

Bluffing and Deception in Negotiations

INTRODUCTION

This chapter discusses deception and bluffing in negotiations and focuses on the following example. I am selling a house and tell a prospective buyer that $350 000 is absolutely the lowest price that I will accept, when I know that I would be willing to accept as little as $320 000 for the house. In this case, I make a deliberate false statement about my intentions and bargaining position.

Despite the strong presumption against harmful lying and deception in commercial transactions established by the arguments of Chapters 6–9, lying and deception in negotiations can sometimes be justified in cases like this for reasons of "self-defense" if others are engaging in lying/deception and thereby gaining an advantage over one.

10.I. IS BLUFFING LYING?

In the US, it is common and often a matter of course for people to deliberately misstate their bargaining positions during business negotiations. Such statements are lies according to standard dictionary definitions of lying—they are intentional false statements intended to deceive others. However, given my first definition of lying, L5 (see p. 30), such cases are not lies unless the negotiator warrants the truth of what he says. Given that misstating one's negotiating position is a common and widely condoned practice, it is unclear that statements about one's negotiating position are generally warranted to be true. Suppose that two "hardened" cynical negotiators who routinely misstate their intentions, and do not object when others do this to them, negotiate with each other. Each person recognizes that the other party is a cynical negotiator, and each is aware of the fact that the other party knows this. In this sort of case, statements about one's minimum or maximum price are not warranted to be true. In many ordinary cases it is unclear whether people warrant the truth of what they say about their negotiating positions, and, thus, on my view, it is unclear whether or not these deliberate false statements about one's intentions are lies. (Most people know that false statements about one's negotiating position are common and widely thought to be acceptable, but often in negotiations one does not know what the other party's understanding and expectations are, see Chapter 1.I.9.)

My alternative definition of lying, L7 (see p. 37), replaces the requirement that the liar warrants the truth of what she says with the requirement that the liar *intends* to warrant the truth of what she says. There are cases of bluffing that count as lies according to L7, but not L5. There are cases in which one fails to actually warrant the truth of what one says about one's intentions on account of conventional norms and expectations of dishonesty in negotiations, but in which one, nonetheless, intends and hopes to give an assurance of the truth of what one says so that others will rely on it. In the case of the two cynical negotiators each of whom recognizes the other as a cynical negotiator, there may not even be the intention to warrant the truth of what one says; neither may be attempting to give the other an assurance of the truth of what she says.

10.II. THE ECONOMICS OF BLUFFING

In negotiations, there is typically a range of possible agreements that each party would be willing to accept rather than reach no agreement at all. For instance, I might be willing to sell my home for as little as $320 000.[1] My range of acceptable agreements extends upward without a limit—I would be willing to accept any price in excess of $320 000 rather than fail to make the sale today. Suppose that a prospective buyer is willing to spend as much as $335 000 for the house. (She prefers to buy the house for $335 000 today rather than not buy it at all today.) The buyer's range of acceptable agreements extends downward without a limit—she would be willing to purchase the house for any price below $335 000. In this case, the two bargaining positions overlap, and an agreement is possible (today). Unless there is some overlap between the minimum bargaining positions of the two parties, no agreement is possible. The best negotiator in the world cannot secure an agreement unless the minimum acceptable positions of the two parties overlap.

If there is an overlap between the bargaining positions of the negotiators, then the actual outcome depends on the negotiations. Consider again our example of a negotiation over the sale of the house. Whether the house sells for $320 000, $335 000, somewhere between $320 000 and $335 000, or not at all will be determined by the negotiations. In this case, it would be very advantageous for either party to know the other person's minimum acceptable position and disadvantageous for either party to reveal her position to the other. For example, if the buyer knows that the lowest price that the seller is willing to accept is $320 000, she can drive him toward the limit of his range of acceptable offers. In negotiations, both buyer and seller will ordinarily have reason to keep their own bargaining positions and intentions secret.

It can sometimes be to one's advantage to deceive others about one's own minimum bargaining position. In the present case, it would be to the seller's advantage to cause the buyer to think that $335 000 is the lowest price that he (the seller) will accept. For in this case the buyer would offer $335 000 for the house—the best possible agreement from the seller's point of view. In this case, it would be to the buyer's advantage to deceive the seller into thinking that he is unable or unwilling to pay more than $320 000 for the house.

Attempting to mislead the other person about one's bargaining position can backfire and prevent a negotiation from reaching a settlement that both parties would have preferred to no agreement at all. For example, suppose that the seller tells the buyer that he will not accept anything less than $375 000 for the house. If the buyer believes him (or believes that his statement is close to the truth), she will break off the negotiations, since, by hypothesis, she is not willing to pay $375 000 for the house. Unless he *knows* the other person's bargaining position, a person who misrepresents his own position risks losing the opportunity to reach an acceptable agreement.

It is possible to engage in the give and take of negotiations without making any false claims. To see this, imagine the following examples. I am selling a house, and my reservation price is $250 000. I offer to sell the house for $300 000. You offer me $250 000, and I say "I don't accept the offer, I want more" and repeat my offer to sell the house for $300 000. One can withhold information about one's reservation price and make offers and counter offers without making any false or deceptive claims about one's reservation price. Making offers and counter offers and rejecting and accepting offers does not necessarily constitute deception. Negotiators can also avoid lying and deception by making sealed offers to buy/sell at a certain price. In making such an offer, one agrees to buy/sell if the other party offers to sell/buy and there is overlap between the two prices offered. The exact price is set by a predetermined formula such as splitting the difference. (The sealed offers are opened at the same time.) This can be done without either party making any explicit or implicit claim that her offer is a statement of her reservation price. Such offers are no more than offers to buy or sell on certain terms.

10.III. IS IT MORALLY PERMISSIBLE TO MISSTATE ONE'S NEGOTIATING POSITION?

Ordinarily, it is permissible to withhold information about one's bargaining position. Revealing this information is contrary to one's self-interest, and, barring special circumstances, one is not obligated to act contrary to one's self-interest in this way. Even if the other party states her reservation price, one has no duty to do this oneself. (As one has reason to be skeptical of claims made by the other party, it is likely to be disadvantageous for one to report her reservation price candidly in response to the claims that other people make about their reservation price.) One is not obligated to reveal one's settlement preferences or answer questions concerning them.

Is it permissible for one to attempt to gain an advantage in a negotiation by making deliberate false statements about one's intentions and reservation price? It is often permissible to misstate one's reservation price when one has good reason to think that one's negotiating partner is doing the same. However, with rare exceptions, it is impermissible to misstate one's reservation price if one does not have good reason to think that the other party is misstating her reservation price.

Whether or not the statements in question are lies, they are often intended to deceive others and thereby give one an advantage over them in the negotiations. Such statements aim at making others worse off and are likely to do so. This is attempted deception that is likely to harm others and there is a presumption that this is morally wrong. However, when others attempt to deceive us and thereby gain an advantage over us we are often justified in deceiving them in "self-defense." It is *prima facie* very wrong to use violence or deadly force against another person, but when doing so is necessary to protect ourselves from the violence or deadly force of others, then it is morally permissible. Generalizing the conditions for the justifiable use of violence in self-defense to lying and deception in negotiations yields the following principle of self-defense:

SD. It is permissible to lie or attempt to deceive others about one's negotiating position provided that: 1. one's negotiating partner is doing the same and is likely to harm one thereby, 2. one can't prevent or substantially mitigate this harm short of lying/attempting to deceive oneself, and 3. the harm one causes the other party does not exceed or greatly exceed the harm that one will suffer if one doesn't lie/attempt to deceive.

We can consistently hold that we and others should follow this and similar moral principles; we do not object to people making it a policy to defend themselves and not allow themselves to be prey for others.

An Objection

Granted that it is reasonable and consistent to accept SD, is it reasonable to reject it? Clearly reasonable and consistent people can and do endorse SD (or similar principles). This means that the view that it is true that it is wrong to lie/deceive in self-defense is mistaken. The question is whether one can reasonably reject SD. If some people can reasonably reject SD, then it follows that reasonable people can disagree about the cases in which it applies and it follows that there are no objectively correct moral judgments about those cases. I think that it is unreasonable to reject SD. Very briefly, here is why. Killing other people in self-defense is sometimes morally permissible and, in light of that, it is reasonable to think that analogous principles of justifiable self-defense, such as SD, apply to other types of actions. Those who hold that killing is wrong even in self-defense almost always appeal to religious claims about God's will. I think that those claims are mistaken (at least we have no good reason to accept them). Clearly, more needs to be said here. Nothing else I say in the book turns on this point.

10.IV. APPLYING THE PRINCIPLE OF SELF-DEFENSE

Now let us apply SD to the example of making deliberate false statements about one's intentions in a negotiation. First, consider a case in which it is clear that the other person is not lying. You and I are negotiating the sale of a house. You do not make any claims about your intentions or negotiating position. You just offer to pay a certain amount for the house. In this case, there is a strong moral presumption against my trying to deceive you by misstating my intentions. Barring unusual circumstances, it would be wrong for me to do this.[2] A mere offer, however low and unrealistic, cannot be a false statement and thus cannot be a lie. Such offers typically are not deceptive, either.

Consider now a case in which it is *clear* that the other person is misstating his intentions. You and I are negotiating the sale of a house. You falsely claim that, because of limitations set by lenders, the most you can possibly pay for the house is $300 000. You do this in the hope of pressuring me to accept a low bid. Several minutes later, you offer me considerably more than $300 000 for the house. In this case, it is clear that your initial claim was false and intended to be deceptive, as the change in your offer cannot be attributed to a change in your own preferences during the heat of the negotiations. If this tends to give you an advantage in the negotiations, then (barring strong countervailing considerations) it is permissible for me to misstate my intentions.

Often in negotiations one suspects that the other party is lying or attempting to deceive one but cannot be sure that this is the case. (Suppose that you make claims that I strongly suspect are false, but do not know this for sure.) I lean toward thinking that it would be wrong for me to lie to you or attempt to deceive you for this reason. The default position should be not to lie or deceive others, but I will not attempt to settle this issue here, and I doubt that my theory of moral reasoning yields a clear answer.

An Objection

One might object that even if something like my SD principle is true and acceptable to rational consistent moral judges, it has very little application to the issue of bluffing in negotiations because its conditions for being justified in making false claims about one's reservation price are never satisfied. Other people's lies and/or misrepresentations in negotiations can hurt one only if one chooses to remain in the negotiations. Therefore, there cannot be cases in which misstating one's own negotiating position or intentions is *necessary* to avoid being harmed by the other person's misrepresentations of her position. Breaking off the negotiations and dealing with someone else is *always* an option. If successful, the foregoing argument shows that SD will never justify a person in misrepresenting her own bargaining position.

Replies

1. Sometimes people have no acceptable alternative to negotiating with a particular party. In labor negotiations, employers and labor unions that have entered into collective bargaining agreements are required by law to negotiate "in good faith" with the other party and cannot decide that they will only talk with parties who scrupulously avoid deception. For either party to refuse to negotiate would be viewed as an "unfair labor practice" by the law; it would constitute a failure to "negotiate in good faith" (see Carson *et al.*, 1982).
2. There are cases in which one can refuse to negotiate with a given party but only at considerable cost to oneself. Suppose that I am trying to buy a house in a tight real-estate market. You own the only house that I can afford within a reasonable commuting distance from my job. In such cases, it is implausible to maintain that I am obligated to bear the (high) costs of refusing to deal with you simply in order to avoid deceiving you (or lying to you) in response to *your* deception (or lies). It would be even less plausible to demand that an employee who has very limited options seek other employment rather than negotiate with an employer whose deceptive negotiating tactics are likely to put him/her at a disadvantage.
3. Even if it would be relatively easy for an individual involved in a negotiation to find someone else to deal with, given the pervasiveness of the deception in negotiations, it might still be very difficult for that person to find another negotiating partner who he *knows* would not practice deception.

A Related Objection

According to SD, a person can justify lying/deception only if (1) she has reason to think that the other party is engaging in lying/deception (or attempted deception), and (2) she has reason to think the other party is thereby harming her. However, the two conditions can never *both* be satisfied. I cannot be harmed by your attempted deception unless I am actually deceived by it, but, in that case, I cannot know that I am being deceived. (I cannot be harmed unless I am deceived and if I am deceived, I cannot know/believe that I am being deceived.) This objection assumes that the only way in which lies or attempted deception can harm me in a negotiation is if they cause me to have false beliefs. However, this is not the case. Attempted deception can pressure one in ways that cause one to reveal one's own preferences (expressions of emotion in response to pressures created by deception can give useful information to the other party). Attempted deception can also create uncertainty or fears that weaken one's resolve and bargaining position, even if one takes those fears to be irrational. Nonetheless, I concede that this objection supports the view that my SD principle *seldom* justifies lying or deception in negotiations.

ENDNOTES

1. I would prefer to sell the house for $320 000 *today*, rather than continue to try to sell the house. I make this qualification because a person's bargaining position often changes over time.
2. For a defense of the view that lying/deception are morally permissible in such cases see Strudler (1995). He argues that, given the uncertainty and lack of trust endemic to negotiations, lying and deception about one's reservation price can be useful devices to signal one's intentions and reach mutually beneficial agreements. According to Strudler, there is no moral presumption against such lying and deception. Also, see Strudler (2005).

11

Honesty, Professionals, and the Vulnerability of the Public

INTRODUCTION

Often, professionals are in a position to advance their own financial interests by means of lying and deception. This creates very serious ethical problems because often clients have no way to assess the truth of what professionals tell them. We are all at the mercy of professionals and need to rely on their honesty. Section 11.I explains and illustrates this important and widespread phenomenon. I argue that the financial benefits professionals often derive from deception create systemic conflicts of interest. Section 11.II discusses the obligations of professionals to provide information to clients/customers. Many professionals work on the understanding that they are acting as fiduciaries (or quasi-fiduciaries) for the benefit of their clients/employers. They are obliged to do much more than refrain from lying and deception. They have positive duties to be candid and provide salient information that clients/customers/employers need. Even professionals who do not have fiduciary obligations have substantial obligations to provide information to clients. At a minimum, they have the duty to warn others of potential health/safety hazards and refrain from steering clients/customers toward decisions they have reason to think will be harmful to them. Perhaps the most fully developed account of the obligation of professionals to give information is found in the principle of informed consent in medicine. I explain this principle in Section 11.III and ask how far it can or should be extended to other professions. Informed consent is a good model for professionals who are hired by their clients and have fiduciary duties to act for their benefit. Because physicians often deal with patients who are incapacitated and because complete candor often robs patients of hope, the case for paternalistic departures from informed consent is stronger in the case of physicians than other professionals who have fiduciary obligations. However, in cases in which members of a profession do not have fiduciary duties to those with whom they deal, they are not obligated to be completely candid or follow anything like the principle of informed consent. Often, doing so would violate their duties to third parties, e.g., their employers.

11.I. THE FREQUENT INCENTIVE/TEMPTATION TO DECEIVE CLIENTS

Often, professionals and others who have specialized knowledge are in a position to advance their financial interests by means of lying and deception, e.g., lying to a client to manipulate her into purchasing unneeded services. This creates very serious ethical problems because often clients cannot verify the truth of what professionals tell them without great difficulty. Professionals ask their clients to trust their judgment and defer to their expertise. Sometimes they pressure their clients to defer to their judgment. Deception in such cases is particularly objectionable. It is treacherous to ask others to trust that one is acting for their benefit when one is planning to deceive them for one's own personal benefit. Because professionals typically have much more knowledge about the matters concerning which they advise their clients, their clients are very vulnerable to being exploited and defrauded. Here are a few examples that illustrate this widespread phenomenon.

1. I have a water leak near my bathtub. A self-employed plumber comes to repair the leak. He discovers that the problem is very simple—the faucet needs a new washer. This sort of repair should cost about $100 (including the cost of the service call). However, the plumber is experiencing financial problems and his business is slow. He lies and tells me that the pipes behind the wall in my bathroom are leaking and need to be replaced. He will charge me about $800 for this. Doing this will require that he destroy part of the wall by the bathtub. It will cost me about $2000 to repair the wall and replace the tiles in the bathroom. Of course, I could seek a "second opinion" from another plumber, but that would take time and cost money. It would be especially difficult for me to do this (and thereby call the plumber's honesty and/or competence into question) if the plumber is an acquaintance or the only plumber in the area.

2. I am a self-employed attorney and am very dissatisfied with my income. A client comes to me seeking my advice as to whether she should file a lawsuit. I know that if the client sues, the case is likely to be very emotionally and financially taxing. The legal precedent is clear and does not favor the plaintiff—the suit is almost certain to fail. However, I lie to my client and say that she has a 95% chance of winning the case. She retains my services and after two months, the suit is unsuccessful. I present her with a bill for $25 000.

3. A physician sees a patient whom he knows to be in perfect health. The physician receives referral fees from other physicians and medical laboratories. He refers the patient to a heart surgeon and orders several very expensive laboratory tests. The physician receives a total of $1000 for these referrals.[1]

The patient's medical insurance pays $10 000 for the tests and consultation, and the patient pays about $1500 out of pocket. The physician knows that the patient is a very nervous and anxious person who will experience great stress and anxiety until he learns the results of the tests in about two weeks.

4. I am a salesperson for a pest control company. A homeowner is worried that the ants he sees in his house are carpenter ants. I manipulate him into agreeing to a very expensive course of treatment. While inspecting his house, I see many ants, but they are not carpenter ants; they are just sugar ants that have come into his house because the kitchen is dirty. The homeowner needs to clean his kitchen. I lie and say that he has carpenter ants and greatly exaggerate the potential damage that carpenter ants can cause. The homeowner agrees to a course of treatment that will cost him $2000. I earn a $300 commission.

In such cases, professionals have clients at their mercy. This is a very serious problem. Because of the asymmetry of knowledge in such cases, there is often little chance of the professional being caught in a lie. It is difficult for anyone outside of the profession to detect lying by professionals and many professionals are very reluctant to criticize members of their own profession. Professional organizations are often very ineffective in disciplining their members and deterring them from unethical conduct. For extensive evidence of this in the cases of the law and medicine, see Bayles (1989) and Rodwin (1993).

A *Reader's Digest* study of dishonesty in the auto repair business illustrates this problem. In 1941, two researchers took a 20 000-mile road trip through 48 states. They visited 347 repair shops.

They kept the car in perfect condition throughout the trip, but before visiting each shop they simply disconnected the wire from one of the car's two coils. Then they brought the car in for diagnosis and repair. Although the problem was minor and obvious, only 37 percent of the mechanics in these garages reattached the wire for nothing or a nominal charge. The majority—63 percent—"overcharged, lied, invented unnecessary work, or charged for work not done, for parts not needed, for parts not installed."

Blumberg (1989, p. 65)

In 1987 *Reader's Digest* repeated this study: "an automotive writer who drove a perfectly maintained three-year-old car on a 10,000 mile [trip] . . . visited 225 garages . . . . Before entering each garage, he disconnected one spark plug wire from the engine, a problem that is as simple and obvious in a repair shop as an unplugged appliance is at home" (Blumberg, 1989, pp. 65). In 56% of the cases "mechanics performed unnecessary work, sold unnecessary parts or charged for repairs not done" (Blumberg, 1989, pp. 65–66). One recent estimate of the annual cost of fraudulent auto repairs in the US is $40 billion (Callahan, 2004, p. 30). (Note that in the *Reader's Digest* studies, most of the mechanics could see by the license plates on the car that the customer was from out of state. These studies indicate that "out of town" and out of state customers are very likely to be treated dishonestly by auto mechanics. However, they do not show anything about how "in town" customers, who might later say things that damage the reputation of the auto shop, are treated in auto repair shops.)

The fact that professionals can often enrich themselves by deceiving clients with very little chance of being caught creates systemic conflicts of interest in many professions. Many professionals have financial interests that they can further by means of lying and deception. These interests make it difficult for them to discharge their duties to their clients/employees. A conflict of interest exists whenever a professional is tempted to deceive a client because she has financial interests that would be furthered by lying (and thinks she can get away with it). In many cases, the financial interests of professionals make it difficult for them to exercise proper judgment and give good advice to clients. Even if the professional makes no conscious attempt to deceive clients or withhold needed information, it is difficult to give good candid advice if giving that advice is contrary to one's own financial interests.

A conflict of interest exists if, and only if:

1. an individual (I) has duties to another party (P) in virtue of holding an office or a position, 2. I is impeded or compromised in fulfilling her duties to P, and 3. the reason why I is impeded or compromised in fulfilling her duties to P is that she has interests that are incompatible (or seem to her to be incompatible) with fulfilling her duties to P.[2]

Professionals are involved in conflicts of interest whenever they are tempted to lie or deceive clients in order to serve their own financial interests. My definition also implies that conflicts of interest exist in cases in which professionals have difficulty fulfilling their duty to give good advice to clients because their judgment is affected by their concern for their own personal interests. Often professionals who contend that their judgment is unaffected or unimpaired by concern for their financial interests are mistaken or self-deceived.

I have defended this definition at length in Carson (2004) and will not repeat myself here. My claim that the financial benefits professionals can obtain by deceiving their clients and the vulnerability of the public to such deception create pervasive conflicts of interest does not depend on this particular definition. Standard definitions of conflict of interest also imply that professionals are involved in conflicts of interest whenever they are tempted to deceive clients in order to promote their own financial interests. Kevin McNunigal says that conflicts of interest are a species of perverse incentives that create substantial and unjustified risk of harm to those to whom one owes fiduciary duties ("Conflict of Interest and Risk Analysis," in Davis and Stark, 2001, p. 69). Being tempted to deceive clients for one's own benefit is such a perverse incentive. Stephen Latham defines conflict of interest as follows: "A person has a conflict of interest when, in the presence of some duty to pursue the interests of another, she is motivated by self-interest to do something inconsistent with that duty" ("Conflict of Interest and Risk Analysis," in Davis and Stark, 2001, p. 283). Being tempted or motivated to deceive clients for the sake of one's self-interest is such a motivation. Probably the most well known and widely cited definition of conflict of interest is that of Michael Davis. Davis has refined his definition in a series of papers. His most recent definition reads as follows:

A conflict of interest is a situation in which some person P (whether an individual or corporate body) stands in a certain relation to one or more decisions. On the standard view, P has a conflict of interest if, and only if, (1) P is in a relationship with another requiring P to exercise judgment on the other's behalf, and (2) P has a (special) interest tending to interfere with the proper exercise of judgment in that relationship.

Davis's Introduction to Davis and Stark (2001, p. 8)

Cases in which professionals knowingly or unknowingly give bad advice to clients because of a personal financial interest contrary to the interests of the client satisfy both conditions of Davis's definition.

The definitions of McNunigal, Latham, and Davis also imply that professionals are involved in conflicts of interest whenever they are tempted to deceive clients in order to serve their own financial interests.

Michael Bayles argues that there exists a "fundamental conflict of interest" in any relationship between a client and a professional person created by the professional's interest in income and leisure. When professionals are paid on a fee for service basis, they have an interest in providing more services than are necessary or desirable for their clients. For example, when physicians are paid according to how much work they do for their patients, many succumb to the temptation to provide their patients with unnecessary, even dangerous treatments. Bayles (1989) continues:

Alternative systems of paying professionals do not remove this conflict but merely reverse the effect on the client. In a capitation payment system, professionals have an interest in having as many clients as possible to maximize their income and in performing as few services as possible to minimize their costs. On a salary system or flat fee for a case, professionals receive the same income no matter the number of clients or services performed, so they have an interest in minimizing clients or services. These payment systems thus encourage professionals not to perform useful services. . . . This fundamental conflict of interest between professional and client cannot be removed. It is inherent in the professional–client relationship.   (p. 89)[3]

11.II. INFORMATION DISCLOSURE AND PROFESSIONAL OBLIGATIONS

Typically, when professionals work for clients who hire and pay them, they are obligated to act as fiduciaries for their clients, i.e., they are obligated to act on behalf of clients and for the benefit of clients. Law and medicine are clear examples of this. These professions have codes of ethics that require their members to act for the benefit of their clients. Often, formal business contracts state fiduciary obligations in detail. Many other professions, including architecture, financial planning, and social work (to name just a few) also have codes of ethics that explicitly require professionals to act for the benefit of their clients (Gorlin, 1990, pp. 33, 79, 271). The codes for these three professions also include explicit requirements that professionals be candid and disclose information that is helpful to clients (see Gorlin, 1990, pp. 35, 77, 271). Since these codes of ethics are publicly stated and used to encourage the public to trust and rely on the judgment and services of members of the profession,[4] professionals have a duty to follow them. Professionals claim to have expertise and ask clients to rely on their advice; the statements that they make in their official capacities are very strongly warranted to be true. Because professionals who ask clients to rely on their advice give a strong assurance of the truth and reliability of what they say, lying and deception by professionals in these situations is a serious betrayal of trust. This strong warranty of truthfulness partly explains why clients are so vulnerable to being harmed by professionals. We strongly object to being harmed by the deceptive promises of others who claim to be acting for our benefit when they are not.

There are often difficult cases in which professionals make claims that they *believe* are true, although they have serious doubts and reservations. Professionals are obligated to be clear in communicating their doubts and reservations about what they say. It is not enough to say what one thinks is true and has reason to think is true. Saying something that one believes to be true (but has serious doubts or reservations about) in a context in which what one says is strongly warranted to be true aims at deceiving others (it aims at causing others to believe that something is *clearly true* when it is not clearly true) and often borders on lying.

The role of being an attorney, architect, or financial planner requires not only that one refrain from lying and deception, it also requires that one be candid and provide one's clients with relevant information that benefits them. Attorneys, architects, and financial planners are obligated to provide clients with such information even if they judge that doing so is likely to persuade the clients not to use their services (or use less of their services). This obligation holds for all of the many professions that have public codes of ethics requiring members to act for the benefit of clients.

Sometimes, individual professionals attempt to secure the trust and reliance of others by implicitly or explicitly promising or assuring others that they are acting on their behalf or for their benefit. Such promises or assurances create the same kinds of fiduciary obligations as formal codes of ethics. Those who give such assurances must deliver on them, absent very important conflicting obligations. It is very wrong to make a pretense of trying to serve the interests of the client/customer if one is not attempting to do so.

Even when no fiduciary duties are involved, it is not enough that professionals refrain from lying and deception. The arguments of Chapter 8 about the duties of salespeople (who typically do not have fiduciary duties to customers) also apply here. At a minimum, members of professions also have *prima facie* duties to warn others of potential health and safety hazards and refrain from steering clients/customers toward decisions they have reason to think will be harmful to them. In principle, it seems that the obligation to answer questions and provide (nonsafety) information can be waived by mutual agreement, provided that the professional and the individual come to an understanding about what they expect of each other.

11.III. INFORMED CONSENT

The principle of informed consent in contemporary medicine is an important view about the duties of professionals *vis-à-vis* their clients. It is worth sketching some of the main features of this principle and asking whether they can or should be extended to other professions.

The principle of informed consent requires that physicians inform their patients about the consequences of medical procedures and obtain the consent of patients before performing those procedures. It also requires that medical and psychological tests be performed only on people who give their informed consent to taking the tests.

In various forms, the principle of informed consent has been adopted in the codes of ethics of the American Medical Association, the American Hospital Association, the Food and Drug Administration, and the American Nurses Association (see Faden and Beauchamp, 1986, pp. 94, 96, 282; Jameton, 1995, p. 1226).

Faden and Beauchamp (1986, p. 274) and Beauchamp and Childress (2001, p. 79) both identify five essential elements of informed consent: (1) the patient is competent; (2) information is disclosed to the patient; (3) the patient understands the information; (4) the patient's decision about whether to consent to the procedure in question is voluntary; and (5) the patient consents to the procedure.

There are serious problems involved in defining the third condition (patient understanding). It would be unreasonable to require complete information or even complete material information, because this would place impossible demands on the time of physicians. There is also a question of whether it is possible for physicians to ensure that patients are *adequately informed* when they give their consent. Gert, Culver, and Clouser (1997) argue that physicians can adequately inform their patients by listing salient benefits and harms of proposed procedures and informing patients of the likelihood or probability of salient harms and benefits.

Some physicians have objected that accurately conveying information about significant harms and benefits is all but impossible, because to do so would require giving patients a medical education. That is not true. The language and level of specificity in which rational patients want harms and benefits explained is in terms of the significant harms that will likely be eliminated, diminished, or caused by any available rational treatment. The basic harms which concern rational persons are: death, pain (psychological as well as physical), disabilities (both mental and physical), and loss of freedom or pleasure . . . Patients almost never care about, say, the chemical structure of a chemotherapeutic agent, or about its postulated mechanism of interference with the metabolism of neoplastic cells. They do care about pain, nausea, weakness, and hair loss—about how likely these are to occur, how severe they are apt to be, and how long they may be expected to last. Technical language is not only not necessary, it is often counter productive . . . .

We believe that information about risks should usually be in numerical form. Rather than using terms and explanations like "common," or "rare," . . . physicians should give reasonably precise numerical information, like "this drug is very good in lowering blood pressure about 80% of the time," or "about 1 in 200 times this operation, even when it's performed technically perfectly, causes a person to become paralyzed from the waist down." (pp. 162–163)

There is a problem in that how information is presented to patients affects how they respond to it. Suppose the death rate for a certain operation is 5%. To say that the death rate is 5% is equivalent to saying that the survival rate is 95%, "Yet psychologists studying decision making have shown that significantly more persons will consent to have the procedure when the survival rate is mentioned than when the death rate is mentioned" (Gert *et al.*, 1997, p. 165). In such cases, Gert *et al.* (1997) claim that the ideal of informed consent requires that the information be presented in both ways: "Any rational person facing such an important decision and knowing that there was a one-in-seven chance she would make a different treatment decision with information presented in both ways rather than with information presented in only one way, would choose to have information in both ways" (p. 167).[5] The presentation of facts and statistics is often misleading. Suppose that a certain course of treatment reduces the patient's chance of suffering a heart attack by 50%. In order to weigh the costs and benefits of this treatment, patients need information about the likelihood of suffering a heart attack. The benefit of reducing a young healthy person's (very low) risk of heart attack by 50% is not nearly as great as the benefit of reducing the risk of a heart attack by 50% in someone that has a very high risk of suffering a heart attack. Physicians must be attentive to these considerations when they talk with patients.

Exceptions

The American Medical Association model of informed consent allows for the following exceptions: (1) public health emergency; (2) medical emergency (for the patient); (3) incompetent patient; (4) "therapeutic privilege" or harmful effects of disclosure, e.g., loss of hope; and (5) patient waiver of the right to be informed (Faden and Beauchamp, 1986, pp. 35–39).

Adequately informed patients are generally in a better position to judge their own interests than physicians because what is best for the patient depends largely on facts about the patient's preferences and the patient's life history that physicians cannot possibly know. Prostate cancer is often fatal, but particularly in older men it often progresses very slowly. Many elderly men who are diagnosed with prostate cancer live with the cancer for a long time and die of other causes. Prostate cancer surgery (which usually involves removal of the entire prostate gland) carries with it serious risks of incontinence and impotence. A celibate man who plans to abstain from sexual intercourse for the rest of his life will view the risks of impotence very differently than a man who has a very active and fulfilling sex life, which is essential for his personal happiness and the success of his marriage (cf. Gert *et al.*, 1997, p. 157). Even with the best intentions, few physicians know enough to make good decisions for their patients in such cases. (In addition, physicians often have financial interests contrary to those of patients that can influence their judgment.)

Because it is not possible for patients to be *fully informed*, it is easy for professionals to give one-sided advice and slant the information they give to favor the decisions they want the patients to make. Physicians must act very carefully and conscientiously. They must take pains to avoid slanting the information they give.

Professionals who have fiduciary duties to their clients would be well advised to adopt something like the principle of informed consent (there are no doubt special considerations that are relevant in the case of each profession). In order to fulfill their duty to promote clients' interests, professionals need to give them the information they need to make reasonably informed choices. Because physicians often deal with patients who are incapacitated and because complete candor often robs patients of hope, the case for paternalistic departures from informed consent is stronger in medicine than other professions. (Note that in some cases, clients might not be willing to spend the time and effort involved in consulting with the professional; they might prefer to waive their right to be given extensive information so that the professional can simply render her services without consulting extensively with them. Codes of ethics for most professions should permit this.)

ENDNOTES

1. Such referral fees or, less politely, "kickbacks" are common practice in medicine. See Rodwin (1993, pp. 19–52).
2. I defend this definition in Carson (2004, p. 165). I have made stylistic revisions in condition 3.

3. Morreim (1995) argues the conflicts of interest arising out the payment of physicians are "inescapable" (pp. 61–62).
4. Cf. Arrow (1997, pp. 124–126). Arrow notes that codes of ethics are intended to cause the public to trust professionals enough to use their services.
5. This is a very helpful suggestion. Also, see Rosati (1995, p. 309).

12

Lying and Deception about Questions of War and Peace: Case Studies

INTRODUCTION

This chapter examines cases in which political leaders and other public figures told lies or engaged in deception as a pretext for fighting wars. My examples include William Randolph Hearst, Franklin Roosevelt, Lyndon Johnson, and George W. Bush and Dick Cheney. I devote particular attention to the case of Bush and Cheney and argue that they lied and attempted to deceive the public. Although this claim will strike many readers as obvious, it has not been adequately defended by those who make it. The public officials and pundits who have accused Bush and Cheney of lying and deception have not made a serious attempt to define lying and deception, much less given a careful application of those definitions to the cases at issue. Certain features of my definition of lying are salient in these cases and help to show that they lied—Bush and Cheney strongly warranted the truth of claims that they knew were open to serious doubts.

In most of these cases, lying and deception led to disastrous consequences and were morally wrong. However, I argue that Franklin Roosevelt was morally justified in his lying and deception in order to aid Britain during the early stages of WWII. I also discuss cases in which Dean Acheson, John Foster Dulles, and Dwight Eisenhower may have engaged in lying and deception in order to *avoid* war. These also seem to be cases of justifiable lying/deception.

These cases are prime examples of a larger phenomenon. Most cases of lying and deception by public officials about matters of public policy fall into one or both of the following categories:

1. Lying and deception to manipulate public opinion and generate support for actions, causes, policies, and political objectives that one wants to promote.
2. Lying and deception to promote one's personal interests, e.g., a politician lying to avoid impeachment or increase his chances of winning an election.

1 and 2 are not mutually exclusive. A politician might lie both to increase her chances of being elected and to promote her policy objectives. Both sorts of lying and deception are profoundly contrary to the ideals of a democratic society. Democratic forms of government tend to promote the general welfare

only insofar as the public has accurate information about policy matters. The choices made by the citizens of a democratic society are valuable only if they have accurate information and can make reliable judgments about whether candidates will pursue the policies that they support. Lying and deception by political leaders are great betrayals of trust in democratic societies; they thwart or subvert the will of the populace. There is a very strong presumption against doing this in a democratic society (cf. Lynch, 2004, chapter 10). This applies to political leaders who deceive their own citizens. Deceiving the leaders or citizens of other countries is rarely a comparable breach of trust. The power of the government and government officials to control and influence the media and its access to information often gives politicians the power to prevent the public from learning the truth.

In *The Republic*, Plato says that the rulers of a state will frequently need to make use "of falsehood and deception for the benefit of those they rule" (459c). He calls such useful falsehoods "noble lies" (414 b–c). However, some hold that political leaders should never lie or deceive the public (Alterman, 2004, p. 22). I disagree. The cases of Franklin Roosevelt, Acheson, Dulles, and Eisenhower seem to be exceptions to this. In a limiting case, surely it would be morally permissible for political leaders to lie if doing so were necessary to avoid a nuclear war that would destroy human civilization. Nonetheless, the moral presumption against leaders lying to the public is very strong.

12.1. LYING AND DECEPTION IN ORDER TO CREATE A JUSTIFICATION OR PRETEXT FOR WAR

The stakes involved in lying and deception are particularly high in cases involving lying/deception in order to bring about or prevent wars. Here are some examples of leaders who lied and/or deceived the public in order to create a justification or pretext for starting wars.

12.1.1. Hearst and the Spanish American War

One of the most brazen attempts to instigate a war by means of lying and deception was the newspaper publisher William Randolph Hearst's attempt to start a war between the US and Spain over Cuba. In 1896, Hearst sent the painter Frederick Remington to Cuba to draw pictures of Spanish atrocities. After a stay in Cuba, Remington failed to find any atrocities. He wired Hearst, "Everything is quiet. There is no trouble here. There will be no war. I wish to return." Hearst replied as follows, "Please remain. You furnish pictures. I'll furnish the war" (Goldberg, 1990, p. 51). Hearst later published Remington's drawings, including a sketch of a naked Cuban girl on an American ship being searched for documents and leered at by Spanish police. These drawings were deeply shocking to the sensibilities of Victorian Americans. Hearst's campaign succeeded in creating hatred for the Spanish government and its colonial rulers in Cuba. Several years later, when the US Battleship Maine exploded in Havana Harbor, the US quickly plunged into war with Spain to free Cuba, without carefully ascertaining the cause of the explosion (many historians now believe the explosion was the result of failure of the boiler rather than a Spanish mine). Remington's drawings were based largely on lies and fabrications. The girl in question had actually been searched by female matrons (Goldberg, 1990, p. 51). Later, during the Spanish Civil War, Hearst newspapers ran photos of atrocities allegedly committed by Loyalists against the followers of Franco, which, in fact, were pictures of atrocities committed by Franco's soldiers against Loyalists (Goldberg, 1990, p. 51).

12.I.2. Franklin Roosevelt and World War II

Roosevelt wanted to help Britain in WWII, and by 1941, he wanted the US to enter the war against Germany. However, American public opinion was strongly opposed to entering the war and many Americans opposed Roosevelt's departures from neutrality to aid Britain. During the 1940 presidential campaign and on many other occasions, Roosevelt assured the public that their sons would not be sent off to fight in "foreign wars." Just before the election on November 2, 1940, he stated "Your president says your country is not going to war" (Dallek, 1979, p. 250). Later he privately expressed very different intentions. According to Robert Dallek (1979):

[although] Roosevelt had now apparently concluded that the United States would have to join the fighting, he remained painfully uncertain about how to proceed. On May 17 [1941] he told Morgenthau [Secretary of the Treasury] that he was "waiting to be pushed into this situation," Morgenthau took him to mean that "he wanted to be pushed into war rather than lead us into it." At a Cabinet meeting on the 23rd, when some participants expressed the hope that the President . . . would declare the country "ready to do something," he replied: "I am not willing to fire the first shot."   (p. 265)

During mid 1941, his Cabinet was debating whether Roosevelt should ask Congress to declare war on Germany. Roosevelt rejected this idea:

Instead, he said that he would wage war, but not declare it, and that he would become more and more provocative. . . . Everything was to be done to force an "incident" which would justify him in opening the hostilities.

(Dallek, 1979, p. 285)

Winston Churchill reports Roosevelt saying almost exactly the same thing to him in their meeting off the coast of Newfoundland in August 1941. According to Churchill, "The President . . . said he would wage war but not declare it . . . and that he would become more and more provocative. If the Germans did not like it, they could attack American forces. . . . Everything was to be done to force an 'incident' that could lead to war" (LaFeber, 1989, pp. 381–382).[1]

In September 1941, Roosevelt secretly ordered the US Navy to escort British convoys as far as Iceland and fire at German submarines on sight, even if the submarines were hundreds of miles away from any convoys. In September 1941 the US Navy ship, *The Greer*, followed a German submarine for 3 hours and signaled its location to the British Navy. After this, the German submarine turned and attacked *The Greer*. In a "fireside chat" radio broadcast on September 11, 1941, Roosevelt denounced this attack and said: "I tell you the blunt fact that this German submarine fired first . . . without warning and with deliberate design to sink her" (Franklin D. Roosevelt, Fireside Chat, September 11, 1941). He failed to explain how the German ship had been provoked. Roosevelt then used this incident as a pretext to state his hitherto unannounced policy of attacking German and Italian submarines on sight.

We have sought no shooting war with Hitler. We do not seek it now. . . .

But when you see a rattlesnake poised to strike, you do not wait until he has struck before you crush him.

These Nazi submarines and raiders are the rattlesnakes of the Atlantic.

. . . From now on, if German or Italian vessels of war enter the waters, the protection of which is necessary for American defense, they do so at their own peril.

Franklin D. Roosevelt, Fireside Chat, September 11, 1941

In light of his earlier statements to his Cabinet and Churchill that he would wage war but not declare it, Roosevelt's claim that "We have sought no shooting war with Hitler. We do not seek it now," seems to be a lie. One might instead conclude that Roosevelt lied to his Cabinet and Churchill, but what Roosevelt said to his Cabinet and Churchill was not a lie; it aptly describes what he did.

12.1.3. Lyndon Johnson and the Gulf of Tonkin Resolution

The Gulf of Tonkin Resolution authorized President Johnson to take "all necessary measures to repel any armed attacks against the armed forces of the United States and to prevent further aggression" (Alterman, 2004, p. 161). Lyndon Johnson used this as an authorization to escalate US involvement in the Viet Nam War. The "Gulf of Tonkin Incident" was represented to the public as an unprovoked North Vietnamese attack on US Naval Forces. On the night of August 4, 1964, the USS *Maddox* reported being under torpedo attack by North Vietnamese boats. Later reports from the naval unit involved in the incident questioned the accuracy of the initial reports. An inexperienced sonar operator on the Maddox filed 21 torpedo reports. Navy pilots flying that evening with perfect visibility saw no North Vietnamese ships in the area (Alterman, 2004, pp. 187–189). When the Johnson administration made the case for the Resolution, Congress was told that there had been an attack but never told the basis for doubting that the attack had occurred. The Johnson administration deceived Congress and the public by representing the incident as an unprovoked attack. In fact, the US had been making secret attacks on North Viet Nam since 1961; several days before the August 4 incident US ships landed commandos on two North Vietnamese islands very near the area of the reported attacks on the *Maddox*. Even if US ships did come under fire that could be plausibly construed as an act of self-defense by the North Vietnamese (Alterman, 2004, pp. 185, 202).

12.II. ANOTHER CASE: GEORGE W. BUSH, DICK CHENEY, AND THE IRAQ WAR OF 2003

Before the Iraq War of 2003, George Bush and his administration aggressively courted support in the UN, the US Congress, and public opinion to gain support for the US invasion of Iraq. In the run up to the war, Bush and his administration repeated two main claims: first, that America and the world were threatened by Iraq's "weapons of mass destruction," and second, that there were close links between Iraq and al Qaeda and that there was a grave danger that Iraq would hand over some of those weapons to al Qaeda. Many people allege that Bush and others in his administration lied and led America into a disastrous war.

12.II.1. Claims About Iraq's "Weapons of Mass-Destruction"

Here are some of the claims repeatedly made by Bush and members of his administration concerning weapons of mass destruction. In August 2002, Vice President Cheney claimed: "Simply stated, there is no doubt that Saddam Hussein now has weapons of mass destruction. There is no doubt he is amassing them to use against our friends, our allies, and against us" (Korn, 2003, p. 208), and "Many of us are convinced that Saddam Hussein will acquire nuclear weapons fairly soon" (p. 213).

On September 8, 2002, Cheney said of Saddam: "we do know, with *absolute certainty* [my emphasis], that he is using his procurement system to acquire the equipment he needs to in order to enrich uranium to build a nuclear bomb" (Rich, 2006, pp. 59, 241–242). The main evidence Cheney cited was Saddam's attempt to acquire aluminum tubes for a centrifuge (p. 59). On September 20, 2002, Cheney claimed:

We now have irrefutable evidence that [Saddam] has once again set up and reconstituted his program to take uranium . . . so that it will function as the base material as a nuclear weapon . . . There's no doubt about what he is attempting. And there's no doubt about the fact that the level of effort has escalated in recent months.

Rich (2006, p. 247)

Shortly before the US invasion began in March 2003, Cheney claimed that Saddam Hussein was trying to produce nuclear weapons (Korn, 2003, p. 239).

In September 2002, Defense Secretary Donald Rumsfeld claimed: "There's no debate in the world as to whether they have those weapons . . . . We all know that a trained ape knows that" (Korn, 2003, p. 211) and "We all know they have weapons of mass destruction . . . . There isn't any debate about it" (Alterman, 2004, p.299). Later, in December and on January 7 he claimed: "It is clear that the Iraqis have weapons of mass destruction. There is no doubt in my mind but that they currently have chemical and biological weapons" (Korn, 2003, p. 211).

On January 9, Bush's Press Secretary, Ari Fleischer claimed: "We know for a fact that there are weapons there" (Korn, 2003, p. 211).

In September 2002, Bush claimed: "when the inspectors went into Iraq [in 1991] and were denied, finally denied access [in 1998], a report came out of the Atomic—the IAEA, that they were six months away from a weapon. I don't know what more evidence we need" (Korn, 2003, p. 213).

On October 7, 2002, Bush gave a televised address in which he claimed: "Iraq has attempted to purchase high-strength aluminum tubes and other equipment needed for gas centrifuges, which are used to enrich uranium for nuclear weapons" (Rich, 2006, p. 252).

In his State of the Union address on January 28, 2003 Bush said: "The British Government has learned that Saddam Hussein recently sought significant quantities of uranium from Africa. And our intelligence sources tell us that he has attempted to purchase high-strength aluminum tubes suitable for nuclear weapons production" (Rich, 2006, pp. 259–260).

On March 17 (three days before he began the war) Bush asserted that: "Intelligence gathered by this and other governments leaves *no doubt* [my emphasis] that the Iraq regime continues to possess and conceal some of the most lethal weapons ever devised" (Alterman, 2004, p. 298).

12.II.2. Claims about the Connection between Iraq and Al Qaeda

In March 2003 (several days before the US invasion of Iraq) Cheney claimed that Saddam Hussein was: "trying once again to produce nuclear weapons and we know that he has a long standing relationship with various terrorist groups, including the al Qaeda organization" (Korn, 2003, p. 239). In July 2002, Daniel Pearl, Chairman of the Defense Policy Board, claimed: "It is likely that chemical weapons, biological weapons in the possession of the Iraqis derived during the Cold War from the Soviet Union, are now being disseminated to terrorists" (p. 215).

Secretary of State Powell claimed: "Iraq today harbors a deadly terrorist network headed by Abu Musab al-Zarqawi, an associate and collaborator of Osama bin Laden and his al Qaeda lieutenants" (p. 232).

George W. Bush claimed: "Iraq is harboring a terrorist network, headed by a senior al Qaeda terrorist planner [Abu Musab al-Zarqawi]" (p. 235).[2]

In order to make the connection between al Qaeda and Iraq, the Bush administration used a dubious story that Mohammed Atta (leader of the 9/11 hijackers) met with an Iraqi intelligence official in Prague. The story originally came from Czech intelligence and was repeated by columnist William Safire who claimed that this meeting was an "undisputed fact" (p. 216). On September 8, 2002, Cheney claimed that: "Mohamed Atta, who was the lead hijacker, did apparently travel to Prague . . . we have reporting that places him in Prague with a senior Iraqi intelligence official a few months before the attack on the World Trade Center" (p. 217). Such a meeting itself would not be direct evidence of Iraqi involvement in or prior knowledge of the 9/11 attacks. Further, the reports of a meeting between Atta and an Iraqi intelligence official shortly before September 11, 2001 are dubious. Later, in October 2002, Czech President Vaclav Havel told the White House that there was no evidence to confirm earlier reports of the meeting. Apparently, Atta had been to Prague in 2000, not 2001, and "some Czech and German officials say that their best explanation of why Mr. Atta came to Prague was to get a cheap airfare to the United States" (Korn, 2003, p. 217). On June 21, 2002, a CIA report raised serious doubts about the Atta–Prague story (Rich, 2006, pp. 237–238).

In a draft resolution to Congress (September 19, 2002) that authorized President Bush to use military force against Iraq, the Bush administration claimed: "Members of al Qaeda, an organization bearing responsibility for attacks on the United States, its citizens, its interests, including the attacks that occurred on Sept. 11, 2001 are known to be in Iraq" (Korn, 2003, p. 218).

12.II.3. The Falsity of the Claims about Iraq's Weapons and its Connections with Al Qaeda

After more than six years of American occupation of Iraq and an intensive search of the entire country, no weapons of mass destruction have been found. Given the extensive search of the entire country and US control over former Iraqi officials, the failure of the US to find weapons of mass destruction is very strong evidence that they did not exist. In addition, the Bush administration's case (such as it was) relied on a misleading classification of chemical weapons as weapons of mass destruction. Had Iraq possessed nuclear or biological weapons and given them to al Qaeda, it would have been a very serious threat to the US, but chemical weapons were not a serious threat to the US. It is true that Iraq possessed and had used chemical weapons in the past; the Iraqi Army used them to kill thousands of Kurdish civilians in Iraq and had used them against the Iranian Army. Given Iraq's past possession and use of chemical weapons, it was reasonable to think that they still possessed some chemical weapons. It was a genuine surprise that no chemical weapons were found.[3] However, it was very misleading to classify them as weapons of mass destruction that were a serious threat to the US. Very large amounts of chemical weapons in the hands of an army can be weapons of mass destruction. However, even if Iraq had possessed large quantities of chemical weapons, they would not have been a major threat to the US because Iraq was not capable of delivering sufficient quantities of chemical weapons to the US to bring about a massive loss of life (cf. Clarke, 2004, pp. 267–268).

The *9/11 Commission Report* issued by the bipartisan group created by the US government to investigate the September 11 attacks did not conclude that Iraq helped al Qaeda plan or carry out its attacks on the US. Shortly after September 11, 2001, Bush asked about possible Iraqi ties to the attacks. Richard Clarke (then National Counterterrorism Coordinator for the National Security Council) submitted a memo to National Security Advisor Condoleezza Rice on September 18, 2001:

The memo found no "compelling case" that Iraq had either planned or perpetrated the attacks . . . Arguing that the case for the links between Iraq and al Qaeda was weak, the memo pointed out that Bin Ladin resented the secularism of Saddam Hussein's regime. Finally, the memo said, there was no confirmed reporting on Saddam co-operating with Bin Ladin on unconventional weapons.

9/11 Commission Report (p. 334)

The *9/11 Commission Report* also discussed connections between Iraq and al Qaeda in the 1990s. The report claimed that during the 1990s:

Bin Ladin had in fact been sponsoring anti-Saddam Islamists in Iraqi Kurdistan, and sought to attract them into his Islamic Army . . . Bin Ladin himself met with a senior Iraqi intelligence officer in Khartoum in late 1994 or early 1995. Bin Ladin is said to have asked for space to establish training camps, as well as assistance in procuring weapons, but there is no evidence that Iraq responded to this request.   (p. 61)

Similar meetings between Iraqi officials and Bin Ladin or his aides may have occurred in 1999 . . . The reports describe friendly contacts and indicate some common themes in both sides' hatred of the United States. But to date we have no evidence that these earlier contacts ever developed into a collaborative relationship. Nor have we seen evidence indicating that Iraq cooperated with al Qaeda in developing or carrying out any attacks against the United States.   (p. 66)

Given the considerable resources available to the Bush administration to find evidence for its claims about the connections between Iraq and al Qaeda (including its control of Iraq, Iraqi government facilities, and most former officials of Saddam Hussein's government during the last 6 years), and given the administration's clear motives for finding such evidence, the absence of credible evidence for Iraqi involvement in the terrorist attacks on the US is strong, but not irrefutable, evidence for the *non-involvement* of Iraq in those attacks. In September 2003, Bush himself finally admitted that there was "no evidence that Iraq was involved in the September 11 attacks" (Clarke, 2004, p. 268).

12.II.4. Reasons to Think that Some of the Claims about Iraq's Weapons and Ties to Al Qaeda Constituted Lying or (Attempted) Deception

Cheney's statement on September 20, 2002, that "there is irrefutable evidence that [Saddam] has once again set up and reconstituted his program to take uranium . . . so that it will function as the base material as a nuclear weapon . . . " was a lie. Cheney may well have believed that Iraq was trying to build nuclear weapons, but his statement is a lie because of his repeated and insistent claims to certainty. The claim that he had "irrefutable evidence" about which there could be "no doubt" (repeated twice) was a lie. Cheney knew that there were reasons to doubt this claim. A few days before, in mid September 2002, CIA chief Tenet told Bush, Cheney, and Rice that a member of Saddam's inner circle said that Iraq had no active programs to build weapons of mass destruction. At this time, Tenet also told Bush that he had doubts about whether the aluminum tubes were suitable for the purpose of enriching uranium (Rich, 2006, p. 246–247).[4] Cheney's claim that there was "no doubt" that Iraq was enriching uranium to make nuclear weapons was false. He knew that it was false and strongly warranted its truth.

The 1998 IAEA (International Atomic Energy Agency) report, which according to Bush (in a statement he made in September 2002—see above) claimed that Iraq was "six months away from developing a [nuclear] weapon," said no such thing. To the contrary, the IAEA report in question said: "There are no indications that Iraq has achieved its programme's goal of producing nuclear weapons . . . There are no indications of Iraq having retained any physical capability for the indigenous production of weapon-usable nuclear material in amounts of any practical significance . . . nor any indication that Iraq has otherwise acquired such material" (Korn, 2003, pp. 213–214).

If Bush read and understood the IAEA memo in question (and recalled its contents when he spoke about it), then he lied when he said that Iraq was six months away from having nuclear weapons. (In that case, Bush strongly warranted the truth of a statement that he knew was probably false.) If, as is very possible, Bush relied on reports from his staff, then it is likely that members of his staff are guilty of lying/deception. It is also possible that Bush was advised by people who were misinformed about the contents of the IAEA report. However, even if Bush's statement was an honest mistake by him and his staff, surely some people in the administration became aware of this mistake after Bush's statement; they are guilty of failing to correct it or asking Bush to correct it (if Bush was made aware of his mistake, then his failing to correct it constitutes deception on his part). If someone knows that she has made an unintentional false claim that caused others to have false beliefs about matters of great importance and she is able to correct that claim, then her failure to correct it counts as deception. By failing to correct the earlier claim, she is intentionally causing others to persist in false beliefs (see Chapter 2.I).

In his 2003 State of the Union Address, Bush also made claims about Iraq attempting to acquire nuclear weapons, citing as evidence the aluminum tubes and Iraqi attempts to purchase uranium in Niger (see above, 12.II.1). He made these claims despite having received several intelligence reports that contradicted or raised grave doubts about these claims. In September and October 2002, he received oral intelligence reports from Tenet that cast grave doubts about the aluminum tubes and the African uranium (Rich, 2006, pp. 246–247, 249–251).[5] On October 6, 2002, the CIA sent a fax to Bush explaining why the reference to Iraq and African uranium should be removed from the speech that Bush was set to give the next day (p. 252). Bush's statements about Iraq's nuclear program and the uranium and aluminum tubes were all false, but these statements may not have been lies because he may have believed them to be true. Were these statements deceptive? If Bush believed what he said then on this occasion, he did not attempt to deceive the public about Iraq's nuclear program. Even if we grant all of this, Bush's statement was still intended to deceive because he strongly warranted the truth of claims that he knew were open to serious doubt. He intended to cause the public to believe something that was false and that he believed to be false, namely, that there were no serious reasons for doubting that the stories about the aluminum tubes and the uranium from Niger were strong evidence that Iraq was attempting to acquire nuclear weapons. On a solemn occasion, such as the State of the Union Address, a democratically elected leader warrants the truth of what he says to a very high degree, especially if the statements are used as a basis for starting a war that will kill thousands of people. Bush knew that there was a basis for doubting these claims. Still, it is possible that he dismissed all of the counter-evidence presented to him as completely unfounded and did not think that it was a serious basis for questioning the truth of the claims he made. If that is the case, then Bush was not guilty of attempted deception by giving a much stronger warranty of truth than he knew was justified. However, in that case, we have strong reasons for questioning his intellectual honesty—he was willful in believing what he wanted to believe (believing what was consistent with his case for going to war) and not giving credence to evidence for things he did not want to believe (not believing or giving credence to what was inconsistent with his case for going to war). On the best construction possible, Bush was intellectually dishonest.

A more cynical interpretation (and one that is very likely correct) is that Bush and other members of his administration were so confident that *some* "weapons of mass destruction" (chemical weapons) would be found, that they did not worry very much about lying or deceiving the public about *other things*. At the end of the day, they expected that some of Iraq's pre-existing chemical weapons (which it had used earlier) would be found so that they could say that they were correct in their claim that Iraq possessed (some) "weapons of mass destruction."

For reasons given above, the classification of chemical weapons as "weapons of mass destruction" was misleading/deceptive.

A number of pundits have claimed that the Bush administration's false claims about "weapons of mass destruction" were honest mistakes because it would have been highly imprudent for them to deceive the public about these matters. Given the likelihood that the truth would come to light and subject the administration to very harsh criticism, members of the administration would not have made the claims they made unless they believed them. This argument is unconvincing. The administration (and almost everyone else) expected that chemical weapons would be found in Iraq. Therefore, the administration's claim that there were (some) "weapons of mass destruction" (or what it called "weapons of mass destruction") in Iraq was not a lie and was not a case of attempted deception. However, the expectation that chemical weapons would be found explains why making the false/exaggerated claims about *other matters* would not have seemed imprudent to the Bush administration. Whatever else happened, Bush and his administration were confident that they could say that they were correct in claiming that there were (some) weapons of mass destruction.

On the most charitable construction possible, Bush and other members of his administration were negligent and reckless in forming and acting on their views about Saddam Hussein's regime. They ignored a great deal of intelligence that pointed to different conclusions than those that they drew.

12.II.5. Lying and Deception about Other Matters Related to the Iraq War

Two days before the invasion of Iraq in March 2003, Bush said "Should Saddam Hussein choose confrontation, the American people should know that *every measure has been taken to avoid war* [my emphasis]" (Rich, 2006, p. 218). This is *clearly* a lie. Bush was aware of many alternatives to war (and alternatives to fighting a war as early as March 2003) that were urged on him by many people inside and outside of his administration. Among the alternative measures that Bush rejected was to allow Hans Blix and the UN weapons inspectors to complete their job before beginning a war.

Here, some will object that I am reading Bush's statements too literally. Bush's use of hyperbole ("every") is obvious and thus not a case of lying or deception. We should take him to be claiming that he took *every reasonable* measure to avoid war—he claimed that he took steps to avoid war and went to war only after all reasonable alternatives were exhausted. Even if it is false that he exhausted all reasonable alternatives to war, some might argue that his statement is not a case of lying or attempted deception because he believed that what he said was true. This argument is unpersuasive. Bush claimed that he tried to avoid war and went to some lengths to avoid going to war, but that is *false*. There is considerable evidence that Bush wanted to go war with Iraq (even before September 11, 2001) and that, rather than taking measures to avoid war, he was seeking a pretext to justify going to war. In a discussion with British Prime Minister Tony Blair, recorded by Blair's foreign policy adviser, Bush "toyed with the idea of staging a deliberate military provocation in order to precipitate a casus belli" (Brzezinski, 2007, p. 143).[6] Former Bush Treasury Secretary and member of the National Security Council, Paul O'Neill reports that this idea was seriously considered at a meeting of the National Security Council on another occasion (Suskind, 2004, p. 96).[7] In the "Downing Street memo," the secret minutes of a meeting between Blair and other high ranking British officials, Richard Dearlove reported on his visit with US intelligence officials in 2002. Dearlove "said that the White House was already determined to go to war, and was working to make sure that 'the intelligence facts' could be 'fixed around the policy' " (Rich, 2006, pp. 175–176). British Foreign Secretary Jack Straw, who was present at the meeting that Dearlove reported on, says the following: "It seemed clear that Bush had made up his mind to take military action, even if the timing was not yet decided. But the case was thin. Saddam was not threatening his neighbors, and his WMD capability was less than that of Libya, North Korea or Iran" (Rich, 2006, p. 239).

Dearlove's recollections are strongly corroborated by Paul O'Neill. According to O'Neill, at the first meeting of the National Security Council after Bush's inauguration in January 2001 (long before September 11, 2001), Powell said that he understood the US position to be that the US should help overthrow the Iraqi regime, and Bush affirmed this (Suskind, 2004, p. 74). O'Neill said that very early in 2001 at National Security Council meetings, "Actual plans . . . were already being discussed to take over Iraq and occupy it—complete with disposition of oil fields . . . " (Suskind, 2004, p. 129). According to O'Neill:

> From the start, we were building the case against Hussein and looking at how we could take him out and change Iraq into a new country. And, if we did that, it would solve everything. It was all about finding *a way to do it*. That was the tone of it. The President saying, "Fine. Go find me a way to do this."
>
> Suskind (2004, p. 86; also see pp. 187–188, 278, 306)

In his statement of March 17, 2003, Bush strongly warranted his claim that he went to war reluctantly and took many measures to avoid going to war with Iraq. This claim was false; he clearly rushed into war. Bush had not forgotten his earlier efforts to bring about a war when he spoke on March 17. Therefore, he knew that his claim was false, and the statement in question is a lie.

In a CNBC interview in 2004, Cheney denied ever having claimed that the connection between Mohamed Atta and Iraqi was "pretty well confirmed." However, there is a videotape of him saying exactly these words on the television news show *Meet the Press* in December 2001 (Rich, 2006, p. 209). Cheney's denial was almost certainly a lie. To suppose otherwise is to impute to him a very impaired memory. He and other members of the administration made this claim more than once, and it was a centerpiece of their case for war. Since he repeated his denial three times, it was not a slip of the tongue or a momentary lapse. One might object that Cheney only denied having used the words "pretty well-confirmed" and that there is no reason to think that he was lying in doing that because he might have forgotten that he used those words. This is possible, but in that case, Cheney's carefully parsed statement is still clearly a case of attempted deception. (By denying that he used those specific words, he was attempting to cause people to believe falsely that he never said anything that meant the same thing.) When making claims that are grounds for starting a war that will kill thousands of people, a leader strongly warrants those claims as true; explicitly saying that such claims "are pretty well confirmed" is redundant. Cheney *knew* perfectly well that his past statements implied that his claims about the Iraq–al Qaeda link were well confirmed. Therefore, even if we take him to be carefully parsing the words "pretty well-confirmed" and not saying anything he believed to be literally false, his denial of having said that the Iraq–al Qaeda connection was "pretty well-confirmed" was a bald-faced attempt to deceive the public about having earlier claimed to have strong evidence about the connection.

Both Bush and Cheney made false statements to the effect that the US had found mobile biological weapons labs in Iraq. (The existence of these mobile labs was one of the main claims stressed by Secretary of State Powell in his February 2003 speech to the United Nations General Assembly.) Bush claimed that this showed the US had found "weapons of mass destruction." On May 29, 2003, Bush answered a Polish interviewer about the failure to find "weapons of mass destruction" as follows: "We found the weapons of mass destruction. We found biological laboratories" (Rich, 2006, p. 269).

On June 5, 2003, he repeated his claim about the mobile biological weapons labs but dropped the claims about having found "weapons of mass destruction," "We recently found two mobile biological-weapons facilities which were capable of producing biological agents" (p. 271).

Cheney repeated Bush's claims about the mobile biological weapons labs on September 14, 2003 and January 22, 2004 (pp. 287, 301). However, two days before Bush's initial claim about the mobile weapons labs, a Defense Intelligence Agency (DIA) report of a fact-finding mission of US and British biological weapons experts was sent to Washington. It concluded that "there was no connection to anything biological" in the two mobile trailers in question (p. 268). If they were aware of this report when they made their claims about the biological weapons labs, it is nearly certain that Bush and Cheney lied. However, we do not know whether Bush and Cheney actually saw or heard about this report. It seems likely that they were aware of the report as it contained important newsworthy intelligence. Even if he was not aware of this report on May 29, it is reasonable to suppose that someone who knew about the report would have brought this to the attention of Bush and Cheney after Bush's initial false claims on May 29. This is a reasonable assumption, though far from certain. The DIA report in question was stamped "secret" and did not come to light until 2006 (p. 268). Given this, Bush's failure to correct his statement of May 29, 2003, is a case of attempted deception. On this assumption, it seems likely that Cheney's statements on September 14, 2003 and January 22, 2004 were lies.

Bush repeatedly lied when he denied that he and his administration selectively leaked classified information from the National Intelligence Estimate (NIE) to support his partisan political aims before the 2003 war. On April 6, 2006, Bush admitted to his press secretary, Scott McClellan, that he had authorized selective leaks from classified NIE documents to discredit Joseph Wilson's rejection of the Bush Administration's claims about Iraq seeking to obtain uranium from Niger. Bush leaked this information in October 2002. At the same time, Rice was denying that the administration engaged in selective leaking. Bush often decried selective leaking and there are news videos of him hypocritically attacking leaks in 2003 and saying "There are too many leaks of classified information" and "If there is a leak out of my administration, I want to know who it is" (McClellan, 2008, pp. 294–296). McClellan resigned his position on account of Bush's admission that he selectively leaked classified documents (pp. 297–301).

After the war and the failure to find any weapons of mass destruction, Bush gave a misleading explanation of his earlier mistaken claims: "Intelligence throughout the decade showed they had a weapons program. I am absolutely convinced, with time, that we'll find out that they did have weapons programs" (Korn, 2003, p. 282).

Rather than candidly admit that his earlier claims were false/mistaken, Bush changed the subject to claim that Iraq had weapons of mass destruction *programs*. Earlier, he claimed that Iraq possessed large *stocks of weapons of mass destruction* and that Iraq would obtain nuclear weapons "fairly soon" (on another occasion, Bush claimed that an IAEA report from 1998 said that Iraq was six months away from acquiring nuclear weapons; Korn, 2003, pp. 213–214). He claimed that there was an urgent need to go to war *very soon*. This carefully parsed statement was clearly an attempt to deceive the public about the extent of his earlier mistakes and suggest that earlier he had only claimed that Iraq had "weapons programs." Surely, Bush had not forgotten his earlier claims to the effect that Iraq already possessed the sorts of weapons in question.

After the war, Bush and members of his administration claimed that they were the victims of bad intelligence reports. In doing this, they conveniently ignored the fact that many intelligence reports available to the administration before the war contradicted what the administration had so confidently claimed.[8] Further, many people in the intelligence community reported being pressured by Cheney and other members of the Bush Administration to give reports favorable to the case for war (Korn, 2003, pp. 213–214).

12.III. A CASE OF LYING/DECEPTION TO AVOID WAR?

The foregoing examples of lying and deception in order to justify fighting wars prompt the question of whether there have been cases in which leaders lied in order to *avoid* wars. It would seem very improbable that none of the thousands and thousands of heads of state in human history have never told lies to avoid fighting wars. Here are the most likely examples of such cases that I have been able to find.

Bruce Cumings gives a detailed account of extensive deception by Dean Acheson (Secretary of State under Truman) and John Foster Dulles (Eisenhower's Secretary of State) concerning US foreign policy in Asia. At least two of the cases he describes seem to be cases of lying/deception to avoid war. On January 12, 1950, Acheson spoke to the Press Club in Washington DC. He excluded South Korea from the "US defense perimeter" (suggesting that the US would not defend South Korea if it was attacked by the communists; Cumings, 1990, volume II, pp. 408, 421–422). This was deceptive, if not a lie, because the Truman Administration had made no clear decision not to defend South Korea in case of an attack (several months later in June of 1950 the US *did* defend South Korea when it was attacked by North Korea). This deceptive statement was intended to deter *South* Korea from starting a war in Korea. Acheson and the Truman administration were greatly displeased by South Korea's belligerent policy toward North Korea and feared that South Korean leader Syngman Rhee would start a war with North Korea. (South Korea made very provocative military incursions into North Korea in June of 1950, shortly before the outbreak of the Korean War (Cumings, 1990, volume II, p. 547).) Acheson and the Truman Administration wanted to constrain Rhee by making him uncertain about US help in case he became embroiled in a war (p. 428).

Cumings also claims that John Foster Dulles systematically engaged in deception by cloaking his cautious foreign policy that aimed at avoiding war while preventing the further expansion of communism (a policy of "containment") in public statements and rhetoric that endorsed the much more risky and aggressive policy of removing communist regimes from power (the policy of "rollback"). Dulles was trying to constrain and "channel" "the rollbackers" in order to keep the peace during a very perilous stage of the Cold War (Cumings, 1990, volume II, pp. 29, 80, 708).

Some people allege that several months after the end of the Korean War President Eisenhower withheld and kept secret information about US prisoners being held after the war because he feared that it being revealed would lead to a resumption of the Korean War and thus risk causing a nuclear war between the US and the USSR. According to an article in the *New York Times*:

[D]ocuments, obtained from the Dwight D. Eisenhower Presidential Library . . . by a Congressional committee, show that the Pentagon knew in December 1953 that more than 900 American troops were alive at the end of the war but were never released by the North Koreans.

Congressional investigators said much of the information was confirmed by a former military aide to President Eisenhower, Col. Phillip Corso.

. . . Colonel Corso . . . said, " . . . in 1953, 500 sick and wounded American prisoners were within 10 miles of the prisoner exchange point at Panmunjom but were never exchanged." Panmunjom was the site of peace negotiations between the United States and North Korea that ended with an armistice on July 27, 1953. One of the documents . . . shows that the Army believed at that time that 610 "Army people" and 300 Air Force personnel were still being held prisoners by the North Koreans, five months after a prisoner exchange between the United States and North Korea.

Al Santoli, a Congressional investigator . . . said that the intelligence information released by the Eisenhower Library . . . showed that the Eisenhower Administration "was trying to do what it could to get the prisoners back" short of war.

Historians of the Korean War have suggested that the Eisenhower Administration chose not to make public much of its intelligence on the issue of missing Americans for fear of whipping up a war hysteria among Americans who would have demanded that the prisoners be returned home.

"In a nuclear age, Eisenhower could not risk telling the Russians or the Chinese that we're willing to go to all-out war to get our prisoners back," Mr. Santoli said.

Shenon (1996)

Eisenhower withheld the information/evidence in question and kept it secret from the public. Did this constitute lying/deception? In order to answer this question, we would need to take a close look at all of Eisenhower's statements about this matter. I have not been able to do this. However, if Eisenhower was asked questions about US prisoners of war (in press conferences and congressional briefings, etc.), then it seems likely that he resorted to deception or lying in order to keep the story secret.

Clearly, this topic requires a great deal more historical research. I hope that this book will prompt others, who are more capable of undertaking it than I, to do that research. I raise this unresolved issue here because of this hope and because I have had so little success in finding examples of lying/deception by leaders in order to prevent or avoid wars—this may be such a case.[9]

12.IV. A MORAL ASSESSMENT OF (SOME OF) THE CASES

12.IV.1. Lyndon Johnson

America's involvement in the Viet Nam War was a disaster for all parties involved. Johnson's dramatic escalation of the war turned out very badly. It did not alter what now seems to be the inevitable outcome of the war. In spite of sending more than half a million US soldiers and using massive firepower, the US was not able to win the war. The Vietnamese communists were clearly a much more competent and disciplined military force than the South Vietnamese. Unlike the US, they were willing to accept huge casualties and fight indefinitely. US involvement did not alter the outcome of the Viet Nam conflict (unification of the country under a communist government). Without US involvement, the Viet Nam conflict would have been a small-scale war (the South Vietnamese government would have collapsed without putting up much of a fight), rather than a terribly destructive war in which several million people were killed. Contrary to many dire predictions, the fall of South Vietnam did not seriously alter the outcome of the Cold War. It would be too strong to say that the deception involved in the Gulf of Tonkin Resolution was *the cause* of America's large-scale involvement in the Viet Nam War. Johnson might have obtained congressional authorization to escalate the war dramatically (in order to stop the advance of communism) without resorting to deception. Further, Johnson could have refrained from sending large numbers of US troops to Viet Nam in spite of the resolution. He felt great political pressure to "stand up to the communists," but he was also very pessimistic about the prospects for success in the war.[10] In any case, the deception in question was dishonesty in the service of a disastrous cause and was clearly morally wrong.[11]

12.IV.2. Bush and Cheney

Bush's decision to invade Iraq has caused immense suffering and destruction and appears to have been a terrible mistake. The war has killed tens/hundreds of thousands of Iraqis and injured many more. Several recent estimates of the total number of Iraqis killed in fighting since the US invasion of March 2003 range between 92 489 and 601 207. The British organization, Iraq Body Count, estimates the number of Iraqi civilians killed by military action between March 2003 and June 2009 at between 92 489 and 100 971.[12] The Associated Press estimates that 110 600 Iraqis were killed between March 2003 and April 2009.[13] The Iraq Health Ministry estimates that 150 000 Iraqi Security Force members and civilians were killed between March 2003 and November 2006.[14] The British medical journal, *The Lancet*, published an estimate by the Johns Hopkins School of Medicine that more than 601 027 Iraqi civilians were killed before the end of 2006 (October 11, 2006, as reported in Brown, 2006). On December 12, 2005, Bush estimated that about 30 000 Iraqis had died as the result of the war (Bumiller, 2005). (Bush has not made any more recent estimates of Iraqi deaths. His estimate would have to be higher as of this writing (43 months later). Bush's estimate was very close to the estimate that Iraq Body Count gave at that time (27 000–30 000). Therefore, his 2005 estimate is consistent with the Iraq Body Count's current estimate of 92 489 to 100 971 Iraqi civilian deaths.) There is very little interest in and discussion of these figures in the US (Iraqi casualties have not been a major issue in recent national elections in the US). That is both troubling and revealing.

Shortly after the US invasion, a very bloody insurgency bordering on a civil war ensued. Despite the tactical successes of the "Surge" of 2007, there is a serious danger that a civil war will erupt when the US Army leaves. There is also a danger that a civil war in Iraq between Sunni and Shiite factions will result in a larger regional war between Sunni and Shiite states. The Iraq War has destabilized a volatile region—instability in nuclear-armed Pakistan is particularly dangerous. (The US invasion of Iraq is extremely unpopular with the Pakistani people.)

Living conditions for ordinary people in Iraq have become worse due to the violence of the insurgency, high unemployment, and lack of electricity and water. Strong evidence for this is the very large number of Iraqis who have fled their homes since the US invasion in 2003. Approximately two million Iraqis have fled their country and another two million internally displaced. Roughly 15% of Iraq's people have fled their homes as result of the war (Rich, 2007).[15] Polls taken in the spring of 2007 reveal that only 21% of the Iraqi people think that the presence of US troops in Iraq makes Iraq more secure; 69% think that it makes security worse. Only 22% of Iraqis support the presence of US troops in Iraq (Kristof, 2007).

The Iraq War of 2003 seems to have been a disaster for US national interests. To date, more than 4245 US soldiers have been killed and more than 45 583 have been wounded.[16] Bush's often repeated claim that "it is better to fight the terrorists there [Iraq] rather than wait for them to attack us here [in the US]" is pure nonsense/bullshit. The presence of US troops in Iraq does *nothing* to prevent terrorists from entering the US. Bush's claim ignores the fact that the US invasion and occupation of Iraq (and the widely publicized mistreatment and torture of Iraqi prisoners at Abu Ghraib Prison and events such as the massacre of 24 unarmed Iraqi civilians by US Marines in Haditha) have inflamed hatred for the US in the Muslim world[17] and help recruit more people into Islamic terrorist groups. Fear and dislike of the US is much more widespread than ever before. A Zogby International poll shows that the number of people in several Middle Eastern counties who rate the US "unfavorably" increased dramatically between 2002 and 2004. The percentage of Egyptians who have negative attitudes toward the US increased from 76% to 98%; in Saudi Arabia the figure is 87% to 94%; and in Morocco the figures are 61% in 2002 and 88% in 2004 ("AntiAmericanism," *Wikipedia*, July 2007). The decline in US standing as a result of the war is even more dramatic in the case of its European allies. The Pew Global Attitudes Project Poll reports that the percentage of people in the United Kingdom who "have favorable attitudes about America" declined from 83% in 2000 to 56% in 2006. In France the percentage reporting favorable attitudes declined from 63% in 2000 to 39% in 2006. In Spain, the figures are 50% to 23%. Most dramatically of all, the percentage of people in Germany who reported a favorable view of America declined from 78% to 37% ("AntiAmericanism," *Wikipedia*, July 2007). The Iraq War has greatly diminished the standing of the US in the world. This greatly diminishes the diplomatic power of the US and makes for a growing conflict between the US and the Islamic world. The war has won Muslim extremist groups many new recruits and has made terrorist attacks on the US more likely, not less likely.

The war has cost the US hundreds of billions of dollars. As of August 2008, the US had spent $550 billion on the Iraq War ("Financial Costs of Iraq War," *Wikipedia*, July 2009). (This figure represents money spent to date; the total costs of the war, which include future medical care and pensions for the wounded, are clearly much greater.) This expenditure has diverted resources needed to protect the US against real terrorist threats. The war has diverted money for such things as better intelligence, border security, port security, emergency medical and civil defense preparation in the US,[18] and securing loose nuclear weapons and nuclear material in the former Soviet Union.[19] In a recent book, Nobel Prize-Winning economist Joseph Stiglitz gives a much higher estimate of the total cost of the war. When indirect and long-term costs (such as wear and tear on military equipment, the increase in the price of oil, and the cost of caring for veterans disabled by the war) are taken into account, he and his co-author Linda Bilmes estimate the total cost of the Iraq War to the US to be roughly three *trillion* dollars (Stiglitz and Bilmes, 2008, as reported by Herbert, 2008). In October 2007, the Congressional Budget Office estimated the total long-term costs of the Iraq War at $1.9 *trillion* dollars ("Financial Costs of Iraq War," *Wikipedia*, July 2009). These figures stand in sharp contrast to Cheney's absurdly low estimate that the war would cost $80 billion.[20]

From the US point of view, the Iraq War is unwinnable in exactly the same way that the Viet Nam War was unwinnable. The "Surge" of 2007 notwithstanding, the US is *clearly not* willing to commit a large enough military force for a long enough time to quell the insurgency, nor is it willing to spend nearly enough money to rebuild the country. In geopolitical terms, the big winner of the war seems to be Iran. Given their long persecution under Saddam Hussein, it is likely that the majority Shiite population of Iraq will want to align their country much more closely with Shiite Iran. As of this writing, Iran is seeking to develop its nuclear power industry and many fear that Iran is intent on developing nuclear weapons. It is very possible that the Iraq War and fear of the US are prompting Iran to try to acquire nuclear weapons. The overall strategic position of the US is much worse than before. Our military, economic, and diplomatic power is greatly diminished and the entire region has been destabilized.

There were several alternative courses of action that would likely have produced much better consequences than the war Bush started in March 2003. Bush could have worked through the UN and other international bodies to make sure that Iraq did not develop weapons of mass destruction and to minimize human rights violations within Iraq. Had he been more patient, Bush might have been able to bring about the peaceful removal of Saddam Hussein from power. Failing that, the Bush Administration could have tried to assassinate Saddam or remove him by bringing about a *coup d'état*. If all these measures failed, Bush could have attacked Iraq later under much more favorable circumstances (and likely fought a war with UN approval and the support of France and Germany and other major allies). The aftermath of such a war would likely have been much better than what actually happened. Contrary to the deceptive claims of the Bush Administration, there was no rush to go to war with Iraq in the spring of 2003. The acts of lying and deception by Bush, Cheney, and others in the Bush Administration precipitated a rush to war and were seriously immoral.

However, particularly in a book on the topic of lying and deception, I should not overstate my case. We will be in a much better position to judge the wisdom of Bush's actions in the distant future when events have played themselves out, but this war is such a major event that we can never be certain about what would have happened if the war had not occurred. (For more on the difficulties of historical counterfactuals see Chapter 13.IV.)

The foregoing notwithstanding, we *can* say the following. The Iraq War of 2003 has caused immense suffering in Iraq—it has killed and injured many thousands of people and caused *millions* of people to lose their homes and livelihoods. The war has caused great suffering to US and coalition soldiers and their families. The war has cost the US a huge amount of money. It has greatly harmed the reputation and standing of the US, inflamed hatred of the US in the Muslim world, and served as a recruitment tool for anti-American terrorist groups. The war has destabilized a volatile region and greatly diminished the ability of the US to deal with future crises.

If Iraq becomes a stable peaceful democracy in the future that will be a huge benefit. However, that outcome is far from certain and, in my view, unlikely—only time will tell. The removal of Saddam Hussein's tyrannical regime was a great benefit of the war, but it is questionable whether that benefit outweighs all of the bad consequences of the war. Even if it does (outweigh the bad consequences), it is likely that US could have removed Saddam or curbed his evil deeds without resorting to war. Many other things short of war should have been tried first. Lying and deception by the Bush Administration brought about a rush to war when war should have been the very last resort.

12.IV.3. Over-optimism as a Major Cause of Wars

Geoffrey Blainey's offers some very plausible speculations about the causes of war. According to Blainey, states do not begin wars unless their leaders think that they will win without paying too great a cost, but states often defend themselves against attack even if their leaders and citizens are not optimistic about their prospects for victory. Clearly, many nations that begin aggressive wars often fail to achieve victory at a cost they deem acceptable. Thus, it seems that over-confidence about one's prospects for victory at an acceptable price is a major cause of wars. Blainey (1973) writes: "If two nations are in disagreement on a vital issue, and if both expect that they will easily win a war, then war is highly likely. If neither nation is confident of victory, or if they expect victory to come only after long fighting then war is unlikely" (p. 55; also see pp. 103–107, 123–124, 141).

A corollary of Blainey's thesis is that deception that leads a country or its leaders to be overly optimistic about their prospects for an easy victory in an aggressive war is dangerous and harmful. These lessons are clearly illustrated in the Iraq War of 2003. The Bush administration greatly underestimated the costs and difficulties of the post-war occupation and administration of Iraq. It also greatly underestimated nationalistic and religious resistance to American occupation. Dismissing such worries, Cheney confidently predicted "we will be greeted as liberators" (Korn, 2003, p. 239). The Bush administration was completely willful in believing what it wanted to believe. General Shinseki told Rumsfeld that the US needed a much larger army to invade Iraq and was forced into retirement. Similarly, it seems clear that Hitler's over-confidence about the prospects for a German victory was a major cause of WWII (see Chapter 13.I).

12.IV.4. Franklin Roosevelt

Robert Dallek (1979) claims Roosevelt's acts of deception were justified:

In light of the national unwillingness to face up fully to the international dangers facing the country, it is difficult to fault Roosevelt for building a consensus by devious means. Had he directly presented his view to the public of what it must do . . . it would have won him few converts and undermined his popularity and ability to lead by confronting ambivalent Americans with choices they did not want to make. Further, if he advised the public of the fact that the U-boat had fired in defense and that Hitler did not then seem intent on attacking America's Atlantic traffic, as Churchill had reported, he would have risked having to wait for the collapse of Russia and Britain's near demise before gaining broad national support for a call to arms . . . that would have been a failure of his responsibility as Commander in Chief.   (p. 289; also see p. 530)

I must reluctantly agree with Dallek. Roosevelt's lies and acts of deception were necessary in order to save the lives and liberty of a great many people and were morally permissible. WWII was a supreme emergency. Monstrous tyrannies threatened to conquer much of the world. There was a serious danger that the Axis Powers would win the war. If Hitler had attacked the Middle East during the summer of 1941 instead of attacking Russia, he likely would have won the war (Shirer, 1960, p. 829; Keegan, 1999, pp. 295–305).[21] It is also likely that the Axis Powers would have won the war if Japan had attacked Russia in coordination with the Germans, instead of attacking the US.[22] Roosevelt had a much better grasp of dangers besetting civilization than did the public. His actions were "noble lies" for the good of the country and civilization. Roosevelt's deception helped Britain and Russia survive the German onslaught and helped the US prepare to enter the war. The risks involved in not pushing the US aggressively toward helping Britain and Russia and preparing for war justified Roosevelt's deception.

Nonetheless, Roosevelt's actions had indirect bad consequences in that they encouraged lying and deception by later Presidents for less pressing reasons. Dallek (1979) writes the following:

> Yet for all the need to mislead the country . . . the President's deviousness also injured the national well-being over the long run. His actions . . . created a precedent for later Presidents in less justifiable circumstances. "The fact that Roosevelt and Truman were substantially right in their assessment of the national interest," Senator William Fullbright asserted in 1971, "in no way diminishes the blamefulness of the precedents they set. FDR's deviousness in a good cause made it easier for LBJ to practice the same kind of deviousness in a bad cause." (p. 289; also see pp. 530–531, and Bok, 1979, pp. 179–180, and Alterman, 2004, p. 21 and elsewhere)

12.IV.5. Acheson, Dulles, and Eisenhower

It is (or can be) morally permissible to tell lies in order to prevent people from being killed. Individuals can be morally justified in telling lies to save the lives of other individuals (see Chapters 3.V and 7.II). Similarly, leaders can be justified in lying or deception to prevent disastrous wars that will kill many people (the cases of Acheson, Dulles, and Eisenhower may be such cases).

ENDNOTES

1. Lafeber's source is Kimball (1984, volume I, pp. 229–231).
2. Further, "CIA Chief George Tenet said that while Zarqawi had received funds from Bin Laden, he and his network were 'independent' of al Qaeda," ibid.
3. On this point see Clarke (2004, p. 267). Clarke was head of the Counterterrorism Security Group under Presidents George W. Bush and Bill Clinton.
4. My claim that this is a lie depends on Rich's reconstruction of the sequence of events and his claim that Cheney received the report from Tenet very shortly *before* making his statement. Even if Rich is mistaken about the exact sequence of events, Cheney never corrected or tempered his very strong claims in light of the evidence that later surfaced. Therefore, in any case, Cheney is still guilty of deception in this case. By failing to correct his past false claims (which caused others to have false beliefs), he intentionally caused others to persist in false beliefs.
5. Parts of Rich's account are contradicted by Bush's former national security advisor Steven Hadley. Hadley claims that Tenet's warning about doubts

concerning Saddam Hussein's alleged attempt to purchase uranium in Africa was given to him, but that he (Hadley) did not pass the information on to Bush. Hadley says that he failed to remember Tenet's report and remind Bush of it before Bush's State of the Union Address in 2003. Hadley offered to resign his position on account of this (McClellan, 2008, p. 177).

6. This incident is also reported in Rich (2006, pp. 190, 218).

7. O'Neill reports this occurred in February 2002.

8. For very extensive evidence of this and a detailed time-line of events, see Rich (2006, in particular, pp. 187, 190, 216–217, 246–247, 249–254, 256–257, and 264).

9. I ask anyone who can shed light on this to contact me at tcarson@luc.edu.

10. See Johnson's taped conversation with Senator Richard Russell on May 27, 1964 transcribed in Beschloss (1997, pp. 363–370; also see pp. 401–403).

11. Here is a possible counter-argument that should be considered. Although the West won the Cold War in spite of losing the Viet Nam War, US participation in the Viet Nam War might have decisively altered the outcome of the Cold War by postponing the defeat of the anti-Communist regime in South Viet Nam and stemming/slowing the advance of Communism. For all that, I can show it is possible that the Cold War would have developed very differently if South Viet Nam had fallen to the Communists in the mid-1960s instead of 1975.

12. Iraq Body Count [on the web]. These figures are also given in "Casualties of the Iraq War," *Wikipedia*, July 2009.

13. "Casualties of the Iraq War," *Wikipedia*, July 2009.

14. NPR The Toll of War [on the web].

15. Rich's figures are confirmed by the UNHCR, which gives the figures of 2 million people having fled the country and 1.9 million people internally displaced: http://www.unhcer.org/accessed June 20, 2007. At least one other source (Foreign Policy in Focus: www.fpif.org) gives higher figures.

16. These figures are as of February 28, 2009. The figures are not in dispute. My source is Iraq Coalition Casualty Count [on the web], which uses US Department of Defense figures. More recent figures from July 10, 2009 list 4300 killed and 46 132 wounded, "Casualties of the Iraq War," *Wikipedia* July 2009.

17. Brzezinski (2007) cites strong evidence for this:

In the fall of 2003, a revealing poll asked responders whether they regretted the initial lack of effective Iraqi military resistance—in effect, whether they regretted that more Americans were not killed. The disappointed numbered 93 percent in Morocco, 91 percent in Jordan, 82 percent in Lebanon, 82 percent in Turkey, 82 percent in Indonesia, 81 percent in Palestine, and 74 percent in Pakistan.   (pp. 149–150)

18. On the woeful unpreparedness of the US to respond to future terrorist attacks, see Clarke (2004, pp. 261–262).
19. See Clarke (2004, pp. 289–290) for a sharp rebuttal to Bush's claim that he is "fighting terrorists in Iraq so that we don't have to fight them in the streets of America."
20. Cheney gave this estimate on *Meet the Press* on March 16, 2003, several days before the war began ("Financial Costs of Iraq War," *Wikipedia*, July 2009).
21. A German attack on the Middle East in 1941 would have easily succeeded with a much smaller army than was needed to invade Russia. Such an attack would have greatly weakened Britain (by depriving it of oil and the Suez Canal and threatening its colonial empire in India). In addition, this would have provided Hitler with much needed oil, and put him in a better position to attack the Soviet Union the following year. Hitler's invasion of Greece and Yugoslavia in the Spring of 1941 delayed his invasion of Russia by about a month. Because of this, the German attack was greatly impeded by the fall rains and winter snows. An invasion of the Soviet Union in 1942, from both Europe and the Middle East, would have had a much greater chance for success.
22. The Soviet counter-attack around Moscow in December 1941 succeeded because the Soviets brought in 30 divisions from the Far East to defend Moscow. This counter-attack was possible because in October 1941 Stalin learned that Japan was preparing to attack the US and thus would not send its army into Manchuria to attack the Soviet Union. John Keegan (1989) thinks that the German attack on Moscow "would have almost certainly resulted in German victory" were it not for the transfer of troops from the far east (p. 209). Also see Bethell (1977, p. 186).

13

Honesty, Conflicts, and the Telling of History: More Case Studies

INTRODUCTION

The main thesis of this chapter is that deception and dishonesty about the historical record often create or aggravate conflicts and sometimes lead to disastrous consequences and, that, therefore, this sort of deception and dishonesty is morally wrong. Section 13.I discusses the myth of the "stab in the back" (*Dolchstosslegende*) and Germany's defeat in WWI. The widespread acceptance of this myth by the German people was one of the central causes of the rise of Nazism and the Holocaust itself. Section 13.II discusses other cases of deception and lying that distorted the historical record and thereby led to very bad consequences. In Section 13.III, I explicate the important concept of "half-truths." Half-truths mislead people, distort the truth but fall short of lying, and often fall short of deception. Even when it falls short of lying and deception, endorsing half-truths is often a form of morally objectionable intellectual dishonesty. I discuss a number of important cases in which half-truths have distorted the historical record and aggravated social/political conflicts. I also show that the concept of half-truths has widespread application in personal relationships. Section 13.IV offers a brief account of the virtue of intellectual honesty (with particular attention to intellectual honesty about political questions).

13.I. GERMANY, WORLD WAR I, AND THE MYTH OF THE "STAB IN THE BACK"

During and after WWI, General Ludendorff, Field Marshall von Hindenburg and other important German leaders lied and made false claims about the causes of Germany's defeat. They denied the plain facts of Germany's military defeat by a coalition of nations (including France, Britain, Russia, the US, Italy, Japan, Belgium, Rumania, Greece, and Serbia) that possessed vastly greater manpower and economic resources. Their actions had catastrophic consequences.

WWI was fought on two main fronts: (1) the "Western Front" where France, Britain, and Belgium fought Germany, and (2) the "Russian Front" where Germany and Austria-Hungary fought against Russia. The war was also fought in Italy, Serbia and Macedonia, the Caucasus, Mesopotamia, and Africa. Throughout the first three years of the war (1914–1917), the fighting on the Western Front was stalemated, and neither side was able to gain a decisive advantage. On the Eastern Front, the Germans prevailed and conquered much of the Russian Empire. In 1917, the US entered the war against Germany and the Bolsheviks took over the government in Russia and began negotiating an end to the war with Germany and Austria-Hungary. In early 1918, Germany and Russia signed a peace treaty. The Germans then moved much of their army from Russia to the Western Front where they enjoyed a temporary advantage before the American Army arrived in strength. In the spring and early summer of 1918, the Germans launched a successful offensive against the British and French. In July, they came close to Paris and seemed (at least to many in Germany) to be on the verge of winning the war. Then, very suddenly, everything collapsed. The American Army put one million soldiers into the battle (three million more American soldiers were on the way or in training), and the Germans were greatly outnumbered and outgunned. The morale of the German Army collapsed; roughly one million German soldiers deserted during the final months of the war (Herwig, 2000, p. 321; on this point also see Deist, 1996, p. 202). The collapse of morale was due to: (1) heavy casualties in the spring/summer offensives (0.75 million German soldiers were wounded between March and July 1918; the casualties were particularly high in the elite units that led the offensive); (2) the cumulative effects of Germany's total military casualties (two million killed, 4.2 million wounded; 2.7 million of the wounded were permanently disabled; Ferguson, 1999, pp. 295, 437); (3) the effects of the 1918 flu epidemic (1.75 million German soldiers caught the flu between March and July 1918); and (4) widespread hunger and starvation in Germany caused by the British naval blockade, which deprived Germany of the imported food it normally depended on.[1]

Hindenburg and Ludendorff were warned by subordinates about the dire situation of the German Army and its lack of resources to continue its offensive successfully in early May 1918, but they chose to ignore these warnings. Ludendorff reacted angrily, rebuking his subordinate, Colonel von Trier, for his "gloom-mongering" (Deist, 1996, pp. 199–200). (Similarly, US Defense Secretary Donald Rumsfeld ridiculed critics of the war for their unwarranted pessimism and worries about Iraqi insurgents who were fighting US forces after the 2003 Iraq war—"Henny Penny the Sky is Falling."[2]) Hindenburg and Ludendorff did not acknowledge the gravity of the military situation until August 1918. On August 8, 1918, British, Canadian, and Australian troops attacked on a 25-mile front. "The German front collapsed; within hours 16,000 prisoners had been taken . . ." (J. Williams, 2005, p. 192). On August 10, General Ludendorff (who together with Hindenburg commanded the army) told the Kaiser (Emperor) that the "war must be ended" (p. 193). The extent and gravity of this defeat were denied in official German press reports. On August 12, Ludendorff issued a brazenly dishonest communiqué stating that the attacks were "completely defeated" (p. 193). Lying and deception about this and other defeats made the German public completely unprepared for the news of Germany's defeat in November (on this point, see Deist, 1996, pp. 206–207). This dishonesty lent credence to the myth of the "stab in the back."

On October 1, 1918, the German high command met and Ludendorff told the Kaiser that Germany no longer had any hope of winning the war. Ludendorff advised the Kaiser and Chancellor to request an armistice immediately. Ludendorff cynically suggested that the Kaiser install liberals and socialists to head the government so that they would have the responsibility for ending the war (Herwig, 1997, p. 425). On October 2, 1918, Hindenburg wrote a letter to the government that begins as follows: "The Supreme Command adheres to its demand made on September 29, for the immediate despatch of the Peace offer to our enemies" (Wheeler-Bennett, 1936, p. 166).

Hindenburg cites as the reason for this the collapse of the Macedonian front in the Balkans, which required that the German Army send reserves from the Western Front thereby making it impossible for the Army to make good its recent heavy losses in France at a time when the enemy was "regularly bringing new and fresh reserves into action." Hindenburg states that "there no longer exists any prospect . . . of forcing peace upon our enemies." The letter makes no mention of the stab in the back and concludes: "In these circumstances it is imperative to stop fighting in order to spare the German people and its allies further useless sacrifices. Every day lost costs thousands of brave soldiers' lives" (Wheeler-Bennett, 1936, p. 166). At this time, the German Army was being quickly driven out of the French and Belgian territories that it had occupied since the beginning of the war. By early November 1918, Germany's allies (i.e., Austria-Hungary, Turkey, and Bulgaria) were out of the war, leaving Germany open to attack from the south by the Italian, British, Serbian, and Greek armies that were fighting Germany's allies.

On November 9, the Kaiser abdicated the throne. Germany was thrown into chaos. There were mutinies in the navy and left-wing/Marxist revolutions in several regions. The socialist government that came to power had the task of ending the war. The blame for the harsh peace was shifted to the leftist government. According to the later Nazi version of the story, Jews were primarily to blame for causing Germany's defeat. Some of the leaders of the socialist/leftist government that came to power were Jewish. Rosa Luxemburg, Karl Liebknecht, and Kurt Eisner were prominent Jewish members of the Marxist political parties that helped instigate labor strikes and resistance to the German war effort during the later stages of the war. (Leibknecht and Luxemburg were in prison between 1916 and 1918 and thus had no direct role in the labor unrest in the later stages of the war.) This much *was* true—little else in the Nazi story about "the stab in the back" was true—and even this needs to be qualified. Hitler greatly exaggerated the role of Jews in the left-wing political parties. Most of the leaders and members of these parties were non-Jewish and most German Jews were not members of far-left political parties. Hitler's perceptions were distorted by his proximity to Kurt Eisner, who organized the overthrow of the Bavarian Government on November 7, 1918 and was briefly Prime Minister of the "Bavarian Soviet Republic." (Hitler returned to Munich after the end of WWI.) (I want to make clear my own view that those Germans on the left (both gentiles and Jews) who sought to end the senseless slaughter of WWI deserve credit not blame.)

Still one might ask whether Jews were "over-represented" in left-wing political parties. There are no definitive data about Jewish political views and voting patterns during WWI or the Weimar Republic. It is clear, however, that Jews were greatly "over-represented" in the leadership positions of the moderate Marxist Social Democratic Party (SDP). Roughly 10% of the SDP Reichstag deputies during the Weimar era were Jewish, even though Jews were less than 1% of the total German population at that time (Niewyk, 2001, pp. 26, 29–30). Because the SDP helped lead strikes during the war, the party was widely held to be implicated in the "stab in the back." The prominence of Jewish Bolsheviks such as Leon Trotsky and Bella Kuhn in the Russian and Hungarian Revolutions might have also lent some credence to the view that Jews supported the leftist parties that undermined the German war effort (p. 28). However, there were very few Jews in leadership positions in the radical left-wing German Communist Party. None of the 100 Communist members of the last Weimar Reichstag was Jewish (p. 32). Ironically, a right-wing Jew, Paul Cossman, editor of a Munich journal "was among the first to spread the story that Jewish Marxists like Kurt Eisner and Rosa Luxemburg had stabbed the undefeated German Army in the back" (p. 99). Cossman later died at the hands of the Nazis in a concentration camp (p. 99).

After the war, the German government held hearings to determine why the war had turned out so badly for Germany. Hindenburg was asked to testify. In November 1919, at the hearing before the Committee of Inquiry of the Reichstag, Hindenburg claimed: "As an English general has very truly said 'The German Army was stabbed in the back.' It is plain enough upon whom the blame lies" (Wheeler-Bennett, 1936, pp. 236–237; also see Shirer, 1960, p. 31).

He claimed that the stab in the back caused Germany's defeat and said "we could have brought the struggle to a favorable issue if determined and unanimous co-operation had existed between the army and those at home" (Wheeler-Bennett, 1936, p. 235). Socialist Chancellor Ebert also lent credence to the myth of the stab in the back when he greeted German soldiers returning to Berlin in December 1918 and told them that they had been undefeated on the battlefield (Bessel, 1993, p. 263).[3] The claim that Germany was undefeated on the battlefield and lost the war because of disloyalty on the home front is patently false.[4]

Germany lost the war because it was overwhelmed by its far more numerous and economically powerful foes. On September 28, 1918, Hindenburg and Ludendorff met with the Kaiser and insisted on an immediate armistice. In his letter of October 2, 1918, Hindenburg wrote that the *military* situation made it imperative to "stop fighting." His letter makes no mention of any "stab in the back" (also see Shirer, 1960, p. 31).

The claim that a British General supported the story of the stab in the back is false. In fact, two British Generals were inadvertently involved in this story. General Sir Frederick Maurice, whose book *The Last Four Months* "was grossly misinterpreted by German reviewers in the German press as proving that the German Army had been betrayed on the home front, and not defeated in the field" (Wheeler-Bennett, 1936, p. 237). General Maurice attempted to correct this misinterpretation in the German press but his correction was ignored and the story took hold in popular consciousness in Germany. The other British General was General Malcolm, who while talking to Ludendorff after the war, asked him to summarize his views and asked Ludendorff, "Do you mean, General, that you were stabbed in the back?" Ludendorff affirmed that this was his meaning, but General Malcolm himself did not endorse the view that Germany was stabbed in the back by traitors on the home front (Wheeler-Bennett, 1936, p. 237; also see Shirer, 1960, p. 31 and Chickering, 1998, p. 190).

Hindenburg's testimony was very self-serving and masked the terrible strategic mistakes of the German high command. These mistakes included initiating a battle of attrition at Verdun, even though Germany was greatly outnumbered by its adversaries, provoking the US into war by initiating unrestricted submarine warfare in 1917, and gambling everything on a massive offensive in 1918 against numerically and materially superior foes who were being reinforced by the arrival of a huge American Army. During the hearing in question, Hindenburg was repeatedly asked about the [disastrous] decision to begin unrestricted submarine warfare: "Hindenburg resolutely ignored the Committee's technical questions concerning the U-boat campaign and instead read a prepared statement [which included the claim about the stab in the back] . . . A stunned Committee of Inquiry was barely able to cross-examine the 'witness' " (Herwig, 1997, pp. 447–448).[5]

In addition, Wilhelm II's arrogance and bungling before WWI created a balance of power very unfavorable to Germany by alienating both Russia and Britain. Germany was so greatly outnumbered by its adversaries that, during the crisis that arose after the assassination of Franz Ferdinand, it felt compelled to mobilize for war and carry out the Schlieffen Plan (which required Germany to mobilize quickly and attack and defeat France before Russia mobilized its very large army), rather than patiently trying to negotiate a settlement to the crisis. The monarchists and militarists were also to blame for continuing to fight such a terrible war rather than seek peace much earlier and for continuing the war for three months after Ludendorff said that all was lost and more than one month after Hindenburg had written that it was "imperative" to stop the fighting, that further fighting would involve "useless sacrifices," and that "each day lost" would cost "thousands of brave soldiers' lives" (Wheeler-Bennett, 1936, p. 166).

The historical record is clear and unambiguous; the German monarch and military leaders, rather than the socialists or the Jews, brought about the catastrophe that befell Germany during and after WWI. Still, we might ask how much lying and deception were involved in the creation of the *Dolchstosslegende*. Ludendorff and other military leaders clearly lied to the German press and public about the many military defeats suffered by the German Army in the later stages of the war. It is not as clear what we should say about Hindenburg's testimony in 1919. Near the end of the war, he told the Kaiser that the military situation required that the war be ended immediately and did not cite treason or disloyalty on the home front as a crucial reason to end the war. It is possible that he later came to believe that Marxists on the home front had played a major part in undermining support for the German war effort. Nonetheless, he *knew* that the army had collapsed in early August 1918, long before leftist groups on the home front succeeded in greatly undermining support for the government and war effort. He *knew* that America's entry into the war dramatically altered the military situation and balance of power (and that America's entry into the war was a result of his decision to resume unrestricted submarine warfare). He *knew* that huge numbers of German soldiers were deserting late in the war. His evasion of the questions about the resumption of unrestricted submarine warfare and public statements about the *Dolchstoss* were clearly intended to deceive the public about the extent of his own personal responsibility for Germany's disastrous defeat in the war.

There is no reason to think that Hindenburg was motivated by anti-Semitism. He knew that German Jews were very patriotic and had sacrificed themselves for the war effort as much as gentiles did. In response to allegations from the far right that German Jews were not doing their part in the war effort, the army began a "Jew count" in 1916 to ascertain the truth of these charges. This "count" showed that roughly the same proportion of German Jews and gentiles served in the army, served in the front lines, were killed, were decorated, and promoted. The rumors that Jews were shirking danger in the front lines were completely untrue and Hindenburg knew this (Herwig, 2000, pp. 322–323). Hindenburg was simply trying to avoid being personally blamed for the catastrophe that befell Germany as a result of WWI. This example provides an important lesson. If someone lies or engages in deception in order to avoid being held responsible for some very bad outcome, it is likely that someone else will be unjustly blamed or punished for what s/he did.

The Nazis took the original popular story of the stab in the back and gave it a decidedly anti-Semitic spin,[6] but the myth of the stab in the back (and the anti-Semitic version of that myth) began *before* the end of WWI: "By the summer of 1918, Pan-Germans had already laid the foundation for the *Dolchstoss* myth—even identifying the guilty party. In a harrowing statement, the chairman of the Pan-German League declared on October 19 that Germany's impending collapse 'should be used for a fanfare against Jewry and the Jews as lightning conductors for all injustices' " (Astore and Showalter, 2005, p. 72; also see Deist, 1996, p. 207).

The myth of the stab in the back is a grotesque distortion of the clear historical record. Unfortunately, the story had great resonance with popular consciousness in Germany, in part, because of its similarity to the very well known story in the *Niebelungenleid* in which the great hero Siegfried is stabbed in the back by the spear of the evil Hagen. Hindenburg alludes to this story in his autobiography, *Aus Meinem Leben*, which was published shortly after the war in September 1919 (Wheeler-Bennett, 1936, pp. 226–227).

The consequences of the widespread belief in the myth of the stab in the back were very grave. Hitler passionately believed that Germany was "stabbed in the back" by Jews and leftists. Many of Hitler's contemporaries commented on the utter sincerity and conviction of his early speeches and informal talks; his rage at the "November Criminals" was heartfelt (see Weinberg, 1995, p. 185). Biographers concur that learning of Germany's defeat while convalescing in a military hospital was a shattering experience for Hitler (see, for example, Bracher, 1970, p. 66; Fest, 1974, pp. 78–80; Kershaw, 1998, pp. 97–98). Hitler gives a very vivid description of this in *Mein Kampf*:

everything went black before my eyes . . . I . . . threw myself on my bunk, and dug my burning head into my blanket and pillow.

Since the day when I had stood at my mother's grave, I had not wept. . . .

And so it had all been in vain. In vain all the sacrifices and privations; in vain the hunger and thirst of months which were often endless; in vain the hours in which, with mortal fear clutching at our hearts, we nevertheless did our duty; and in vain the two millions who died. . . . Was it for this that boys of seventeen sank into the earth of Flanders? . . .

. . . Was it for this that he had lain in the hell of the drumfire and in the fever of gas attacks without wavering, always thoughtful of his one duty to preserve the fatherland from enemy peril?

The more I tried to achieve clarity on the monstrous event in this hour, the more the shame of indignation and disgrace burned in my brow. . . .

There followed terrible days and even worse nights—I knew that all was lost. Only fools, liars, and criminals would hope in the mercy of the enemy. In these nights hatred grew in me, hatred for those responsible for this deed.

Kaiser William II was the first German Emperor to hold out a conciliatory hand to the leaders of Marxism without suspecting that scoundrels have no honor. While they still held the imperial hand in theirs, their other hand was reaching for the dagger. There is no making pacts with Jews; there can only be the hard: either–or.

I, for my part, decided to go into politics. (Hitler, 1943, pp. 204–206)

During 1918–1919, Hitler became *violently* anti-Semitic (he was, by most accounts, anti-Semitic before 1918, but he was not consumed by hatred for the Jews). Hitler's wholehearted belief in the myth of "the stab in the back" seems to be the main explanation for this dramatic change in his attitudes about the Jews in 1918–1919. In *Mein Kampf* and his speeches, he returns over and over to denunciations of the "November Criminals" who stabbed Germany in the back. The widespread acceptance of the myth of "the stab in the back" (and the credibility that Hindenburg's dishonest statements gave it) made Nazi anti-Semitism more popular and seem more reasonable (or less unreasonable) than it would have otherwise.

Heinrich Himmler appeals to the *Dolchstoss* as a justification for the extermination of the Jewish people in his infamous speech to the SS officers in Posen in October 1943. Speaking with respect to the "extermination of the Jewish people," he says:

This is a page of glory in our history . . . for we all know how difficult we should have made it for ourselves if . . . we had Jews today in every town as secret saboteurs, agitators, and trouble mongers. We would now probably have reached the 1916/1917 stage when Jews were still in the German national body.
. . . We had the moral right, we had the duty to our people, to destroy this people which wanted to destroy us.   (pp. 563–4)

A number of major historians believe that the *Dolchstosslegende* was a decisive and essential cause of the rise of Nazism and the Holocaust. William L. Shirer writes: "Thus emerged for Hitler, as for so many Germans, a fanatical belief in the legend of the 'stab in the back' which, *more than anything else* [my emphasis], was to undermine the Weimar Republic and pave the way for Hitler's ultimate triumph" (Shirer, 1960, p. 31; also see Bracher, 1970, p. 66).

Hitler biographer Ian Kershaw (2006) claims that Hitler's wholehearted acceptance of the myth of the stab in the back was "at the heart" of his murderous hatred for the Jews (p. 8).[7] Kershaw says that from the beginning of his career, Hitler pursued two goals, restoring Germany's greatness and "punishing those responsible for the revolution that followed ['the capitulation in 1918'] and the national humiliation that was fully revealed in the Treaty of Versailles." He continues:

These goals could only be attained . . . "by the sword." Since in his eyes the Jews were to blame for the worst crimes of all time—for the "stab in the back" of 1918, the capitulation, the revolution, for Germany's misfortune . . . and since in his belief in the legend of the "Jewish World Conspiracy" they would always block his path and pose the most dangerous enemy to his plans, it followed logically that war for him had to be a war against the Jews.   (p. 10)

Lucy Dawidowicz (1975) thinks it "likely" that Hitler's radical anti-Semitism dates from November 1918 (p. 155). She claims that the "Final Solution grew out of" three main factors: "traditional anti-Semitism," the widespread belief in the *Dolchstoss* in Germany, and "the emergence of Hitler and the National Socialist Movement" (p. 163). "Without the paranoid delusion of the Dolchstoss that masses of Germans shared in the wake of Germany's defeat, political upheavals, economic distress, and humiliations of the Versailles Treaty, Hitler could not have transformed the German brand of conventional anti-Semitism into a radical doctrine of mass murder" (p. 163). Holger Herwig (2000) asks: "Is it too far off the mark to suggest that the 'twisted road to Auschwitz' began with the *Dolchstosslegende?*" (p. 323).

Gerhard Weinberg speculates that the acceptance of the myth of the stab in the back caused Hitler and his entourage to be much too optimistic about Germany's chances of winning WWII and greatly underestimate the military power of the US. Hitler and his followers believed that Germany almost single-handedly defeated Britain, France, Russia, the US, and Italy during WWI. "The belief that Germany had lost World War I at home rather than having been defeated at the front almost automatically led to speculation about a possible successful repetition" (Weinberg, 1995, p. 75). Acceptance of the myth commits one to thinking that the entry of the US into WWI was not a decisive event that caused Germany's defeat (Weinberg, 1995, pp. 185, 188, 196). Hitler rashly declared war on the US on December 11, 1941 to honor the terms of his alliance with Japan—the very moment at which his invasion of Russia was encountering grave problems.

Karl Bracher speculates that the currency of the myth inhibited members of the German resistance movement in their actions against Hitler and the Nazis. Knowing the terrible consequences of the myth in Germany, they were afraid that their actions would give rise to similar destructive myths in the future (Bracher, 1970, pp. 397–398, 446).

Another important consequence of Hitler's acceptance of the myth of the stab in the back is this. Because he genuinely believed that Germany was defeated because of treason on the home front in WWI, Hitler was afraid to do things he thought would hurt civilian morale. As a result, he was reluctant to do things that would require economic sacrifices of German civilians. Substantial production of consumer goods continued in Germany during the first three years of the war. Ian Kershaw (2000) writes:

Hitler shored up by Goering had, however, resisted imposing increased hardship and material sacrifice on the civilian population. He was conscious as ever of the collapse of morale on the home front during the First World War, certain that this had undermined the war effort and paved the way for revolution. His anxiety about the impact on the morale of their men-folk at the front, coupled with his traditionalist views about the domestic role of women, had led him to oppose the conscription of female labour to work in the hard-pressed armaments industries.   (p. 563)

The German economy was put on a war footing only after the defeat at Stalingrad and Goebbels' call for "total war" in February 1943.

American Versions of the *Dolchstosslegenge*?

William Astore argues that Bush, Cheney, McCain, and others are laying the groundwork for their own American *Dolchstosslegenge* in order to deflect the blame that is properly theirs for the disastrous war in Iraq. Astore (2007) writes:

The world's finest military launches a highly coordinated shock-and-awe attack that shows enormous initial progress . . . But the war unexpectedly drags on. As fighting persists into a third, and then a fourth year, voices are heard calling for negotiations, even "peace without victory." Dismissing such peaceniks and critics as defeatists, a conservative and expansionist regime—led by a figurehead who often resorts to simplistic slogans and his Machiavellian sidekick who is considered the brains behind the throne—calls for one last surge to victory. Unbeknownst to the people on the home front, however, this duo has already prepared a seductive and self-exculpatory myth in case the surge fails.

The United States in 2007? No, Wilhelmine Germany in 1917 and 1918, as its military dictators, Field Marshal Paul von Hindenburg and his loyal second, General Erich Ludendorff, pushed Germany toward defeat and revolution in a relentless pursuit of victory in World War I. Having failed with their surge strategy on the Western Front in 1918, they nevertheless succeeded in deploying a stab-in-the-back myth, or *Dolchstosslegende*, that shifted blame for defeat from themselves and Rightist politicians to Social Democrats and others allegedly responsible for losing the war by their failure to support the troops at home.

Astore faults Bush for refusing to call upon the nation to make any sacrifices for the war effort and says:

. . . Now, they are getting ready to claim that it was all *our* fault. *We* were the ones who lost our patience and will to victory. . . .
  . . . Now, despite dramatic setbacks over the last four years, they still refuse to mobilize our national will . . .
  So let me be clear: If we lose in Iraq, the American people will not be to blame. We cannot be accused of lacking a will that was never wanted or called upon to begin with. Yet the stab-in-the-back myth gains credibility precisely because so few high-level people either in government or the military are being held accountable for failures in Iraq.

The parallels Astore draws between Bush and Cheney and the *Dolchstosslegende* are striking and frightening. It is clear, as of this writing (July 2009), that many Republicans claim that the "Surge" of 2007 led by General Petraeus has succeeded to the extent that the Iraq War of 2003 has been, or can be, a "victory" for the US. It is also clear that if President Obama withdraws US troops from Iraq and the situation there falls to pieces, many Republicans will blame Obama and the Democrats for betraying those who fell and for turning victory into defeat. However, it is open to debate whether the claims they are prepared to make under those circumstances would be myths (false) (has the surge ensured or made possible a successful outcome for the war?). It is also open to debate to what extent such claims by Republicans would be honest or sincere. One factor that greatly complicates this is that the term "victory" or "success" is ambiguous. No doubt, a superpower such as the US *could*, if it chose and had the will to do so, prevail for a very long time on the battlefield in Iraq. However, that would not, by itself, constitute victory/success. The question is whether it is possible to achieve a favorable military *and political* outcome that is worth the enormous humanitarian and economic price (paid by both Iraqis and Americans) of the war (and continuing the war). For my own part, I think not. I think that Astore is largely correct in his views quoted above. I also think that he is correct in thinking that there is another mistaken *Dolchstosslegende* about the Viet Nam War that is widely accepted in America, but I will not attempt to defend his views (or assume their correctness) here.

Regardless of the correctness of Astore's analyses of these two wars, we should expect destructive and harmful myths of "stabs in the back" to be common phenomena. The following are clearly true:

1. Political leaders often lead their nations into disastrous, foolish, and unjustified wars, indeed most wars are disastrous, foolish, and unjustified.
2. Military and political leaders often make mistakes while fighting wars that lead their nations to disaster.
3. Often, when wars go badly and cause the nations fighting them great harm, anti-war sentiments and movements arise in those countries.
4. Human beings are reluctant to admit their own errors, particularly errors that lead to disaster and great loss of life.

Therefore,

5. When wars go badly and leaders are to blame, they are reluctant to admit responsibility for the disasters they have caused and, when it is an option for them, they will be very tempted to blame opponents of the war on the home front.

There is no reason for patriots of any stripe to think that their own leaders are exempt from these motivations.

Myths of stabs in the back are very dangerous and destructive. They unfairly deflect blame for failed disastrous wars from leaders and popular nationalistic sentiments to others who rightly and justly opposed those disastrous wars. The scapegoating of the Jews by the Nazis is a particularly striking and horrific result of the German myth of the stab in the back. In addition (and I think more commonly), myths of stabs in the back are likely to facilitate the continuation of disastrous wars and blind leaders and peoples to the dangers of fighting or continuing wars by making them overly optimistic about chances for success (see Chapter 12.IV.3). Such myths are extremely harmful in that they deter and inhibit anti-war movements from effectively opposing foolish and disastrous wars.

13.II. REWRITING HISTORY

13.II.1. Feel-Good Confederate History and the Post-Civil War South

Prominent in this version of history are the kindly paternalistic slave masters of *Gone with the Wind* and W. D. Griffith's film *Birth of a Nation*. This version of history downplays or denies the evils of American slavery; e.g., the exploitation of slave labor, the lack of freedom/autonomy inherent in slavery, the horrors of the "middle passage" from Africa to the New World, the separation of families, harsh corporal punishment, and the rape of and sexual exploitation of slave women by their masters. It justifies and glorifies the KKK.

In the late nineteenth and early twentieth centuries, the United Confederate Veterans and the United Daughters of the Confederacy lobbied very aggressively and successfully to make sure that their version of history was taught in Southern schools and colleges. They sought to represent the Confederate cause as a valiant "lost cause" that fought for states' rights and constitutional liberties, not to defend the institution of human slavery (McPherson, 2007, p. 93). According to this view:

> Confederate soldiers . . . fought for a noble cause, the cause of state's rights, constitutional liberty, and the consent of the governed. Slavery had nothing to do with it. "Think of it, soldiers of Lee!" declared a speaker at a reunion of the United Confederate Veterans in 1904. "You were fighting, they say, for the privilege of holding your fellow man in bondage! Will you for a moment acknowledge the truth of that indictment? Oh no! . . . You could not have followed a banner that was not a banner of liberty."
>
> McPherson (2007, p. 94)

These groups fought to make sure that history textbooks used in Southern schools portrayed the Confederate cause and American slavery in a very favorable light. A number of Southern states enacted laws to ensure this (McPherson, 2007, pp. 99–100). One important textbook written by Susan Pendelton Lee made the following claims about American slavery: "the evils connected with it were less than those of any other system of labor. Hundreds of thousands of African savages had been Christianized under its influence — the kindest relations existed between [the slaves] and their owners . . . They were better off than any other menial class in the world" (McPherson, 2007, p. 99). The "historian general" of the United Daughters of the Confederacy, Mildred Rutherford, wrote several widely distributed pamphlets. Among the claims she made are the following:

> Southern men were anxious for the slaves to be free. They were studying earnestly the problems of freedom, when Northern fanatical Abolitionists took matters into their own hands.

More slaveholders and sons of slaveholders fought for the Union than for the Confederacy . . .

Gen. Lee freed his slaves before the war began and Gen. Ulysses S. Grant did not free his until the war ended . . .

Union forces outnumbered Confederate forces five to one . . . .

McPherson (2007, pp. 102–103)

In another pamphlet written for teachers and librarians Rutherford wrote:

Reject a book that says the South fought to hold her slaves,

Reject a book that speaks of the slaveholder of the South as cruel and unjust to his slaves.

McPherson (2007, p. 102)

Pendelton Lee, Rutherford, and other like-minded neo-Confederates were extremely successful in banishing books critical of the antebellum slavery and the Confederate cause from southern schools and libraries. "One target of these committees was the *Encyclopedia Britannia*, which contained an article stating that slavery was exploitative rather than paternal and another maintaining that secession was revolutionary rather than constitutional" (McPherson, 2007, p. 100).

Offending books were burned at one Southern college (p. 101). At Roanoke College in Virginia there was a huge outcry over Professor Herman Thorstenberg's use of Henry Elson's *History of the United States* as a textbook. Elson's book was offensive to neo-Confederates, because it claimed that "the slavery issue was the main factor in provoking secession and war . . . which he called the 'slaveholders' rebellion" (McPherson, 2007, p. 104). Particularly offensive to their sensibilities were two passages in which Elson quoted a sister of James Madison, who said that although "Southern ladies were complimented with the name of wife, they were only the mistresses of seraglios," and quoted another southern woman who told Harriet Martineau that "the wife of many a planter was but the chief slave of his harem" (McPherson, 2007, p. 104).

A measure of the power of the neo-Confederate attempt to squelch opposing views is the furor created over Woodrow Wilson's *History of the American People*, which claimed that the Union ship USS *Monitor* won its famous battle with the Confederate ship CSS *Merrimac*. This innocuous claim was widely denounced in the Southern press. Wilson who was then (1911) Governor of New Jersey was elected President the next year. He felt compelled to write "a letter of apology on the official stationary of the New Jersey executive mansion, expressing himself 'very much mortified' by his mistake" (McPherson, 2007, pp. 100–101).

The views in question represent an absurd and grotesque distortion of the historical record. This dishonest "feel-good" version of history blinded many people to the terrible injustices of slavery in the post-Reconstruction American South. These myths and distortions of history helped to allow great injustices to continue for a very long time. The terrible reversion of the American South from Reconstruction to Jim Crow (roughly from 1880 until 1970) was facilitated by this dishonest retelling of history. Jim Crow ended in the light of the truth—the truth of the grievances articulated by the civil rights movement and such books as John Howard Griffin's *Black Like Me* and Martin Luther King's *Why We Can't Wait*.

Many educated people and historians in the South propounded and endorsed the feel-good Confederate version of history. It would be rash to say that all of them were engaged in lying and deception, especially since I am not privy to their actual beliefs and intentions. The claim that the Confederates were not fighting to preserve slavery can be spun so as to have some plausibility, but only if certain evidence is selectively emphasized and other evidence is selectively ignored. At the beginning of the war, the Union was not aiming to abolish slavery (and thus the Confederacy was not fighting to preserve slavery). However, after the Emancipation Proclamation, which proclaimed the freedom of the slaves behind Confederate lines as of January 1, 1863, and, even more clearly, by the summer of 1864, when Lincoln ran for re-election on a platform calling for the adoption of a Constitutional Amendment to totally abolish slavery, the Union fought the Civil War largely for the purpose of reducing/ending slavery.[8] Even this way of putting it concedes far too much. The Confederate states seceded because of Lincoln's policy to prohibit the institution of slavery in federal territories and new states admitted to the Union. Despite their states' rights rhetoric, they demanded that new states and territories *not* have the right to prohibit slavery. In this demand they were emboldened by the Dred Scot decision, which, on some understandings, gave slaveholders the right to bring "their property" anywhere in the US. The war came because the militant deep South demanded that the US government permit the territorial enlargement of slavery. Therefore, the Confederates *were* fighting for the institution of slavery—not to preserve it, but to *extend* it. Lincoln put it best in his Second Inaugural Address:

[the institution of slavery] constituted a peculiar and powerful interest. All knew that this interest was somehow the cause of the war. To strengthen, perpetuate, and extend this interest was the object for which the insurgents would rend the Union even by war; while the government claimed no right to do more than restrict the territorial enlargement of it . . .

Lincoln (volume II, p. 686)

Rutherford's claims cited above—her claim that (prior to the beginning the Civil War) [many] people in the Confederate states were looking for ways to end slavery, her claim that more slave owners fought for the North than the South, her claim that the Confederates were outnumbered five to one, and her claim that Grant owned slaves during the Civil War—are preposterous and demonstrably false. But, were these statements lies? Did she know or believe that they were false? Did she believe that what she said was true? I cannot claim to know what she believed about each of these points. However, it is demonstrable that she was a liar and extremely dishonest in her telling of history. She *made up* the following quotation, which she dishonestly attributed to the famous Civil War historian James Ford Rhodes: "Emancipation Proclamation was not issued from a humane standpoint. He [Lincoln] hoped that it would incite the negroes to rise against women and children. His Emancipation Proclamation was intended only as a punishment for the seceding states" (McPherson, 2007, p. 103). This fabricated quotation is doubly dishonest. Not only is it a lie that Rhodes said this, the substance of the quotation flatly contradicts what Lincoln says in the Emancipation Proclamation. Near the end of the Proclamation, Lincoln says: "I hereby enjoin the people so declared to be free to abstain from all violence, unless in necessary self-defense . . ." (volume II, p. 425). Rutherford made up many other quotations "out of whole cloth."[9] Since Rutherford and others militantly fought to suppress and exclude other accounts of history from southern schools and libraries it is fair to question their intellectual honesty. In this connection, it is well to remember that the antebellum South went to great lengths to limit free discussion and criticism of the institution of slavery. Southern states passed laws against inciting slave insurrections and used them as legal grounds for suppressing anti-slavery writings (Miller, 1995, p. 104). In addition, there was a "gag rule" in effect in the US House from 1836 until 1844 prohibiting Representatives from reading aloud to the Congress anti-slavery petitions signed by their constituents (this is discussed at great length in Miller, 1995).

13.II.2. Lying About the Crimes of Joseph Stalin

Beginning in 1929, Joseph Stalin set out to collectivize all of the farms in the Soviet Union. Between 1929 and 1933, approximately 15 million people were killed or died as a result of the collectivization. Stalin intentionally sought to kill off the more prosperous farmers, the "Kulaks." Stalin's terror famine fell particularly hard on the Ukraine where 7 million people died. These crimes were long denied by many in the West. Some Western journalists, who knew first hand what was going on, lied and denied the existence of Stalin's crimes against Soviet farmers. The actions of *New York Times* correspondent Walter Duranty were particularly odious. Reporting from the Soviet Union, Duranty repeatedly denied the existence of any starvation there. Not only was what Duranty said completely false, his claims were lies. In 1933, he told a British diplomat in Moscow that he thought that as many as 10 million may have died of hunger in the previous year. Duranty's dishonesty was very well rewarded. He received interviews with Stalin and was awarded the Pulitzer Prize in 1932 for "dispassionate interpretive reporting from the Soviet Union" (Conquest, 1986, pp. 304, 309, 319–321).

These were very consequential and immoral lies. They helped many of those on the political left maintain their wildly inaccurate view of Stalin's regime.

This was relevant and vital information for politicians and voters throughout the world; it was also information relevant to debates about the Cold War. As a reporter for a respected newspaper, Duranty had a great potential to influence public opinion, all the more so because he wrote at a time when much of the public was justifiably skeptical of ideologically driven assessments of the Soviet Union from both the far left and far right.

13.II.3. An Objection

One might object that dishonest renderings of history that involve denying or downplaying past wrongs can sometimes *diminish* conflicts between groups. Suppose that nation X has done horrible things to nation Y in the past. People in Y deeply resent this and this memory of past wrongs is a source of strife and conflict between the two nations. Couldn't defending a dishonest account of history be justified if it reduced conflicts between two peoples? In principle, lying and deception can be justified if they are necessary in order to save lives. This issue is no exception. However, lying about past wrongs in order to minimize conflict is likely to be counterproductive. In the present example, lying about the past wrongs is very unlikely to persuade people in Y who have their own memory of wrongs they suffered. Further, any attempt to deny those past wrongs is likely to anger them. If there is a concerted effort within nation X to deny or downplay past wrongs that it committed, this version of history is likely to be accepted by the people in country X—many people are inclined to believe the best about their own country. However, to the extent to which this is possible, it is also a prescription for conflict between the two nations. Country X's denial or downplaying of its past wrongdoing will infuriate people in Y and people in X will feel anger against Y, since they will think that their country is being unfairly slandered by the other country.

Reconciliation between hostile peoples is compatible with giving an honest account of historical wrongs; indeed, it seems to require such an account. Consider the honest and forthright way that Germany and South Africa have dealt with their historical pasts. This has promoted reconciliation between the peoples in question. The victims of historical wrongs (and their descendants who maintain vivid memories of those wrongs) need an acknowledgment and recognition of those wrongs to put their enmity behind them (often more is required, but an honest acknowledgment of the past is part of what is required).

By contrast, schools and the media in Japan and Turkey give dishonest accounts of the histories of those countries. Japanese schools and textbooks downplay or ignore the numerous large-scale Japanese atrocities and human rights violations during WWII. Many Japanese have little knowledge of the extent of these atrocities. This is greatly resented in Asia and has done much to undermine relations between Japan and China and Japan and Korea (on this, see French,

2001; Onishi and French, 2005). In Turkey, the government and schools deny the clear fact that more than one million Armenians were systemically slaughtered in Turkey during WWI (many put the number killed at 1.5 million). There are severe limitations on freedom of expression in Turkey; people who state the truth about the Armenian genocide are subject to prosecution for "anti-national agitation." Recently, Turkish novelist Orham Pamuk spoke about the mass killing of Armenians in a newspaper interview and was prosecuted for "insulting Turkish identity."[10] There have been some hopeful developments of late. The Turkish government has made many Ottoman Era documents available to historians. In 2005, a Turkish university hosted an academic conference at which the Armenian genocide was freely discussed and debated. However, government meddling delayed the conference for several months and the Turkish Minister of Justice accused the university that hosted the conference of "treason" (see Boland, 2005; Burrows, 2005). In 2006, the Turkish novelist Elif Shafak was prosecuted because *a fictional character* in one of her novels claimed that Turkey committed genocide against the Armenians (Freely, 2006).

13.III. HALF-TRUTHS AND GROUP CONFLICT

13.III.1. Half-Truths

This topic was broached earlier in Chapter 2.IV. A narrative or interpretation of an issue constitutes a "half-truth" if it emphasizes facts that tend to support a particular assessment of the issue and ignores, minimizes, or denies other relevant facts that tend to support different or contrary assessments. Half-truths need not involve any false claims—they are characterized by the omission of countervailing truths/evidence. Half-truths need not involve an outright denial of facts that weigh against one's convictions—a selective attention to and focus on those relevant facts and considerations that support one's views (and a selective inattention to and lack of focus on relevant facts and considerations that weigh against one's views) are sufficient for that. Often, for the purposes of assessing a controversial issue, knowing or accepting a half-truth puts one in a worse cognitive position than knowing nothing.

The narratives that we construct to defend prior beliefs and assessments about controversial matters often constitute half-truths. In the case of conflicts between hostile groups, half-truths often involve a kind of selective indignation, being moved by some things, but not others: in particular, being indignant about wrongs done to one's own group but not about wrongs it does to other groups.

Half-truths about national, ethnic, religious, and political conflicts are particularly harmful and destructive. Often, in cases of long-standing conflicts, each party to the conflict tells half-truths (or quarter-truths) about the conflict. Each party can give a graphic account of its own sufferings and grievances at the hands of the other party, but each party ignores, minimizes, or even denies the sufferings and grievances of the other party.

To tell or relate a half-truth is to say something misleading, but this need not involve lying or deception. Individuals who accept half-truths bear varying degrees of responsibility and culpability for this. Some accept half-truths because of self-deception or a stubborn unwillingness to believe the obvious or take seriously ostensible counter-evidence to what they believe. Such individuals are responsible and often culpable for accepting half-truths. People familiar with the historical record who deliberately craft half-truths, such as a lawyer drafting a brief, engage in deception and are often very culpable for endorsing or accepting half-truths. Other individuals accept half-truths because of systematic distortions or restrictions on the information available to them. An illiterate person whose only sources of information are one-sided has a greatly diminished responsibility for accepting half-truths. In some totalitarian societies, government controls on the media are designed to foster the acceptance of half-truths by the general population. The citizens of such states have little responsibility or culpability for their views. George Orwell's *1984* explores some of the possibilities for this.

Half-truths are narratives or interpretations about *controversial issues* that systematically favor a particular interpretation or assessment of those issues by selectively emphasizing certain facts/considerations and downplaying or ignoring other facts/considerations. In cases of conflicts where others offer criticisms of one or criticisms of a group with which one strongly identifies, the natural tendency of many people is to justify oneself or the group with which one identifies. Many people are very reluctant to admit to themselves or others their own faults and shortcomings (or the faults or shortcomings of groups to which they belong). Half-truths are general narratives or interpretations. Short statements of fact should not be classified as half-truths even if what they state is part of some larger half-true narrative. Suppose that a journalist covering a controversial conflict correctly and honestly reports facts that support the half-truths of one particular party to the dispute without mentioning anything else. The journalist's report is not itself a half-truth, although it can be used to construct or augment a half-truth. In debates in which both sides are ably represented, it may be defensible and appropriate for each debater to craft half-truths, since the debate itself will yield a reasonably accurate account of the whole truth.

13.III.2. Examples of Harmful Half-Truths

The Israeli–Palestinian Conflict

The present Middle Eastern conflict between Israel and the Palestinians provides good illustrations of the phenomenon of half-truths, or if you prefer, one-quarter truths. Many of the parties to this conflict and their supporters in other countries base their understandings and narratives of the conflict on half-truths. They are able to cite a long list of grievances against the other group and able to point to ways in which their group has been harmed and victimized by the other group. However, at the same time, they downplay, ignore, or deny the grievances of the other group. Here are some salient truths that are downplayed or ignored by many Palestinian critics of Israel who have a detailed knowledge of Palestinian grievances against Israel: (1) the Arab riots and murders of Jews in the 1920s and 1930s (including the massacre of 66 ultra-Orthodox Jews by Arabs in Hebron in 1929; Morris, 2004, p. 10); (2) numerous terrorist attacks on Israel; (3) the expulsion/persecution of hundreds of thousands of Jews from/in many Arab countries after the founding of the state of Israel and the Suez War of 1956; and (4) the pronouncements of many Arab and Islamic leaders calling for the destruction of the state of Israel (and the kind of fear those pronouncements would be likely to arouse in a people with such a long history of persecution as the Jews). Some salient truths ignored or downplayed by many Israelis and supporters of Israel are the following: (1) the terrorist attacks by the Jewish group, the Irgun, against Arabs and the British prior to the independence of Israel; (2) the membership of prominent Israeli politicians, including prime ministers Menachem Begin and Yitzhak Shamir, in the Irgun; (3) the massacre of 254 Arab villagers in Deir Yassin by the Israeli Army in 1948 (Morris, 1999, pp. 207–209);[11] (4) the fact that Israel did not allow the 700 000 Arabs who fled from Israel during the 1948 war to return to their homes or retain their property; and (5) the large number of Arab civilians killed by the Israeli military in retaliation for Arab attacks on Israel.

The US and Iran

Many Americans expressed tremendous animosity for Iran during the Hostage Crisis of 1979–1981, and some displayed bumper stickers that said "Nuke Iran." Nearly all Americans knew of America's grievances against Iran (the 52 Americans were held as hostages in the US Embassy in Tehran). However, this animosity was based on the acceptance of half-truths (or, I would argue, 1/8th or 1/16th truths). Few Americans knew that Iran had serious grievances against the US and Britain. Britain long controlled the Iranian oil industry and paid almost nothing to Iran for its oil. As late as 1947, the Anglo-Iranian Oil Company, which at that time operated the largest oil facility in the world, paid Iran only 7 million pounds a year for the huge amount of Iranian oil it produced (Kinzer, 2003, p. 67). In 1950 a nationalist government headed by Mohammad Mossadegh came to power in Iran. The new government nationalized the Iranian oil industry. This action made Mossadegh extremely popular with the Iranian people (Kinzer, 2003, p. 80) but greatly angered the British government. The British prodded the US to help them depose Mossadegh, but President Truman declined to do this (Kinzer, 2003, pp. 127–129). Truman tried to arrange a compromise between Britain and Iran. US policy changed when Eisenhower became President. In 1953, a CIA *coup d'état* led by Kermit Roosevelt overthrew the democratically elected Mossadegh and installed the repressive kleptocratic government of Shah Mohammad Reza Pahlavi. The Shah did the bidding of the US government for 25 years and built a huge military, which was allied with the US against the USSR during the Cold War. The Shah's brutally repressive and much feared secret police, the Savak, helped him to maintain power.

It is very dangerous to misunderstand one's adversaries. This past history is very relevant today. In the very recent past, the US and Israel were openly discussing pre-emptive attacks on Iran to prevent Iran from developing nuclear weapons. Israel planned an attack on Iran to destroy its nuclear program in 2008. The Israeli government asked the US to: (1) give it "bunker buster" bombs with which to destroy underground nuclear sites in Iran; (2) allow its planes to fly over Iraq; and (3) give it equipment for the in-flight refueling of aircraft. The Bush Administration rejected these requests and refused to grant approval for an Israeli attack on Iran (Sanger, 2009). For their part, Iranian leaders are making very provocative threats against Israel and have aided Hezbollah and Hamas in their large-scale rocket attacks on Israel.

Hitler and Germany's Suffering after WWI

Belief in the uniquely tragic and unfair position of Germany in the wake of WWI was an important part of Nazi ideology and rhetoric. Those who read Hitler's writings and speeches before WWII will be struck by the centrality of the themes of German suffering and national self-pity. Much of what Hitler said was true, but his narrative omits any mention of the fact that Germany was prepared to inflict a very harsh peace on the other side if it won WWI. In the Treaty of Brest-Litovsk in early 1918, Germany imposed a very harsh peace on Russia.[12] The Russian territorial losses from this treaty were much greater than those Germany suffered after WWI. The peace imposed on Germany was arguably less harsh than the peace that it tried to impose on Russia. Because of the horrendous suffering and casualties in WWI, it was clear that any victor would, for internal political reasons, be inclined to impose a very harsh peace on the vanquished.

13.III.3. Half-Truths in Personal Relations

Half-truths and one-sided selective memory and indignation for harms and injustices done to oneself are an important factor in many personal conflicts. This kind of one-sided memory is a prescription for strife and conflict in personal relations. Consider disputes between husbands and wives. Each may have vivid and accurate memories of unkind words and acts of his/her spouse but a much less vivid memory of his/her own unkind words and deeds. This kind of selective memory will tend to result in one's viewing the other party as a villain—a selfish, nasty, unkind person—and make it seem that the marriage is a one-sided affair. If in all areas of conflict in my marriage, I have a vivid memory of my wife's shortcomings and the unkind things she has said and done to me and a dim awareness of my own shortcomings and unkindness, then (unless she is a saint) I cannot help but have a negative view of her and view her as a kind of villain. In addition, we sometimes selectively remember the nice things we have done for others and forget the nice things they do for us. It is difficult to have a happy marriage if the partners view conflicts through the lens of these kinds of half-truths.

Similar remarks apply to other kinds of personal conflicts. Telling oneself half-truths about one's own job performance is likely to leave one with a sense of being unfairly treated on the job. Many people think themselves underpaid and underappreciated relative to their colleagues. A study of university professors found that 94% (!) thought that they performed their jobs better than the average colleague (Bishop and Trout, 2005, p. 44).[13] To avoid half-truths, we must honestly acknowledge our failures and shortcomings on the job, as well as our virtues and successes. If one views things through the lens of half-truths, it is likely that one will feel unfairly treated relative to others.

People who accept these kinds of half-truths about their marriages, friendships, or careers will be almost certain to feel *unwarranted resentment* against their spouses, friends, or colleagues/supervisors. That resentment is very harmful and destructive and it creates and aggravates conflicts.

13.IV. INTELLECTUAL HONESTY

Let me offer a brief incomplete account of intellectual honesty (with particular attention to intellectual honesty about political questions). An intellectually honest person will seek the whole truth (or at least a balanced view) about controversial matters and take the evidence where it leads her. She will not be unduly quick to discount or deny evidence that tends to undermine her cherished beliefs. She will seek out relevant evidence and not simply look for evidence that supports what she believes. She will not be unduly credulous in accepting reports or claims that support her beliefs or prejudices. She will apply the same evidential standards to claims and reports that tend to support her views that she applies to claims and reports that tend to count against her views. She will subject all evidence to critical scrutiny. She will look at all evidence holistically, not just at what supports her own prejudices and preconceptions.

A minimal condition of my honestly debating and disagreeing with you about something is that I strive to understand and represent your views accurately. A plausible test of this requirement is that I am able to state your views in ways that you find acceptable.

One common means of dishonestly dismissing the views of those who disagree with one is to distort their views and turn them into caricatures and "straw men" that do not need to be taken seriously. For example, suppose that there is a wide range of views held by those who hold views contrary to one's own. It is always tempting to find the most implausible and outlandish versions of those views and hold that all who disagree with one are committed to those outlandish views.

For example, some Americans who opposed the Viet Nam War likened Lyndon Johnson and Richard Nixon to Adolf Hitler. However, most Americans who opposed the Viet Nam War did not believe that Johnson and Nixon were evildoers on a par with Adolf Hitler. Defenders of the US role in the Viet Nam war cannot succeed in defending their position simply by answering the *least plausible* of their critics. In debates about specific issues, it is often easy to find opponents whose reasons for holding the views in question are patently absurd and/or reprehensible. However, it is not legitimate to criticize a view by pointing to the bad reasons that some people have for holding it. An intellectually honest person will seek to find and assess the *strongest versions* of opposing views and not content herself with responding to the weakest and most outlandish formulations of contrary views. There are usually enough rash and unreasonable defenders of contrary views that it is often very easy to dismiss contrary views in this way.

An intellectually honest person will have a healthy sense of her own intellectual fallibility and not view herself as immune to the dishonesty and folly that it is so easy for her to recognize in others. She need not be, nor can she be, completely impartial. Her emotions may exhibit partiality toward certain groups and causes, but she will be aware of her partiality and try to take it into account.

Intellectual honesty is in short supply in many political controversies. For many people, political affiliations are a part of one's identity as a person or one's identity as a member of a particular ethnic or religious group. Those who make their political beliefs central to their identity as persons will be very reluctant to change their political allegiances and may have difficulty in seriously considering objections to their political views. (For many of us, radically altering our political views would invite the scorn and incomprehension of those near and dear to us.) In contemporary America, many/most people belong to groups that reinforce each other's political/ideological views. Vigorous political debate and being subjected to serious intelligent criticisms of one's own political views seem to be the exception rather than the rule. Many of us who often associate with people with whom we have deep political disagreements avoid talking about politics with them because we think that it is very rude to criticize other people's political views. Recall the old adage that we should avoid discussing religion or politics. The recent fragmentation and segmentation of the media allows many people to cut themselves off from opposing points of view. (At its best, the mass media of the1940s and 1950s confronted people with able and articulate representatives of very different points of view, e.g., CBS radio with Edward R. Murrow and Eric Severeid.) Nicholas Kristof (2009) worries that the very segmented range of views available in cyberspace will lead many people to limit their sources of information and opinions to those with whom they agree:

When we go online, each of us is our own editor, our own gatekeeper. We select the kind of news and opinions that we care most about. Nicholas Negroponte of M.I.T. has called this emerging news product The Daily Me. And if that's the trend, God save us from ourselves because there's pretty good evidence that we generally don't truly want good information—but rather information that confirms our prejudices. We may believe intellectually in the clash of opinions, but in practice we like to embed ourselves in the reassuring womb of an echo chamber.

Because most of us claim that certain empirical facts confirm or support our political views (and falsify or discredit opposing views), we must concede that there are empirical beliefs on which our political beliefs depend and that any evidence *against* those empirical beliefs is evidence that falsifies or at least counts against the political beliefs in question. Many of us regard the political views of others as falsified/falsifiable or discreditable but refuse to think seriously that our own political views might be falsified/falsifiable or discredited/discreditable in exactly the same way.

A general limitation of the falsifiability/discreditability of our political beliefs by empirical evidence is the following. In the case of any historically significant event or policy, it is very difficult, if not impossible, to know what would have happened if it had not taken place. In time, we will know much about what happened in the aftermath of the Iraq War of 2003, but we will never know what would have happened if the war had not taken place. Therefore, however badly (or well) things turn out after the war, it is always possible for someone to say that things would have turned out even worse (or better) if Bush had not ordered the invasion of Iraq. Here is another example that illustrates this point. Some people claim that the historical record falsifies or at least seriously discredits Marxism/socialism. Even if *all* Marxist societies, such as the Soviet Union and Mao's China, have turned out very badly, it is perfectly fair for many Marxists to claim that their preferred form of socialism (perhaps something like democratic market socialism) has not yet been put into practice and would produce much better results than the types of socialism that have existed to date. This is perfectly honest and fair as far as it goes. Many critics of Marxism greatly overstate what follows from the colossal failures of Soviet and Maoist style Marxism. However, critics of socialism/Marxism *can* fairly claim that there is no case of *an entire society* that has successfully practiced certain types of socialism (such as democratic market socialism), and thus that there is no conclusive empirical evidence that proves that the type of socialism in question will/can work out well in practice.[14]

In order to be intellectually honest we must always heed Oliver Cromwell's plea "I beseech you, in the bowels of Christ, think it possible you may be mistaken . . ."[15]

ENDNOTES

1. Roughly one million Germans died from hunger and malnutrition caused by the British naval blockade. I take these figures from Gilbert (1994). According to Gilbert, 762 106 Germans died during the war because of the blockade. The British naval blockade continued after the Armistice of November 11, 1918 until Germany signed the Treaty of Versailles in May of 1919. Several hundred thousand more deaths were caused by the blockade during this time (p. 256). The blockade was used to compel Germany to accede to the harsh terms of the Versailles Treaty. Gilbert (1994) quotes Count Brockdorff-Rantzau, the senior Germany delegate to the treaty negotiations: "The hundreds of thousands of non-combatants who have perished since November 11 by reason of the blockage were killed with cold deliberation, after our adversaries had conquered and victory had been assured them. Think of that when you speak of guilt and punishment" (p. 511).

2. He said this on April 11, 2003 and April 11, 2006, see http://www.thebluestate.com/2006/04/video_rumsfeld_.html.

3. Bessel says that Ebert believed that saying this was "politically necessary." In his memoirs written during the 1920s, Kaiser Wilhelm II claimed: "For thirty years the army was my pride. For it I lived, upon it I labored, and now after four and a half years of war with unprecedented victories, it was forced to collapse by the stab-in-the-back from the dagger of the revolutionist, at the very moment peace was within reach!" (Quoted in Welch, 2000, p. 253). This is a preposterous and self-serving statement by the man, who, more than anyone else, brought ruin on Germany in WWI (see below). Peace (and a much better peace for Germany than it got in 1918) was an option for the Kaiser for most of the war, but to get this peace the Kaiser would have had to have been willing to give up the territory that Germany conquered during the war and he was unwilling to do that.

4. Deist (1996) states the definitive case for this.

5. Hindenburg was treated with great deference and respect by the Committee of Inquiry, which allowed him to ignore its repeated questions about the resumption of unrestricted submarine warfare. Hindenburg was an immensely popular and revered figure in Germany during and after WWI. He was widely credited with saving Germany from a Russian invasion early in the war. He, more than anyone else, was the popular symbol of Germany and the German war effort during WWI. At many rallies, at which German citizens were encouraged to support the war effort and purchase war bonds, there were giant wooden statues of Hindenburg. People would acknowledge their support for the war by pounding nails into the statue of Hindenburg. This was also done at rallies in the US. Also see

Wheeler-Bennett (1936), *Hindenburg: The Wooden Titan*, pp. 236–238 (note the title of the Wheeler-Bennett's book).

6. I thank Bill Astore for this point.

7. With respect to Hitler's first and last political statements, which include vicious angry attacks against the Jews, Kershaw writes:

> There can be no doubt that they represent fervently held core beliefs. At their heart was the link in Hitler's mind between the war and the Jews—there from the beginning to the end of his political "career". In a terrible passage in *Mein Kampf*, Hitler expressed his belief that "the sacrifice of millions at the front" [during WWI] would not have been necessary if twelve or fifteen thousand of these Hebrew corrupters of the people had been held under poison gas.   (p. 8)

8. Oddly, after Lincoln's re-election, Confederate President Jefferson Davis offered to abolish slavery in the Confederate States of America in exchange for diplomatic recognition from Britain and France; see Donald (1995, p. 547).

9. E-mails from James McPherson to Thomas Carson, June 6 and June 8, 2009. In response to my question about Rutherford's alleged quotation from Rhodes, McPherson replied "Yes, she made up that quotation (and a good many others) out of whole cloth."

10. Arsu (2006). Article 301 of the Turkish penal code "recommends sentences of up to three years for those convicted of 'denigrating Turkishness' " (Freely, 2006).

11. The number of victims is in dispute. Morris puts the number of Arabs murdered at 100–110.

12. A Jewish Professor, Hans Nawiasky, pointed this out in 1931 and rioting led by Nazis ensued. The Nazis tried without success to get him removed from his position at the University of Munich (Niewyk, 2001, p. 67).

13. This goes a long way to explaining the extraordinary level of conflict and jealousy that prevails in many university faculties.

14. Although he agrees with me that there is no case of *an entire society* that has successfully practiced democratic market socialism, David Schweickart still thinks that there are compelling reasons to think that a successful version of market socialism is feasible—and desirable (see Schweickart, 2002).

15. Letter to the General Assembly of the Church of Scotland, August 3, 1650 (*Bartlett's Familiar Quotations*, 15th edn. Boston: Brown and Little, 1980, p. 272).

14

Honesty as a Virtue

INTRODUCTION

Honesty is generally regarded as a cardinal virtue, and calling someone a "dishonest person" is usually taken to be a severe criticism or condemnation of the person. In order to assess this conventional wisdom, it will be helpful to examine the arguments of dissenters who question it. Some argue that because lying and deception are frequently justified in certain spheres of life/activity (particularly to protect privacy and avoid conflicts in close personal relationships) honesty is not a virtue in those spheres of life/activity.

I again *stipulate* that "honesty" and "dishonesty," as I use these terms, have to do only with lying, deception, withholding information, and the like. In ordinary language, the terms "honesty" and "dishonesty" are used more broadly. In this broader sense, whether a person is honest or dishonest is partly a function of whether she keeps her promises and refrains from stealing and bribery. We take the fact that someone is a thief to be incompatible with his being an honest person. My purpose here is not to capture the ordinary language meaning of the words "honesty" and "dishonesty," but to assess whether honesty/dishonesty in my narrow sense (a character trait that is directly related to lying, deception, and withholding/providing information) is a virtue/vice.

We need to distinguish between what, for lack of better terms, I will call "honesty in a negative sense" (having a strong principled disinclination to tell lies or deceive others) and "honesty in a positive sense," which (in addition to involving being disinclined to tell lies or deceive others) involves being candid, open, and willing to reveal information. I argue that honesty in the negative sense (or something that closely resembles it) is a cardinal virtue in ordinary circumstances, but often honesty in the positive sense is not a virtue. I also identify spheres of activity in which candor and openness are virtues.

Surprisingly, philosophers have written very little about the concept of honesty and the idea of honesty as a virtue. Aristotle's long analysis of moral virtues does not include a discussion of anything like our concept of honesty. He discusses the virtue of "truthfulness," which he takes to be a mean between the vices of boastfulness and self-deprecation. Truthfulness, as Aristotle understands it, only concerns the truthfulness of what one says about oneself (see Aristotle, IV.7,

1127a114–1127b33). Very little has been written on the idea of honesty as a virtue in recent and contemporary philosophy.

14.1. DISSENTERS FROM CONVENTIONAL WISDOM

14.1.1. Lying, Deception, and Privacy

Sometimes people justify lying and deception in order to protect their privacy, the privacy of others, or secrets they have promised to keep. This justification is greatly overused. Often, the morally appropriate way to protect privacy is to evade or refuse to answer questions. Sometimes people who ask about things that are "none of their business" should be rebuked for doing so. Important exceptions to this arise in cases in which the people who ask the questions are in positions of power and authority over those they question (in such cases the person being asked the question may be afraid to refuse to answer). In such cases, lying is often justified. Lying is also often justified in cases in which people are likely to be unfairly subject to severe sanctions and punishments if the information being hidden is revealed. This is often the case in very unjust and intolerant societies in which people are subject to imprisonment or execution for their religious or political affiliations. There is little presumption against lying and deception in such cases; one should not hesitate to lie to protect the innocent. Similarly, subject peoples living under the military occupation of tyrannical conquering powers such as Nazi Germany are permitted to lie to and deceive their occupiers.

Lying is often justified in cases in which evading or refusing to answer a question will be construed as having given a certain kind of answer. For example, if I am asked whether someone is having an extramarital affair, failing to answer the question may be tantamount to answering in the affirmative. In such cases, the option of failing to answer the question is not substantially different from that of answering truthfully. The case for lying/deception is strengthened if one has promised to keep a secret.[1]

Gossiping often puts us in compromising situations in which we must choose between lying/deception and revealing things that we should not reveal. We should avoid compromising situations such as the following. A friend of mine, X, has told me a deep dark secret that I have solemnly promised to keep. An acquaintance of mine, Y, who is unaware of the closeness of my relationship with X, gossips about X's private life among a group of people when I am present. It would be best for me to avoid entering into this gossip or doing anything to reveal the extent of my knowledge of X because that is likely to cause me to be subject to intrusive questions. Garrulous people are often forced to choose between lying/deception and betraying confidences that they ought to keep. Often, it is a mistake to broach certain topics in a conversation or allow certain conversations to continue. An underutilized option in such situations is to end the conversation abruptly—usually this can be done without lying. One can truthfully say things such as "Something just occurred to me; I should leave." Another option is to be adamant in refusing to divulge confidences.

Discretion involves anticipating and avoiding inappropriate conversations. We should avoid making claims that can only be substantiated by violating confidences. Discretion sometimes requires that we lose debates rather than make cogent arguments that involve making claims that violate confidences or that cannot be substantiated without violating confidences.

14.I.2. Lying, Honesty, and Interpersonal Conflicts

Some argue that complete honesty is objectionable because it leads to personal conflicts; for example, Karl Scheibe says that for young married couples, being utterly honest with each other, practicing complete candor, and having no secrets is a recipe for a quick separation.

> The straight out moral case against lying fails to appreciate the requirements of genuine human relationships. A universal insistence on the cold hard truth is basically unfriendly, really destructive of human relationships. I have heard it said by psychologists counseling young married couples that the advice to complete and utter honesty, with no secrets and constant candor, is advising toward quick separation. This does not mean that friendship or love is built on false understandings, but rather that the requirements of fidelity to another person include requirements of tact, discretion, protection, kindness, forbearance, and sensitivity. These requirements are more complex than the simple principle of always telling "the truth."
>
> Scheibe (1980, p. 18)

Scheibe begins this passage by questioning the prohibition against lying, but what follows does not contradict my claim that there is a strong presumption against lying. The acts of tact and discretion that he recommends are not cases of permissible lying/deception. Rather, they are cases in which it is permissible not to express one's beliefs or attitudes. No doubt, a fully unrestrained expression of *all* of one's thoughts and feelings on all occasions is likely to lead to serious conflicts in most friendships and marriages. However, the policy of not lying or deceiving others does not require this; it does not require that one tell everything on one's mind or express every criticism and every petty and angry thought one has. Saying nothing is not tantamount to lying or deception; neither is a partial circumspect expression of one's thoughts, e.g., "I am angry and upset; let me cool off before I say something that I might regret." There is a duty to *refrain* from acts of lying and deception, but there is no general duty to reveal information or fully express one's views or attitudes to others.

The same comments apply to many of the examples in David Nyberg's book, *The Varnished Truth* (1993). Nyberg gives many cases in which he thinks we should avoid being "truthful" in order to avoid conflicts with others. Nyberg's examples are interesting and convincing. However, they do not count against my claim that there is a strong presumption against lying and deception. Nyberg presents a number of cases in which lying and/or deception are necessary to avoid *very bad* consequences. His claim that lying and deception are justified in those cases is perfectly consistent with my claim that there is a strong presumption against lying and deception.

Throughout his book, Nyberg focuses on "truthfulness" and the alleged need to state *the whole truth*. In many of his cases, the question is not about the permissibility of lying and deception but, rather, about the permissibility of withholding information and refraining from saying everything on one's mind. Here are some of Nyberg's (1993) examples:

Your two closest friends offer to tell you, with unchecked candor and without regard for your feelings, everything they think about you. Would you want them to do it? (p. 8)

Have you ever disliked and disrespected someone you worked for, and told them so—while you still needed the job? (p. 9)

Should we give frank expression to every strong feeling of contempt, envy, lust, and self-pity? Should we tell our friends the truth when we believe it would shatter their self-confidence? (pp. 25–26)

Nyberg is right to hold that the whole truth ought not (or need not) be told in these cases. However, failing to tell the whole truth is not tantamount to lying or deception. Similar comments apply to the following statement by Thomas Nagel (1993, p. 29): "Just as social life would be impossible if we expressed all our lustful, aggressive, greedy, anxious, or self-obsessed feelings in ordinary public encounters, so would inner life be impossible if we tried to become wholly persons whose thoughts, feelings, and private behavior could be safely exposed to public view." Nagel's statement (with which I completely concur) is perfectly compatible with the view that there is a strong moral presumption against both lying and deception. We can usually keep our thoughts and feelings private without resorting to lying or deception.

In the foregoing argument, I appeal to the distinction between lying/deception and withholding information, a distinction Scheibe and Nyberg obscure by their frequent use of the terms "truth" and "truthfulness." In some contexts, people legitimately expect to be told certain information. In such cases, withholding the information is tantamount to deception (see 2.III.2). However, there are many cases in which there is no clear understanding that one party must provide that sort of information to the other party. In such cases, withholding information does not involve deception.

Here are some cases in which withholding information constitutes deception. In an "encounter group" in which family members promised to air all of their serious concerns, it is deceptive not to express one's feelings. Withholding information can be deceptive if the other person has a legitimate claim or expectation that the information be provided to him. Failing to inform my fiancée of my five prior divorces is deceptive. It is reasonable for her to assume that, since I did not mention any of my previous marriages, I have not been married before. When clients have a legitimate expectation that professionals will provide them with certain kinds of information, failing to provide that information is tantamount to deception. My attorney would be deceiving me if he were to recommend a strategy for me to minimize my taxes but neglected to tell me that the actions in question are illegal and likely to lead to my being caught and imprisoned.

Often, the *combination* of particular actions and withholding certain information is deceptive. Suppose that I offer an unfavorable evaluation of the work of a junior colleague as part of a confidential formal review process. I do not inform the colleague of my evaluation. I know that this evaluation will be held against the colleague in his application for promotion and tenure. This, in itself, is not tantamount to deception. However, if I do this and, *in addition*, frequently compliment the colleague on the quality of his work in all areas, then I am attempting to deceive him. Expressing dislike and disdain for someone behind her back is not deceptive in itself, but it is deceptive if it is combined with flattery and expressions of esteem and good will for the other person. My being reticent about expressing my petty annoyances with my wife is not deceptive in itself, but it would be deceptive if she and I have agreed to be completely open in expressing all of our feelings about each other.

In personal relations, there is often no clear understanding or convention about what sort of information each person owes the other. This frequently makes it unclear whether withholding information is tantamount to deception or keeping someone in the dark. Consider the following case. Nora has a close friend who is an ardent admirer of former President George W. Bush and his policies. Nora is extremely critical of Bush and thinks that he is one of the worst Presidents in the history of the US. Her friend often expresses hostility toward Bush's critics. It would not be deceptive for Nora to withhold information about her views on Bush and avoid the topic of President Bush and his policies when speaking with her friend. On the other hand, it would be a case of deception if Nora were to frequently and selectively express her (sincere) criticisms of certain unfair criticisms of Bush but scrupulously refrain from ever criticizing Bush and his policies in the presence of the friend, even though their conversations frequently broach the topic of Bush's actions and policies of which Nora is very critical.

14.1.3. Lying, Deception, and Self-Esteem

Some defend lying and deception, especially to children, because it can promote people's self-esteem. The idea is that unmerited praise can enhance a person's self-esteem and that self-esteem/self-respect is an important constituent of (or requirement for) a good life.[2] Lack of self-esteem is held to be responsible for such things as poor academic performance, murder, rape, substance abuse, and prostitution (Slater, 2002, p. 45; also see Dawes, 1996, p. 234). Many people advocate that children should be given huge amounts of praise regardless of their actual accomplishments.

Some parents and educators attempt to raise their children's self-esteem by exaggerating their abilities and achievements. This sort of praise is likely to clash with objective impersonal measures of ability/achievement, e.g., batting averages for Little League players, scholastic aptitude tests, and report cards (especially when they include one's class rank). Parents who lie and mislead their children about their abilities and achievements create unrealistic hopes and expectations and set the children up for a fall. Parents and educators should give children non-deceptive praise (often praise for effort and hard work can be non-deceptive) and encouragement in areas of genuine strength. The best evidence suggests that there is no reason to think that low self-esteem is a cause of poor academic performance (Dawes, 1996, p. 246; also, see Patterson, 2006).

Excessive praise can make people complacent and unwilling to work to improve. Excessive and dishonest praise can also make children hostile and defensive in the face of legitimate criticism. Many educators report this as a consequence of grade inflation. Lauren Slater quotes the following:

People who believe themselves to be in among the top 10 percent on any dimension may be insulted and threatened whenever anyone asserts that they are in the 80th or 50th or 25th percentile. In contrast, someone with lower self-esteem who regards himself or herself as merely in the top 60 percent would only be threatened by the feedback that puts him or her at the 25th percentile . . . In short, the more favorable one's view of oneself, the greater the range of external feedback that will be unacceptably low.

Slater (2002, p. 47)

The distinction between refraining from lying and deception and being completely candid is relevant here. Brutally frank uncensored criticism can be very harmful to people's self-esteem and self-confidence. Prohibitions against lying and deception proscribe trying to build up someone's self-esteem by dishonest means, but they do not require complete brutal candor in itemizing all of her shortcomings.

Slater argues that the importance and benefits of self-esteem have been greatly exaggerated in popular culture and pop psychology. She quotes Nicholas Emler of the London School of Economics who finds that "There is absolutely no evidence that low self-esteem is particularly harmful . . . It's not at all a cause of poor academic performance; people with low self-esteem seem to do just as well in life as people with high self-esteem. In fact they may do better because they try harder" (Slater, 2002, p. 46). Slater also cites empirical evidence that people with high self-esteem are more willing to engage in ostensibly harmful behavior (e.g., subjecting others to blasts of ear-piercing noise) than those with lower self-esteem. To the extent that pop psychology has overrated that value of self-esteem, the case for promoting self-esteem by dishonest means is greatly weakened. Further, the attitudes instilled and encouraged by dishonest praise (or by refraining from giving justified criticism) are likely to be harmful. The kind of love that children need from their parents need not involve the use of dishonesty to promote their self-esteem.

14.II. IN WHAT SENSE HONESTY IS AND IS NOT A VIRTUE

The arguments of Chapters 6 and 7 and the book as a whole attempt to show that there is a strong moral presumption against harmful lying and deception. These arguments also illustrate the harmfulness of lying and deception in a wide range of settings. If successful, these arguments show that honesty in the negative sense is a cardinal virtue in ordinary circumstances. We may need to make exceptions for people who are spies, diplomats, and people who live under repressive governments[3] (this list of exceptions is not complete). Such people often need to engage in lying and deception in order to protect innocent people from great harm.[4] Still, even for those people, there is still an important range of settings in which honesty is a virtue, e.g., a diplomat's dealings with her family. Honesty in the negative sense is compatible with tact, discretion, and politeness.

Here, it might be objected that because my arguments in the earlier parts of the book only show that there is a strong presumption against lying and deception that *harm others*, I cannot claim that honesty in the negative sense (having a strong principled disposition to refrain from lying and deception) is a virtue. Given what I say in Chapters 6 and 7, I can only claim that something that *resembles* honesty in the negative sense is a virtue. I can only claim that having a strong principled disposition to refrain from lying and deception *when they have bad consequences on balance* is a virtue.

Lying and deception *do* tend to have bad consequences. Lying and deception often have bad consequences that one cannot anticipate at the time one acts. These bad consequences include prudential problems created by the difficulties involved in remembering one's acts of lying and deception and avoiding being found out (see Chapter 4.III). Making it a policy not to lie or deceive even when lying and deception do not have bad consequences is likely to help us avoid lying and deception when they do have bad consequences. This reply raises the following question: is it empirically possible for many/most people to have the disposition to refrain from lying and deception *when they have bad consequences* without being honest in the negative sense, i.e., without having the disposition to refrain from all lying and deception? Because we often have to act quickly in situations of stress in which we cannot directly calculate the consequences of our actions, the answer seems to be "no." In practice, we are not able to calculate the consequences of lying and deception before acting well enough for the answer to be "yes." However, more needs to be said here. Ultimately, this question needs to be addressed by experimental psychology.

Suppose that this empirical question remains open. In that case, whether honesty in the negative sense is a virtue depends partly on the answers to questions in ethical theory. If what I call "Ross3" (the view that both lying and deception are *prima facie* wrong—see Chapter 7.1) is true, then honesty in the negative sense is a virtue regardless of the answer to the empirical question at issue.[5] On the other hand, suppose that act-utilitarianism is true and that it is possible for most people to have a strong principled disposition to refrain from lying and deception when they have bad consequences on balance without being honest in the negative sense. If both of those assumptions were true, then being honest in the negative sense would not be a virtue.

Whether or not being strongly disposed not to lie or deceive (even when they do not have bad consequences) is a virtue depends on the answers to empirical questions and questions in ethical theory that I have not provided in this book. Some possible answers to these questions may force us to modify the conventional view that honesty is a virtue. So, for all I have shown, it is open to debate in what sense honesty in the negative sense is and is not a virtue. There is more than one reasonable view about the virtue of honesty in the negative sense. However, those reasonable views overlap/converge to a considerable degree. At a minimum, an analogue of honesty in the negative sense (being disposed to refrain from lying and deception when they cause more harm than good on balance) *is* a virtue and, thus, the view that honesty in the negative sense is a virtue is not too far off the mark. Even if honesty in the negative sense is not a virtue, anyone who is honest in the negative sense will (necessarily) have the virtue of having a strong principled disposition to refrain from lying and deception when they have bad consequences on balance.

What should we say about honesty in the positive sense (candor, openness, and being willing to reveal information)? Complete unrestrained candor that involves expressing every petty annoyance and nasty thought that enters one's mind is not a virtue. Many of our involuntary thoughts and impulses are not things that we reflectively endorse. Barring special circumstances, there is no reason why we are obligated to express such thoughts to others. To the contrary, there are reasons why we should make it a policy not to express such thoughts freely—doing so can be very hurtful to others and very destructive of friendships and family ties. That degree of candor and openness is not a virtue in anyone.

What about candor and openness in personal life that fall short of callous hurtfulness to others but involve openly disclosing important facts about oneself? Sometimes people disclose facts about their emotions, motivations, and past actions, although doing so causes them to feel deeply embarrassed or even humiliated. This kind of candor and openness can be desirable in some situations and undesirable in other situations. Whether it is desirable for me to be open and forthright with you depends on the nature of our relationship. Most of us seek intimate relationships in which we are open and candid with at least some other people, but few people want to be open and candid with everyone, and there is no reason why they should be. It is perfectly permissible to want to keep much of one's life secret from other people. (Among other reasons for keeping things private, people often have the justified fear that what they tell others will be made public and held against them.)

We usually make it a condition of our being open with someone that she *not* tell others everything that we have told her. Openness, candor, and self-disclosure are things to be *negotiated* in personal relationships. Often, in relationships one party desires greater openness and intimacy and takes the risk of disclosing something very personal and embarrassing in the hope that others will reciprocate and open up to her. The other person can choose whether to reciprocate. There is no reason to think that one ought to be intimate with every other person who wants to be intimate with one. Your opening up to someone does not necessarily obligate her to open up to you. In personal relations, this kind of candor and openness is largely optional.

Being open and forthright and willing to provide relevant information when others seek it is almost always desirable when one has fiduciary duties to others; it is almost always beneficial to those one advises. People who have fiduciary duties to others, e.g., physicians and attorneys, are obligated to be candid and open with those to whom they owe fiduciary duties when they act in their professional roles (see Chapter 11.II). When fiduciary duties are not involved, the benefits of this kind of candor in professional and commercial activity need to be weighed against one's obligations to one's employer and family and the legitimate claims of one's own self-interest.

Honesty in the negative sense (or something that closely resembles it) is a virtue in ordinary circumstances. Candor or honesty in the positive sense is a virtue (and morally obligatory) in the case of those who have fiduciary obligations to others. However, in personal relations, candor and openness are often unnecessarily hurtful to others. In those cases, they are morally impermissible and contrary to virtue. Even when candor and openness are permissible in personal relations, they are generally morally optional and are, therefore, neither constitutive of virtue nor contrary to virtue.

ENDNOTES

1. Here, we need to say something about the import of such promises. Is a promise to keep a secret a promise to lie (if necessary) to keep the secret, or is it a promise to do things short of lying to keep the secret? I am not sure what to say here and suspect that this is a matter about which there is considerable disagreement. There are also further issues about the permissibility of making promises to keep secrets, or keep them at all costs.

2. John Rawls holds that self-respect is "perhaps the most important primary good" (Rawls, 1971, p. 440). Primary goods are "things that every rational

man is presumed to want. These goods normally have a use whatever the person's rational plan of life" (p. 62).

3. In such societies parents often need to lie to their children and deceive them in order to hide secrets (for example, that the family listens to forbidden radio broadcasts) that are likely to be revealed by the children when they are questioned at school.

4. In difficult situations such as those in question, lying and deception are often justified. A person who frequently engages in lying and deception in such circumstances can still be honest in the negative sense. However, an honest person will find it difficult to function in such situations, since she will feel compunction when she engages in lying/deception.

5. Given appropriate empirical assumptions, Ross's theory (according to which lying, but not deception, is *prima facie* wrong) implies that the disposition not to lie even when lying does not result in more harm than good is a virtue, but that the disposition not to deceive others even when deception does not result in more harm than good is not a virtue.

Bibliography

Adler, J. (1997). Lying, deceiving, or falsely implicating. *Journal of Philosophy* **94**: 435–452.

Alterman, E. (2004). *When Presidents Lie*. New York: Viking.

Anscombe, E. (1997). Modern moral philosophy. In *Value and the Good Life*, T. Carson and P. Moser (Ed.), pp. 248–260. Oxford: Oxford University Press.

Aquinas, T. (1920/2006). *The Summa Theologica of St. Thomas Aquinas*. 2nd and Revised Edition, 1920. Literally translated by Fathers of the Dominican Province, Online Edition, 2006 http://www.newadvent.org/summa.

Aristotle (1962). *Nicomachean Ethics*. Translated by M. Ostwald. Indianapolis, IN: Bobbs-Merrill, 1962.

Arrington, R. (1989). *Rationalism, Realism, and Relativism*. Ithaca, NY: Cornell University Press.

Arrow, K. (1997). Business codes and economic efficiency. In *Ethical Theory and Business*, 5th edn, T. Beauchamp and N. Bowie (Ed.), pp. 124–126. Upper Saddle River, NJ: Prentice Hall.

Arsu, S. (2006). Court drops charges against author for "insulting" Turkey. *New York Times International Edition*, January 23.

Astore, W. J. (2007). Tomgram: William Astore, If We Lose Iraq, You're to Blame. TomDispatch.com, November 6. http://www.tomdispatch.com/post/174859.

Astore, W. and Showalter, D. (2005). *Hindenburg: Icon of German Militarianism*. Washington, DC: Potomac Books.

Augustine (1965). "Lying" and "against lying." In *Treatises on Various Subjects, Fathers of the Church*, Vol. 16, R. J. Deferrari (Ed.). Washington, DC: Catholic University Press.

Baier, A. (1990). Why honesty is a hard virtue. In *Identity, Character, and Morality*, O. Flanagan and A. Rorty (Ed.), pp. 259–282. Cambridge, MA: The MIT Press.

Barnes, A. (1997). *Seeing Through Self-Deception*. Cambridge: Cambridge University Press.

Barnes, J. A. (1993). *A Pack of Lies*. Cambridge: Cambridge University Press.

Baron, M. (1995). *Kantian Ethics Almost Without Apology*. Ithaca, NY: Cornell University Press.

Bayles, M. (1989). *Professional Ethics*, 2nd edn. Belmont, CA: Wadsworth.

Beauchamp, T. (1983). *Case Studies in Business, Bociety, and Ethics*. Englewood Cliffs, NJ: Prentice Hall.

—— and Childress, J. (2001). *Principles of Biomedical Ethics*, 5th edn. Oxford: Oxford University Press.

Belasco, A. (2007). The cost of Iraq, Afghanistan, and other global war on terror operations since 9/11. *Congressional Research Services Report*, Updated June 28.

Beschloss, M. (1997). *Taking Charge*. New York: Simon & Schuster.

Bessel, R. (1993). *Germany After the First World War*. Oxford: The Clarendon Press.

Bethell, N. (1977). *Russian Besieged*. New York: Time Life Books.

Bishop, M. and Trout, J. D. (2005). *Epistemology and the Psychology of Human Judgment*. Oxford: Oxford University Press.

Black, M. (1983). *The Prevalence of Humbug and Other Essays*. Ithaca, NY: Cornell University Press.

Blackburn, S. (1984). *Spreading the Word*. Oxford: Oxford University Press.

—— (1993). *Essays in Quasi-Realism*. Oxford: Oxford University Press.

Blainey, G. (1973). *The Causes of War*. New York: The Free Press.

Blumberg, P. (1989). *The Predatory Society*. Oxford: Oxford University Press.

Bok, S. (1979). *Lying: Moral Choice in Public and Private Life*. New York: Vintage Books.

Boland, V. (2005). Turkish academics grasp the nettle on Armenians. *Financial Times of London*, September 23.

Bracher, K. D. (1970). *The German Dictatorship*. New York: Praeger.

Brandt, R. (1954). The definition of an "ideal observer" in ethics. *Philosophy and Phenomenological Research* 15: 407–413.

—— (1959). *Ethical Theory*. Englewood Cliffs, NJ: Prentice Hall.

—— (1992). *Morality, Utilitarianism, and Rights*. Cambridge: Cambridge University Press.

—— (1997). The real and alledged problems of utilitarianism. In *Morality and the Good Life*, T. Carson and P. Moser (Ed.), pp. 373–383. New York: Oxford University Press.

Brentano, F. (1969). *The Origin of Our Knowledge of Right and Wrong*. Translated by R. Chisholm and E. Schneewind. New York: Humanities Press.

—— (1973). *The Foundation and Construction of Ethics*. Translated by E. Schneewind. New York: Humanities Press.

Brink, D. (1989). *Moral Realism and the Foundations of Ethics*. Cambridge: Cambridge University Press.

Brown, D. (2006). Faces of the fallen. *The Washington Post*, October 11.

Brzezinski, Z. (2007). *Three Presidents and the Crisis of American Superpower*. New York: Basic Books.

Bumiller, E. (2005). The reach of war: home front. *New York Times*, December 13.

Burrows, D. (2005). Turkey won't say genocide but U documentary does. *Minnesota Daily*, September 29.

Callahan, D. (2004). *The Cheating Culture: Why More Americans are Doing Wrong to Get Ahead*. New York: Harcourt World and Brace.

Carson, T. (1984). *The Status of Morality*. Dordrecht: Kluwer.

—— (1986). Hare's defense of utilitarianism. *Philosophical Studies* 50: 97–115.

—— (1988). On the definition of lying: a reply to Jones and revisions. *Journal of Business Ethics* 7: 509–514.

—— (1989). Could ideal observers disagree: a reply to Taliaferro. *Philosophy and Phenomenological Research* 50: 115–124.

—— (1993a). Hare on utilitarianism and intuitive morality. *Erkenntnis* 39: 305–331.

—— (1993b). Second thoughts on bluffing. *Business Ethics Quarterly* 3: 317–341.

—— (1998). Ethical issues in sales: two case studies. *Journal of Business Ethics* 17: 725–728.

—— (2000). *Value and the Good Life*. Notre Dame, IN: Notre Dame University Press.

—— (2001). Deception and withholding information in sales. *Business Ethics Quarterly* 11: 275–306.

—— (2004). Conflicts of interest and self-dealing in the professions: a review essay. *Business Ethics Quarterly* 14: 161–182.

—— (2006). The definition of lying. *Nous* 40: 284–306.

—— (2008). Liar liar. *International Journal of Applied Philosophy* 22: 189–210.

—— Wokutch, R., and Murrmann, K. (1982). Bluffing in labor negotiations: legal and ethical issues. *Journal of Business Ethics* 1: 13–22.

CBC News (2006). July Deadliest Month for Iraqi Civilians: report. CBC News, August 16. http://www.cbc.ca./story/world/national/2006/08/15/iraq-civilian.html.

Chickering, R. (1998). *Imperial Germany and the Great War, 1914–1918*. Cambridge: Cambridge University Press.

Chisholm, R. and Feehan, T. (1977). The intent to deceive. *Journal of Philosophy* 74: 143–159.

Clarke, R. A. (2004). *Against All Enemies*. New York: Free Press.

Coleman, L. and Kay, P. (1981). Prototype semantics: the English verb "lie." *Language* 57: 26–44.

Conquest, R. (1986). *The Harvest of Sorrow*. Oxford: Oxford University Press.

Cromwell, O. (1980). Letter to the General Assembly of the Church of Scotland, August 3, 1650. In *Bartlett's Familiar Quotations*, 15th edn, p. 272. Boston, MA: Brown and Little.

Cumings, B. (1990). *The Origins of the Korean War*, Volume II. Princeton, NJ: Princeton University Press.

Cumminsky, D. (1996). *Kantian Consequentialism*. Oxford: Oxford University Press.

Dallek, R. (1979). *Franklin D. Roosevelt and American Foreign Policy 1932–1945*. New York: Oxford University Press.

Davis, M. and Stark, A. (Ed.) (2001). *Conflict of Interest in the Professions*. New York: Oxford University Press.

Dawes, R. (1996). *House of Cards*. New York: Free Press.

Dawidowicz, L. (1975). *The War Against the Jews 1933–1945*. New York: Holt, Rinehart and Winston.

Dees, J., and Cramton, P. (1991). Shrewd bargaining on the moral frontier: towards a theory of morality in practice. *Business Ethics Quarterly* 1: 135–167.

Deist, W. (1996). The military collapse of the German Empire: the reality behind the stab-in-the-back myth. Translated by E. J. Feuchtwanger. *War in History* 3: 186–207.

DePaul, M. (1993). *Balance and Refinement: Beyond Coherence Methods of Moral Inquiry*. New York: Routledge.

Dietrichson, P. (1969). Kant's criteria of universalizability. In *Kant: Foundations of the Metaphsics of Morals*, R.P. Wolff (Ed.), pp. 163–207. Indianapolis, IN: Bobbs-Merrill.

Donald, D. H. (1995). *Lincoln*. New York: Random House.

Eckman, P. (1985). *Telling Lies*. New York: Norton.

Ewing, A. C. (1959). *Second Thoughts in Moral Philosophy*. London: Routledge & Kegan Paul.

Faden, R. and Beauchamp, T. (1986). *A History of Informed Consent*. New York: Oxford University Press.

Fallis, D. (2009). What is lying? *Journal of Philosophy* CVI: 29–56.

Feldman, F. (1984). Hare's proof. *Philosophical Studies* 45: 269–283.

Ferguson, N. (1999). *The Pity of War*. New York: Basic Books.

Fest, J. (1974). *Hitler*. Translated by R. Wilson and C. Wilson. New York: Harcourt Brace Jovanovich.

Finnegan, W. (1999). The invisible war. *The New Yorker*, January 25: 50–73.

—— (2000). A slave in New York. *The New Yorker*, January 24: 50–61.

Firth, R. (1954). Reply to Professor Brandt. *Philosophy and Phenomenological Research* 15: 414–421.

—— (1997). Ethical absolutism and the ideal observer. In *Morality and the Good Life*, T. Carson and P. Moser (Ed.), pp. 40–60. New York: Oxford University Press.

Foot, P. (1978). *Virtues and Vices*. Berkeley, CA: University of California Press.

Frankena, W. (1973). *Ethics*, 2nd edn. Englewood Cliffs, NJ: Prentice Hall.

Frankfurt, H. (1992). The faintest passion. *Proceedings and Addresses of the American Philosophical Association* 66: 5–16.

—— (2005). *On Bullshit*. Princeton, NJ: Princeton University Press.

Freely, M. (2006). Writers on trial. *New York Times Book Review*, August 13: 27.

Frege, G. (1959). *Posthumous Writings*. Translated by P. Long and R. White. Oxford: Blackwell.

French, H. (2001). Japan's refusal to revise textbooks angers its neighbors. *New York Times*, July 10: p.A3.

Fried, C. (1978). *Right and Wrong*. Cambridge, MA: Harvard University Press.

FTC Policy Statement on Deception. On the web at: http://www.ftc.gov/bcp/guides/guides.htm then click on FTC Policy Statement on Deception.

FTC Decisions 95. Sears, Roebuck, and Co., Et. Al, 1980, pp. 406–527. On the web at ftc.gov/as/decisions/vol95.shtm.

FTC Decisions 113. R. J. Reynolds Tobacco Company, 1990, pp. 344–366. On the web at ftc.gov/as/decisions/vol113.shtm.

Gaut, B. (2002). Justifying moral pluralism. In *Ethical Intuitionism: Re-Evaluations*, P. Stratton-Lake (Ed.), pp. 137–160. Oxford: Oxford University Press.

Gensler, H. (1986). A Kantian argument against abortion. *Philosophical Studies* 49: 83–98.

—— (1996). *Formal Ethics*. London: Routledge.

—— (1998). *Ethics*. London: Routledge.

Gert, B., Culver, C., and Clouser, K. D. (1997). *Bioethics: A Return to the Fundamentals*. Oxford: Oxford University Press.

Gibbard, A. (1990). *Wise Choice and Apt Feelings*. Cambridge, MA: Harvard University Press.

Gilbert, M. (1994). *The First World War*. New York: Henry Holt.

Glover, J. (1977). *Causing Death and Saving Lives*. London: Penguin Books.

—— (1999). *Humanity: A Moral History of the Twentieth Century*. New Haven, CT: Yale University Press.

Goldberg, M. H. (1990). *The Book of Lies*. New York: William Morrow.

Goldman, A. (1970). *A Theory of Human Action*. Englewood Cliffs, NJ: Prentice-Hall.

Gorlin, R. (Ed.) (1990). *Codes of Professional Responsibility*, 2nd edn. Washington, D.C.: The Bureau of National Affairs, Inc.

Green, R. (2006). Direct-to-consumer advertising and pharmaceutical ethics: the case of Vioxx. *Hofstra Law Review* 35: 749–759.

Grice, P. (1989). *Studies in the Way of Words*. Cambridge, MA: Harvard University Press.

Griffiths, P. (2004). *Lying: An Augustinian Theology of Duplicity*. Grand Rapids, MI: Brazos Press.

Grossman, R. (1995). Chicago's Schindler honored. *Chicago Tribune*, February 18, p.5.

Grotius, H. (1925). *On the Law of War and Peace*. Translated by F. W. Kelsey. Indianapolis, IN: Bobbs Merrill.

Hare, R. M. (1952). *Language of Morals*. Oxford: Oxford University Press.

—— (1963). *Freedom and Reason*. Oxford: Oxford University Press.

—— (1981). *Moral Thinking*. Oxford: Oxford University Press.

—— (1989). *Essays in Ethical Theory*. Oxford: Oxford University Press.

—— (1997). *Sorting Out Ethics*. Oxford: Oxford University Press.

Hartman, N. (1975). *Ethics*. Translated by S. Coit. Atlantic Highlands, NJ: Humanities Press.

Herbert, B. (2008). Sharing the pain. *New York Times*, March 11, p.A23.

Herman, B. (1993). *The Practice of Moral Judgment*. Cambridge, MA: Harvard University Press.

Herwig, H. (1997). *The First World War Germany and Austria-Hungary 1914–1918*. New York: Arnold.

—— (2000). Of men and myths: the use and abuse of history and the Great War. In *The Great War and the Twentieth Century*, J. Winter *et al.* (Ed.), pp. 299–330. New Haven, CT: Yale University Press.

Himmler, H. (1946). Speech to SS Officers in Posen, Poland (October 1943). Document 1919-PS; included in *Nazi Conspiracy and Aggression*, Vol. IV, Office of United States Chief of Counsel for Prosecution of Axis Criminality (Washington: United States Government Printing Office), pp. 558–578.

Hitler, A. (1943). *Mein Kampf*. Translated by R. Manheim. Boston, MA: Houghton Mifflin Company.

Holley, D. (1993). A moral evaluation of sales practices. In *Ethical Theory and Business*, 4th edn, T. Beauchamp and N. Bowie (Ed.), pp. 462–472. Englewood Cliffs, NJ: Prentice Hall.

Hooker, B. (2000). *Ideal Code, Real World*. Oxford: Oxford University Press.

Hurka, T. (1993). *Perfectionism*. Oxford: Oxford University Press.

Hurley, S. (1989). *Natural Reasons*. Oxford: Oxford University Press.

Iraq Body Count, on the web at iraqbodycount.org.

Iraq Coalition Casualty Count, on the web at icasualties.org.

Isenberg, A. (1964). Deontology and the ethics of lying. *Philosophy and Phenomenological Research* 24: 465–480.

Jameton, A. (1995). Information disclosure: ethical issues. In *Encyclopedia of Bioethics*, W. T. Reich (Ed.), pp.1225–1230. New York: Macmillan.

Kagan, S. (1998). *Normative Ethics*. Boulder, CO: Westview Press.

Kant, I. (1996). *Critique of Practical Reason*. Translated by M. Gregor. In *Immanuel Kant: Practical Philosophy*. Cambridge: Cambridge University Press.

—— (1959). *Foundations of the Metaphysics of Morals*. Translated by L. White Beck. Indianapolis, IN: Bobbs-Merrill Co.

—— (1993a). *Grounding for the Metaphysics of Morals*. Translated by James Ellington, 3rd edn. Indianapolis, IN: Hackett.

Kant, I. (1993b). On a supposed right to tell lies because of philanthropic concerns. In Kant, *Grounding for the Metaphysics of Morals*. Translated by J. Ellington, 3rd edn. Indianapolis, IN: Hackett.

——(1996a). *Metaphysics of Morals*. Translated by M. Gregor. In Kant, *Practical Philosophy*. Cambridge: Cambridge University Press.

——(1996b). On the miscarriage of all philosophical trials in theodicy. Translated by G. di Giovanni. In *Religion and Rational Theology*, edited and translated by A. W. Wood and G. di Giovanni. Cambridge: Cambridge University Press.

——(1997). *Lectures on Ethics*. Translated by P. Heath. Cambridge: Cambridge University Press.

Kawall, J. (2002). Virtue theory and ideal observers. *Philosophical Studies* **109**: 197–222.

Keegan, J. (1989). *The Second World War*. New York: Viking.

——(1999). How Hitler could have won the war. In *What If?*, R. Cowley (Ed.), pp. 295–305. New York: G. P. Putnam and Sons.

Kershaw, I. (1998). *Hitler, 1889–1936: Hubris*. New York: Norton.

——(2006). Hitler's role in the Final Solution. *Yad Vashem Studies* **34**: 7–43.

Kinzer, S. (2003). *All the Shah's Men*. Hoboken, NJ: John Wiley & Sons.

Knobe, J. (2003). Intentional action and side effects in ordinary language. *Analysis* **63**, 190–193.

Korsgaard, C. (1996). *Creating the Kingdom of Ends*. Cambridge: Cambridge University Press.

Korn, D. (2003). *The Lies of George W. Bush*. New York: Crown Books.

Kristof, N. (2007). "Inspiring Progress" on Iraq? *New York Times*, July 12.

——(2009). The Daily Me. *New York Times*, March 18.

LaFeber, W. (1989). *The American Age*. New York: Norton.

Lemos, N. (2004). *Common-Sense*. Cambridge: Cambridge University Press.

Lincoln, A. (1989). *Abraham Lincoln: Speeches and Writings*. New York: The Library of America.

Linsky, L. (1963). Deception. *Inquiry* **6**: 157–169.

Lycan, W. (2006). On the Gettier problem. In *Epistemology Futures*, S. Hetherington (Ed.), pp. 148–168. Oxford: Oxford University Press.

Lynch, M. (2004). *True to Life: Why Truth Matters*. Cambridge, MA: MIT Press.

Lyons, D. (1994). *Rights, Welfare, and Mill's Moral Theory*. Cambridge: Cambridge University Press.

MacIntyre, A. (1995). Truthfulness, lies, and moral philosophers: what can we learn from Mill and Kant? *The Tanner Lectures on Human Values* **16**: 308–361.

Mahon, J. (2007). A definition of deceiving. *International Journal of Applied Philosophy* **21**: 181–194.

——(2006). Kant and the perfect duty to others not to lie. *British Journal for the History of Philosophy* **14**: 653–685.

——(2008). The definition of lying and deception. *Stanford Online Encyclopedia of Philosophy*. February.

——(2009). The truth about Kant on lies. In *The Philosophy of Deception*, C. Martin (Ed.), pp. 201–224. New York: Oxford University Press.

Manison, D. S. (1969). Lying and lies. *Australasian Journal of Philosophy* **47**: 132–144.

McClellan, S. (2008). *What Happened: Inside the Bush White House and Washington's Culture of Deception*. New York: Public Affairs.

McNaughton, D. (1996). An unconnected heap of duties. *Philosophical Quarterly* **46**: 433–447.

McPherson, J. (2007). *This Mighty Scourge: Perspectives on the Civil War*. Oxford: Oxford University Press.

Mendola, J. (2006). *Goodness and Justice and Consequentialist Moral Theory*. Cambridge: Cambridge University Press.

Mele, A. (2001). *Self-Deception Unmasked*. Princeton, NJ: Princeton University Press.

Mill, J. S. (1963). Bentham. In *The Collected Works of John Stuart Mill*. Volume X, pp. 77–115. Toronto: University of Toronto Press.

—— (1979). *Utilitarianism*. Indianapolis, IN: Hackett.

Miller, W. L. (1995). *Arguing About Slavery*. New York: Knopf.

Moore, G. E. (1965). *Ethics*. Oxford: Oxford University Press.

—— (1968). A reply to my critics. In *The Philosophy of G. E. Moore*, 3rd edn, P.A. Schilpp (Ed.), pp. 535–577. La Salle, IL: Open Court.

Morreim, H. (1995). *Balancing Act: The New Medical Ethics of Medicine's New Economics*. Washington, DC: Georgetown University Press.

Morris, B. (1999). *Righteous Victims: A History of the Zionist Arab Conflict, 1881–1999*. New York: Alfred A. Knopf.

—— (2004). *The Birth of the Palestinian Refugee Problem Revisited*. Cambridge: Cambridge University Press.

Nagel, T. (2002). *Concealment and Exposure and Other Essays*. Oxford: Oxford University Press.

Niewyk, D. L. (2001). *The Jews in Weimer Germany*. New Brunswick, NJ: Transaction Publishers.

9/11 Commission Report. New York: Barnes and Noble Books.

NPR (National Public Radio). The Toll of War, on the web at npr.org/News/specials/tollofwar/tollofwarmain.htm

Nussbaum, M. (2001). Non relative virtues. In *Moral Relativism: A Reader*, P. Moser and T. Carson (Ed.), pp. 199–225. Oxford: Oxford University Press.

Nyberg, D. (1993). *The Varnished Truth: Truthtelling and Deceiving in Ordinary Life*. Chicago, IL: University of Chicago Press.

Oakes, G. (1990). *The Soul of the Salesman*. Atlantic Highlands, NJ: Humanities Press.

Onishi, N. and French, H. (2005). Ill will rising between China and Japan as old grievances fuel new era of rivalry. *New York Times*, August 3.

Outka, G. (1972). *Agape: An Ethical Analysis*. New Haven, CT: Yale University Press.

Oxford English Dictionary, 2nd edn. Oxford: The Clarendon Press, 1989.

Patterson, O. (2006). A poverty of the mind. *New York Times*, March 26.

Platts, M. (1980). Moral reality and the end of desire. In *Reference, Truth and Reality*, M. Platts (Ed.), pp. 69–81. London: Routledge & Kegan Paul.

Polgreen, L. (2008). Court rules Niger failed by allowing girl's slavery. *New York Times*, October 28.

Preston, I. (1975). *The Great American Blow-Up: Puffery in Advertising and Selling*. Madison, WI: University of Wisconsin Press.

—— (1994). *The Tangled Web They Weave: Truth, Falsity, and Advertisers*. Madison, WI: University of Wisconsin Press.

Preston, I. (1998). Puffery and other "loophole" claims: how the law's "don't ask don't tell" policy condones fraudulent falsity in advertising. *Journal of Law and Commerce* 18: 49–114.

Putnam, H. (2002). *The Collapse of the Fact/Value Dichotomy and Other Essays*. Cambridge, MA: Harvard University Press.

Ramsey, F. (1931). *The Foundations of Mathematics*. London: Routledge & Kegan Paul.

Rashdall, H. (1928). *Theory of Good and Evil*. Oxford: Clarendon Press.

Rawls, J. (1971). *Theory of Justice*, 1st edn. Cambridge, MA: Harvard University Press.

Rich, F. (2006). *The Greatest Story Ever Sold*. New York: Penguin.

—— (2007). Operation freedom from Iraqis. *New York Times*, May 27.

Rodwin, M. (1993). *Medicine and Moral: Physicians' Conflicts of Interest*. New York: Oxford University Press.

Rodzinski, W. (1979). *A History of China*. Oxford: Pergamon Press.

Roosevelt, Franklin D. Radio fireside chat. September 11, 1941. www.usmn.org/fdr/rattlesnake.html.

Rosati, C. (1995). Persons, perspectives, and full information accounts of the good. *Ethics* 105: 296–325.

Ross, W. D. (1930). *The Right and the Good*. Oxford: Oxford University Press.

Sanger, D. (2009). US rejects aid for the Israeli raid on Iranian nuclear site. *New York Times*, January 10.

Sawyer, R. (1986). *Slavery in the Twentieth Century*. London: Routledge & Kegan Paul.

Scheibe, K. (1980). In defense of lying. *Berkshire Review* 15: 15–24.

Schweickart, D. (2002). *After Capitalism*. Lanham, MD: Rowman Littlefield.

Searle, J. (1968). How to derive "ought" from "is." In *Theories of Ethics*, P. Foot (Ed.), pp. 101–114. Oxford: Oxford University Press.

Shenon, P. (1996). US knew in 1953 North Korea held American P.O.W.s. *New York Times*, September 17.

Shibles, W. (1985). *Lying: A Critical Analysis*. Whitewater, WI: The Language Press.

Shirer, W. L. (1960). *The Rise and Fall of the Third Reich*. New York: Simon and Schuster.

Sidgwick, H. (1966). *The Methods of Ethics*. New York: Dover.

Siegler, F. A. (1966). Lying. *American Philosophical Quarterly* 3: 128–136.

Singer, M. (1963). The golden rule. *Philosophy* 38: 293–314.

Slater, L. (2002). The trouble with self esteem. *New York Times Magazine*, February 3: 44–47.

Smart, J. C. and Williams, B. (1973). *Utilitarianism: For and Against*. Cambridge: Cambridge University Press.

Smith, M. (1994). *The Moral Problem*. Boston, MA: Blackwell.

Sorensen, R. (2007). Bald-faced lies! Lying without the intent to deceive. *Pacific Philosophical Quarterly* 88: 251–264.

Soyinka, W. (1998). Heart of darkness. *New York Times Book Review*, October 4, p. 11.

Stevenson, C. (1945). *Ethics and Language*. New Haven, CT: Yale University Press.

Stiglitz, J. and Bilmes, L. (2008). *The Three Trillion Dollar War: The True Cost of the Iraq Conflict*. New York: Norton.

Stone, C. (1975). *Where the Law Ends*. New York: Harper & Row.

Stowe, H.B. (1965). *Uncle Tom's Cabin*. New York: Harper & Row.

Strawson, P. (1949). Truth. *Analysis* 9: 83–97.

Strudler, A. (1995). On the ethics of deception in negotiation. *Business Ethics Quarterly* 5: 805–822.

—— (2005). Deception unraveled. *Journal of Philosophy* 102: 458–473.

Suskind, R. (2004). *The Price of Loyalty*. New York: Simon & Schuster.

Sweetser, E. (1987). The definition of *lie*. In *Cultural Models in Language and Thought*, D. Holland and N. Quinn (Ed.), pp. 43–66. Cambridge: Cambridge University Press.

Thomas, H. (1997). *The Slave Trade*. New York: Simon and Schuster.

Walzer, M. (1977). *Just and Unjust Wars*. New York: Harper & Row.

Warnock, G. J. (1971). *The Object of Morality*. London: Methuen.

Wattles, J. (1996). *The Golden Rule*. New York: Oxford University Press.

Weinberg, G. (1995). *Germany, Hitler, and World War II*. Cambridge: Cambridge University Press.

Welch, D. (2000). *Germany Propadanda and Total War, 1914–1918*. New Brunswick, NJ: Rutgers University Press.

West, H. (2004). *An Introduction to Mill's Utilitarian Ethics*. Cambridge: Cambridge University Press.

Wheeler-Bennett, J. W. (1936). *Hindenburg: The Wooden Titan*. London: Archon Books.

Wikipedia (2007). Anti-Americanism. July.

—— (2009). Casualties of the Iraq War. July.

—— (2009). Financial costs of Iraq War. July.

Williams, B. (2002). *Truth and Truthfulness: An Essay in Genealogy*. Princeton, NJ: Princeton University Press.

Williams, J. F. (2005). *Corporal Hitler and the Great War 1914–1918*. New York: Frank Cass.

Wood, A. (2008). *Kantian Ethics*. Cambridge: Cambridge University Press.

Zagzebski, L. (2004). *Divine Motivation Theory*. Cambridge: Cambridge University Press.

Index